Psychopathology and Addictive Disorders

Psychopathology and Addictive Disorders

Edited by

Roger E. Meyer

The Guilford Press

New York   London

© 1986 The Guilford Press
A Division of Guilford Publications, Inc.
200 Park Avenue South, New York, N.Y. 10003

Printed in the United States of America

Library of Congress Cataloging-in-Publication Data
Main entry under title:

Psychopathology and addictive disorders.

Includes bibliographies and index.
1. Substance abuse. 2. Psychology, Pathological.
I. Meyer, Roger E. [DNLM: 1. Mental Disorders—
complications. 2. Substance Dependence—complications.
WM 270 P9739]
RC564.P83   1986   616.86   85-30547
ISBN 0-89862-680-3

To Jessica, Stephanie, Tobie, and Sheila Meyer;
and to the memory of Carl Meyer

Contributors

MICHAEL H. ALLEN, MD, Department of Psychiatry, Cornell University Medical College, New York Hospital, Westchester Division, White Plains, New York

MARGARET BEAN-BAYOG, MD, Department of Psychiatry, Cambridge Hospital, Harvard Medical School, Cambridge, Massachusetts

JAMES T. BECKER, PhD, Alzheimer's Disease Research Center, Departments of Psychiatry and Neurology, University of Pittsburgh School of Medicine, Pittsburgh, Pennsylvania

DOMENIC A. CIRAULO, MD, Department of Psychiatry, Tufts University School of Medicine, Boston, Massachusetts; Veterans Administration Medical Center, Boston, Massachusetts

RICHARD J. FRANCES, MD, Department of Clinical Psychiatry, Cornell University Medical College, New York Hospital, Westchester Division, White Plains, New York; Alcohol Treatment Service, The New York Hospital–Cornell Medical Center, Westchester Division, White Plains, New York

MARC GALANTER, MD, Division of Alcohol and Drug Abuse, Department of Psychiatry, Albert Einstein College of Medicine, Bronx, New York

MICHIE N. HESSELBROCK, PhD, Department of Psychiatry, University of Connecticut Health Center, Farmington, Connecticut

VICTOR M. HESSELBROCK, PhD, Department of Psychiatry, University of Connecticut Health Center, Farmington, Connecticut

JACOB H. JACOBY, MD, PhD, Department of Psychiatry, Albert Einstein College of Medicine, Bronx, New York

JEROME H. JAFFE, MD, Addiction Research Center, National Institute on Drug Abuse, Baltimore, Maryland; Department of Psychiatry, University of Connecticut Health Center, Farmington, Connecticut

RICHARD F. KAPLAN, PhD, Alcohol Research Center, Department of Psychiatry, University of Connecticut Health Center, Farmington, Connecticut

EDWARD J. KHANTZIAN, MD, Department of Psychiatry, Harvard Medical School at the Cambridge Hospital, Cambridge, Massachusetts

HERBERT D. KLEBER, MD, Department of Psychiatry, Yale School of Medicine, New Haven, Connecticut; Drug Dependence Unit, Connecticut Mental Health Center, New Haven, Connecticut

LESTER LUBORSKY, PhD, Department of Psychiatry, Hospital of the University of Pennsylvania, Philadelphia, Pennsylvania

A. THOMAS MCLELLAN, PhD, Substance Abuse Treatment Unit, Veterans Administration Medical Center, Philadelphia, Pennsylvania; Department of Psychiatry, University of Pennsylvania, Philadelphia, Pennsylvania

ROGER E. MEYER, MD, Department of Psychiatry, University of Connecticut Health Center, Farmington, Connecticut

JACQUELINE MICHAEL, ACSW, Drug Dependence Treatment Unit, McLean Hospital, Belmont, Massachusetts

STEVEN M. MIRIN, MD, Westwood Lodge Hospital, Westwood, Massachusetts; Alcohol and Drug Abuse Research Center, McLean Hospital, Belmont, Massachusetts; Department of Psychiatry, Harvard Medical School, Boston, Massachusetts

CHARLES P. O'BRIEN, MD, PhD, University of Pennsylvania School of Medicine, Veterans Administration Medical Center, Philadelphia, Pennsylvania

BRUCE J. ROUNSAVILLE, MD, Department of Psychiatry, Yale School of Medicine, New Haven, Connecticut; Drug Dependence Unit, Connecticut Mental Health Center, New Haven, Connecticut

ROBERT J. SCHNEIDER, MEd, North Charles Institute for the Addictions, Cambridge, Massachusetts

ROGER D. WEISS, MD, Drug Dependence Treatment Unit, McLean Hospital, Belmont, Massachusetts; Department of Psychiatry, Harvard Medical School, Boston, Massachusetts

GEORGE E. WOODY, MD, Veterans Administration Medical Center, Philadelphia, Pennsylvania

Contents

Psychopathology and Addictive Disorders

I

Introduction

1

How to Understand the Relationship between Psychopathology and Addictive Disorders: Another Example of the Chicken and the Egg

ROGER E. MEYER

DEFINITIONS

The terms "psychopathology" and "addictive disorder" each suffer from a lack of precision and a variety of interpretations that sometime seem more to confuse than to enlighten. Efforts by a single author to clarify the collected literature on these subjects in a new volume will inevitably fall short in some area or discipline. The diversity of current research in the field is one point in favor of a multiauthored text. Definitions of "psychopathology" range from the categorically based disease concepts of the *Diagnostic and Statistical Manual of Mental Disorders*, third edition (DSM-III; American Psychiatric Association, 1980) to the dimensionally based trait constructs of psychological inventories; the symptom-based rating scales employed in psychopharmacological and other treatment outcome studies; and the clinically derived and meaningfully rich formulations of psychoanalysis, family therapy, and other psychotherapy-based schools of practice. It is relatively easy for a reviewer to criticize the specific limitations of the psychopathology literature from the vantage point of an "outsider." It is more difficult for a writer in any one discipline to convince colleagues in another discipline about the veracity of observations and nomenclature derived from his or her perspective. Yet it is likely that no single mode of observation or description in the area of psychopathology can account for enough of the relevant variance to claim for itself an exclusive "validity."

The definitions of "addictive disorder" have also ranged widely, from nomenclature based upon the presence or absence of physiological dependence to constructs relying on legal, social, and/or psychological problems associated with substance use; definitions based on the quantity, frequency, and/or intensity of consummatory behaviors; and/or definitions based upon the use of an illegal substance. In attempting to make sense of the interface between psychopathology and addictive disorders, one is challenged like a child making sand castles on the beach. Such formulations can be destroyed by the feet of an unkindly critic, or by the natural forces of a high tide of new information.

At this writing, definitions of "psychopathology" and "additive disorder" are again in the process of change. DSM-III represents the apotheosis of atheoretical descriptive psychiatry in the United States in this century. Yet movements are already under way to consider the usefulness of new axes based upon psychodynamic and family process variables, as well as new formulations of Axis I and Axis II categories devolving from the subsequent years of clinical experience. In terms of addictive disorders, current DSM-III criteria for substance use disorders are based upon three dimensions: (1) a pattern of pathological use, (2) substance use associated with social impairment, and (3) physiological tolerance and withdrawal. These three dimensions result in two categories: alcohol or drug *abuse*, and alcohol or drug *dependence*. The former is defined by the first two criteria; the latter requires the presence of tolerance or withdrawal symptoms. Alcohol dependence and cannabis dependence also require the presence of pathological use and/or impairment, along with the presence of tolerance and withdrawal symptoms.

There are rumors that the DSM-III criteria for abuse and dependence will be superseded by definitions of alcohol and drug dependence syndromes derived from the concept of an alcohol dependence syndrome proposed by Edwards and Gross (1976). The seven elements of this syndrome are described in Table 1-1. Rather than defining substance use disorders as abuse or dependence, individuals are classified along two dimensions: severity of dependence, and severity of psychosocial disabilities. While severity of dependence would be expected to correlate with the quantity, frequency, and intensity of substance use, the severity of disability should be influenced by cultural factors, the presence of

TABLE 1-1   Elements of the Alcohol Dependence Syndrome Proposed by Edwards and Gross (1976)

Element	Description
Narrowing of the drinking repertoire	Increasing severity of dependence is marked by increasingly sterotyped drinking, with little day-to-day variability of beverage choice; drinking is scheduled so as to maintain a high blood alcohol level.
Salience of drink-seeking behavior	Increasing severity of dependence is marked by the individual granting highest priority to maintaining alcohol intake, with a failure of negative social consequences to deter drinking behavior.
Increased tolerance	Increasing severity of dependence is marked by the individual's ability to function at blood alcohol levels that would incapacitate the nontolerant drinker. In later stages of the illness, the individual begins to lose his or her previously acquired tolerance because of liver damage, aging, and/or brain damage.
Repeated withdrawal symptoms	With increasing severity of dependence, the individual manifests more frequent and severe withdrawal symptoms. Four key symptoms include tremor, nausea, sweating, and mood disturbance.
Relief avoidance of withdrawal symptoms	With increasing severity of dependence, the individual will take to drinking earlier in the day—and may even awaken in the middle of the night.
Subjective awareness of a compulsion to drink	With increasing severity of dependence, the individual will experience a sense of "loss of control" or impaired control over alcohol intake, and a subjective sense of "craving" or desire to drink. Cues for craving may include the feeling of intoxication, withdrawal, affective discomfort, or situational stimuli.
Reinstatement after abstinence	With increasing severity of dependence, the individual will feel "hooked" within a few days of starting to drink, and his or her drinking will revert to the old stereotyped pattern. The six elements of the syndrome will rapidly reappear.

other psychopathology, and/or the severity of dependence. While some studies have appeared to support the validity of an alcohol dependence dimension in terms of prediction of treatment outcome and psychophysiological responsiveness in the laboratory (Kaplan, Meyer, & Stroebel, 1983; Polich, Armor, & Braiker, 1980; Vaillant, 1983), there have been no systematic studies that would describe the validity of any other drug dependence syndrome so constructed. Moreover, some studies have failed to find a strong correlation between treatment outcome and severity of alcohol dependence as defined by questionnaire data (Heather, Rollnick, & Winton, 1983; Litman, Eiser, Rawson, & Oppenheim, 1977). Nevertheless, the biaxial construct that derives from the formulation of Edwards and Gross may turn out to be a useful reference point for the analysis of the interaction of psychopathology with the development, maintenance, and recurrence of a variety of addictive disorders.

POSSIBLE TYPES OF RELATIONSHIPS BETWEEN PSYCHOPATHOLOGY AND ADDICTIVE DISORDERS

In considering the relatedness between psychopathology and addictive disorders, it is important to differentiate among a correlational relationship, a meaningful relationship, and an etiological relationship. As described in the chapter by Allen and Frances in this volume, certain psychiatric disorders occur more frequently in alcoholics and drug addicts than one would necessarily predict from their prevalence in the general population (a *correlational* relationship). Affective illness and antisocial personality (ASP) disorder are two such conditions; their relationships to addictive disorders are considered in the chapters by Jaffe and Ciraulo and by Michie Hesselbrock. The correlation between ASP disorder and a variety of addictive disorders has led some individuals to postulate that ASP is a risk factor for addictive disorders and/or that some addictive individuals develop antisocial characteristics as a consequence of their substance use disorder (Robins, Bates, & O'Neil, 1962; Schuckit, 1983). These issues are considered in greater detail below and in subsequent chapters.

Individuals understand their own behavior, and put it into a *meaningful* context, on the basis of their culture, personal history and psychodynamics, family and other object relations, psychopathology, and other specific and nonspecific factors. Physical dependence upon a drug or upon alcohol also produces meaningful relationships between time and/or space, and subjective mood and behavior. Election Day, when bars and liquor stores are closed, becomes a highly stressful occasion for a severely dependent alcoholic. In her sensitive chapter on the traumatic ravages of alcoholism, Bean likens alcoholism to other overwhelming human experiences that require the healing effects of time and altered circumstances. Khantzian and Schneider, in their chapter, describe the importance of psychodynamic understanding in their empathic approach to opiate addicts; while the chapter by Woody, O'Brien, McLellan, and Luborsky describes impressive evidence for the efficacy of psychotherapy (vs. simple drug counseling) in the rehabilitation of some heroin addicts in methadone maintenance treatment programs. It is clear that when the biological components of the addictive process are addressed, as in a methadone maintenance program for opioid addicts, individual patients can benefit substantially from *meaningful* therapeutic interventions. While the study by Woody *et al.* has focused upon two types of individual psychotherapy, it is likely that some patients might also benefit from family therapy, couples, and/or group therapy that would help them to move beyond the trauma of their addictive experience.

The traditional clinical literature on psychopathology and addictive disorders has tended to presume that the presence of a substance use disorder is a consequence of psychopathology. The psychopathology has been thought to be *etiologically* related to the substance use disorder. Despite efforts to identify an addiction-prone personality, addictive disorders have not been etiologically linked to specific antecedent psychopathology. In contrast, data from long-term longitudinal studies of individuals who became alcoholic (Kammeier, Hoffman, & Loper, 1973; Vaillant, 1983), as well as studies of chronic alcohol and drug intoxications in the clinical research laboratory (Mendelson & Mello, 1966; Meyer & Mirin, 1979; Nathan, Titler, Lowenstein, Solomon, & Rossi, 1970), indicate that the relationship may not simply be one of cause and effect.

There are five possible relationships (and one non-relationship) between addictive behavior and coexisting psychopathology; these are summarized in Table 1-2. To some extent, this book has been organized into sections based upon the 5 possible relationships between addictive

TABLE 1-2   The Possible Relationships between Addictive Behavior and Coexisting Psychopathology

1. Axis I and II. Psychopathology may serve as a risk factor for addictive disorders.
2. Psychopathology may modify the course of an addictive disorder in terms of rapidity of course, response to treatment, symptom picture, and long-term outcome.
3. Psychiatric symptoms may develop in the course of chronic intoxications.
4. Some psychiatric disorders emerge as a consequence of use and persist into the period of remission.
5. Substance-using behavior and psychopathological symptoms (whether antecedent or consequent) will become meaningfully linked over the course of time.
6. Some psychopathological conditions occur in addicted individuals with no greater frequency than in the general population, suggesting that the psychiatric disorder and the addictive disorder are not specifically related.

disorders and coexisting psychopathology. The next chapter (by Allen & Frances) describes the kinds of psychiatric disorders that have been found in patients with addictive disorders. Allen and Frances highlight the persistent questions about cause and effect. It appears that issues of cause and effect are clearer for those disorders that are consequent to drug or alcohol use (e.g., acute psychotic reactions to stimulants and/ or hallucinogenic drugs, and cognitive disorders secondary to alcoholism) than for psychopathology as a distinct cause of addictive disorder.

PSYCHOPATHOLOGY AS A RISK FACTOR

⌐In general, epidemiological and cross-cultural studies suggest that the principal determinant of the use of an intoxicant in any group is the availability of the intoxicant and the attitude of the population toward its use. The more normative drug or alcohol use is in a population, the less important psychopathology is as a predictor of use⅃ Where heavy drinking is normative in a society (as in France), psychopathology appears to be a less significant risk factor for alcoholism. In this country, psychopathology may be a more significant determinant of alcoholism among Jews than among the Irish. The changing importance of psychopathology as a risk factor for addictive disorders also emerges in studies of marijuana and heroin use. As marijuana use has become widespread in the United States over the past two decades, use per se is no longer limited to deviant or peripheral groups, and psychopathology has become less important as a risk factor for use. Psychopathology was also a less significant determinant of heroin use by American servicemen in Vietnam (Robins, 1973) (and probably is less significant among inner-city youths) than among suburban teenagers. Family pedigree studies of psychopathology in substance abusers (see the chapter by Mirin, Weiss, and Michael) and in alcoholics (see the chapter by Victor Hesselbrock) may suggest a genetic basis for the risk of addictive disorders in some individuals and families.

⌐ASP disorder is the psychiatric disorder that is most prevalent among alcoholic and substance-abusing male patients⅃Frequencies of occurrence of ASP vary, depending upon the type and socioeconomic class of the sample, and upon the diagnostic criteria used. Several recent studies report a prevalence rate of 16–49% of ASP among alcoholics (Hesselbrock *et al.,* 1984; Schuckit, 1973; Cadoret, Troughton, & Widmer, 1984), and a similarly high prevalence of this disorder among heroin addicts (Rounsaville, Weissman, Kleber, & Wilber, 1982). A diagnosis of ASP disorder in an adult, based upon DSM-III criteria, requires that antisocial behavior begin prior to age 15. All adults carrying this diagnosis must have had a history of childhood conduct disorder. The criteria are based upon the longitudinal studies conducted by Robins and colleagues on the adult outcomes of children with childhood conduct disorder (Robins *et al.*, 1962). Gunderson (1983), for one, believes that the relatively broad definition given to antisocial personality within the DSM-III framework must include persons with a variety of different personality types. Two recent studies reporting on the prevalence of ASP in two separate cohorts of alcoholics (Cadoret *et al.*, 1984; Hesselbrock *et al.*, 1984) identified much higher rates of ASP using DSM-III criteria than earlier work using other diagnostic criteria (e.g., Schuckit, 1973). These issues are addressed in the chapter by Michie Hesselbrock in this volume, and in the excellent review article by Brantley and Sutker (1984). Michie Hesselbrock (this volume) contrasts the childhood histories of alcoholics with and without a diagnosis of ASP.

The etiology of ASP (sociopathy) remains controversial, although it may be genetically linked in a manner that is distinct from the inheritance of alcoholism or drug abuse (Cloninger & Reich, 1983). It is predominantly a disorder of males, with a suggestion that the diagnosis of hysteria in females constitutes an equivalent (albeit gender-linked) disorder. There also appears to be an environmental component to the etiology, and there is evidence of pathological levels of cortical and autonomic arousal (Fowles, 1980; Gorenstein & Newman, 1980) and other neurological abnormalities (Elliott, 1978) in the sociopath. These individuals experience dysphoric moods and evidence impulsive behavior rooted in sensation-seeking attitudes (Brantley & Sutker, 1984). They also have poor and unstable object relations, and generally have a history of underachievement despite normal to above-normal intelligence. One could postulate a relationship between substance use and any of a variety of these characteristics in individuals with ASP.

PSYCHOPATHOLOGY AS A MODIFIER OF THE COURSE OF
ADDICTIVE DISORDER

In general, ASP and other psychiatric disorders may modify the course of an addictive disorder in terms of rapidity of course (ASP), response to treatment, symptom picture (ASP, depression) and long-term out-

come (Hesselbrock *et al.*, 1984).⌐Where psychiatric disorders are asso-
ⱴ ciated with negative mood states, poor object relations, and/or poor
impulse control, one would predict a more rapid progression from substance use to addictive behavior, poor bonding to treatment personnel
in programs, and rapid relapse to dependent patterns of substance use
once drug or alcohol consumption resumes after a period of abstinence.⌐

McLellan, in his chapter in this volume and in his extensive research
on alcoholics and drug addicts, has provided impressive documentation
on the relationship between severity of psychopathology and treatment
outcome. In this regard, McLellan's work does not support a hypothetical relationship between *specific* psychiatric diagnoses and treatment outcome. Rather, it has been the general severity of psychopathological symptoms that has anticipated the results, with severity of
psychopathology predicting response to treatment as well as general
outcome. In a study of the contexts of "craving" in the alcoholic, Ludwig
and Stark (1974) found that alcoholics reported high levels of craving
for alcohol in those circumstances associated with dysphoric moods,
supporting the general premise that alcoholics who experience more
frequent dysphoric mood states may be at greater risk of relapse following a period of treatment.⌐My colleagues and I (Hesselbrook, Meyer,
& Keener, 1985) recently reported that the symptom picture in the
alcoholic is influenced by the presence or absence of other psychiatric
disorders. In our study, we found that the presence of psychological and
social disabilities correlated with the presence of ASP disorder and/or
affective disorder. In general, these findings support the notion that
psychopathology may influence the course and symptom picture in the
alcoholic.⌐

Psychiatric Symptoms of Chronic Intoxications

Psychiatric symptoms and/or aberrant behavior may emerge during the
course of drug or alcohol intoxication. Mirin reviews the literature on
laboratory-based studies of drug and alcohol intoxication in a chapter
of this volume. His review suggests that most chronic intoxications are
marked by increasing depression, anxiety, and belligerence. This appears paradoxical, in light of the hedonistic rationale that is often in-
voked to explain drug and alcohol abuse. It is remarkable that a variety
of intoxicated states share dysphoric mood as part of their pattern. In

their chapter in this volume, Jacoby and Galanter examine the question of the role of the intoxicant in producing aberrant behavior, which has been called "pathological intoxication" or "alcohol idiosyncratic intoxication." Their scholarly review is a strong argument for continued research in this area.

PSYCHIATRIC DISORDERS AS A CONSEQUENCE OF USE

Three areas of psychopathology have been described as consequences of addictive disorder that may persist beyond the period of alcohol and/or drug consumption. Cognitive impairment, depression, and "personality change" have all been associated with alcoholism. Consequent psychopathology has also been associated with opiate addition. Zinberg (1975) has argued that the manifest personality disturbances in heroin addicts result from the loss of varied contact with social and familial relationships, the necessity to hustle in order to procure drugs, and the "deviant" label. Secondary depression has been described in opiate addicts (Weissman *et al.*, 1977), and cognitive dysfunction has been reported in polydrug abusers (Grant *et al.*, 1978).

Cognitive impairment in the alcoholic, as described by Becker and Kaplan in this volume, is a significant consequence of chronic alcohol use. This impairment may have a major impact upon treatment response and recovery of function. As described in detail by Becker and Kaplan, chronic alcoholics show three kinds of cognitive impairment: deficits in abstraction, in short-term memory, and in visual–spatial performance. Alcoholics also show a paucity of alpha activity on the electroencephalogram (EEG), and abnormalities of synchrony and coherence in the computerized EEG. Computerized tomography (CT) scan studies reveal ventricular enlargement and frontal cortical shrinkage (Carlen, Wortzman, Holgate, Wilkinson, & Rankin, 1978). While there is recovery in some areas of cognitive functioning after 1 year of abstinence, it is possible that persisting cognitive deficits make it difficult for some individuals to continue successfully in their usual occupations. It is also possible that this cognitive impairment contributes, to some extent, to the depressed mood seen in some alcoholic patients.

As described by Jaffe and Ciraulo in this volume, depression constitutes a special case in any reconsideration of the relationship between psychopathology and addictive disorders. The Washington University group has emphasized the distinction between primary and secondary depressive disorder (Guze, Woodruff, & Clayton, 1971). Primary depression exists in the absence of other significant psychopathology or physical disorders. Secondary depression may occur as a consequence of other psychopathologies, including alcohol and drug abuse. In an effort to document the prevalence of secondary depression in alcoholics, Weissman, Myers, and Harding (1980) reviewed the frequency of depression across a series of clinical research studies in alcoholics. They reported depressive symptoms in 59% of 61 alcoholic outpatients in New Haven; this result was consistent with a review of the clinical research literature indicating the existence of secondary depression in alcoholics. Dorus and Senay (1980) and Rounsaville, Weissman, Wilber, Crits-Cristoph, and Kleber (1982) also found significant depressive symptomatology in opioid addicts. Our recent report (Hesselbrock *et al.*, 1985) pointed out the high prevalence of primary depression in female alcoholics, whereas secondary depression was as prevalent as primary depression in males. In their review, Jaffe and Ciraulo discuss aspects of assessment of depression in the alcoholic, possible etiological factors in secondary depression, and approaches to treatment. Similar issues apply to the assessment of depression in association with other drug use disorders.

The consequent personality deterioration of individuals who have become alcoholic has been described by Vaillant in his follow-up studies (1983) (also, Vaillant & Milofsky 1982) and by Kammeier *et al.* (1973). Bean's description of the trauma of alcoholism to individuals (this volume) describes one potential mechanism involved in this personality deterioration. Kammeier *et al.* compared Minnesota Multiphasic Personality Inventory (MMPI) profiles of 38 men admitted for alcohol treatment with the profiles of these same men while they were in college 10 years earlier. At the time of their hospitalization for alcoholism, these individuals had pathological MMPI profiles, with the highest elevations in depression and sociopathy. Their profiles in college were normal.

The question of personality change in association with drug use has been a controversial area of study. Is there, for example, an amotivational syndrome consequent to chronic marijuana use (Meyer, 1978)? There have been too few longitudinal studies with data on personality prior to the development of drug- and alcohol-using behaviors. It is also not clear how resilient consequent personality changes will be in individuals who recover from alcohol and drug dependence. Schuckit's (1973) concept of secondary sociopathy suggests that alcoholics with consequent personality changes might have a different prognosis in response to treatment from that of individuals with ASP disorder who become alcoholics. Rounsaville and Kleber (this volume) describe the changes in psychopathology observed in a cohort of opioid addicts over time. Their data suggest that some types of psychiatric disorder will remit with improvement in addictive behavior.

CONCLUSION

We are clearly at an early stage in determining the degree to which psychopathology can modify the course of addictive disorders, their prognosis, and their response to treatment. This volume represents an amalgam of literature reviews and presentations of specific ongoing research. The authors who have been asked to prepare chapters for this volume represent the state of the art in their fields. Some of the chapters are literature reviews on aspects of psychopathology; other chapters represent new research findings being presented for the first time. None of the authors presumes to report the final statement on the issue. In a sense, the separate chapters constitute part of a continuing dialogue and inquiry, rather than a definitive statement.

In the past, some investigators have endeavored to explain addictive behavior on the basis of hypothetical, pre-existing psychopathology, while other, more behaviorally oriented researchers have sought to explain the same behavior without any consideration of psychopathology in the individual. We have moved a good distance beyond the notion of a simple cause-and-effect relationship between psychopathology and additive disorders. We have come to appreciate the multivariate complexity of these conditions. It is paradoxical, in view of the growing body of data on the diversity of individuals who constitute drug- and alcohol-addicted patients, that most programs offer one or another generic package of services that fails to differentiate the needs of individual patients. The originally proposed system of reimbursement for care of addicted individuals based upon diagnostic-related groups even failed to differentiate between the treatment of withdrawal states and the requirements for rehabilitation. We may hope that as our assessments of patients become more thorough and offer clear directions for treatment, the treatment system will respond to the heterogeneity of addicted patients, and the reimbursement system will recognize the elements of essential long-term care (inpatient, residential, partial hospital, and outpatient) that may be required by patients with different levels of severity of dependence and coexisting psychiatric disorders.

REFERENCES

American Psychiatric Association. (1980). *Diagnostic and statistical manual of mental disorders* (3rd ed.). Washington, DC: Author.

Brantley, P., & Sutker, P. P. (1984). Antisocial behavior disorders. In H. E. Adams & B. P. Sutker (Eds.), *Comprehensive handbook of psychopathology* (pp. 439–478). New York: Plenum Press.

Cadoret, R., Troughton, E., & Widmer, R. (1984). Clinical differences between antisocial and primary alcoholics. *Comprehensive Psychiatry, 25,* 1–8.

Carlen, P. L., Wortzman, G., Holgate, R. C., Wilkinson, D. A., & Rankin, J. G. (1978). Reversible cerebral atrophy in recently abstinent chronic alcoholics measured by computed tomograph scans. *Science, 200,* 1076–1078.

Cloninger, C., & Reich, T. (1983). Genetic heterogeneity in alcoholism and sociopathy. In S. Kety, L. Roland, R. Sidman, & S. Matthysse (Eds.), *Genetics of neurological and psychiatric disorders* (pp. 145–166). New York: Raven Press.

Criteria Committee, National Council on Alcoholism. (1972). Criteria for the diagnosis of alcoholism. *Annals of Internal Medicine, 77,* 249–258.

Dorus, W., & Senay, E. C. (1980). Depression, demography dimension, and drug abuse. *American Journal of Psychiatry, 137,* 699–704.

Edwards, G., & Gross, M. M. (1976). Alcohol dependence: Provisional description of a clinical syndrome. *British Medical Journal, 1,* 1058–1061.

Elliott, F. A. (1978). Neurological aspects of antisocial behavior. In W. H. Reid (Ed.), *The psychopath: A comprehensive study of antisocial disorders and behaviors.* New York: Brunner/Mazel.

Fowles, D. C. (1980). The three arousal model: Implications of Gray's two-factor learning theory for heart rate, electrodecimal activity, and psychopathology. *Psychophysiology, 17,* 87–104.

Gorenstein, E. E., & Newman, J. P. (1980). Disinhibitory psychopathology: A new perspective and a model for research. *Psychological Review, 87,* 301–315.

Grant, I., Adams, K. M., Carlin, A. S., Rennick, P. M., Judd, L. L., & Schooff, K. (1978). The collaborative neuropsychological study of polydrug users. *Archives of General Psychiatry, 35,* 1063–1074.

Gunderson, J. G. (1983). DMS-III diagnoses of personality disorders. In J. Frosch (Ed.), *Current perspectives on personality disorders* (pp. 20–39). Washington, DC: American Psychiatric Press.

Guze, S., Woodruff, R., & Clayton, T. (1971). Preliminary communication—secondary affective disorder: A study of 95 cases. *Psychological Medicine, 1,* 426–428.

Heather, N., Rollnick, S., & Winton, M. (1983). A comparison of objective and subjective measures of alcohol dependence as predictors of relapse following treatment. *British Journal of Clinical Psychology, 22,* 11–17.

Hesselbrock, M. N., Hesselbrock, V. M., Babor, T. F., Stabenau, J. R., Meyer, R. E., & Weidenman, M. A. (1984). Antisocial behavior, psychopathology and problem drinking in the natural history of alcoholism. In D. Goodwin, K. Van Dusen, & S. Mednick (Eds.), *Longitudinal research in alcoholism* (pp. 197–214). Boston: Kluwer-Nijhoff.

Hesselbrock, M. N., Meyer, R. E., & Keener, J. J. (1985). Psychopathology in hospitalized alcoholics. *Archives of General Psychiatry, 42,* 1050–1055.

Kammeier, M. L., Hoffman, H., & Loper, R. G. (1973). Personality characteristics of alcoholics as college freshman and at the time of treatment. *Quarterly Journal of Studies on Alcohol, 34,* 309–399.

Kaplan, R. F., Meyer, R. E., & Stroebel, C. F. (1983). Alcohol dependence and responsivity to an ethanol stimulus as predictors of alcohol consumption. *British Journal of Addition, 78,* 259–267.

Litman, G. K., Eiser, J. R., Rawson, N. S. B., & Oppenheim, A. N. (1977). Towards a typology of relapse: A preliminary report. *Drug and Alcohol Dependence, 2,* 157–162.

Ludwig, A. M., & Stark, L. A. (1974). Subjective and situational aspects of craving. *Quarterly Journal of Studies on Alcohol, 35,* 899–904.

Mendelson, J. H., & Mello, N. K. (1966). Experimental analysis of drinking behavior of chronic alcoholics. *Annals of the New York Academy of Sciences, 133,* 828–845.

Meyer, R. E. (1978). Behavioral pharmacology of marijuana. In M. A. Lipton, A. Dimascio., & K. F. Killam (Eds.), *Psychopharmacology: A generation of progress* (pp. 1639–1652). New York: Raven Press.

Meyer, R. E., & Mirin, S. M. (1979). *The heroin stimulus.* New York: Plenum Press.

Meyer, R. E., Babor, T. F., Hesselbrock, M. N., Hesselbrock, V. M., & Kaplan, R. F. (in press). *New directions in the assessment of the alcoholic patient* (NIAAA Research Monograph). Washington, DC: U.S. Government Printing Office.

Nathan, P. E., Titler, N. A., & Lowenstein, L. M., Solomon, P., & Rossi, A. M. (1970). Behavioral analysis of chronic alcoholism. *Archives of General Psychiatry, 22,* 419–430.

Polich, J. M., Armor, D. J., & Braiker, H. B. (1980). *The course of alcoholism four years after treatment* (Report No. R-2433-NIAAA). Santa Monica, CA: Rand Corporation.

Robins, L. N. (1973). *A follow-up of Vietnam drug users.* Washington, DC: Special Action Office of Drug Abuse Prevention.

Robins, L. N., Bates, W., & O'Neil, P. (1962). Adult drinking patterns of former problem children. In D. J. Pittman & C. R. Snyder (Eds.), *Society, culture and drinking patterns* (pp. 395–412). New York: Wiley.

Rounsaville, B. J., Weissman, M. M., Kleber, H., & Wilber, C. H. (1982). The heterogeneity of psychiatric diagnosis in treated opiate addicts. *Archives of General Psychiatry, 39,* 161–166.

Rounsaville, B. J., Weissman, M. M., Wilber, C. H., Crits-Cristoph, K., & Kleber, H. D. (1982). Diagnosis and symptoms of depression in opiate addicts: Course and relationship to treatment outcome. *Archives of General Psychiatry, 39,* 151–166.

Schuckit, M. A. (1973). Alcoholism and sociopathy—diagnostic confusion. *Quarterly Journal of Studies on Alcohol, 34,* 157–164.

Schuckit, M. A. (1983). Alcoholism and other psychiatric disorders. *Hospital and Community Psychiatry, 34,* 1022–1026.

Vaillant, G. E. (1983). *The natural history of alcoholism: Causes, patterns and paths of recovery.* Cambridge, MA: Harvard University Press.

Vaillant, G. E., & Milofsky, E. S. (1982). The natural history of male alcoholism: Paths to recovery. *Archives of General Psychiatry, 39,* 127–133.

Weissman, M. M., Myers, J. K., & Harding, P. S. (1980). Prevalence and psychiatric heterogeneity of alcoholism in the United States urban community. *Journal of Studies on Alcohol, 41,* 672–681.

Weissman, M. M., Pottenger, M., Kleber, H., Ruben, H. L., Williams, D., & Thompson, W. D. (1977). Symptom patterns in primary and secondary depression: A comparison of primary depressives with depressed opiate addicts, alcoholics and schizophrenics. *Archives of General Psychiatry, 34,* 854–862.

Zinberg, N. E. (1975). Addiction and ego function. *Psychoanalytic Study of the Child, 30,* 567–588.

2

Varieties of Psychopathology Found in Patients with Addictive Disorders: A Review

MICHAEL H. ALLEN
RICHARD J. FRANCES

There has been a renewed interest in the relationship between substance use disorders and other psychopathology over the past 15 years. A positive result of the implementation of the multiaxial diagnostic system set forth in the third edition of the *Diagnostic and Statistical Manual of Mental Disorders* (DSM-III; American Psychiatric Association, 1980) has been a more careful assessment of patients who present with psychiatric disorders in association with substance abuse. Longitudinal studies, adoption studies, and family studies (Goodwin, VanDusen, & Mednick, 1984) call into question a simple a causal relationship between manifest psychopathology and addictive behavior. The challenge to clinicians and researchers has been to separate primary traits or disorders from symptoms secondary to acute and chronic intoxication, toxicity, idiosyncratic reactions, withdrawal, and the psychosocial effects of the addiction process. The work of McCord and McCord (1960), Vaillant (1984), and Pettinati, Sugerman, and Maurer (1982) suggests that the majority of psychopathology is secondary. Still, the high prevalence of severe psychiatric symptoms in patients with addictive disorders points to the need for careful psychiatric assessment in all patients with substance abuse (Woody et al., 1984). Because alcoholism and substance abuse both mimic and interact with all mental illnesses, to know substance abuse is to know all of psychiatry. This chapter reviews the literature on the varieties of psychopathology found in patients with addictive disorders.

AFFECTIVE DISORDERS

Historically, discussions of the etiology of addiction have related it to disturbances of affect. Thus, in his *Lectures on Clinical Psychiatry*, Kraepelin (1904/1968) described "that form of alcoholism which is usually called dipsomania . . . The starting point of every attack of this kind as can easily be proved is a state of depression, a feeling of discomfort and restlessness within, which patients try to escape by drinking" (p. 178). Rado (1932) described addicts as suffering from a "tense depression," the relief of which resulted in a sharp rise in self-esteem, which he felt to be the essential feature. Such thinking has intuitive appeal, and is reflected in concepts such as "depressive-equivalent behavior" and "self-medication" of painful affective states (Woody *et al.*, 1984). In fact, the issues are much more complex.

The apparent strength of the association among affective states, true affective illness, and addictive behavior has been found to vary according to population and design, and even within the same cohort evaluated by different criteria. Keeler, Taylor, and Miller (1979) found that the prevalence of depression in alcoholics across a range of studies varied between 3% and 98%. These investigators then administered clinical interviews, the Hamilton Depression Rating Scale, the Zung Self-Rating Depression Scale, and the Minnesota Multiphasic Personality Inventory (MMPI) to a group of recently detoxified alcoholics. They obtained percentages of depression of 8.6% by interview, 28% for the Hamilton, 66% for the Zung, and 43% for the MMPI in the same patients. Rounsaville, Rosenberger, Wilber, Weissman, and Kleber (1980) have reported similar findings in a study of 62 narcotic addicts; 42% of these met the criteria for major depression using the Schedule for Affective Disorders and Schizophrenia (SADS) and Research Diagnostic Criteria (RDC), while only 9% were so diagnosed using an unstructured interview and DSM-III criteria. (See also the chapter by Rounsaville & Kleber, this volume.) The work of Woody and his colleagues (Woody *et al.*, 1983) supports the findings of Rounsaville *et al.* Of 110 opiate addicts entering outpatient treatment, 43% had suffered major depression according to the SADS/RDC. (See also the chapter by Woody, O'Brien, McLellan, & Luborsky, this volume.)

The efforts to specify the relationship between addictive disorders and affective symptoms has led investigators to identify the earlier-onset disorder as "primary" and the later-onset disorder as "secondary." In a large longitudinal community survey, Weissman and Myers (1980) found that of 34 alcoholics, 15 were diagnosed as having major depression at some point, and 60% of these were considered primary depressives (i.e., depression preceded the onset of alcoholism). Schuckit (1983), however, states that only 10–15% of female alcoholics and 5% of male alcoholics have primary affective disorder. In a sample of 157 opiate addicts entering treatment, 48% had a lifetime diagnosis of major depression; 94.5% of these were secondary depressives (i.e., depression succeeded the onset of initial drug abuse) (Rounsaville, Weissman, Crits-Christoph, Wilber, & Kleber, 1982). In a court-referred group of male and female narcotic addicts, Croughan, Miller, Wagelin, and Whitman (1982) found no primary depression, but up to 50% secondary depression. In a large survey of young males, Schuckit (1982a) found that 60% of depressed subjects also acknowledged at least one substance-related problem that antedated the onset of the depression.

The depression associated with substances may also be qualitatively different. Woodruff, Guze, Clayton, and Carr (1973) found that alcoholics with secondary depression were more similar to other alcoholics than to depressed patients. Most of the differences were in delinquent, antisocial, and criminal behavior. Rounsaville et al. (1982) found that the most striking feature of opiate addicts' depressive symptomatology was the fluctuation. Major depressive episodes were relatively mild and not protracted, although 21–26% had some chronic symptoms that did not remit over a 6-month period.

Several studies have examined the relationship between bipolar affective illness, alcohol consumption and related problems. A number of investigators have found that consumption usually decreased during depressive episodes and increased during manic episodes. Mayfield and Coleman (1968) studied 59 bipolar and 21 unipolar males. Of those with cyclic affective disorder, 20% were considered excessive drinkers. Alcohol consumption increased in 19 with elation and 6 with depression. It decreased in 10 with depression, but never decreased with elation. The increase in drinking was not related to euphoria, but to restlessness and impulsivity, while the decrease in drinking with depression was seen as a concomitant of constriction of interest and activity. Reich, Davies, and Himmelhock (1974) retrospectively compared the records of 40 bipolar patients who had been hospitalized and 25 who had never required hospitalization. Of the latter, none had used alcohol excessively. In contrast, 13 of the 40 hospitalized manic patients had a history of excessive drinking during the manic phase of their illness. Of the 40 hospitalized bipolar depressed patients, 7 also had a history of excessive drinking during periods of elation. Thirty percent of these patients with histories of excessive drinking reported using alcohol for insomnia or hyperactivity. Some reported shunning alcohol when depressed, as it worsened their mood.

However, despite the association between bipolar illness and increased alcohol consumption, two studies (Moon & Patton, 1963; Morrison, 1974) failed to find an increased risk of alcohol addiction in bipolar patients. Cassidy, Flanagan, Spellman, and Cohen (1957) found that bipolar patients who increased their drinking during episodes of illness were more likely to have relatives with alcohol-related problems than bipolar patients who did not increase their drinking during these periods. Like Winokur, Clayton, and Reich (1969), Reich *et al.* (1974) concluded that excessive drinking might increase the morbidity of bipolar illness and the likelihood of hospitalization.

Underlying various hypotheses about the association of affect and addiction are assumptions about the psychopharmacology of drugs and alcohol. Experimental studies have shown that the administration of low doses of alcohol improves a number of mood variables (Mayfield, 1979; Tucker, Vuchinich, & Sobell, 1982). This effect is lost with continued drinking. Chronic intoxication is regularly accompanied by deterioration of affective state and by the development of depressive symptoms. This mood disturbance then disappears with abstinence. Paradoxical affective deterioration (increased depression, belligerence, and anxiety) in chronic states of intoxication has also been observed with heroin self-administration (Meyer & Mirin, 1979), experimental amphetamine intoxication (Griffith, Cavanaugh, Held, & Oates, 1972), and cocaine abuse (Wein, Mirin, Michael & Sollogub, 1986). Alcoholics differ from nonalcoholics in their tendency to retain their expectations of the intoxicated state rather than their actual experience (Mayfield, 1979; Tamerin & Mendelson, 1969). Mayfield has hypothesized that alcoholics anticipate affective improvement and then continue drinking because the resulting dysphoria intensifies the pursuit.

The link between affective illness and addiction has also been considered in behavioral genetics and family studies. Amark (195), in a study of psychiatric morbidity in male alcoholics and their relatives, found risk for "psychopathy" and "psychogenic psychoses" to be increased in these families. The latter category included a number of disorders, including affective illness. Winokur and Pitts (1965) studied the same phenomenon in the families of patients with affective disorder. These authors compared the prevalence of affective and other disorders in the parents of 366 patients diagnosed as having manic depression, involutional psychosis, or psychotic depressive reaction, with the prevalence of these disorders in the parents of 382 patients with other diagnoses and matched controls. The parents of affectively ill probands showed a significantly higher prevalence of affective disorder and alcoholism. The prevalence of alcoholism was 9.5% in fathers and 1.1% in mothers of affectively ill patients compared to 1.7% and 0%, respectively, in the comparison group. Affective illness was more common in female relatives, and alcoholism and sociopathy in male relatives. It was observed that if one combined the prevalence of alcoholism and affective disorder in male relatives of affectively disordered patients, one would approximate the combined prevalence of the same disorders in female relatives. However, alcoholism in fathers was also related to several other diagnoses, including schizophrenia, psychoneurosis, and personality disorders.

Focusing on the association of alcoholism and affective disorder more closely, Pitts and Winokur (1966) compared the families of affectively ill probands, primary alcoholic probands, and controls. Of affectively ill probands, brothers had disproportionately more alcoholism, while sisters manifested more affective disorder. Of primary alcoholic probands, fathers had significantly more alcoholism, but no more affective disorder or other psychiatric illness than controls while siblings showed excesses of both alcoholism and affective disorder, with most of the excess alcoholism in brothers and excess affective disorder in sisters.

Schuckit, Pitts, Reich, King, and Winokur (1969) described a study of 39 women with primary alcoholism and 19 with affective disorder antedating problem drinking; they noted differences between the two groups and their families. The primary alcoholic group was older and had been ill longer, while the affectively disordered group had made significantly more suicide attempts. The rate of psychiatric illness in close relatives was identical, and male first-degree relatives of both were alcoholic. However, significantly more female relatives of primary alcoholic probands were alcoholic while those of primary affective disorder probands were depressed. When the primary alcoholics with affective symptoms were removed from that group, the difference became even more significant. ⌈These findings suggested that two distinct types of alcoholism could be identified in females: primary alcoholism and alcoholism secondary to affective disorder.⌋

Winokur and his colleagues extended the series of alcoholics (Winokur, Reich, Rimmer, & Pitts, 1970) and unipolar depressed patients (Winokur, Cadoret, Dorzab, & Baker, 1971) and their families using personal interviews rather than family history methods. Employing RDC and clearly distinguishing primary and secondary diagnoses, 73% of 156 alcoholic males were considered to have primary alcoholism. Of the remainder, in which another psychiatric disorder preceded the onset of alcoholism, 20% had a diagnosis of personality disorder, mainly sociopathy; 3% had a diagnosis of affective disorder; and 4% had other diagnoses. Of 103 females, 61% were primary alcoholics, and among the remainder the most common antecedents were affective disorder (25%) and personality disorder (7%). The higher prevalence of sociopathy in males and primary affective disorder in females with secondary alcoholism was quite significant. This difference also held for morbid risk of affective disorder in female relatives, and for sociopathy and alcoholism in male relatives. Male relatives were much more likely to be ill than females and, if the affected proband was female, there was a greater likelihood of illness in first-degree relatives.

Considering age at onset, Winokur and his colleagues analyzed the data on 100 unipolar depressive patients for onset before or after age 40 and came to the conclusion that there were two, and possibly three, discrete groups of depressive patients. First, there were early-onset male and female depressives with an increased risk of alcoholism and sociopathy in male relatives. Second, late-onset male depressives were found to have equal numbers of male and female relatives with depression, minimal amounts of alcoholism and sociopathy in family members, and less depression and total psychiatric illness in all first-degree relatives. Late-onset female depressives were thought to represent a third group related to late-onset male depressives, in which there was a higher frequency of affective disorder but not of alcoholism or sociopathy in the family.

Winokur, Cadoret, Dorzab, and Baker (1974) reviewed these findings and concluded that depression is etiologically heterogeneous. They proposed a subtype, "depression spectrum disease," characterized by early onset predominantly in females, with an increased frequency of alcoholic and antisocial male relatives. Winokur's group's findings have received some support from Mendlewicz and Baron (1981), who partially replicated data on morbid risk for alcoholism, sociopathy, and depression in the families of depressed patients. They found, as did Winokur's group, an increased frequency of alcoholism, sociopathy, and unipolar depression in relatives of early-onset probands. Early-onset females had twice as much depression in female relatives as male relatives (17% and 8%, respectively), while late-onset males had equal amounts of depression in male and female relatives (8% in both).

This suggests the possibility of a genetic vulnerability to certain forms of mental illness with different phenotypic expression in men and women, perhaps related to environmental variables. The recent findings of the Amish study (Egeland & Hostetter, 1983) support this concept. In this culturally and genetically homogeneous population without alcoholism and sociopathy, rates of unipolar depression were equal for men and women.

On the other hand, Cloninger, Reich, and Wetzel (1979) cite data from Winokur's group showing that alcoholism is more frequent in families of nondepressed alcoholics than in families of primary depressives with alcoholism. This should not be the case if the two have the same underlying familial predisposition. The issue of mode of transmission is too complex for this discussion, but Cloninger *et al.* feel that alcoholism, sociopathy, and depression are genetically distinct. They postulate that any overlap is due to intervening environmental variables. Adoption studies are consistent with this result. Biological sons of alcoholics adopted away at an early age manifest a higher frequency of alcoholism, but not antisocial personality or affective disorder, than biological sons of nonalcoholics (Goodwin, Schulsinger, Hermansen, Guze, & Winokur, 1973; Goodwin *et al.*, 1974) Biological daughters of alcoholics reared away have excess alcoholism but not depression (Goodwin, Schulsinger, Knop, Mednick, & Guze, 1977).

Considering environmental variables, Vaillant (1984) has observed that if one controls for the effect of parental alcoholism, the effect of chaotic home life vanishes. Of 57 men with an alcoholic parent but few environmental weaknesses in childhood, 27% became alcohol-dependent as adults, while only 5% of 56 men with nonalcoholic parents became dependent, despite many psychosocial stressors.

[A final link between affective disorder and addiction is the finding that the majority of successful suicides suffer from one or both of these disorders (Baraclough, Bunch, Nelson, & Sainsbury, 1974; Dorpat & Ripley, 1960; (Robins, Murphy, Wilkinson, Gassner, & Keyes, 1959).] Suicide, at least in cases identified by coroners' reports, appeared as a late complication of a long history of drinking. Murphy, Armstrong, Hermele, Fisher, and Clendenin (1979) reported that depression was not a universal finding in suicidal alcoholics. They found that 11 of 50 successful suicides in their sample were suffering from uncomplicated alcoholism. The majority had alcoholism with secondary depression.] Only 8% were reported to have primary affective disorder with secondary alcoholism. Although depression was not universal, 26% of their sample had experienced a major loss within the previous 6 weeks. Of those with uncomplicated alcoholism, 45% had suffered a major loss within the previous 6 weeks and 64% within the past year.

PERSONALITY

A fairly large number of studies have attempted to relate personality traits or constructs to the risk of addictive disorder (Clopton, 1978; Morey & Blashfield, 1981; Sutherland, Schroeder, & Tordella, 1950; Syme, 1957). [Despite this serious and important effort, no single personality type, group of traits, or disorder is now thought to be specific for addiction.] Morey and Blashfield (1981) observed that attempts to identify personality characteristics of alcoholics may depict a composite personality that obscures differences and fails to be representative of any existing types.\

If rigorous criteria requiring antisocial behavior in four life areas before age 16 are employed (Schuckit, 1983), 10–20% of male and 5–10% of female alcoholics requiring admission can be diagnosed as having antisocial personality disorder. When DSM-III criteria are applied, the prevalence of antisocial personality disorder may be higher than when other criteria are utilized (Gunderson, 1983). Among opiate addicts, Woody *et al.* (1983) identified 15% of an outpatient male veteran cohort as antisocial according to the RDC, which are more restrictive than DSM-III criteria. Rounsaville *et al.* (1980) found 20% antisocial using

RDC in a mostly male community inpatient service. In a court referral service, 73% of males and 61% of females were so diagnosed (Croughan *et al.*, 1982). The association between antisocial personality disorder and addictive behavior will appear strongest in court-referred patient groups, and studies employing DSM-III criteria for antisocial personality disorder.

Other personality findings include schizotypal features (RDC) in 8% of opiate addicts; borderline personality disorder (DSM-III) in 3%; dependent personality (DSM-III) in 2%; and Briquet's syndrome (RDC) in 0.7% of females and 0% of males (Rounsaville *et al.*, 1980). Woody *et al.* (1983) similarly reported schizotypal features in 6%.

A number of atheoretical instruments have been used to study personality in addict populations. Apfeldorf (1974) has reviewed the assumptions implicit in the MMPI literature and describes two basic approches to the use of the MMPI. These are typified by the work of Rosen (1960), who concluded that there were no marked differences between alcoholics and comparable psychiatric patients, and McAndrew (1965), who felt that alcoholism is a distinct entity with unique personality characteristics. McAndrew developed an item pool that in a number of studies was able to distinguish alcoholics from other psychiatric patients. Finney, Smith, Skeeters, and Auvenshine (1971) have described high scorers on the McAndrew Alcoholism Scale as bold, uninhibited, self-confident, sociable, rebellious, and resentful of authority. Brown (1950) on the other hand, divided alcoholic MMPIs into psychopathic and psychoneurotic subgroups, and observed that these subgroups were more similar to psychoneurotics and psychopaths who did not drink than they were to each other.

Morey and Blashfield (1981) reviewed the recent literature that has attempted to divide alcoholics into meaningful subtypes using cluster analysis of data gathered with objective instruments, including the MMPI, the Differential Personality Inventory (DPI), and the 16 Personality Factor Questionnaire (16 PF). The number of subtypes identified by different authors has varied, but generally two subtypes, first identified by Goldstein and Linden (1969), have been found by subsequent authors. Goldstein and Linden's Type I was characterized by an elevated 4 (*Pd*) scale and was described as an emotionally unstable personality type, exhibiting a trait disturbance marked by poorly controlled anger, with "temper tantrums" and other overt forms of emotional expression in response to frustration. The nosological entity associated with this was psychopathic personality. Type II, having a 278 (*D*, *Pt*, and *Sc*) profile, was marked by the presence of either anxiety reaction or reactive depression, with somatic complaints and suicidal ideation. These persons were described as psychoneurotic. Subsequent studies (Clopton, 1978; Donovan, Chaney, & O'Leary, 1978; Whitelock, Overall, & Patrick, 1971) have generally found a cluster with a high 4 scale and have noted that these tend to be moderately heavy users who come to attention as a result of poor impulse control and antisocial behavior. The 278 cluster has consistently been associated with the heaviest use of alcohol, more severe consequences, and severe psychopathology. Similar results have been obtained in drug-dependent populations (Eshbaugh, Dick, & Tosi, 1982). Dimensional analysis of empirically derived personality subtypes suggests that an important dimension reflecting a major difference between the 278 and 4 clusters is the dimension of subjective distress (Skinner, Jackson, & Hoffman, 1974). This dimension contrasts emotional, highly anxious subjects with those exhibiting shallow affect and denial.

One limitation of the aforementioned studies is that the subjects have generally been males in treatment at Veterans Administration hospitals or state hospital facilities. Data were usually collected shortly after admission to a treatment unit. Thus, the results reported in these studies may not be generalizable to other alcoholics and substance abusers. The methodological flaws in the work were highlighted by comparison with data that have been collected in longitudinal research designs. For example, Kammeier, Hoffmann, and Loper (1973) compared college entrance MMPI profiles of a control group to those of a group who entered treatment for alcoholism an average of 13 years later. They were impressed by the lack of obvious deviance in the college orientation group. The most frequent scale with *T* scores of 70 or above in the orientation group was the 9 (*Ma*) scale. By the time of entering treatment, however, the classic alcoholic MMPI profiles had emerged, with 50% scoring 70 or above on the 4 scale. The treatment group appeared to be suffering from increases in irritability, depression, hostility, anxiety, impulsivity, resentment, instrumentality, and difficulties in interpersonal relationships. On admission to treatment, these individuals appeared to be self-centered, immature, dependent, resentful, irresponsible, and unable to face reality.

Rohan, Tatro, and Rotman (1969) followed the MMPIs of a group of alcoholic inpatients over a period averaging 72 days. Approximately half presented with *T* scores above 70 on scale 4. Of these, two-thirds dramatically improved on other scales while scale 4 remained elevated; the remaining third improved on scale 4 also. The first group was described as exhibiting stable psychopathic personality, and the second as exhibiting psychopathic reaction type. Another group of depressed somatic patients with 213 (*D*, *Hs*, and *Hy*) profiles lost many of their somatic complaints as they felt healthier. Patients followed over longer periods of either complete abstinence or occasional slips tended to show continued improvement (Pettinati *et al.*, 1982).

ORGANIC CONDITIONS

Alcoholism and drug addiction have long been identified in a variety of ways with organic conditions. The earliest descriptions of alcoholism include organic psychoses (Kraepelin, 1904/1968), and there is a large body of literature describing neurological syndromes, more subtle neuropsychological impairment and post mortem findings in addicts (Fitzhugh, Fitzhugh, & Reitan, 1965; Victor, 1962). It has always been suspected as well that one of the bases for familial transmission of alcoholism was a direct toxic effect on either the germ cells or the developing embryo. Recent efforts have begun to focus on populations at risk, attempting to identify differences in premorbid brain functioning that might predispose persons to the development of addiction or explain the great individual variation in its consequences (Porjesz & Begleiter, 1981). Although this is still a controversial area, there is a body of evidence that a heterogeneous group of organic conditions may be associated with an increased risk of addiction and more severe consequences. The neuropsychological deficits consequent to alcohol addiction are described in greater detail in the chapter by Becker and Kaplan, this volume.

MINIMAL BRAIN DYSFUNCTION AND ATTENTION DEFICIT DISORDER

Wender (1971) has described minimal brain dysfunction (MBD) in children and its persistence as attention deficit disorder (ADD), residual type, in adults. The condition is a fairly common disorder of childhood, affecting as many as 3% of prepubertal children. It is characterized by inattention, distractability, overactivity, impulsivity, mood lability, and low frustration tolerance. There may be neurological soft signs, although only about 5% of cases will have a clear neurological disorder (American Psychiatric Association, 1980). For the remainder, the etiology is not known and may not be structural.

Stewart, Pitts, Craig, and Dieruf (1966) described a group of such children in whom they found prevalent delayed speech development, speech problems, poor coordination, and strabismus. The children had an increased frequency of antisocial problems, including persistent lying, stealing, vandalism, fire setting, and cruelty to animals. The symptons, once thought to wane and disappear spontaneously in adolescence, may persist into late adolescence and early adulthood, when the condition is said to be associated with an increased risk of sociopathy, drug and alcohol abuse, and addiction (Wender, Reimherr, & Wood, 1981).

Retrospective studies have noted an increased frequency of signs and symptoms of childhood hyperactivity in a number of adult psychiatric disorders, including early-onset severe alcoholism, impulsive character disorders, explosive personality, violent dyscontrol, depression, anxiety, and certain subgroups of schizophrenia (Wender *et al.*, 1981). Tarter and his colleagues (Tarter, McBride, Buonpane, & Schneider, 1977) divided a cohort of alcoholic patients into primary and secondary groups based on presence or absence of a precipitant. Primary alcoholics reported significantly more symptoms of MBD and a younger age at onset of drinking than did secondary alcoholics, who did not differ from the normal controls. Psychiatric patients were more similar to primary alcoholics. High scores for MBD were correlated with "essential alcoholism," using the Rudie–McGaughran scale. Essential alcoholics have been described by Rudie and McGaughran (1969) as dependent, passive, and psychosexually immature. They begin drinking early in life without specific precipitating cause, and demonstrate a history of long-standing maladjustment and social incompetency. Tarter (1982) postulated that the disturbed developmental history observed in "essential alcoholics" may be the product of neuropsychological factors such as hyperactivity or MBD. He found that 42% of the variance of the essential–reactive score was attributable to characteristics of MBD, and that when this was also correlated with alcohol use inventory scales, 46.8% of the variance of alcoholism severity could be predicted using combined MBD and essential–reactive scores. Hale, Hesselbrock, and Hesselbrock (1982) have reported a similarly high frequency of MBD symptoms in childhood among alcoholics; 20% of their sample also reported items associated with conduct disorder in childhood and antisocial behavior in adulthood.

Family studies by Cantwell (1972) and Morrison and Stewart (1971) have shown an increased risk of hyperactivity, alcoholism, sociopathy, and hysteria in the relatives of hyperactive children. Of the relatives diagnosed as hyperactive themselves, a particularly high frequency also suffered from major psychiatric illness. Goodwin, Schulsinger, Hermansen, Guze, and Winokur's (1975) retrospective study of Danish male adoptees found that more than half of the alcoholics demonstrated antisocial behavior and/or childhood hyperactivity. The relationship between familial alcoholism and childhood MBD and hyperactivity may, in some cases, represent a variant of fetal alcohol effects (Clarren & Smith, 1978; Lippmann, 1980).

Mendelson, Johnson, and Stewart (1971) prospectively studied a group of 83 hyperactive children between the ages of 12 and 16 who had been diagnosed as hyperactive from 2 to 5 years earlier. Although half were markedly improved, rebellious attitude had replaced overactivity as the most frequent complaint; 59% had had some contact with the police, 18% had already been before juvenile court, 15% were drinking excessively, 15% were setting fires, and 13% were enuretic. Of the children with the most antisocial problems, 22% of their fathers and 4% of their mothers were problem-drinkers.

A controlled prospective 10-year study of 25 hyperactive children (Weiss, Hechtman, Perlman, Hopkins, & Wener, 1979) found that immature and impulsive traits persisted but that court referrals did not significantly increase. More hyperactives had used certain drugs, mainly "hash" and "grass," but hyperactives did not differ from controls in use of "speed" or narcotics or in severity of drug use. Hallucinogen use was more common in controls.

Residual symptoms of childhood MBD or ADD may persist into adulthood. These individuals may then be at increased risk for substance use, especially in adolescence, but the basis and outcome have not been established prospectively.

PSYCHOSIS

Like organic conditions, psychosis has been cited more frequently as a condition secondary to addiction. Schuckit (1982b) has described the psychotic symptomatology of alcoholics, noting that the symptoms are not distinct from those of functional disorders. Most are associated with active drinking. In Schuckit's study, none of the alcoholics met the criteria for schizophrenia; schizophrenia was rare in their families as well. Antisocial personality and polysubstance abuse correlated more closely with psychotic symptomatology than did drinking history.

Ellinwood and Petrie (1976) have reviewed the literature on psychiatric syndromes associated with stimulants and hallucinogens. A number of reaction types have been described with psychotomimetics (Ellinwood & Petrie, 1976; Frosch, 1969; Meyer, 1978). Anxiety and panic may occur in both naive and experienced drug users (Frosch, 1969) in response to the loss of cognitive control or the emergence of disturbing material (Ellinwood & Petrie, 1976). Recurrent reactions or flashbacks without further drug ingestion have been reported in a third of LSD users (Frosch, 1969) and in marijuana users (Meyer, 1978). Prolonged reactions described include chronic anxiety states (Frosch, 1969), "amotivational syndrome" (McGlothlin & West, 1978), and prolonged psychoses (S. Cohen, 1960; S. Cohen & Ditman, 1963; Glass & Bowers, 1970).

Psychotic reactions have been a focus of controversy. Adverse reactions of any type were reported in a very small number of approximately 5000 cases of LSD administration under experimental or therapeutic conditions (S. Cohen, 1960). Glass and Bowers's (1970) patients had used LSD 50–250 times over periods of 18–24 months before coming to attention. Psychosis is probable in any individual given high doses of amphetamine over a long enough period (Ellinwood & Petrie, 1976). All of Griffith *et al.*'s (1972) subjects became psychotic within 5 days of repeated amphetamine administration, and all rapidly remitted following discontinuation.

ʃThe role of pre-existing psychopathology or vulnerability to adverse reactions is complex⌡ Antisocial personality accounted for an average of 45% of amphetamine psychoses in a review of six series (Ellinwood, 1969). Prolonged psychoses (S. Cohen, 1960; S. Cohen & Ditman, 1963; Glass & Bowers, 1970) suggest an interaction of drug and premorbid vulnerability to schizophrenia.ʃHekimian and Gershon (1968) found that 50% of psychotic drug abusers showed signs of schizophrenia and 9% showed schizoid features prior to initial exposure. Patients diagnosed as schizophrenic more commonly abuse psychotomimetics, rarely central nervous system depressants (McLellan & Druley, 1977), despite recent interest in the relationship of endogenous opioids and psychosis (Emrich, *et al.*, 1977) {Breakey, Goodell, Lorenz, and McHugh (1974) compared drug-abusing to non-drug-abusing schizophrenics and found a 4-year-earlier onset of symptoms in the drug abusers despite better premorbid personality, suggesting a role for drug abuse in the precipitation of schizophrenia.] Such findings are consistent with Hollister's view that LSD does not induce permanent psychosis, but, rather, attracts emotionally disturbed individuals (Hollister, quoted in Ellinwood & Petrie, 1976).

ANXIETY DISORDERS

Anxiety as affect may occur as a symptom of affective disorders, psychosis, personality, and organic disorders. [Anxiety is also the major symptom of a group of discrete disorders of relatively low frequency but possibly overrepresented among addicts.] In their survey, Weissman, Myers, and Harding (1980) found generalized anxiety disorder in 9% and phobias in 3% of alcoholics. In an inpatient addict population, Rounsaville *et al.* (1980) found 11% with generalized anxiety disorder, 5% with phobic disorder, 5% with panic, and 4% with obsessive–compulsive disorder.

PANIC DISORDER

Panic disorder, marked by onset in the teens and 20s of discrete panic attacks with multiple autonomic signs including cardiorespiratory symptoms and tremulousness, has previously come under the rubric of "anxiety neurosis" or "neurocirculatory asthenia." Shader, Goodman, and Gever (1982) describe the condition, distinguishing it from generalized anxiety disorder and citing a prevalence of 1–2% in the general population. There may be genetic vulnerability to it (Crowe, Pauls, Slymen, & Noyes, 1980; Noyes, Clancy, Crowe, Hoenk, & Slymen, 1970). It is unclear from the existing literature whether its frequency is increased in addict populations. Rounsaville *et al.* (1980) found that 3 of 62 narcotic addicts had had panic disorder at some point, while 7 had had generalized anxiety disorder.

Although the numbers in addict populations are small, there is a high familial prevalence of panic disorder and an increased prevalence of alcoholism among the male relatives of probands with panic disorder (M. E. Cohen, Badal, Kilpatrick, Reed, & White, 1951). Noyes *et al.* (1970) found the morbid risk in 112 probands and their families to be significantly increased for both panic disorder and alcoholism. The risk of alcoholism among male relatives was 10% for subjects and 5% for controls. Crowe *et al.* (1980) found an even higher risk with 15% of the index population and only 4% of controls manifesting either alcohol abuse or dependence. Other anxiety disorders and depression were not increased.

POSTTRAUMATIC STRESS DISORDER

Posttraumatic stress disorder (PTSD) is a syndrome marked by the development of symptoms following a traumatic event outside the range of usual human experience. Characteristic symptoms include re-experiencing of the traumatic event; numbing of responsiveness to or reduced involvement with the external world; and a variety of autonomic and cognitive symptoms, including hyperalertness, exaggerated startle response, insomnia, and dysphoria. Onset may be immediate or may occur with a latency of months or years. Substance abuse disorders are listed as a complication of PTSD in DSM-III (American Psychiatric Association, 1980). The association of substance use with PTSD is, however, controversial.

Archibald and Tuddenham (1965) were the first to report the persistence of symptoms in World War II combat fatigue patients. Although the diagnosis of PTSD was not in use at the time, the syndrome they described is very similar to the current nosological entity. They noted that although there was actually an increase in symptomatology in their sample over time, alcoholism was nearly as frequent among noncombat patients as among combat patients. During the Vietnam War, with high availability of alcohol and drugs in a stressful environment, there were reports of heavy substance use among troops, with a high percentage of veterans giving up drugs on return to civilian life. It has also been reported that those returning from Vietnam felt betrayed and alienated, and had higher incidences of arrests and alcoholism (Egendorf, 1982). Sierles, Alan, McFarland, and Taylor (1983) report that in a sample of 25 patients with PTSD, 64% had alcoholism and 20% were drug-dependent. The question remains as to whether variations in the pattern of abuse or addiction are directly related to the stress response, or to an underlying vulnerability to addiction, or as Roy (1983) suggests, to the nonrandom effect of assignment to combat.

CONCLUSION

The interactions between psychopathology and the addictions are often difficult to differentiate clinically and are only beginning to be researched. The following are still controversial questions raised in the research reported in this chapter.

1. Is substance abuse or addiction inherited distinctly, or does it interact with a broad-based genetic vulnerability to psychiatric illness?
2. To what degree is familial substance abuse predictive of psychiatric illness?
3. To what degree can substance abuse be secondary to psychiatric illness?
4. What is the contribution of substance abuse in exacerbation or causation of other psychiatric symptomatology?
5. In what ways can substance abuse mask, "treat," or alter the expression of other psychiatric illness?

The use of multiaxial diagnoses and of reliable diagnostic criteria is important in improving our ability to classify patients and heighten awareness of interactions. Better understanding of the relationships between psychopathology and addiction will help us further improve the classification system in the revised DSM-III, and future editions of the *International Classification of Diseases*.

REFERENCES

Amark, C. (1951). A study in alcoholism. *Acta Psychiatrica Scandinavica, 70*, 1–283.
American Psychiatric Association. (1980). *Diagnostic and statistical manual of mental disorders* (3rd ed.). Washington, DC: Author.
Apfeldorf, M. (1974). Contrasting assumptions and directions in MMPI research on alcoholism. *Quarterly Journal of Studies on Alcohol, 35*, 1374–1379.
Archibald, H. C., & Tuddenham, R. D. (1965). Persistent stress reaction after combat. *Archives of General Psychiatry, 12*, 475–481.

Baraclough, J., Bunch, J., Nelson, D., & Sainsbury, P. (1974). 100 cases of suicide: Clinical aspects. *British Journal of Psychiatry*, *125*, 355–373.

Breakey, W. R., Goodell, H., Lorenz, P. C., & McHugh, P. R. (1974). Hallucinogenic drugs as precipitants of schizophrenia. *Psychological Medicine*, *4*, 255–261.

Brown, M. A. (1950). Alcoholic profiles on the Minnesota Multiphasic Personality Inventory. *Journal of Clinical Psychology*, *6*, 266–269.

Cantwell, D. P. (1972). Psychiatric illness in the families of hyperactive children. *Archives of General Psychiatry*, *27*, 414–417.

Cassidy, W. L., Flanagan, M. B., Spellman, B. A., & Cohen, M. E. (1957). Clinical observations in manic–depressive disease. *Journal of the American Medical Association*, *164*, 1535–1546.

Clarren, S. K., & Smith, D. W. (1978). The fetal alcohol syndrome. *New England Journal of Medicine*, *298*, 1067.

Cloninger, R. C., Reich, T., & Wetzel, R. (1979). Alcoholism and affective disorders. Familial associations and genetic models. In D. W. Goodwin & C. K. Erickson (Eds.), *Alcoholism and affective disorders* (pp. 57–86). Jamaica, NY: Spectrum.

Clopton, J. R. (1978). Alcoholism and the MMPI: A review. *Journal of Studies on Alcohol*, *39*, 1540–1551.

Cohen, M. E., Badal, D. W., Kilpatrick, A., Reed, E. W., & White, P. D. (1951). The high familial prevalence of neurocirculatory asthenia. *American Journal of Human Genetics*, *3*, 126–158.

Cohen, S. (1960). Lysergic acid diethylamide: Side effects and complications. *Journal of Nervous and Mental Disease*, *130*, 30–40.

Cohen, S., & Ditman, K. S. (1963). Prolonged adverse reactions to lysergic acid diethylamide. *Archives of General Psychiatry*, *8*, 71–81.

Croughan, J. L., Miller, P., Wagelin, D., & Whitman, G. Y. (1982). Psychiatric illness in male and female narcotic addicts. *Journal of Clinical Psychiatry*, *43*, 225–228.

Crowe, R. R., Pauls, P. L., Slymen, D. J., & Noyes, R. (1980). A family study of anxiety neurosis: Morbidity risk in families of patients with or without mitral valve prolapse. *Archives of General Psychiatry*, *37*, 77–79.

Donovan, D. M., Chaney, E. F., & O'Leary, M. R. (1978). Alcohol MMPI subtypes: Relationship to drinking styles, benefits and consequences. *Journal of Nervous and Mental Disease*, *166*, 553–561.

Dorpat, T. L., & Ripley, H. S. (1960). A study of suicide in the Seattle area. *Comprehensive Psychiatry*, *1*, 349–359.

Egeland, J. A., & Hostetter, M. A. (1983). Amish study I: Affective disorders among the Amish, 1976–1980. *American Journal of Psychiatry*, *140*, 56–61.

Egendorf, A. (1982). The post-war hell of Vietnam veterans: Recent research. *Hospital and Community Psychiatry*, *35*, 901–907.

Ellinwood, E. H. (1969). Amphetamine psychosis: A multi-dimensional process. *Seminars in Psychiatry*, *1*, 208–226.

Ellinwood, E. H., & Petrie, W. M. (1976). Psychiatric syndromes induced by non-medical use of drugs. In R. J. Gibbons, Y. Israel, H. Kalant, R. E. Popham, W. Schmidt, & R. C. Smart (Eds.), *Research advances in alcohol and drug problems* (Vol. 3, pp. 177–222). New York: Wiley.

Emrich, H. M., Cording, C., Pirée, S., Kölling, A., Möller, H. J., vonZerssen, D., & Herz, A. (1977). Actions of naloxone in different types of psychosis. In E. Usdin, W. W. Bunney, & M. S. Kline (Eds.), *Endorphins in mental health research* (pp. 452–460). New York: Macmillan.

Eshbaugh, T. M., Dick, K. V., & Tosi, D. J. (1982). Typological analysis of MMPI personality patterns of drug dependent females. *Journal of Personality Assessment, 46*, 488–494.

Finney, J. C., Smith, D. F., Skeeters, D. E., & Auvenshine, C. D. (1971). MMPI alcoholism scales: Factor structure and content analysis. *Quarterly Journal of Studies on Alcohol, 32*, 1055–1060.

Fitzhugh, E. C., Fitzhugh, K. B., & Reitan, R. M. (1965). Adaptive abilities and intellectual functioning of hospitalized alcoholics: Further considerations. *Quarterly Journal of Studies on Alcohol, 26*, 402–411.

Frosch, W. A. (1969). Patterns of response to self-administration of LSD. In R. E. Meyer (Ed.), *Adverse reactions to hallucinogenic drugs* (pp. 74–79). Washington, DC: U.S. Government Printing Office.

Glass, G. S., & Bowers, M. B. (1970). Chronic psychosis associated with long-term psychomimetic drug abuse. *Archives of General Psychiatry, 23*, 97–103.

Goldstein, S. G., & Linden, J. D. (1969). Multivariate classification of alcoholics by means of the MMPI. *Journal of Abnormal Psychology, 74*, 66–669.

Goodwin, D. W., Schulsinger, F., Hermansen, L., Guze, S. B., & Winokur, G. (1973). Alcohol problems in adoptees raised apart from alcoholic biological parents. *Archives of General Psychiatry, 28*, 238–243.

Goodwin, D. W., Schulsinger, F., Hermansen, L., Guze, S. B., & Winokur, G. (1975). Alcoholism and the hyperactive child syndrome. *Journal of Nervous and Mental Disease, 160*, 349–533.

Goodwin, D. W., Schulsinger, F., Knop, J., Mednick, S., & Guze, S. B. (1977). Alcoholism and depression in adopted-out daughters of alcoholics. *Archives of General Psychiatry, 34*, 751–755.

Goodwin, D. W., Schulsinger, F., Miller, N., Hermansen, L., Winokur, G., & Guze, S. B. (1974). Drinking problems in adopted and nonadopted sons of alcoholics. *Archives of General Psychiatry, 31*, 164–169.

Goodwin, D. W., VanDusen, K. T., & Mednick, S. A. (Eds.). (1984). *Longitudinal research in alcoholism.* Boston: Kluwer-Nyhoff.

Griffith, J. D., Cavanaugh, J., Held, J., & Oates, J. A. (1972). Dextroamphetamine: Evaluation of psychomimetic properties in man. *Archives of General Psychiatry, 26*, 97–100.

Gunderson, J. P. DSM-III diagnoses of personality disorders. (1983). In J. P. Frosch (Ed.), *Current perspectives on personality disorders* (pp. 19–39). Washington, DC: American Psychiatric Press.

Hale, M. S., Hesselbrock, M., & Hesselbrock, V. (1982). Childhood deviance in sociopathy and alcoholism. *Journal of Psychiatric Treatment and Evaluation, 4*, 33–36.

Hekimian, L. J., & Gershon, S. (1968). Characteristics of drug abusers admitted to a psychiatric hospital. *Journal of the American Medical Association, 205*, 125–130.

Kammeier, M. L., Hoffman, H., & Loper, R. G. (1973). Personality characteristics of alcoholics as college freshmen and at the time of treatment. *Quarterly Journal of Studies on Alcohol, 34*, 390–399.

Keeler, M. H., Taylor, C. I., & Miller, W. C. (1979). Are all recently detoxified alcoholics depressed? *American Journal of Psychiatry, 136*, 586–588.

Kraepelin, E. (1968). *Lectures on clinical psychiatry* (T. Johnstone, Rev. and Ed.). New York: Hafner. (Original work published 1904).

Lippmann, S. (1980). Prenatal alcohol in minimal brain dysfunction. *Southern Medical Journal, 73*, 1173–1174.

Mayfield, D. G. (1979). Alcohol and affect: Experimental studies. In D. W. Goodwin & C. K. Erickson (Eds.), *Alcoholism and affective disorders, clinical, genetic, and biochemical studies* (pp. 99–107). Jamaica, NY: Spectrum.

Mayfield, D. G., & Coleman, L. L. (1968). Alcohol use and affective disorder. *Diseases of the Nervous System, 29,* 467–474.

McAndrew, C. (1965). The differentiation of male alcoholic outpatients from nonalcoholic psychiatric outpatients by means of the MMPI. *Quarterly Journal of Studies on Alcohol, 26,* 238–246.

McLellan, A. T., & Druley, K. A. (1977). Non-random relation between drugs of abuse and psychiatric diagnosis. *Journal of Psychiatric Research, 13,* 179–184.

McCord, W., & McCord, J. (1960). *Origins of alcoholism.* Stanford, CA: Stanford University Press.

McGlothlin, W. H., & West, L. J. (1978). The marihuana problem: An overview. *American Journal of Psychiatry, 125,* 126–134.

Mendelson, W., Johnson, N., & Stewart, M. A. (1971). Hyperactive children as teenagers: A follow-up study. *Journal of Nervous and Mental Disease, 153,* 273–279.

Mendlewicz, J., & Baron, M. (1981). Morbidity risk in subtypes of unipolar depressive illness. *British Journal of Psychiatry, 139,* 463–466.

Meyer, R. E. (1978). Behavioral pharmacology of marihuana. In M. A. Lipton, A. DiMascio, & K. F. Killam (Eds.), *Psychopharmacology: A generation of progress* (pp. 1639–1652). New York: Raven Press.

Meyer, R. E., & Mirin, S. M. (1979). *The heroin stimulus.* New York: Plenum Press.

Moon, L. E., & Patton, R. E. (1963). The alcoholic psychotic in the New York State mental hospitals, 1951–1960. *Quarterly Journal of Studies on Alcohol, 24,* 664–681.

Morey, L. C., & Blashfield, R. K. (1981). Empirical classifications of alcoholism. *Journal of Studies on Alcohol, 42,* 925–937.

Morrison, J. R. (1974). Bipolar affective disorder and alcoholism. *American Journal of Psychiatry, 131,* 1130–1133.

Morrison, J. R., & Stewart, M. A. (1971). A family study of the hyperactive child syndrome. *Biological Psychiatry, 3,* 189–195.

Murphy, G. E., Armstrong, J. W., Hermele, S. L., Fisher, J. R., & Clendenin, W. W. (1979). Suicide in alcoholism. *Archives of General Psychiatry, 36,* 65–69.

Noyes, R., Clancy, J., Crowe, R., Hoenk, P. R., & Slymen, D. J. (1970). The familial prevalence of anxiety and neurosis. *Archives of General Psychiatry, 35,* 1057–1059.

Pettinati, H. N., Sugerman, A., & Maurer, H. S. (1982). Four year MMPI changes in abstinent and drinking alcoholics. *Alcoholism: Clinical and Experimental Research, 6,* 487–494.

Pitts, F. N., & Winokur, G. (1966). Affective disorders VII: Alcoholism and affective disorder. *Journal of Psychiatric Research, 4,* 37–50.

Porjesz, B., & Begleiter, H. (1981). Human evoked brain potentials and alcohol. *Alcoholism: Clinical and Experimental Research, 5,* 304–316.

Rado, S. (1932). The psychoanalysis of pharmacothymia. *Psychoanalytic Quarterly, 2,* 1–23.

Reich, L. H., Davies, R. K., & Himmelhock, J. N. (1974). Excessive alcohol use in manic–depressive illness. *American Journal of Psychiatry, 131,* 83–86.

Robins, E., Murphy, G. E. Wilkinson, Jr., R. H., Gassner, S., & Keyes, J. (1959). Some clinical considerations in the prevention of suicide based on a study of 134 successful suicides. *American Journal of Public Health, 49,* 888–899.

Rohan, W. P., Tatro, R. L., & Rotman, S. R. (1969). MMPI changes in alcoholics during hospitalization. *Quarterly Journal of Studies in Alcohol, 30*, 389–400.

Rosen, A. C. (1960). A comparison study of alcoholic and psychiatric patients with the MMPI. *Quarterly Journal of Studies in Alcohol, 21*, 253–266.

Rounsaville, B. J., Rosenberger, P., Wilber, C., Weissman, M. M., & Kleber, H. D. (1980). A comparison of the SADS/RDC and the DSM-III. *Journal of Nervous and Mental Disease, 168*, 90–97.

Rounsaville, B. J., Weissman, M. M., Crits-Christoph, K., Wilber, C., & Kleber, H. (1982). Diagnosis and symptoms of depression in opiate addicts: Course and relationship to treatment outcome. *Archives of General Psychiatry, 39*, 151–156.

Roy, R. (1983). Alcohol misuse and posttraumatic stress disorder delayed: An alternative interpretation of the data. *Journal of Studies on Alcohol, 44*, 198–202.

Rudie, R., & McGaughran, L. (1969). Differences in developmental experiences, defensiveness and personality organization between two classes of problem drinkers. *Journal of Abnormal and Social Psychology, 62*, 659–665.

Schuckit, M. A. (1982a). Prevalence of affective disorder in a sample of young men. *American Journal of Psychiatry, 139*, 1431–1436.

Schuckit, M. A. (1982b). The history of psychotic symptomatology in alcoholics. *Journal of Clinical Psychiatry, 43*, 53–57.

Schuckit, M. A. (1983). Alcoholism and other psychiatric disorders. *Hospital and Community Psychiatry, 34*, 1022–1026.

Schuckit, M., Pitts, F. N., Reich, T., King, L. J., & Winokur, G. (1969). Alcoholism I: Two types of alcoholism in women. *Archives of General Psychiatry, 20*, 301–306.

Shader, R. I., Goodman, N., & Gever, J. (1982). Panic disorders: Current perspectives. *Journal of Clinical Psychopharmacology, 2*, 2–10.

Sierles, F., Alan, J. J., McFarland, R. F., & Taylor, M. A. (1983). Post-traumatic stress disorder in concurrent psychiatric illness: A preliminary report. *American Journal of Psychiatry, 140*, 1177–1179.

Skinner, H. A., Jackson, D. N. & Hoffman, H. (1974). Alcoholic personality types: Identification and correlates. *Journal of Abnormal Psychology, 83*, 658–666.

Stewart, M. A., Pitts, F. N., Craig, A. G., & Dieruf, W. (1966). The hyperactive child syndrome. *American Journal of Orthopsychiatry, 36*, 861–867.

Sutherland, E. H., Schroeder, H. G., & Tordella, C. L. (1950). Personality traits of the alcoholic: A critique of existing studies. *Quarterly Journal of Studies on Alcohol, 11*, 547–561.

Syme, L. (1957). Personality characteristics in the alcoholic: A critique of current studies. *Quarterly Journal of Studies on Alcohol, 18*, 288–302.

Tamerin, J. S., & Mendelson, J. H. (1969). The psychodynamics of chronic inebriation: Observations of alcoholics during the process of drinking in an experimental group setting. *American Journal of Psychiatry, 125*, 886–889.

Tarter, R. E. (1982). Psychosocial history in minimal brain dysfunction in differential drinking patterns of male alcoholics. *Journal of Clinical Psychology, 38*, 867–873.

Tarter, R. E., McBride, H., Buonpane, N., & Schneider, D. (1977). Differentiation of alcoholics: Childhood history of minimal brain dysfunction, family history, and drinking pattern. *Archives of General Psychiatry, 34*, 761–768.

Tucker, J. A., Vuchinich, R. E., & Sobell, M. B. (1982). Alcohol's effect on human emotions: A review of the stimulation/depression hypothesis. *International Journal of the Addictions, 17*, 155–180.

Vaillant, G. E. (1984). The course of alcoholism and lessons for treatment. In L. Grinspoon (Ed.), *Psychiatry update, III* (pp. 311–319). Washington, DC: American Psychiatric Press.

Victor, M. (1962). Alcoholism. In A. B. Baker (Ed.), *Clinical neurology* (pp. 1084–1129). New York: Harper.

Washton, A., Wein, R., Mirin, S., Michael, J. & Sollogub, A. (1986). Psychopathology in chronic cocaine abusers. *American Journal of Drug and Alcohol Abuse, 12*, 17–29.

Weiss, G., Hechtman, L., Perlman, T., Hopkins, J., & Wener, A. (1979). Hyperactives as young adults: A controlled prospective ten year follow-up of 75 children. *Archives of General Psychiatry, 36*, 675–681.

Weissman, M. M., & Myers, J. K. (1980). Clinical depression in alcoholism. *American Journal of Psychiatry, 137*, 372–373.

Weissman, M. M., Myers, J. J., & Harding, P. S. (1980). Prevalence and psychiatric heterogeneity of alcoholism in a U.S. urban community. *Journal of Studies on Alcohol, 41*, 672–681.

Wender, P. H. (1971). *Minimal brain dysfunction in children*. New York: Wiley.

Wender, P. H., Reimherr, F. W., & Wood, D. R. (1981). Attention deficit disorder (minimal brain dysfunction) in adults: A replication study of diagnosis in drug treatment. *Archives of General Psychiatry, 38*, 449–456.

Whitelock, P. R., Overall, J. E., & Patrick, J. H., (1971). Personality patterns in alcohol abuse in a state hospital population. *Journal of Abnormal Psychology, 78*, 9–16.

Winokur, G. A., Cadoret, R., Dorzab, J. A., & Baker, M. (1971). Depressive disease: A genetic study. *Archives of General Psychiatry, 24*, 135–144.

Winokur, G. A., Cadoret, R., Dorzab, J. A., & Baker, M. (1974). The division of depressive illness into depression spectrum disease and pure depressive illness. *International Pharmacopsychiatry, 9*, 5–13.

Winokur, G. A., Clayton, P. G., & Reich, T. (1969). *Manic depressive illness*. St. Louis: C. V. Mosby.

Winokur, G. A., & Pitts, F. N. (1965). Affective disorders VI: A family history study of prevalence of sex differences and possible genetic factors. *Journal of Psychiatric Research, 3*, 113–123.

Winokur, G. A., Reich, T., Rimmer, J., & Pitts, F. N. (1970). Alcoholism III: Diagnosis and familial psychiatric illness in 259 alcoholic probands. *Archives of General Psychiatry, 23*, 104–111.

Woodruff, R. A., Guze, S. B., Clayton, P. J., & Carr, D. (1973). Alcoholism and depression. *Archives of General Psychiatry, 28*, 97–100.

Woody, G. E., Luborsky, L., McLellan, A. T., O'Brien, C. P., Beck, A. T., Blaine, J., Herman, I., & Hole, A. (1983). Psychotherapy for opiate addicts: Does it help? *Archives of General Psychiatry, 40*, 639–645.

Woody, G. E., McLellan, A. T., Luborsky, L., O'Brien, C. P., Blaine, J., Fox, S., Herman, I., & Beck, A. T. (1984). Severity of psychiatric symptoms as a predictor of benefits from psychotherapy: The Veterans Administration–Penn study. *American Journal of Psychiatry, 141*, 1172–1177.

II

Psychopathology as a Risk Factor

3

Family History of Psychopathology in Alcoholics: A Review and Issues

VICTOR M. HESSELBROCK

Patients with alcoholism do not form a homogeneous group, from either a clinical or a research perspective. An important source of heterogeneity among alcoholic patients can be found in the variety of additional psychopathology they manifest and in the range of psychopathology found among their biological relatives. Additional psychopathology in the alcoholic proband provides an indicator of risk for future psychiatric illness in biological family members, provides clues regarding etiology, and may suggest strategies for prevention. On the other hand, the presence of a specific disorder or treatment response in affected family members may provide valuable information for making a differential diagnosis or in formulating a treatment plan for the proband (Weissman *et al.*, 1984).

METHODOLOGICAL ISSUES IN RESEARCH ON THE FAMILY HISTORY OF PSYCHOPATHOLOGY

A variety of methodological problems can limit the external validity of studies of the family history of psychopathology, particularly among psychiatric probands. External validity speaks to the question of the generality of a study's findings: To what extent can this study's results generalize to other samples, settings, and situations (Campbell & Stanley, 1963)?

A primary issue is the ascertainment of the proband. How was the index case identified (e.g. through a random sampling of the general population, or based on a patient population)? Generally speaking, if a general population sampling method is used, a range of severity of the disorder of interest (e.g., alcoholism) will be obtained. On the other hand, when a treated sample is used, the severity of the disorder found in the probands tends to be truncated toward the more extreme end of the range. The generality of the findings of identified, severely affected treated samples to unidentified, untreated, mildly affected probands is an issue. In addition, when treated samples are used, the probability of a family's being ascertained depends directly on the number of affected individuals in the family. Families with a large number of affected members have a greater probability of being selected than families with few or a single affected member.

A second issue is the presence of multiple diagnoses in the proband. As described by other authors in this volume and elsewhere (Penick *et al.*, 1984; Weissman *et al.*, 1984), multiple syndromes often exist within the same individual. How are the diagnoses to be ordered; which diagnosis is to be considered the principal problem? Often the probands have received treatment for several psychiatric problems. One solution, proposed by the Washington University group, is to classify the disorders based on the primary–secondary distinction (E. Robins & Guze, 1969). Generally, a primary disorder is the first occurring diagnosable psychiatric disorder, unless it occurs in the presence of a life-threatening or incapacitating medical illness. Disorders that occur after another diagnosable psychiatric condition is present or following a life-threatening or incapacitating medical illness are classified as secondary. A second possible approach would be to develop a diagnostic hierarchy based on exclusion criteria, primacy of the disorder, or the like. This approach would also reduce the diagnostic heterogeneity of the groups being compared. The importance of distinguishing between principal diagnoses is evident, for example, when the family history data for alcoholism in alcoholic probands with depression is compared to data obtained from depressed probands who may also have alcoholism. Alcoholism shows a familial aggregation in the first group of probands (cf. Woodruff, Guze, Clayton, & Carr, 1973) but does not necessarily do so in the former (Gershon *et al.*, 1982; Weissman *et al.*, 1984).

The age of the proband and of the proband's family members is an important demographic variable when evaluating family history data. The age at which a person is most likely to become affected (i.e., the age of "risk") varies across psychiatric disorders. Therefore, the proportion of family members who are not at risk, who have entered the risk period, or who have passed through the risk period varies according to the age of the individual family members and according to the disorder of interest. It is possible to age-correct rates of the disorder among relatives—for example, by using the Stromgren method (Slater & Cowie, 1971), which involves weighing the number of persons at risk by the proportion of the risk period through which they have passed. Such a correction is often necessary in order to make accurate comparisons of samples from multiple generations or from different populations. Consider, for example, a comparison of the family history data from two probands: a patient with antisocial personality (ASP) and secondary alcoholism, and a patient with alcoholism only. The first patient is likely to be younger and to have an early-onset type of alcoholism (see chapter by Michie Hesselbrock, this volume). The relatives are also likely to be young and just entering or just into the period of risk for alcoholism. The patient with primary alcoholism, in comparison, is likely to be somewhat older. Further, the relatives of this patient are also likely to be older and either well into or beyond the risk period for alcoholism. The family history data for alcoholism from the first proband will provide an underestimate of the true lifetime risks, because the age-of-onset distribution most often used for alcoholism is biased toward older ages.

A final issue is the method of determining the psychiatric status of the individual family members: history methods versus direct interview. Undoubtedly, the most accurate method of obtaining a psychiatric history of an individual is via a direct interview. The reliability and validity of the diagnoses made are often further enhanced when the information is obtained using a structured interview (Endicott & Spitzer, 1978; V. Hesselbrock, Stabenau, Hesselbrock, Mirkin, & Meyer, 1982; L. Robins, Helzer, Croughan, & Ratcliff, 1981). However, in large-sample studies, interviewing all relatives can be time-consuming and costly. Many investigators opt to use the family history method to gather information about the extended family. With the history method, one family member, usually the proband, provides as much information as possible about the psychiatric status of each relative. Systematic interviewing methods and specific criteria have been developed to increase the reliability of this procedure (Andreasen, Endicott, Spitzer, & Winokur, 1977). The economy produced by using family history methods has a cost, however, in terms of reliability of the diagnoses made. Most studies comparing information obtained from the proband (history) to that obtained from a direct interview of the relative report only a modest amount of agreement for most diagnoses. Probands tend to underestimate the level of psychiatric illness of relatives, but this varies as a function of the relationship with the relative (Mendlewicz, Fleiss, Cataldo, & Rainer, 1975). Reliability also improves when collateral information is obtained from more than one informant (Gershon & Guroff, 1984; Mendlewicz *et al., 1975*). Further, reliability is usually higher for the more prevalent disorders than for disorders that occur more infrequently (Leckman, Sholomskas, Thompson, Belanger, & Weissman, 1982). The reliability of the diagnosis of alcoholism using family history methods tends to be quite high (K = .91–1.00), compared to that obtained using a direct interview (Andreasen *et al.*, 1977; Mendlewicz *et al.*, 1975; V. Hesselbrock, Stabenau, & Hesselbrock, 1985). Andreasen *et al.* found lower reliabilities for ASP (K = .52–.93). A similar range of reliability has been reported for affective disorder, but varies according to the number of subtyping distinctions made (Gershon & Guroff, 1984). Andreasen *et al.* (1977) and V. Hesselbrock *et al.* (1985) report kappas for depression in the .74–.88 range, although Gershon and Guroff (1984) report a lower reliability when history and record data are compared.

PSYCHOPATHOLOGY IN THE BIOLOGICAL RELATIVES OF ALCOHOLIC PROBANDS

Family studies and family pedigree studies have found a variety of different types of psychopathology among the biological relatives of alcoholic probands. The disorders most frequently noted in the pedigrees of alcoholics include depression and ASP, in addition to alcoholism itself. Interestingly, these disorders also are strongly familial. Because of their close association, the question has sometimes been raised as to whether alcoholism is a separate diagnostic entity or only a different manifestation of these disorders. Occasionally an association has also been noted between alcoholism and a family history of schizophrenia. The following subsections examine the relevance of each of the diagnoses to the development of alcoholism.

Schizophrenia

Schizophrenia is seldom found in alcoholic probands, but has been suggested as an etiological factor in alcoholic hallucinosis. However, the literature is quite scant on this issue. Schuckit and Winokur (1971) found a similar number of alcoholics with a previous diagnosis of schizophrenia (about 1%) admitted with and without alcoholic hallucinosis. Furthermore, the family histories of first-degree relatives for schizophrenia, affective disorder, and alcoholism did not differentiate the two groups. Similar findings were reported by Scott (1967). He found no excess of schizophrenia in probands with and without alcoholic hallucinosis or in their biological family members.

A question remains as to whether the presence of schizophrenia in a parent places the proband's offspring at greater risk for developing alcohol-related problems later in life. Several studies (e.g., Gottesman & Shields, 1972; Heston, 1966) clearly document the risk of developing schizophrenia in these offspring, but the risk for developing alcohol problems has received little attention. A recent report by Worland, Weeks, Janes, and Hesselbrock (1985), based on a longitudinal study of families of hospitalized psychiatric patients, has examined the prevalence of psychopathology in their young adult offspring. The probands included patients with schizophrenia or affective disorder, in addition to patients hospitalized with a physical illness and a general population control group. The young adult offspring (aged 17–35) of parents with a mental disorder, including schizophrenia, had substantially greater rates of alcohol abuse/dependence (11–18%) than children of normal parents (2%). (The criteria used for abuse/dependence were those of the *Diagnostic and Statistical Manual of Mental Disorder,* third edition [DSM-III; American Psychiatric Association, 1980].) Eleven percent of the offspring of schizophrenic parents received a diagnosis of alcohol abuse/dependence. These rates are quite high, given the fact that most of the sample was just entering the age of risk for alcohol-related problems. These data are supported by a 10-year follow-up study of children of schizophrenic mothers reported by H. Schulsinger (1976). Using data from the Danish birth cohort study, Schulsinger found that 13% of the sons between the ages of 23 and 31 of schizophrenic mothers met the *International Classification of Diseases,* eighth edition (ICD-8 1966) criteria for alcoholism, compared to 4% of the sons in the control group. No alcoholism was found among the daughters of either group in this age range. In the 18–24 age range, 3% of the daughters and 6% of the sons of schizophrenic mothers were alcoholic, while no alcoholism was found in the offspring of control parents. However, this age group was just entering the age of risk for alcoholism. Future follow-up studies of both Worland et al.'s and H. Schulsinger's samples are likely to find even higher rates of alcohol problems in these offspring.

Both studies indicate that offspring of a schizophrenic parent are at increased risk not only for schizophrenia, but also for alcohol problems later in life. Neither study provides any evidence for a genetic relationship between schizophrenia and alcoholism. However, the increased prevalence rate of alcoholism found for children of a schizophrenic parent does suggest the existence of a cultural or environmental risk factor in these families.

MAJOR DEPRESSIVE DISORDER

As indicated earlier, the association of alcoholism and major depressive disorder in alcoholic probands is widely known from both clinical observation and from research data (cf. V. Hesselbrock, Tennen, Stabenau, & Hesselbrock, 1983; Weissman & Myers, 1980; Winokur, Cadoret, Dorzab, & Baker, 1971; Winokur, Rimmer, & Reich, 1971; Woodruff, Guze, & Clayton, 1973; Woodruff, Guze, Clayton, & Carr, 1973). Further, depression occurs more frequently in the biological family members of alcoholic probands than expected by chance. Pitts and Winokur (1966) found that the sisters of alcoholic probands had an affective disorder more frequently than the sisters of medically ill matched controls. In a later study, Winokur, Reich, Rimmer, and Pitts (1970) examined the parents and siblings of alcoholic probands. This study found that depression occurred frequently in the female relatives of alcoholic probands, regardless of the gender of the proband. For both male and female probands, there was an almost fourfold increase in the frequency of affective disorder found among female versus male relatives. More recently, Cloninger, Reich, and Wetzel (1979) found that the first-degree relatives of primary alcoholics were more than four times more likely to have early onset primary depression than the general population (14.6% vs. 3.1%), but only about two-thirds as likely as the first-degree relatives primary depressive probands (14.6% vs. 20.3%).

Cloninger et al. (1979), in their review of other studies of alcoholism and depression in the same family, have concluded that, although both disorders are frequently found in the same families, the disorders have different etiologies and are genetically distinct. Additional support for this hypothesis can be found in studies that have examined the family histories of depressed probands for the presence of alcoholism. Gershon *et al.* (1982), for example, examined the families of schizoaffective, bipolar I, bipolar II, unipolar, and normal control probands and found that alcoholism did not occur more frequently in the first-degree relatives of affectively ill patients than in those of controls. A similar finding was reported by Weissman *et al.* (1984) in a study of probands with either bipolar illness or major depression compared to normal controls. Alcoholism did not show familial aggregation with affective disorders in the pedigrees of probands with a principal diagnosis of affective disorder.

Differences in findings between studies that report an excess of depression in biological family members and those that do not are probably not due to just differences in ascertainment of the probands. V. Hesselbrock, Tennen, Stabenau, and Hesselbrock (1983) examined the family histories of a sample of patients being treated for alcoholism, some of whom also had depression as diagnosed by the Research Diagnostic Criteria (RDC). This study found that alcoholic patients with depression were almost two times more likely to have a depressed biological relative, and also were more likely to have depression in two consecutive generations than nondepressed probands. No difference in the rate of alcoholism in the family members of alcoholic probands with primary depression, secondary depression, concurrent depression, or no depression was found.

ASP

A second disorder that frequently occurs with alcoholism, both in the proband and in the proband's family, is ASP. However, the literature in this area must be viewed with caution, since it is often difficult to distinguish alcoholism and ASP on the basis of phenomenology (Schuckit, 1973). Persons with alcoholism often display antisocial behavior, while persons with ASP often abuse alcohol (M. Hesselbrock *et al.*, 1984). The distinction between alcoholism and ASP can be quite difficult to make during a direct interview of the subject, but is doubly difficult using history methods.

ASP occurs frequently among alcoholic probands (Powell, Penick, Othmer, Bingham, & Rice, 1982), with one study citing a frequency rate of 49% among male alcoholic patients (M. Hesselbrock, Meyer, & Keener, 1985). But what about the relatives of alcoholic ASP probands?

Are they at increased risk for both alcoholism and ASP? Two adoption studies suggest that the two traits are independent. Goodwin, Schulsinger, Hermansen, Guze, and Winokur (1973) examined the adult, adopted-away sons of Danish alcoholics and found an increased prevalence of alcoholism but not ASP. F. Schulsinger (1972), on the other hand, found an increased rate of criminality and psychopathy, but not alcoholism, among the adopted-away offspring of psychopathic parents. Cloninger *et al.* (1979) reviewed a number of studies to examine the familial aggregation of a number of psychiatric disorders. In general, the studies cited by Cloninger *et al.* suggested that alcoholism and ASP aggregate according to the primary diagnosis of the proband; that is, the prevalence of relatives with the same primary diagnosis as the proband was greater than that of relatives with other diagnoses. Primary alcoholism was most frequently found among primary alcoholics, while primary ASP was most frequently found among probands with primary ASP. However, this finding appeared to be true for the relatives of probands with only alcoholism or only ASP. If a proband happened to have both disorders, the relatives showed an increased risk for both disorders (Reich, Cloninger, Lewis, & Rice, 1981). Reich *et al.* have concluded that alcoholism and ASP are transmitted separately; however, the presence of ASP in a family tends to increase the risk of alcoholism for the family members.

Bohman and associates have examined the relationship between alcoholism and criminality in adopted Swedish men (Bohman, Cloninger, Sigvardsson, & von Knorring, 1982; Cloninger, Sigvardsson, Bohman, & von Knorring, 1982). Criminality was defined in two ways and distinguished to some extent from ASP. The first type was similar to the DSM-III definition of ASP requiring repetitive antisocial behavior and included violent alcohol-related crime. The second type, petty criminality, was characterized by the commission of infrequent, minor property offenses. Based on information about the genetic and environmental backgrounds of the adoptees, Bohman and colleagues were able to identify two types of alcohol abuse in his sample. The first type of alcoholic manifested alcohol abuse only when reared in particular postnatal environments. Both mildly and severely affected alcoholics of this type had both parents affected with alcohol abuse and criminality. A second type of alcoholism was identified that seemed to have a male-limited pattern. Probands of this type had a moderate number of registrations with the Swedish Temperance Board, but also had fathers with a combination of alcoholism and criminality. The female relatives were normal. Bohman's group's study supports Reich *et al.*'s (1981) contention that ASP and alcoholism in the same family increases the risk for alcoholism in family members, but adds a qualifier. The type of postnatal environment experienced by the family member, particularly unstable preadoptive placements, influences the development of the second type of alcoholism (Cloninger *et al.*, 1982).

ALCOHOLISM

The familial nature of alcoholism has been long recognized and is well documented (Amark, 1951; Cotton, 1979; Goodwin, 1976; Jellinek, 1945). The finding of much higher rates of alcoholism among the relatives of alcoholic probands than in the general population is no longer an arguable point. In fact, a number of studies reviewed by Goodwin (1976) indicate that about 25% of fathers and brothers are themselves affected with alcoholism. Although there is no direct evidence that alcoholism is transmitted genetically, several studies have provided indirect support for this hypothesis. In a series of studies based on the Danish adoption registers, Goodwin and associates (Goodwin, Schulsinger, Hermansen, Guze, & Winokur, 1973; Goodwin *et al.*, 1974) were able to show that sons of an alcoholic parent had a similar risk for developing alcoholism whether raised with an alcoholic parent or not, and were four times more likely to develop alcoholism than adopted-away sons of nonalcoholics. Schuckit, Goodwin, and Winokur (1972) found similar rates of alcoholism in a study of half-siblings of an alcoholic parent raised with an alcoholic parent, compared to their half-siblings adopted away (50% vs. 46%). Taken together, the studies of Goodwin *et al.* (1973, 1974) and Schuckit *et al.* (1972) indicate that the risk of developing alcoholism in male offspring of an alcoholic is not reduced, even when the children are raised in a nonalcoholic environment.

Goodwin, Schulsinger, Knop, Mednick, and Guze (1977a, 1977b) also compared the adopted-away daughters of alcoholic parents raised by nonalcoholic adoptive parents with daughters raised by their own alcoholic parents. The data from these studies were less clear. Although the adopted-away daughters of alcoholic parents had a higher prevalence rate of alcoholism than found in the general population, a similar high rate of alcoholism was found in the adopted-away daughters of nonalcoholic parents.

Further evidence for a genetic component to the transmission of alcoholism can be found in studies of monozygotic and dizygotic twins. Kaij (1960) examined the concordance of drinking styles, including alcoholism, in 214 pairs of Swedish twins. Using Temperance Board data, Kaij found that monozygotic twins were about two times more concordant for "alcoholism" than dizygotic twins. Kaij's definition of alcoholism has been questioned by Grove and Cadoret (1983), who conducted a reanalysis of Kaij's data. In the reanalysis, a higher correlation of drinking styles ($r = .76 - .81$) was found for monozygotic twins versus dizygotic twins ($r = .61 - .76$). A study of twins drawn from the general population of Finland by Partanen, Brunn, and Markkaven (1966) also found a high concordance rate for drinking styles of monozygotic twins compared to dizygotic twins. However, no difference in drinking problems was found between the two types of twins. In a reanalysis of this data, Cloninger et al. (1979) and Cloninger and Reich (1983) cite the failure to find higher estimates of heritability as a consequence of selecting subjects from the general population, which included many abstinent and light-drinking individuals. Once quantity and frequency of drinking were considered, estimates of the heritability of problem drinking increased.

Even though alcoholism is recognized as a familial disorder, there have been few attempts to use family history for alcoholism to differentiate the type of alcoholism found in the proband. The best-known formulation is the notion of "familial alcoholism" (Goodwin, 1979; Jellinek & Jolliffe, 1940). There are four basic features: (1) a family history of severe, unequivocal alcoholism; (2) early onset of the disorder; (3) drinking in binges, requiring treatment at an early age; and (4) an absence of other conspicuous psychopathology, including other substance abuse. Goodwin cites the Danish studies as supporting the notion of familial alcoholism.

More recently, studies by Penick, Read, Crowley, and Powell (1978), Frances, Timm, and Bucky (1980), McKenna and Pickens (1981), and V. Hesselbrock, Stabenau, Hesselbrock, Meyer, and Babor (1983) have also tended to support aspects of the formulation. Penick et al. (1978) found that alcoholics with an alcohol-abusing parent or grandparent began drinking at an earlier age and had more social and personal problems than nonfamilial alcoholics or alcoholics reporting a relative other than a parent or grandparent with an alcohol problem. Frances *et al.* (1980) defined familial alcoholism on the basis of having a parent or sibling with an alcohol problem. Their study found that familial alcoholics had a more severe form of alcoholism and were more antisocial (including poor academic performance and poor work histories) than nonfamilial alcoholics, in addition to having more psychopathology in their extended families. McKenna and Pickens's (1981) study examined the course and severity of alcoholism in probands with either one or both parents affected with alcoholism. Probands with two alcoholic parents experienced their first intoxication at an earlier age, had more behavioral problems, and progressed more rapidly from first intoxication to treatment than the other alcoholic probands. V. Hesselbrock, Stabenau, Hesselbrock, *et al.* (1983) divided their sample of probands on the basis of a unilineal–bilineal pedigree distinction. A unilineal pedigree was defined as either parent or a sibling of either parent being affected with alcoholism. A bilineal pedigree for alcoholism was defined as a parent or sibling of a parent on both the maternal and paternal sides of the family being affected with alcoholism. Patients with a bilineal pedigree for alcoholism reported greater social and physical consequences of alcohol abuse than other alcoholic probands. These differences based on family history persisted even after effects due to the presence of ASP in the proband were removed.

In summary, these four studies support the notion of familial alcoholism. Furthermore, the presence of alcoholism in a pedigree not only increases the risk for developing alcoholism in the individual family members, but also seems to increase the severity of problems experienced once an individual becomes affected with alcoholism.

CONCLUSIONS

In this chapter, a number of methodological issues are first identified that have implications for the gathering of pedigree data for research or clinical purposes. The method of data collection (history vs. interview), age of the proband and family members, and treatment status of the informant are important determinants of the validity and reliability of the information collected. In general, family history methods can provide an acceptable way of quickly collecting large amounts of pedigree information when the proper safeguards are used. The economy of the method, however, is often provided at the expense of the quality and quantity of the data obtained.

The review of the literature on psychopathology in the biological relatives of alcoholic probands does have implications both for prevention efforts and for treatment. For the purposes of identifying individuals with a higher level of risk of developing alcohol-related problems, knowledge of psychopathology in the family pedigree can be quite important. It is well documented that alcoholism is a familial disorder (i.e., runs in the same family), so that having biological relatives with alcoholism increases the risk in unaffected individuals. More recently, studies by Bohman, Cloninger, and associates (Bohman *et al.*, 1982; Cloninger *et al.*, 1982) suggest that petty criminality in fathers increases the risk of alcoholism for sons. They distinguish this mild type of antisocial behavior from the more traditional notion of psychopathy and DSM-III-defined ASP. The latter does not seem to increase the risk for alcoholism in unaffected family members unless the proband also has alcoholism (Reich *et al.*, 1981). Schizophrenia has traditionally not been thought to increase the risk for alcoholism in unaffected family members, but recent evidence provides a challenge to this view. Studies by Worland *et al.* (1985) and H. Schulsinger (1976) suggest that the offspring of a schizophrenic but nonalcoholic parent also have an increased risk for developing alcohol problems in early adulthood. A family history of depression without alcoholism, however, does not seem to provide an increased risk for the family members. In summary, a family history of several types of psychopathology, in addition to alcoholism, seems to increase the risk for developing alcoholism in unaffected relatives. Information about the presence of psychopathology in biological relatives may be useful in identifying those individuals most vulnerable to alcoholism and targeting them for primary prevention efforts.

Knowledge of a patient's family history of psychopathology may also be of value to the clinician. Patients who consume large quantities of alcohol often have a variety of symptoms that mimic other psychiatric disorders. Making a differential diagnosis and planning treatment for such patients can be difficult. Antisocial behavior and symptoms indicative of major depression, for example, are frequently found in alcohol-abusing patients. Family pedigree information may be helpful to the clinician in deciding whether the depressive symptoms are likely to abate after detoxification. Furthermore, patients with "familial alcoholism" may also need special treatment planning. The review above indicates that these individuals not only tend to have an early onset of the disorder, but also tend to have a more severe form of alcoholism. Such patients may need intervention in several areas (social, psychological, physical) of their lives and extended aftercare in order to promote abstinence and recovery.

Information about psychopathology in the family members of alcoholics probands has been most frequently used by researchers interested in the transmission of the disorder. I hope that this review and discussion have indicated ways in which pedigree data can also be utilized by clinicians and persons working in primary prevention.

ACKNOWLEDGMENT

The writing of this chapter was supported by the National Institute on Alcohol Abuse and Alcoholism (Grant No. 2-P50-AA-03510-07).

REFERENCES

Amark, C. (1951). A study in alcoholism: Clinical, social-psychiatric and genetic investigations. *Acta Psychiatrica et Neurologica Scandinavica, 70* (Suppl.), 1–283.

American Psychiatric Association. (1980). *Diagnostic and statistical manual of mental disorders* (3rd ed.). Washington, DC: Author.

Andreasen, N., Endicott, J., Spitzer, R., & Winokur, G. (1977). The family history method using diagnostic criteria. *Archives of General Psychiatry, 34,* 1229–1235.

Bohman, M., Cloninger, C., Sigvardsson, S., & von Knorring, A. (1982). Predisposition to petty criminality in Swedish adoptees. *Archives of General Psychiatry, 39,* 1233–1241.

Campbell, D., & Stanley, J. (1963). *Experimental and quasi-experimental designs for research.* Chicago: Rand McNally.

Cloninger, C., & Reich, T. (1983). Genetic heterogeneity in alcoholism and sociopathy. In S. Kety, L. Rowland, R. Sidman, & S. Matthysse (Eds.), *Genetics of neurological and psychiatric disorders* (pp. 145–166). New York: Raven Press.

Cloninger, C., Reich, T., & Wetzel, R. (1979). Alcoholism and affective disorders: Familial associations and genetic models. In D. Goodwin & C. Erickson (Eds.), *Alcoholism and affective disorders* (pp. 57–86). New York: SP Medical & Scientific Books.

Cloninger, C., Sigvardsson, S., Bohman, M., & von Knorring, A. (1982). Predisposition to petty criminality in Swedish adoptees: Cross-fostering analysis of gene–environment interaction. *Archives of General Psychiatry, 39,* 1242–1247.

Cotton, N. (1979). The familial incidence of alcoholism. *Journal of Studies on Alcohol, 40,* 89–116.

Endicott, J., & Spitzer, R. (1978). A diagnostic interview. *Archives of General Psychiatry, 35,* 837–844.

Frances, R., Timm, S., & Bucky, S. (1980). Studies of familial and nonfamilial alcoholism. *Archives of General Psychiatry, 37*, 564–566.

Gershon, E., & Guroff, J. (1984). Information from relatives. *Archives of General Psychiatry, 41*, 173–180.

Gershon, E., Hamovit, J., Guroff, J., Dibble, E., Leckman, J., Sceery, W., Targum, S., Nurnberger, J., Golden, L., & Bunney, W. (1982). A family study of schizoaffective, bipolar I, bipolar II, unipolar, and normal controls. *Archives of General Psychiatry, 39*, 1157–1167.

Goodwin, D. W. (1976) *Is alcoholism hereditary?* New York: Oxford University Press.

Goodwin, D. W. (1979). Alcoholism and heredity: A review and hypothesis. *Archives of General Psychiatry, 36*, 57–61.

Goodwin, D. W., Schulsinger, F., Hermansen, L. Guze, S., & Winokur, G. (1973). Alcohol problems in adoptees raised apart from alcoholic biological parents. *Archives of General Psychiatry, 28*, 238–243.

Goodwin, D. W., Schulsinger, F., Knop, J., Mednick, S., & Guze, S. (1977a). Alcoholism and depression in adopted-out daughters of alcoholics. *Archives of General Psychiatry, 34*, 751–755.

Goodwin, D. W., Schulsinger, F., Knop, J., Mednick, S., & Guze, S. (1977b). Psychopathology in adopted and nonadopted daughters of alcoholics. *Archives of General Psychiatry, 34*, 1005–1009.

Goodwin, D. W., Schulsinger, F., Moller, N., Hermansen, L., Winokur, G., & Guze, S. (1974). Drinking problems in adopted and nonadopted sons of alcoholics. *Archives of General Psychiatry, 31*, 164–169.

Gottesman, I., & Shields, J. (1972). *Schizophrenia and genetics: A twin study vantage point*. New York: Academic Press.

Grove, W., & Cadoret, R. (1983). Genetic factors in alcoholism. In B. Kissin & H. Begleiter (Eds.), *The biology of alcoholism: Vol. 7. The pathogenesis of alcoholism* (pp. 31–56). New York: Plenum Press.

Hesselbrock, M., Hesselbrock, V., Babor, T., Stabenau, J., Meyer, R., & Weidenman, M. (1984). Antisocial behavior, psychopathology and problem drinking in the natural history of alcoholism. In D. Goodwin, K. Van Dusen, & S. Mednick (Eds.), *Longitudinal research in alcoholism* (pp. 197–214). Boston: Kluwer–Nijhoff.

Hesselbrock, M., Meyer, R., & Keener, J. (1985). Psychopathology in hospitalized alcoholics. *Archives of General Psychiatry, 42*, 1050–1055.

Hesselbrock, V., Stabenau, J., & Hesselbrock,, M. (1985). Subtyping of alcoholism in male patients by family history and antisocial personality. *Journal of Studies on Alcohol, 49*, 89–98.

Hesselbrock, V., Stabenau, J., Hesselbrock, M., Meyer, R., & Babor, T. (1983). The nature of alcoholism in patients with different family histories for alcoholism. *Progress in Neuropsychopharmacology and Biological Psychiatry, 6*, 607–614.

Hesselbrock, V., Stabenau, J., Hesselbrock, M., Mirkin, P., & Meyer, R. (1982). A comparison of two structured interviews: The SADS-L and NIMH-DIS. *Archives of General Psychiatry, 39*, 674–677.

Hesselbrock, V., Tennen, H., Stabenau, J., & Hesselbrock, M. (1983). Affective disorder in alcoholism. *International Journal of the Addictions, 18*, 435–444.

Heston, L. L. (1966). Psychiatric disorders in foster home reared children of schizophrenic mothers. *British Journal of Psychiatry, 112*, 819–825.

Jellinek, E. M. (1945). Heredity of the alcoholic. *Quarterly Journal of Studies on Alcohol, 7*, 106–114.

Jellinek, E. M., & Jolliffe, N. (1940). Effect of alcohol on the individual: Review of the literature of 1939. *Quarterly Journal of Studies on Alcohol, 1*, 110–181.

Kaij, L. (1960). *Alcoholism in twins.* Stockholm: Almquist & Wiksell.

Leckman, J., Sholomskas, D., Thompson, W., Belanger, A., & Weissman, M. (1982). Best estimate of lifetime psychiatric diagnosis. *Archives of General Psychiatry, 39,* 879–883.

McKenna, T., & Pickens, R. (1981). Alcoholic children of alcoholics. *Journal of Studies on Alcohol, 42,* 1021–1029.

Mendlewicz, J., Fleiss, J., Cataldo, M., & Rainer, J. (1975). Accuracy of the family history method in affective illness. *Archives of General Psychiatry, 32,* 309–314.

Partanen, J., Brunn, K., & Markkaven, T. (1966). *Inheritance of drinking behavior.* Helsinki: Finnish Foundation for Alcohol Studies.

Penick, E., Powell, B., Othmer, E., Bingham, S., Rice, A., & Liese, B. (1984). Subtyping alcoholics by coexisting psychiatric syndromes: Course, family history, outcome. In D. W. Goodwin, K. T. Van Dusen, & S. A. Mednick (Eds.), *Longitudinal research in alcoholism* (pp. 167–196). Boston: Kluwer-Nijhoff.

Penick, E., Read, M., Crowley, P., & Powell, B. (1978). Differentiation of alcoholics by family history. *Journal of Studies on Alcohol, 39,* 1944–1948.

Pitts, F., & Winokur, G. (1966). Affective disorder VII: Alcoholism and affective disorder. *Journal of Psychiatric Research, 4,* 37–50.

Powell, B., Penick, E., Othmer, E., Bingham, S., & Rice, A. (1982). Prevalence of additional psychiatric syndromes among male alcoholics. *Journal of Clinical Psychiatry, 43,* 404–407.

Reich, T., Cloninger, C., Lewis, C., & Rice, J. (1981). Some recent findings in the study of genotype–environment interaction in alcoholism. In R. Meyer (Ed.), *Evaluation of the alcoholic* (NIAAA Research Monograph 5, pp. 145–166). Washington, DC: U.S. Government Printing Office.

Robins, E., & Guze, S. (1969, 30 April). *Classification of affective disorders: The primary– secondary, endogenous–reactive, and the neurotic–psychotic concepts.* Paper presented at the NIMH Workshop on Psychology of Depression, Williamsburg, VA.

Robins, L., Helzer, J., Croughan, J., & Ratcliff, K. (1981). National Institute of Mental Health diagnostic interview schedule. *Archives of General Psychiatry, 38,* 381–389.

Schuckit, M. (1973). Alcoholism and sociopathy—diagnostic confusion. *Quarterly Journal of Studies on Alcohol, 34,* 157–164.

Schuckit, M., Goodwin, D., & Winokur, G. (1972). A study of alcoholism in half siblings. *American Journal of Psychiatry, 128,* 1132–1136.

Schuckit, M., & Winokur, G. (1971). Alcoholic hallucinosis and schizophrenia: A negative study. *British Journal of Psychiatry, 119,* 549–550.

Schulsinger, F. (1972). Psychopathy, heredity and environment. *International Journal of Mental Health, 1,* 190–206.

Schulsinger, H. (1976). A ten-year follow-up of children of schizophrenic mothers. Clinical assessment. *Acta Psychiatrica Scandinavica, 53,* 371–386.

Scott, D. (1967). Alcoholic hallucinosis—an aetiological study. *British Journal of Addiction, 62,* 113–125.

Slater, E., & Cowie, V. (1971). *The genetics of mental disorders.* London: Oxford University Press.

Weissman, M., Gershon, E., Kidd, K., Prusoff, B., Leckman, J., Dibble, E., Hamovit, J., Thompson, D., Pauls, D., & Guroff, J. (1984). Psychiatric disorders in the relatives of probands with affective disorders. *Archives of General Psychiatry, 41,* 13–21.

Weissman, M., & Myers, J. (1980). Clinical depression in alcoholism. *American Journal of Psychiatry, 137,* 372–373.

Winokur, G., Cadoret, R., Dorzab, J., & Baker, M. (1971). Depressive disease: A genetic study. *Archives of General Psychiatry, 24,* 135–144.

Winokur, G., Reich, T., Rimmer, J., & Pitts, F. (1970). Alcoholism III: Diagnosis and familial psychiatric illness in 259 alcoholic probands. *Archives of General Psychiatry, 23,* 104–111.

Winokur, G., Rimmer, J., & Reich, T. (1971). Alcoholism IV: Is there more than one type of alcoholism? *British Journal of Psychiatry, 118,* 525–531.

Woodruff, R., Guze, S., & Clayton, P. (1973). Alcoholics who see a psychiatrist compared to those who do not. *Quarterly Journal of Studies on Alcohol, 34,* 1162–1171.

Woodruff, R., Guze, S., Clayton, P., & Carr, D. (1973). Alcoholism and depression. *Archives of General Psychiatry, 28,* 97–100.

Worland, J., Weeks, D., Janes, C., & Hesselbrock, V. (1985). *Prospective, longitudinal evaluation of childhood functioning and young adult diagnosis.* Manuscript submitted for publication.

World Health Organization. 1966. Manual of the international statistical classification of diseases, injuries, and causes of death. (ICD-8). Geneva: WHO.

4

Family Pedigree of Psychopathology in Substance Abusers

STEVEN M. MIRIN
ROGER D. WEISS
JACQUELINE MICHAEL

Among patients who present for treatment of substance abuse problems, it is estimated that 30–50% are concurrently suffering from some form of nondrug psychopathology—in particular, affective illness, and, less commonly, panic or generalized anxiety disorder (Rounsaville, Weissman, Kleber & Wilber, 1982; Weissman, Pottenger, Kleber, et al., 1977). Moreover, data from a number of recent studies suggest that the distribution of various types of nondrug psychopathology is, in part, predicted by drug of choice. For example, the prevalence of concurrent affective disorder appears to be higher in abusers of central nervous system (CNS) stimulants, compared to those who abuse opiates or CNS depressants (Helfrich, Crowley, Atkinson, et al., 1982; Mirin, Weiss, Sollogub, & Michael, 1984a; Post, Kotin, & Goodwin, 1974), while panic and anxiety disorders appear to be more common among depressant abusers (Mirin et al., 1984a). Finally, antisocial personality (ASP) disorder, though found across a variety of substance-abusing individuals, may be more common in those who abuse alcohol (Schuckit & Morrissey, 1979; Stabenau & Hesselbrock, 1984) and opiates (Craig, 1979).

The high prevalence of nondrug psychopathology in substance abusers frequently complicates the clinical assessment of these patients. For example, in individuals experiencing withdrawal from CNS stimulants, depression, anxiety, guilt, and low self-esteem are common findings. It is often unclear, however, whether these signs and symptoms are a consequence of drug withdrawal; the unmasking of an underlying primary affective disorder; or an expectable response to the social, financial, and occupational sequelae of chronic drug use. Similarly, it is often difficult to discern whether the antisocial behavior observed in many substance abusers is a manifestation of a pre-existing underlying ASP disorder or a learned behavorial adaptation to the vicissitudes of the drug-abusing life style.

Questions of causality and the diagnostic dilemma posed by the existence of multiple forms of psychopathology in an individual substance abuser can be addressed in a number of ways. Of these, the most useful is the clinical evaluation of detoxified patients who have remained abstinent for an extended period of time (i.e., a month or more). In this regard, studies in opiate addicts (Dackis & Gold, 1984; Rounsaville, Weissman, Wilbur, Crits-Cristoph, & Kleber, 1982; Shaw, Steer, Beck, *et al.*, 1979) suggest that much of the depressive symptomatology seen in the early postwithdrawal period fades as patients continue treatment in a drug-free environment. On the other hand, some patients who continue to manifest signs and symptoms of depression may benefit from treatment with antidepressant medication (Kleber & Gold, 1978; Kleber, Weissman, & Rounsaville, 1983; Woody, O'Brien, & Rickels, 1975).

FAMILY STUDIES IN ALCOHOLICS

Yet another method of enhancing diagnostic specificity in substance abusers is suggested by data from family pedigree, twin, and adoption studies, indicating that familial and/or genetic factors play an important role in the development of alcoholism (Goodwin & Guze, 1974; Winokur, Reich, Rimmer, & Pitts, 1970), affective disorder (Cadoret, 1978; Winokur, Tsuang, & Crowe, 1982), and ASP (Cloninger, Reich, & Wetzel, 1981; Reich, Cloninger, Collin, *et al.*, 1980).

With respect to alcoholism, family pedigree studies reveal that the prevalence rate for this disorder in the first-degree relatives of alcoholics is approximately 30–40%, compared to 5–10% in the general population (Goodwin & Guze, 1974; Hirsch, 1955; Mirin *et al.*, 1984a). Studies in twins (Partanen, Brunn, & Markkanen, 1966; Schuckit, 1980) reveal a higher concordance rate for alcoholism in monozygotic (i.e., identical) than in dizygotic twins. Finally, studies of adoptees (Bohman, 1978; Goodwin, Schulsinger, Knop, Mednick, & Guze, 1977) reveal a fourfold increase in the risk for alcoholism in the male, but not the female, offspring of alcoholic parents. In this context, Goodwin (Goodwin, 1971) has used the term "familial alcoholism" to describe an inherited syndrome characterized by strong genetic loading, early onset of pathological drinking behavior, and then the rapid development of alcohol dependence in the absence of other forms of psychopathology. In summary, among males at least, genetic factors appear to play a pivotal role in the genesis of alcoholism, while among females, developmental and/or environmental factors assume more etiological importance (Frances, Timm, & Bucky, 1980; Goodwin et al., 1977).

In addition to the demonstrated role of genetic heritability in alcoholism itself, there are data to suggest that in some cases, this disorder is causally, and perhaps genetically, linked to other forms of psychopathology—in particular, affective disorder (i.e., depression) and ASP disorder. For example, Winokur (Winokur, Cadoret, Dorzals and Babier 1974; Winokur et al., 1970) and others (Behar, Winokur, Van Valkenburg, et al., 1980) have reported a greater than expected prevalence of alcoholism in the male relatives of females with depression, suggesting that the two clinical entities may be part of a "depression spectrum" disorder. On the other hand, Cloninger et al. (1981) and our group (Mirin, Weiss, Sollogub, & Michael, 1984b) have presented data to support a separate mode of inheritance for each of these clinical entities.

The relationship between alcoholism and ASP has also been the subject of several family pedigree studies (Cloninger & Reich, 1983; Cloninger et al., 1981; Schuckit, Rimmer, Reich, et al., 1970; Winokur et al., 1970; Winokur, Rimmer, & Reich, 1971). In one such study, Winokur et al. (1970) interviewed the first-degree relatives of 259 alcoholic probands and found a relatively high prevalence of sociopathy in the male relatives of these patients, compared to the general population. Subsequently, Cloninger et al. (1981) reanalyzed these data and concluded that alcoholism and ASP were each transmitted separately in the families of these patients, although environmental factors may have accounted for the clustering of the two disorders within individual families. Data from subsequent studies (Cloninger & Reich, 1983; Lewis,

Rice, & Helzer, 1983) suggest that the concurrent finding of alcoholism and ASP within a family increases the risk for the subsequent development of alcoholism in the offspring. Moreover, this is apparently true for females as well as males.

Finally, Stabenau and Hesselbrock (1984) used criteria from the third edition of the *Diagnostic and Statistical Manual of Mental Disorders* (DSM-III; American Psychiatric Association, 1980) to determine a lifetime diagnosis of alcoholism, ASP, substance abuse, and depression in 227 alcoholic probands. They found that approximately 40% were free of other types of psychopathology (i.e., ASP, depression, or substance abuse). Among the remaining 60%, primary depression was more common in females, while ASP was significantly more common in males. Indeed, ASP was found in 48% of the male alcoholics, compared to 15% of the female alcoholics. Moreover, alcoholics with ASP experienced a significantly earlier onset of problem drinking than did individuals without ASP, a finding also reported by Frances *et al.* (1980) and others (Schuckit & Morrissey, 1979). Finally, in approximately two-thirds of alcoholics with concurrent ASP, drug abuse was also a problem.

In exploring the role of familial factors, Stabenau and Hesselbrock (1984) assigned psychiatric diagnoses to the relatives of these patients according to the Research Diagnostic Criteria (RDC; Spitzer, Endicott, & Robins, 1978) using the family history method with the proband as informant (Andreasen, Endicott, Spitzer, & Winokur, 1977). In so doing, they found that alcoholics who had a positive family history of alcoholism on both the paternal and maternal sides reported more alcohol-associated psychopathology, including earlier loss of control over drinking, physical and psychosocial problems, and pathological symptoms associated with chronic alcohol use, than did either alcoholics with no alcoholic first-degree relatives or alcoholics with one or more alcoholic relatives on either the paternal or maternal side (but not both). In this study, probands who had alcoholic relatives on both sides of the family also had more male relatives with ASP.

In summary, in patients who exhibit problem drinking, family history data may be helpful in assessing the probability of those individuals' developing alcoholism and its associated adverse sequelae; the rapidity with which this might occur; and the likelihood of the illness's being transmitted to subsequent generations. The presence of other types of psychopathology—particularly ASP, and perhaps affective disorder—may also have some prognostic significance.

FAMILY STUDIES IN SUBSTANCE ABUSERS: METHODOLOGICAL ISSUES

With respect to other forms of substance use disorders (i.e., other than alcoholism), a logical question to ask is whether their development is also influenced by familial and/or genetic factors. Unfortunately, data with which to answer this question are as yet unavailable, since, in contrast to patients with affective disorder and/or alcoholism, family pedigree studies in substance abusers are quite rare. There are several reasons for the paucity of such studies. Though substance abuse has been present among certain subgroups of society throughout recorded history, it is only since 1970 that it has been recognized as a major public health problem. Consequently, research funding for this area is relatively new. Moreover, the major research emphasis thus far has been on developing psychosocial and/or pharmacological approaches to treatment. At the same time, those studies that have been concerned with etiology have focused more on social and cultural factors than on biological and genetic aspects.

Yet another set of factors mitigating against family studies in substance abusers has to do with issues of methodology and the patient population involved. The problems of accurate diagnosis and heterogeneity, which have plagued studies of patients with affective disorder and alcoholism (and their families), are even more pronounced among substance abusers. Indeed, even drug of choice can be an elusive concept, given the propensity of these patients to abuse more than one psychoactive substance (including alcohol) simultaneously. Substance abusers' suspiciousness, crisis orientation, and general reluctance to participate in clinical research add to the difficulties in studying this population. Finally, with regard to family pedigree studies, the propensity of chronic drug use and drug-associated illicit activity to promote transience in substance abusers and their families, and the resulting disruption of family ties, make such studies particularly difficult to carry out.

Thus far, studies of the families of substance abusers have focused in the interpersonal and psychodynamic aspects of family life that may contribute to the development of substance-abusing behavior. Many of these studies have been carried out in opiate abusers and their families, where the triad of a passive, dependent patient, an overinvolved, masochistic mother, and a physically or emotionally absent father has been repeatedly described (Harbin & Maziar, 1975; Mason, 1958; Schwartzman, 1975). Studies of family dynamics in other types of substance abusers (with the exception of alcoholics) are relatively rare.

From the standpoint of methodology, most studies done thus far have relied on the index patient (i.e., the proband) for information about the presence or absence of psychopathology in his or her family members. Most investigators in this field, however, would agree that data derived in this fashion are difficult to interpret, since probands generally tend to underreport psychopathology in family members (Mendelewicz & Rainer, 1974). Moreover, since many substance abusers come from disrupted families, there may be an additional impetus toward underreporting psychopathology, since absent relatives may represent an especially high-risk group. For these reasons, the most accurate and reliable data on the prevalence of familial psychopathology, in this (or any) patient population, are derived by combining information from the proband with data derived from direct clinical evaluation of all available first- and second-degree relatives.

Having reviewed the clinical relevance and methodological difficulties inherent in family pedigree studies of substance abusers, we focus in the remainder of this chapter on a family pedigree study currently underway on the Drug Dependence Treatment Unit at McLean Hospital in Belmont, Massachusetts. In this study, we are attempting to quantitate the prevalence of alcoholism, affective disorder, and other types of nondrug psychopathology in both substance abusers and their first-degree relatives. In the hope of avoiding the methodological pitfalls described above, family pedigree data have been generated through direct clinical evaluation of patients and all their available first-degree relatives using standardized diagnostic criteria. The data presented here were gathered as part of a larger study designed to explore the role of biological, psychosocial, and familial factors in the development of substance use disorders; some of our findings have been published elsewhere (Mirin *et al.*, 1984a, 1984b).

THE MCLEAN HOSPITAL STUDY

THE PATIENT POPULATION

The patient group was composed of 160 consecutively admitted substance abusers. Grouped by drug of choice, they consisted of opiate abusers (56.7%), abusers of CNS stimulants (primarily cocaine) (22.3%), and abusers of CNS depressants (20.3%). Approximately 74% of the patients were men. The mean age of the entire sample was 30.4 years (range 21–61). More than a third of the patients were married, and approximately two-thirds were employed at the time of admission. The average duration of drug experience in these patients was 10.3 years; however, as a group, stimulant abusers began drug use about 3 years later, and had less heavy drug experience, than did those who abused opiates or depressants.

ASSESSMENT PROCEDURES

Upon admission, all patients completed a 280-item questionnaire designed to gather demographic data, quantitate the extent and duration of drug and alcohol use, and assess current social adjustment. Patients also completed the 90-item Symptom Checklist (SCL-90) (Derogatis, Rickels, & Rock, 1976) and the Beck Depression Inventory (BDI; Beck, Ward, Mendelson, Mock, & Erbaugh, 1961) on admission and every 2 weeks thereafter during a 4- to 6-week hospital stay. The Hamilton Depression Rating Scale (Hamilton, 1960) was completed by a nurse/ clinician on the same schedule. Diagnostic judgments using DSM-III criteria (American Psychiatric Association, 1980) were made by the ward psychiatrist and were based on direct clinical interviews, psychiatric rating scale data, and observation of the patients in the ward milieu over an average hospital stay of 28 days. In patients with substantial depressive symptomatology (i.e., Hamilton score > 15), we also carried out a series of laboratory tests currently thought to be useful in evaluating and classifying patients with presumptive affective disorder. These included measurement of the 24-hour urinary excretion of 3-methoxy-4-hydroxyphenylglycol (MHPG) (Schildkraut, Orsulak, Schatzberg, *et al.*, 1978), platelet monoamine oxidase (MAO) activity (Davidson, McLeod, Turnbull, *et al.*, 1980), and the overnight dexamethasone suppression test (Carroll, Curtis, & Mendels, 1976). Preliminary findings on the utility of both the rating scale data and these biological measures in the clinical evaluation of substance abusers have been published elsewhere (Mirin *et al.*, 1984a).

FAMILY INTERVIEWS

Family pedigree data were gathered through the use of structured clinical interviews carried out by the unit social worker (Jacqueline Michael) with all available first-degree relatives, including at least one member of each patient's nuclear family. Complete family pedigree data were obtained from the families of 150 probands (93.7%). The remaining 10 patients either were adoptees or had lost contact with their families. The final data set encompassed 636 relatives, of whom 296 (46.5) were interviewed at least once. The interviewed group included 77.3% of the mothers, 64.8% of the fathers, 27% of the sisters, and 22.9% of the brothers. Both interviewed and noninterviewed family members received DSM-III diagnoses where interview data and/or information supplied by their immediate relatives (i.e., parents, spouses, siblings, or children) suggested a clear clinical picture. For purposes of data analysis, all relatives under age 20 were deleted from the sample to adjust for age-related risk factors, and the results were adjusted for half-siblings. To partially compensate for the hazards involved in assigning diagnoses to noninterviewed individuals, only broad diagnostic categories (e.g., alcoholism, affective disorder) were used to characterize the psychopathology found in these relatives.

PSYCHOPATHOLOGY IN SUBSTANCE-ABUSING PROBANDS

As summarized in Table 4-1, 42.5% ($n = 66$) of the total patient sample met DSM-III criteria for a *current* diagnosis of alcohol abuse or alcohol dependence. Within this alcoholic sub-group, 50% also met DSM-III criteria for at least one additional Axis I diagnosis exclusive of drug or alcohol dependence. Of these, more than half were suffering from some form of affective illness, most often major depression. In contrast, among substance abusers without alcohol problems, only 25% received an additional Axis I diagnosis.

Of the entire patient sample, 40% received at least one Axis I diagnosis exclusive of substance abuse or alcohol abuse/dependence. Almost 29% met DSM-III criteria for a current diagnosis of affective disorder; about two-thirds of this group were suffering from either major or atypical depression. The remainder of the affectively ill patients were

TABLE 4-1   Percentage Distribution of Axis I Diagnoses in 160 Substance Abusers

Diagnoses	Drug of choice			Total $(n = 160)$
	Opiates $(n = 91)$	Stimulants $(n = 36)$	Depressants $(n = 33)$	
Alcohol abuse/dependence	45.1	41.6	36.4	42.5
Major/atypical depression	17.6	30.6	18.2	20.6
Bipolar/cyclothymic disorder[a,b]	3.3	22.2	6.1	8.1
Other Axis I diagnoses [c]	5.5	11.1	27.2	11.35
All nondrug diagnoses[d,e]	26.4	63.9	51.4	40.0

Source: From "Affective Illness in Substance Abusers" by S. M. Mirin, R. D. Weiss, A. Sollogub, and J. Michael, 1984, in S. M. Mirin (Ed.), *Substance Abuse and Psychopathology*, Washington, DC: American Psychiatric Press. Copyright 1984 by American Psychiatric Press, Inc. Reprinted by permission.

[a] Significant difference in stimulant vs. opiate abusers ($\chi^2 = 11.68, p < .001$).

[b] Significant difference in stimulant vs. depressant abusers ($\chi^2 = 3.63, p < .10$).

[c] Significant difference in depressant vs. opiate abusers ($\chi^2 = 11.45, p < .001$).

[d] Significant difference in opiate vs. stimulant abusers ($\chi^2 = 15.57, p < .001$).

[e] Significant difference in opiate vs. depressant abusers ($\chi^2 = 6.97, p < .01$).

diagnosed as having either bipolar (i.e., manic–depressive) or cyclothymic disorder. In comparison, the overall rate of affective disorder in the general population has been variously reported to range from 6% to 15% (Weissman, Kidd, & Prusoff, 1982).

When patients were grouped by drug of choice, some interesting patterns emerged with respect to the prevalence of psychopathology in the different subgroups. As summarized in Table 4-1, alcoholism was equally distributed across the three groups of substance abusers; however, affective disorder in general, and bipolar and cyclothymic disorders in particular, were far more common among stimulant abusers than among those who abused opiates or CNS system depressants. Other Axis I diagnoses, particularly anxiety and/or panic disorder, occurred more frequently among patients who abused CNS depressants. In general, opiate abusers were found to have a significantly lower prevalence of nondrug psychopathology (DSM-III, Axis I), compared to the stimulant or depressant abusers. On the other hand, almost all of the patients who received an Axis II diagnosis of ASP disorder were opiate abusers.

PSYCHOPATHOLOGY IN THE RELATIVES OF SUBSTANCE ABUSERS

General Findings

Table 4-2 summarizes our data on the lifetime expectancy rate (i.e., the number ill divided by the number at risk) for Axis I (DSM-III) psychopathology in the 636 first-degree relatives of 150 substance abusers. Slightly more than 30% of all relatives met DSM-III criteria for at least one Axis I diagnosis, exclusive of substance abuse, during their lifetimes. As seen in Table 4-2, male relatives received an Axis I diagnosis significantly more often than female relatives. Expectably, the lifetime prevalence of alcohol abuse or dependence was significantly greater in the male than in female relatives (19.5% vs. 7.7%). Both these rates are clearly higher than those reported among males (3–5%) and females (0.5–2%) in the general population (Goodwin & Guze, 1974; Hirsch, 1955; Weissman, Myers, & Harding, 1980), but they are comparable to rates reported elsewhere for the relatives of opiate addicts (Ellinwood, Smith, & Vaillant, 1966; Hill, Cloninger, & Ayre, 1977), who, like our patients, probably had some alcoholics in their midst.

TABLE 4-2   Expectancy Rates for Psychopathology among the Relatives of 150 Substance Abusers

Diagnoses	Males ($n = 338$)	Females ($n = 298$)
Alcohol abuse/dependence	19.5%[c]	7.7%
Substance abuse disorders	8.6	5.7
Affective disorder [a]	5.6	14.8[d]
Anxiety/panic disorder	2.4	3.0
Other DSM-III Axis I diagnoses	7.1	5.0
All DSM-III Axis I diagnoses[b]	35.2[e]	25.8

Source: From "Psychopathology in the Families of Drug Abusers" by S. M. Mirin, R. D. Weiss, A. Sollogub, and J. Michael, 1984, in S. M. Mirin (Ed.), *Substance Abuse and Psychopathology*, Washington, DC: American Psychiatric Press. Copyright 1984 by American Psychiatric Press, Inc. Reprinted by permission.

[a] Includes major or atypical depression and bipolar/cyclothymic disorder.

[b] Corrected for multiple diagnoses within a single relative.

[c] Significant between-group difference ($\chi^2 = 18.35, p < .001$).

[d] Significant between-group difference ($\chi^2 = 14.84, p < .001$).

[e] Significant between-group difference ($\chi^2 = 6.52, p < .02$).

As indicated in Table 4-2, the lifetime expectancy of primary affective disorder (i.e., major or atypical depression, bipolar disorder, or cyclothymic disorder) was significantly greater in the female compared to the male, relatives (14.6% vs. 5.6%). Among those relatives found to be suffering from affective disorder, major depression was by far the most frequent diagnosis. Substance use disorders, anxiety disorders, and other Axis I DSM-III diagnoses were evenly distributed among the male and female relatives of our patients.

When relatives were grouped according to the drug of choice of the proband, some interesting intergroup differences emerged with respect to the extent and type of psychopathology found. For example, alcohol abuse and/or dependence was somewhat more frequent in the male relatives of opiate addicts (23.6%) than in the male relatives of stimulant (15.2%) or depressant (11.4%) abusers, though the differences among the three groups did not reach statistical significance. On the other hand, affective disorder (i.e., major or atypical depression, bipolar disorder, or cyclothymic disorder) was significantly more common among both the male and female relatives of stimulant abusers than among the same-sex relatives of those who abused either opiates or depressants (chi-square p values all < .05).

In an attempt to determine whether substance use disorders followed a pattern of familial transmission similar to that reported in alcoholics, we also calculated the expectancy rate for these disorders among the first-degree relatives of the three drug-using subgroups. In so doing, we found that substance abuse disorders were significantly more prevalent among the female relatives of stimulant abusers (15.0%) than among the female relatives of those who abused opiates (2.5%) or depressants (4.2%). This difference was accounted for by the relatively high prevalence of stimulant and depressant abuse in the mothers and sisters of these patients.In contrast, we also found that the male relatives of depressant abusers had a significantly lower lifetime expectancy rate for substance abuse disorders (1.6%), compared to the male relatives of either opiate (10.8%) or stimulant (12.2%) abusers. This finding was part of an overall trend toward less psychopathology of all types (including alcoholism) among the relatives of patients who abused CNS depressants. Indeed, depressant abuse (exclusive of alcoholism) seemed to be much less tied to familial factors than the other two types of substance abuse. Whereas approximately 25% of all relatives of opiate and stimulant abusers were given a lifetime diagnosis of alcoholism and/

or substance abuse, the overall combined expectancy rate for these two disorders in the relatives of depressant abusers was less than 10%. Depressant abuse, where it developed, appeared to be more closely tied to peer-influenced recreational use in the case of methaqualone abusers, or an attempt at self-treatment of some underlying psychiatric disorder (i.e., anxiety or panic disorder).

Expectancy Rates for Alcoholism

In light of previous studies (Goodwin, 1971; Goodwin *et al.*, 1977; Pitts & Winokur, 1966; Schuckit, 1982) suggesting that genetic heritability plays a role in the development of alcoholism, we felt it would be useful to compare the lifetime expectancy rate for this disorder among the first-degree relatives (i.e., parents and siblings) of alcoholic and nonalcoholic substance abusers. As seen in Table 4-3, a cross-group comparison of the relatives of alcoholics with the relatives of nonalcoholics (see Table 4-4), revealed that alcoholism was significantly more prevalent in both the male and female relatives of alcoholic substance abusers than in the same-sex relatives of nonalcoholic substance abusers. Moreover, with the exception of the mothers, this difference was significant (chi-square) for each relative subgroup.

As seen in Table 4-4 within-group comparisons for the sample as a whole revealed that the overall expectancy rate for alcoholism was significantly higher in the male relatives, with fathers having a significantly higher rate than mothers and brothers having a significantly higher rate than sisters. Interestingly, while the expectancy rate for alcoholism was significantly higher in the mothers than in the sisters of our patients, the rate of alcoholism in the fathers and brothers was almost identical. One possible explanation for this finding is that many of these men have what Goodwin (1971) has called "familial alcoholism," characterized by strong genetic loading, early onset, and a rapid downhill course, thus minimizing any age-related differences in expectancy rates.

Expectancy Rates for Affective Disorder

As previously noted, almost 29% of our drug-abusing patients satisifed DSM-III criteria for a current diagnosis of affective disorder. In an attempt to define patterns of familial transmission of affective illness in these patients, we calculated the expectancy rate for the lifetime oc-

TABLE 4-3   Expectancy Rates for Alcoholism among the Relatives of 150 Substance Abusers

Relatives	Total sample (n = 150)		Probands with substance abuse only (n = 88)		Probands with substance abuse and alcoholism (n = 62)		Cross-group comparison (chi-square)
	No. at risk	% Ill	No. at risk	% Ill	No. at risk	% Ill	
Fathers	148	20.3	87	12.6	61	31.1	7.59***
Brothers	190	18.9	105	12.4	85	27.1	6.59**
Mothers	150	11.3	88	8.0	62	16.1	2.42
Sisters	148	4.1	91	1.1	57	8.8	5.31*
All males	338	19.5	192	12.5	146	28.8	13.97****
All females	298	7.7	179	4.5	119	12.6	6.64***

Source: From "Psychopathology in the Families of Drug Abusers" by S. M. Mirin, R. D. Weiss, A. Sollogub, and J. Michael, 1984, in S. M. Mirin (Ed.), *Substance Abuse and Psychopathology*, Washington, DC: American Psychiatric Press. Copyright 1984 by American Psychiatric Press, Inc. Reprinted by permission.

*p < .05.
**p < .02.
***p < .01.
****p < .001.

TABLE 4-4   Within-Group Comparisons (Chi-Squares) of Expectancy Rates for Alcoholism among the Relatives of 150 Substance Abusers

	Total sample (n = 150)	Probands with substance abuse only (n = 88)	Probands with substance abuse and alcoholism (n = 62)
Fathers vs. mothers	4.48*	1.04	3.85*
Brothers vs. sisters	16.35****	9.36***	7.21**
Fathers vs. brothers	0.09	0.01	0.29
Mothers vs. sisters	5.54**	4.92*	1.46
Males vs. females	18.35****	7.58***	10.14*

Source: From "Psychopathology in the Families of Drug Abusers" by S. M. Mirin, R. D. Weiss, A. Sollogub, and J. Michael, 1984, in S. M. Mirin (Ed.), *Substance Abuse and Psychopathology*, Washington, DC: American Psychiatric Press. Copyright 1984 by American Psychiatric Press, Inc. Reprinted by permission.

*p < .05.
**p < .02.
***p < .01.
****p < .001.

currence of affective illness in their first-degree relatives. As summarized in Table 4-5, the overall expectancy rate for affective illness in the first-degree relatives of our patients was 5.6% in the males and 14.8% in the females. In comparison, Weissman and colleagues (Weissman *et al.*, 1982; Weissman, Myers, & Harding, 1978) reported rates of possible, probable, and definite major depression of 3% in the male and 9% in the female relatives of normal probands. As seen in Table 4-6, within-group comparisons for the sample as a whole revealed that the lifetime expectancy rate of affective illness was significantly higher in mothers than in fathers and higher in sisters than in brothers. Moreover, as Table 4-5 indicates, the illness rate for mothers was about twice that of the sisters (19.3% vs. 10.1%), which is not surprising, considering that the mothers had spent considerably more time in the period of risk for these disorders. In contrast, there was no difference in the expectancy rate for affective illness between fathers and brothers (see Table 4-6), perhaps due to the overall low prevalence of these disorders in male relatives as a whole.

TABLE 4-5   Expectancy Rates for Affective Disorder among the Relatives of 150 Substance Abusers

Relatives	Total sample ($n = 150$)		Probands without affective disorder ($n = 106$)		Probands with affective disorder ($n = 44$)		Cross-group comparison (chi-square)
	No. at risk	% Ill	No. at risk	% Ill	No. at risk	% Ill	
Fathers	148	6.8	104	2.9	44	15.9	8.32*
Brothers	190	4.7	130	1.5	60	11.7	9.33*
Mothers	150	19.3	106	12.3	44	36.4	11.58**
Sisters	148	10.1	101	7.9	47	14.8	1.71
Males	338	5.6	234	2.1	104	13.5	17.46**
Females	298	14.8	207	10.2	91	25.0	11.49**

Source: From "Psychopathology in the Families of Drug Abusers" by S. M. Mirin, R. D. Weiss, A. Sollogub, and J. Michael, 1984, in S. M. Mirin (Ed.), *Substance Abuse and Psychopathology*, Washington, DC: American Psychiatric Press. Copyright 1984 by American Psychiatric Press, Inc. Reprinted by permission.

*p < .01.

**p < .001.

TABLE 4-6 Within-Group Comparisons (Chi-Squares) of Expectancy Rates for Affective Illness among the Relatives of 150 Substance Abusers

	Total sample (n = 150)	Probands without affective disorder (n = 106)	Probands with affective disorder (n = 44)
Mothers vs. fathers	10.36***	6.56**	4.77*
Sisters vs. brothers	3.67***	5.59**	0.24
Mothers vs. sisters	5.01*	1.07	5.55**
Fathers vs. brothers	0.64	0.50	0.39
Females vs. males	14.84****	4.41*	12.69****

Source: From "Psychopathology in the Families of Drug Abusers" by S. M. Mirin, R. D. Weiss, A. Sollogub, and J. Michael, 1984, in S. M. Mirin (Ed.), *Substance Abuse and Psychopathology*, Washington, DC: American Psychiatric Press. Copyright 1984 by American Psychiatric Press, Inc. Reprinted by permission.

*$p < .05$.
**$p < .02$.
***$p < .01$.
****$p < .001$.

As in our analysis of the alcoholism data, we also compared the expectancy rate for affective disorder in the relatives of substance abusers *with* affective illness to that found in the relatives of substance abusers *without* affective illness. In this cross-group comparison (see Table 4-5), we found that the overall rate of affective illness (males and females combined) was more than three times higher in the relatives of patients without affective disorder (18.9% vs. 5.9%). Furthermore, as indicated in Table 4-5, the overall rate of affective disorder in the female relatives of affectively ill patients was 25.0%, compared to 10.2% in the female relatives of patients without affective illness. For male relatives, the lifetime expectancy rates were 13.5% and 2.1%, respectively.

Expectancy Rates for Affective Disorder in the Relatives of Alcoholics

In exploring the suggestion of Winokur (Winokur, 1974; Winokur *et al.*, 1970) and others (Behar *et al.*, 1980) that in some instances alcoholism may represent a sex-linked variant of so-called "depression spectrum disease," we compared the expectancy rate for affective disorder in the relatives of alcoholic substance abusers with that found in the relatives of nonalcoholic substance abusers. We found no significant difference between the two groups. Similarly, when we compared the expectancy rate for alcoholism in the relatives of patients with and without affective disorder, there was also no significant difference between groups. Finally, since approximately one-third of our substance abusers with concomitant alcohol problems were also suffering from affective disorder, we looked at the rate of affective disorder and/or alcoholism in the relatives of this potentially high-risk subgroup. However, the expectancy rates for alcoholism or affective disorder, respectively, were no higher than in the relatives of those who were currently suffering from either disease alone. Thus, in this population of substance abusers, being alcoholic did not increase the probability that a patient would have a relative with affective disorder. Conversely, having affective disorder did not increase the probability that a patient would have one or more alcoholic relatives.

Sex-Linked Distribution of Familial Psychopathology

Alcoholism

To explore the possibility that the propensity to develop alcoholism and/ or affective disorder might be transmitted in a sex-linked fashion, we reanalyzed our data separately for male and female probands and their relatives. Despite the small number of relatives in each subgroup, we found that the male relatives of male alcoholics had almost twice the expectancy rate for alcoholism, compared to the male relatives of female alcoholics (33.9% vs. 17.5%; $\chi^2 = 3.41$, $p < .10$). Similarly, male relatives of men without alcohol problems also had a higher rate of alcoholism than the male relatives of women without alcohol problems (14.4% vs. 7.5%). Though these findings did not reach statistical significance (perhaps due to the small sample size), they are consistent with the findings of Goodwin *et al.* (1977) and suggest that in males, genetic factors play an important role in the transmission of alcoholism to their same-sex relatives, whereas in women, developmental and environmental contingencies are causally more important.

Affective Disorder

With respect to the issue of sex linkage in the transmission of affective disorder, we found that the female relatives of male substance abusers had a considerably higher expectancy rate for affective illness, compared to the female relatives of female substance abusers (12.7% vs. 3.5%; $\chi^2 = 3.8$, $p < .10$). Similarly, female relatives of men with affective disorder had a rate of affective illness that was more than twice that found in the female relatives of women with affective disorder (33.3% vs. 14.6%; $\chi^2 = 4.24$, $p < .05$). While these preliminary data fail to distinguish the relative contribution of nature and nurture to this pattern of occurrence, they do suggest that the development of affective illness in males may require significantly more genetic loading, and that it is the female relatives of these patients who contribute most in this regard.

MODELS OF FAMILIAL–GENETIC TRANSMISSION OF PSYCHOPATHOLOGY IN SUBSTANCE ABUSERS

In a clinical setting, the precise causal relationships linking substance abuse, alcoholism, and affective disorder are often murky. From the standpoint of genetic heritability, the frequent concordance of these disorders in the same individual might lead one to suspect that these clinical entities may be different phenotypic expressions of the same inherited disorder, with alcoholism and substance abuse occurring primarily in males, and affective disorder (especially depression) occurring mostly in females.

Family pedigree data are useful in testing this hypothesis. For example, if substance abuse, alcoholism, and affective disorder were merely sex-linked variants of the same illness, one might expect to find an equal, though sex-linked, distribution of these disorders among first-degree relatives, regardless of the diagnosis of the proband. In our population of substance abusers, this was not the case. Being alcoholic did not increase the probability that a patient would have a relative with affective disorder. Conversely, having affective disorder did not increase the probability that a patient would have one or more alcoholic relatives. Indeed, the prevalence of alcoholism and/or affective disorder in the relatives of these substance abusers was correlated solely with the presence of the same clinical entity in the probands.

In our sample, 57% of all patients had at least two diseases (i.e., substance abuse and alcoholism, or substance abuse and affective disorder), and 14% were suffering from all three disorders concurrently. If one hypothesized that these three clinical entities were different phenotypic expressions of the same disorder, and then sought to apply a multiple threshold model of genetic heritability (Baron, Klotz, Mendlewicz, *et al.*, 1981) to the family history data, it would be reasonable to expect that probands with milder forms of the disorder (i.e., those with substance abuse alone) would have fewer pathological relatives than would probands with more severe illness (i.e., those with substance abuse plus alcoholism and/or affective disorder). Indeed, probands with two or more forms of illness might be expected to have not only an increased number of first-degree relatives with any form of the illness, but also more relatives with multiple forms of the illness.

In our study, the relatives of substance abusers with alcoholism and/or affective disorder did have a higher rate of similar nondrug psychopathology when compared to the relatives of substance abusers without these disorders, but the overall rate of substance abuse was not increased in the relatives of these patients. Moreover, patients with all three disorders were at no greater risk for having similarly ill relatives than those whose substance abuse was accompanied by either alcoholism or affective disorder alone. Thus, the data are not consistent with a multiple-threshold model of inheritance for these three disorders. Rather, our data seem to fit a model of inheritance in which alcoholism and affective disorder correspond to two or more different genotypes that are separately transmitted.

With respect to substance abuse itself, the data suggest that alcoholism and substance abuse are more prevalent in the families of opiate addicts and stimulant abusers than in the families of depressant abusers and the general population. The relative contributions of nature and nurture to the development of substance abuse problems in these families are still difficult to discern. Future studies employing more sophisticated methods of data analysis may help to clarify this issue further.

ACKNOWLEDGMENT

Portions of the research data reported in this paper were analyzed with the support of the Engelhard Foundation.

REFERENCES

American Psychiatric Association. (1980). *Diagnostic and statistical manual of mental disorders* (3rd ed.). Washington, DC: Author.

Andreasen, N., Endicott, J., Spitzer, R., & Winokur, G. (1977). The family history method using diagnostic criteria. *Archives of General Psychiatry, 34,* 1229–1235.

Baron, M., Klotz, J., Mendlewicz, J., et al. (1981). Multiple-threshold transmission of affective disorders. *Archives of General Psychiatry, 38,* 79–84.

Beck, A. T., Ward, C. H., Mendelson, M., Mock, J. E., & Erbaugh, J. K. (1961). An inventory for measuring depression. *Archives of General Psychiatry, 4,* 561–571.

Behar, D., Winokur, G., Van Valkenburg, C., et al. (1980). Familial subtypes of depression: A clinical view. *Journal of Clinical Psychiatry, 41,* 52–56.

Bohman, M. (1978). Some genetic aspects of alcoholism and criminality: A population of adoptees. *Archives of General Psychiatry, 37,* 747–751.

Cadoret, R. J. (1978). Evidence for genetic inheritance of primary affective disorder in adoptees. *American Journal of Psychiatry, 135,* 463–466.

Carroll, B. J., Curtis, G. C., & Mendels, J. (1976). Neuroendocrine regulation in depression. *Archives of General Psychiatry, 33,* 1051–1058.

Cloninger, C., & Reich, T. (1983). Genetic heterogeneity in alcoholism and sociopathy. In S. Kety, L. Rowland, R. Sidman, & S. Matthysse (Eds.), *Genetics of neurological and psychiatric disorders* (pp. 145–166). New York: Raven Press.

Cloninger, C., Reich, T., & Wetzel, R. (1981). Alcoholism and affective disorders: Familial associations and genetic models. In D. Goodwin & C. Erickson (Eds.), *Alcoholism and affective disorders: Clinical, genetic and biochemical studies* (pp. 57–86). New York: SP Medical & Scientific Books.

Craig, R. J. (1979). Personality characteristics of heroin addicts: I. A review of the empirical literature with critique. *International Journal of the Addictions, 14,* 513.

Dackis, C. A., & Gold, M. S. (1984). Depression in opiate addicts. In S. M. Mirin (Ed.), *Substance abuse and psychopathology* (pp. 21–35). Washington, DC: American Psychiatric Press.

Davidson, J. R., McLeod, M. N., Turnbull, C. D., et al. (1980). Platelet monoamine oxidase activity and the classification of depression. *Archives of General Psychiatry, 37,* 771–773.

Derogatis, L., Rickels, K., & Rock, A. (1976). The SCL-90 and the MMPI: A step in the validation of a new self report scale. *British Journal of Psychiatry, 128,* 280–289.

Ellinwood, E. H., Jr., Smith, W. G., & Vaillant, G. E. (1966). Narcotic addiction in males and females: A comparison. *International Journal of the Addictions, 1,* 33–45.

Frances, R., Timm, S., & Bucky, S. (1980). Studies of familial and nonfamilial alcoholism: I. Demographic studies. *Archives of General Psychiatry, 37,* 564–566.

Goodwin, D. W. (1971). Is alcoholism hereditary?: A review and critique. *Archives of General Psychiatry, 25,* 545–549.

Goodwin, D. W., Schulsinger, F., Knop, J., Mednick, S., & Guze, S. (1977). Alcoholism and depression in adopted-out daughters of alcoholics. *Archives of General Psychiatry, 34,* 751–755.

Hamilton, M. (1960). A rating scale for depression. *Journal of Neurology, Neurosurgery and Psychiatry, 23,* 56–62.

Harbin, H. T., & Maziar, H. M. (1975). The families of drug abusers: A literature review. *Family Process, 15,* 411–431.

Helfrich, A. A., Crowley, T. J., Atkinson, C. A., et al. (1982). A clinical profile of 136 cocaine abusers. In L. S. Harris (Ed.), *Problems of drug dependence* (pp. 343–350). Washington, DC: U.S. Government Printing Office.

Hill, S. H., Cloninger, C. R., & Ayre, F. R. (1977). Independent familial transmission of alcoholism and opiate abuse. *Alcoholism: Clinical and Experimental Research, 1,* 335–342.

Hirsch, J. (1955). Public health and social aspects of alcoholism. In G. N. Thompson (Ed.), *Alcoholism* (pp. 3–100). Springfield, IL: Charles C Thomas.

Kleber, H. D., & Gold, M. S. (1978). Use of psychotropic drugs in the treatment of methadone maintained narcotic addicts. *Annals of the New York Academy of Sciences, 331,* 81–89.

Kleber, H. D., Weissman, M. M., & Rounsaville, B. J. (1983). Imipramine as treatment for depression in addicts. *Archives of General Psychiatry, 40,* 649–653.

Lewis, C., Rice, J., & Helzer, J. (1983). Diagnostic interactions: Alcoholism and antisocial personality. *Journal of Nervous and Mental Disease, 171,* 105–113.

Mason, P. (1958). The mother of the addict. *Psychiatry Quarterly, 32*(Suppl. 2), 189–199.

Mendelewicz, J., & Rainer, J. R. (1974). Morbidity risk and genetic transmission in manic depressive illness. *American Journal of Human Genetics, 26,* 692–701.

Mirin, S. M., Weiss, R. D., Sollogub, A., & Michael, J. (1984a). Affective illness in substance abusers. In S. M. Mirin (Ed.), *Substance abuse and psychopathology* (pp. 57–74). Washington, DC: American Psychiatric Press.

Mirin, S. M., Weiss, R. D., Sollogub, A., & Michael, J. (1984b). Psychopathology in the families of drug abusers. In S. M. Mirin (Ed.), *Substance abuse and psychopathology* (pp. 80–101). Washington, DC: American Psychiatric Press.

Partanen, J., Brunn, K., & Markkanen, T. (1966). *Inheritance of drinking behavior.* New Brunswick, NJ: Rutgers University Center of Alcohol Studies.

Pitts, F. N., & Winokur, G. (1966). Affective disorder, VII: Alcoholism and affective disorder. *Journal of Psychiatric Research, 4,* 37–50.

Post, R. M., Kotin, J., & Goodwin, F. R. (1974). The effects of cocaine on depressed patients. *American Journal of Psychiatry, 131,* 511–517.

Reich, T., Cloninger, C., Collin, L., et al. (1980). Some recent findings in the study of genotype environment interaction in alcoholism. In R. Meyer (Ed.), *Evaluation of the alcoholic: Implications for research, theory and treatment* (NIAAA Research Monograph 5, pp. 145–165). Rockville, MD: U.S. Department of Health and Human Services.

Rounsaville, B. J., Weissman, M. M., Kleber, H. D., & Wilber, C. H. (1982). Heterogeneity of psychiatric diagnosis in treated opiate addicts. *Archives of General Psychiatry, 39,* 161–166.

Rounsaville, B. J., Weissman, M. M., Wilber, C. H., Crits-Cristoph, K., & Kleber, H. D. (1982). Diagnosis and symptoms of depression in opiate addicts: Course and relationship to treatment outcome. *Archives of General Psychiatry, 39,* 151–156.

Schildkraut, J. J., Orsulak, P. J., Schatzberg, A. F., et al. (1978). Toward a biochemical classification of depressive disorders: I. Differences in urinary excretion of MHPG and other catecholamine metabolites in clinically defined subtypes of depression. *Archives of General Psychiatry, 35,* 1427–1433.

Schuckit, M. A. (1980). Alcoholism and genetics: Possible biological mediators. *Biological Psychiatry, 15,* 437–447.

Schuckit, M. A. (1982). A study of young men with alcoholic close relatives. *American Journal of Psychiatry, 139,* 791–794.

Schuckit, M. A., & Morrissey, E. (1979). Psychiatric problems in women admitted to an alcohol detoxification center. *American Journal of Psychiatry, 136,* 611–617.

Schuckit, M. A., Rimmer, J., Reich, T., *et al.* (1970). Alcoholism: Antisocial traits in male alcoholics. *British Journal of Psychiatry, 117,* 575–576.

Schwartzman, J. (1975). The addict, abstinence, and the family. *American Journal of Psychiatry, 132,* 154–157.

Shaw, B. F., Steer, R. A., Beck, A. T., *et al.* (1979). The structure of depression in heroin addicts. *British Journal of Addition, 74,* 295–303.

Spitzer, R. L., Endicott, J., & Robins, E. (1978). Research diagnostic criteria: Rationale and reliability. *Archives of General Psychiatry, 35,* 773–782.

Stabenau, J. R. & Hesselbrock, V. M. (1984). Psychopathology in alcoholics and their families and vulnerability to alcoholism: A review and new findings. In S. M. Mirin (Ed.), *Substance abuse and psychopathology* (pp. 108–127). Washington, DC: American Psychiatric Press.

Weissman, M. M., Kidd, K. K., & Prusoff, B. A. (1982). Variability in rates of affective disorders in relatives of depressed and normal probands. *Archives of General Psychiatry, 39,* 1397–1403.

Weissman, M. M., Myers, J., & Harding, P. (1978). Psychiatric disorders in a U.S. suburban community, 1975–1976. *American Journal of Psychiatry, 135,* 459–462.

Weissman, M. M., Myers, J., & Harding, P. (1980). Prevalence and psychiatric heterogeneity of alcoholism in a United States urban community. *Journal of Studies on Alcohol, 41,* 672–680.

Weissman, M. M., Pottenger, M., Kleber, H., *et al.* (1977). Symptom patterns in primary and secondary depression: A comparison of primary depressives with depressed opiate addicts, alcoholics, and schizophrenics. *Archives of General Psychiatry, 34,* 854–862.

Winokur, G., Cadoret, K. J., Dorzals, & Baker, (1974). The division of depressive illness into depression spectrum disease and pure depressive disease. *International Pharmacopsychiatry, 9,* 5–13.

Winokur, G., Reich, T., Rimmer, J., & Pitts, F. (1970). Alcoholism, III: Diagnosis of familial psychiatric illness in 259 alcoholic probands. *Archives of General Psychiatry, 23,* 104–111.

Winokur, G., Rimmer, J., & Reich, T. (1971) Alcoholism, IV: Is there more than one type of alcoholism? *British Journal of Psychiatry, 118,* 525–531.

Winokur, G., Tsuang, M. T., & Crowe, R. R. (1982). The Iowa 500: Affective disorder in relatives and depressed patients. *American Journal of Psychiatry, 139,* 209–215.

Woody, G. E., O'Brien, C. P., & Rickels, K. (1975). Depression and anxiety in heroin addicts: A placebo controlled study of doxepin in combination with methadone. *American Journal of Psychiatry, 132,* 447–450.

5

Childhood Behavior Problems and Adult Antisocial Personality Disorder in Alcoholism

MICHIE N. HESSELBROCK

There is abundant evidence indicating an association between the diagnosis of antisocial personality (ASP) disorder and the development of alcoholism. Lewis, Rice, and Helzer (1983) found a strong positive relationship between ASP disorder and the development of alcoholism in medical–surgical inpatients who were referred to a psychiatric consultation service. In his study, the prevalence of alcoholism was higher among antisocial individuals than nonantisocial individuals. The antisocials were more likely to have been exposed to heavy drinking, and, once exposed, tended to develop the full alcoholism syndrome. Several other prospective studies have found a relationship between childhood conduct disorder and alcoholism in adulthood. McCord and McCord (1960) identified aggressiveness and sadistic behavior in delinquent boys as risk factors for the later development of alcoholism. Similarly, childhood sociopathic behavior was associated with adult alcoholism in a child guidance clinic sample (Robins, 1966). The findings have been replicated in nonclinic samples. Kellam, Stevenson, and Rubin (1983) found that aggressiveness in first-grade males predicted heavy drug, alcohol, and cigarette use, as well as delinquency in teenagers. Calahan and Room (1974) also identified youthful rashness and "hell raising" as early predictors of problem drinking in adulthood.

In addition to predicting alcohol abuse in adulthood, childhood behavior problems have been associated with ASP disorder in adulthood. In separate studies examining several different populations, Robins and colleagues found a strong relationship existing between sociopathic behavior in childhood and sociopathy in adulthood in black men (Robins, Murphy, & Breckenridge, 1968; Robins, Murphy, Woodruff, & King, 1971), Vietnam veterans (Robins, 1978), and children attending a child guidance clinic (Robins, 1966). Several conclusions can be drawn from her studies: (1) Violent and aggressive behavior does not appear in adulthood if it has been absent in childhood; (2) while the diagnosis of ASP disorder by definition requires childhood ASP behavior, not all children with a conduct disorder problem become antisocial adults (Robins, 1979).

Similarly, not all children with behavior problems grow up to be alcoholics. While childhood problem behavior can be a risk factor for adult ASP disorder and/or alcoholism, it is not clear why some children become alcoholics and/or antisocial adults while others do not develop either disorder. Efforts to separate the two diagnostic entities based on risk factors have not been entirely successful. We (Hesselbrock, Hesselbrock, Babor, *et al.*, 1984) attempted to separate these two diagnoses by examining retrospective data of alcoholics with or without the additional diagnosis of ASP. It was found that ASP alcoholics were characterized by an early onset of alcoholism, followed by a more severe and chronic course. Factors discriminating ASP and non-ASP alcoholics included current age (ASP alcoholics being younger), family history of alcoholism, and childhood behavior problems.

An in-depth examination of childhood behavior problems may help to increase our understanding of the separate pathways to alcoholism and ASP disorder. Childhood problem behavior, including hyperactivity and minimal brain dysfunction, has been associated with adult psychiatric problems. Tarter, McBride, Buonpane, Dorothea, and Schneider (1977) have found that primary alcoholics (defined as severe drinkers on the basis of drinking patterns and subjective response to alcohol) reported having had more hyperactivity/minimal brain dysfunction symptoms in childhood than secondary alcoholics. Similarly, DeObaldia, Parsons, and Yohman (1983) reported that primary alcoholics reported more hyperactivity/minimal brain dysfunction symptoms, performed poorly on cognitive tests and experienced more severe symptoms of alcohol dependence. This finding led the authors to hypothesize that chronic alcoholics may have had minimal brain dysfunction/hyperactivity symptoms that predisposed them to adult psychopathology.

However, it should be noted that "hyperactivity/minimal brain dysfunction" is a rather general concept used to define a broad range of behavior problems in children. Hyperactivity and minimal brain dysfunction include such symptoms as attention deficit disorder, overactivity, poor perceptual motor coordination, poor socialization, and aggressiveness. P. H. Wender (personal communication, 1983) has suggested that childhood behavior problems can be classified into four categories: attention deficit disorder, impulsivity, hyperactivity, and conduct problems. The diagnosis of attention deficit disorder and hyperactivity in the *Diagnostic and Statistical Manual of Mental Disorder*, third edition (DSM-III; American Psychiatric Association, 1980) includes the first three categories, while conduct problems are classified as a separate diagnosis. Some investigators have distinguished hyperactive children with and without conduct problems and have found a different adult outcome for the two groups of children. August, Stewart, and Holmes (1983) found that both groups of hyperactive boys continued to be inattentive and impulsive, but few purely hyperactive boys showed aggressive and antisocial behavior at their 4-year follow-up evaluation. Hyperactive boys who were undersocialized and aggressive, on the other hand, continued to be aggressive, noncompliant, and antisocial, and used alcohol as teenagers. By classifying childhood problem behaviors according to these specific types, one could hypothesize that certain childhood behavior problems are risk factors for adult antisocial behavior and/or alcoholism, while others are not. The study reported in the present chapter examined the association of a variety of childhood behaviors reported retrospectively and the diagnosis of ASP in hospitalized alcoholics. By comparing retrospective data of childhood behaviors between ASP and non-ASP alcoholics, my colleagues and I hoped to distinguish childhood behaviors that are unique to ASP disorder among hospitalized alcoholics.

METHODS

The subjects and the procedures of this study have been described in detail elsewhere (Hesselbrock, Babor, Hesselbrock, Meyer, & Workman, 1983; Hesselbrock, Choquette, Margoles, & Keener, 1984; Hesselbrock, Meyer, & Keener, 1985), but are described briefly here. Subjects were recruited from three inpatient alcoholism treatment centers in the greater Hartford, Connecticut, area. Randomly selected patients who were admitted to an alcoholism treatment program were asked to participate in a multidisciplinary research project. Informed consent was obtained from each volunteer, and assurance of confidentiality was given. The sample included 231 men and 90 women. Approximately 55% of the sample came from an alcoholism treatment unit in a university-affiliated medical center, 21% from a Veterans Administration medical center, and 24% from a state-funded substance abuse treatment facility. These facilities were selected to permit generalization of the results to patients from a broad range of socioeconomic backgrounds.

PROCEDURES

As part of a multidisciplinary research protocol, a complete psychiatric history was obtained from each subject using the National Institute of Mental Health Diagnostic Interview Schedule (NIMH-DIS; Robins, Helzer, Croughan, Spitzer, & Bennett, 1979). The interviews were conducted by trained research technicians. All interviews were audio-recorded and monitored for consistency. Lifetime psychiatric diagnoses and assessment of age of onset were made according to the DSM-III criteria, utilizing computer programs developed by Robins, Helzer, Croughan, and Ratcliff (1981). One exception to this was made in the present study. Since alcohol intoxication at an early age is a part of the diagnosis for ASP disorder, the diagnosis of ASP in this study was modified to exclude two symptoms that were directly related to or caused by alcohol use— that is, alcohol intoxication before age 15, and trouble driving because of drinking (having an accident or being arrested for drunk driving).

Retrospective information on indicators of childhood problem behavior was collected using items from Tarter *et al.*'s (1977) and Wender's (1971) behavior checklists. Each subject reported on the occurrence of these behaviors prior to the age of 12. Of 29 items used, 7 items were classified as attention deficit disorder, 8 items as hyperactivity, 4 items as impulsivity, and the remaining 10 items as conduct problems (see Table 5-1).

SUBJECTS

The sample consisted of 231 men and 90 women, as noted above, and was 17% black and 83% white. Most subjects (67%) in the study were high school graduates, while 10% had a college or graduate degree.

TABLE 5-1   Childhood Behavior Problems in ASP and Non-ASP Alcoholics

| | % positive in childhood behavior | | | |
| | Males | | Females | |
Childhood behavior	ASP (n = 108)	Non-ASP (n = 112)	ASP (n = 16)	Non-ASP (n = 67)
Attention deficit				
Daydreaming	78	63*	81	63
Didn't work up to ability	54	41	56	41
Didn't complete projects	41	23**	44	28
Short attention span	60	41**	75	39**
Difficulty in math	36	30	69	40*
Difficulty in reading	26	16	19	12
Poor coordination	12	5	13	13
Hyperactivity				
Talked too much	35	25	38	25
Overactive	54	44	38	25
Fidgety	49	43	75	49
Unable to sit still	60	42**	50	44
Hard to get to bed nights	46	29**	38	28
Got into things	78	63**	81	42**
Accident-prone	29	13**	25	27
Wore out toys	54	43	44	21
Impulsivity				
Impulsive	73	55**	69	55
Could not tolerate delay	70	55*	73	54
Unpredictable	68	49**	69	45
Easily frustrated	61	47*	81	53*
Conduct Problems				
Angered friends	20	11	25	12
Trouble accepting corrections	58	34**	68	43
Demanded attention	43	30	63	43
Unresponsive to discipline	53	20**	56	13**
Lied a lot	56	22**	56	13**
Fought a lot	53	36**	56	33
Stealing	31	9**	50	6**
Overly aggressive	33	22*	50	22*
Temper tantrums	34	21*	50	22*
Truant	38	13**	31	9*

*$p < .05$.

**$p < .01$.

Nearly one-third of the men (30%) and one-fourth of the women (22%) were single; 27% of the men and 34% of the women were married; the remainder were divorced or widowed (43% for both sexes). The men were slightly older than the women at the time of hospitalization ($\bar{x}$ =

39.5 and $\bar{x} = 37.3$, respectively), but the difference was not statistically significant. The men were found to have been abusing alcohol more than twice as long as the women (15 and 7 years, respectively).

RESULTS

The classification of individual childhood behaviors into the four categories, and the proportion of items endorsed as positive, are shown in Table 8-1. Each item was more frequently rated as positive by subjects with ASP, compared to non-ASP subjects. Nearly half of the items in the attention deficit disorder and hyperactivity categories, all the items in the impulsivity category, and all but two items in the conduct problems category were endorsed more frequently by the ASP men compared to the non-ASP men. A similar trend was found for the women. However, most differences between ASP and non-ASP in women were not statistically significant, due to the small number of female subjects who met criteria for the diagnosis of ASP and who completed the questionnaire ($n = 16$).

Large differences were found between ASP and non-ASP alcoholics with regard to overall summary measures of attention deficit problems, hyperactivity, impulsivity, and conduct problems. The relationship of antisocial personality and gender to the sum total score of each of the four childhood behavior problem areas was examined using univariate analysis of variance (see Table 5-2). The diagnosis of ASP and gender were examined as main effects. As expected, a significant main effect was found for ASP on all four scales, with higher scores for ASP than

TABLE 5-2   Childhood Behavior Problems, ASP, and Gender

Behavior problems	ASP ($n = 126$)	Non-ASP ($n = 185$)	Male ($n = 227$)	Female ($n = 84$)
Attention deficit disorder	2.98	2.26**	2.50	2.69
Impulsivity	2.59	2.05**	2.28	2.25
Hyperactivity	3.27	2.45**	2.92	2.41*
Conduct problem	4.05	2.18**	2.94	2.93

Note. The figures in the table represent $\underline{x}$'s adjusted for independence.

*$p < .05$.

**$p < .01$.

non-ASP alcoholics. Gender differences were found on the hyperactivity scale, with males scoring higher than femals. No gender and ASP interactions for any of the four overall measures were found.

In order to distinguish which childhood behaviors are specific to ASP alcoholics, items from the behavior checklist were reclassified according to the rate of positive responses among ASP and non-ASP men and women. Each behavior was classified under one of three headings; behaviors endorsed by 30% or more were considered to be high. Childhood behaviors endorsed by both ASP and non-ASP subjects included most items related to attention deficit problems (i.e., "daydreaming," "didn't work up to ability," "short attention span," and "difficulty in math"), hyperactivity (i.e., "overactive," "fidgety," "unable to sit still," "got into things," "wore out toys"), and impulsivity (i.e., "impulsive," "could not tolerate delay," "unpredictable," "easily frustrated"), but only a few items related to conduct problem (i.e., "trouble accepting corrections," "demanded attention," and "fought a lot"). On the other hand, behaviors endorsed more frequently by ASP but not by non-ASP subjects included many conduct problem items (i.e., "hard to get to bed nights," "unresponsive to discipline," "lied a lot," "stealing," "overly aggressive," "temper tantrums," "did not complete projects"), and can be described as aggressive behavior. Items not endorsed by either ASP or non-ASP subjects included "difficulty in reading," "poor coordination," "accident-prone," "angered friends," and "talked too much."

While the childhood behavior checklist solicited behaviors with an onset prior to age 12, more seriors and aggressive conduct problems prior to age 15 were included in the DIS. Childhood conduct problems occurring before age 15 were examined in the DIS interview. The behaviors included in the DIS can be divided into two groups: school problems and predelinquent behaviors. The relationship of DSM-III childhood conduct disorder (before age 15) to the diagnosis of ASP in male and female alcoholics is shown in Table 5-3. School problems included "truancy," "poor grades," "trouble with teachers in school," and "expelled or suspended." Delinquent behaviors included "arrested" (as a juvenile), "stealing," "vandalism," "started fights," "running away," "lying," "sexually active before age 15," and "used nonalcoholic drugs" (before age 15). Poor grades in school were a frequent occurrence for both ASP and non-ASP subjects and for both men and women alcoholics, while truancy, trouble with teachers, and being expelled or suspended from school were more unique to those subjects with ASP. The

TABLE 5-3   DSM-III Childhood Conduct Disorder before Age 15

	Males		Females	
Problem behaviors	ASP (%)	Non-ASP (%)	ASP (%)	Non-ASP (%)
School problems				
Truancy	72	24**	81	28**
Poor grades	82	60**	81	47*
Trouble with teachers in school	65	13**	69	10**
Expelled or suspended	73	21**	75	15**
Delinquent behaviors				
Arrested	30	5**	63	7**
Stealing	75	29**	81	22**
Vandalism	46	12**	31	4**
Started fights	47	9**	38	7**
Runaway	47	10**	50	6**
Lying	50	23**	63	25**
Sexually active before 15	58	33**	31	10*
Used nonalcoholic drugs	25	5**	31	6**

*$p < .05$.

**$p < .01$.

experiences of men and women were similar, except that poor grades were reported less frequently by non-ASP women. As for predelinquent activities, stealing was the most frequently reported behavior by ASP men and women. ASP men frequently reported early sexual activities, lying, running away, fights, and vandalism, while ASP women frequently reported lying and arrests. Vandalism, fights, and early sexual activities were less common among ASP women.

The relationship of childhood problem behaviors occurring before age 12 to conduct problems occurring before age 15 is shown in Table 5-4. All childhood behavior problem scales were positively correlated with school problems and delinquency problems before 15, as well as the total number of conduct problems listed in the NIMH-DIS. Furthermore, the best predictor of conduct problems before 15 was the level of conduct problems in childhood (before age 12).

A variety of behavior problems are included in the DSM-III criteria of adult ASP disorder. The nine different types of symptoms listed in the DIS and their relationship to the diagnosis of ASP and gender of the proband are shown in Table 5-5. Most alcoholic men and women experienced difficulty maintaining employment, but this problem was significantly more prominent for ASP than for non-ASP subjects. In

TABLE 5-4   Correlation of Behavior Checklist and DIS Conduct Problems

Behavior checklist problems	DIS conduct problems					
	School problems		Delinquency		Total	
	Male	Female	Male	Female	Male	Female
Attention deficit	.33	.30	.23	.37	.31	.38
Hyperactivity	.43	.25	.32	.35	.40	.35
Impulsivity	.32	.23	.28	.31	.34	.30
Conduct problems	.45	.46	.43	.63	.51	.61
Total (sum of four scales)	.49	.42	.40	.57	.50	.56

Note. All correlations were significant at $p \leq .01$.

addition, alcoholic men, regardless of the diagnosis of ASP, often experienced multiple arrests, earned money illegally, had alcohol-related driving problems (driving while intoxicated, accidents), had multiple fights, and were promiscuous. The proportion of subjects reporting these symptoms was much higher among ASP men than non-ASP men. While many ASP women also experienced arrest, fighting, and driving problems, and earned money illegally, the proportion reporting these behaviors was less than that reported by the ASP men but generally higher than that of the non-ASP men. However, more women (regardless of ASP) were involved in domestic violence and lying than men. Child neglect was rare in this population of alcoholics, and very few reported being sued for bad debts. Vagrancy and lying were quite common among ASP alcoholics, but less frequent among non-ASP men and women. The relationship among childhood problem behavior, DIS conduct problems, and the total number of adult antisocial symptoms is shown in Table 5-6. All childhood behaviors were positively related to the total number of adult antisocial behaviors. Childhood aggression was the best childhood predictor of adult antisocial behavior for both men and women, but only moderate correlations were found. The strongest relationships were found between the DSM-III symptoms of school and conduct problems prior to age 15.

Regression analysis was used to determine the usefulness of the childhood problem behaviors occurring before age 12 and conduct problems occurring prior to age 15 in predicting the age of onset of alcoholism and the number of alcohol-related symptoms reported on the NIMH-

TABLE 5-5   Adult Antisocial Behaviors

	Males		Females	
Behaviors	ASP (%)	Non-ASP (%)	ASP (%)	Non-ASP (%)
Group 1: Job troubles				
3 different jobs in 5 years	73	55**	53	31
Can't find or keep job	73	45**	60	36*
Late or missed work 3 times a month	17	10	27	17
	(54)[a]	(34)[a]	(53)[a]	(19)[a]
Quit job more than once before finding another	68	35**	73	23**
Group 2: Neglecting children				
Left young children alone	0	1	0	2
Neighbor had to feed children	2	1	0	0
Social worker said children not fed	2	0	0	0
Ran out of money for food	15	4*	27	2**
Group 3: Criminal activity				
Arrested more than once	75	42**	38	12**
Felony conviction	39	9**	13	3**
Paid for sex	18	12	25	3**
Found customers for sex	19	7**	6	0
Made money illegally	61	21**	56	18**
Group 4: Difficulty in interpersonal relationships				
Separated more than twice	25	12**	31	25*
Separated more than twice in common law	26	9**	56	12**
Walked out on spouse	23	13*	38	21
Sex with 10 different people a year	67	32**	38	10**
Group 5: Violence				
Hit spouse	24	12*	50	29
Hit child	3	4	7	5
Involved in more than one fight	86	41**	75	34**
Used weapon in fights	43	16**	38	9**
Group 6: Bad debts				
Sued for bad debts	7	5	19	8
Group 7: Vagrancy				
Traveled around	58	20**	44	11**
No regular place to live	53	19**	44	19*
Group 8: Lying				
Used alias	24	11*	25	5**
Lied often	51	26**	63	23**
Group 9: Traffic problems				
Multiple traffic tickets	46	21*	31	4*
Problems driving—alcohol-related	77	53*	44	25

[a] Late or missed work because of drinking.

*$p < .05$.

**$p < .01$.

TABLE 5-6 Correlation of Childhood Behavior and Adult ASP Behavior

| | Childhood behavior checklist | | | | | | | | DSM-III | | | |
| | Attention deficit | | Impulsivity | | Hyperactivity | | Aggression | | School | | Conduct | |
ASP behavior	Male	Female	Male	Female	Male	Female	Male	Female	Male	Female	Male	Female
Total ASP symptoms	.26	.29	.30	.27	.36	.22	.38	.40	.54	.52	.59	.53
Job problems	.20	.22	.17	—	.26	—	.24	.24	.41	.50	.28	.34
Criminal activities	.20	—	.20	—	.30	.26	.30	.34	.47	.45	.58	.47
Personal relationships	.13	.28	.16	.18	.23	—	.20	—	.29	—	.37	.30
Violence	.12	—	.22	.18	.19	—	.26	—	.36	.21	.45	.33
Vagrancy	.15	.20	.23	.30	.22	.28	.20	.35	.30	.46	.34	.48
Lying	.24	.22	.18	.19	.17	—	.28	.29	.26	.31	.27	.26

Note. Only statistically significant correlations ($p < .05$) are reported.

DIS. When the total sample was used, no linear combination of these variables was found to be significantly related to the total number of DSM-III alcohol abuse/dependence symptoms reported by the subjects. However, three variables were found to account for 42% (R = .644) of the variance (F = 74.87, df = 3, 317, p < .05) in the age of onset of alcoholism. The patients' current age (B = .43), school problems before age 15 (B = −.18), and conduct problems before 15 (B = −.15) were each significant contributions to the regression model. This model indicates that a higher frequency of school and conduct problems is associated with an earlier onset of alcohol abuse.

Finally, a discriminant-function analysis was performed to determine whether a linear combination of the childhood variables could be formed to distinguish the two types of adult outcome. This analysis was conducted in order both to summarize and to supplement the previous analyses. First, the discriminant-function analysis was conducted using the total sample. Wilk's criteria for variable selection were used, and the probability of group membership was based on group size. The final solution yielded three variables: .13, childhood aggression; .52, school problems (NIMH-DIS); and .61, conduct problems (NIMH-DIS); F = 104.80, df = 3, 307, p < .01; Wilk's lambda = .49. This function correctly classified 81.4% of all cases. Of the alcoholic-only subjects, 85.9% were correctly classified, while 75% of the alcoholic ASP cases were correctly classified (χ^2 = 115.96, df = 1, p < .01).

The analyses were conducted again with the sample divided according to the gender of the patients. The results were very similar to those found for the entire sample, suggesting that gender did not influence the results. For the male sample, the variables and weights of the final solution were as follows: .12, childhood aggression; .56, school problems (NIMH-DIS); and .60, conduct problems (NIMH-DIS); Wilk's lambda = .52, F = 690.12, df = 3, 223, p < .01. This function correctly classified 80.6% of the men. Of the alcoholic men, 83.8% were correctly classified, while 77.3% of the alcoholic men with ASP were correctly identified (χ^2 = 85.07, df = 1, p < .01). For the female subjects, the final discriminant function was as follows: .51, childhood aggression; .53, school problems (NIMH-DIS); .57, conduct problems (NIMH-DIS); Wilk's lambda = .51, F = 253.58, df = 3, 80, p < .01. This function correctly classified 88.1% of all the women subjects. Female alcoholics were correctly classified 94.1% of the time, while female alcoholics with

ASP were correctly classified 62.5% of the time ($\chi^2 = 29.89$, $df = 1$, $p < .01$).

DISCUSSION

The principal focus of this study was an attempt to identify behaviors in childhood that are unique to adult ASP among alcoholics. This task was complicated by the difficulty in establishing a clear differential diagnosis between the two disorders based on phenomenology. The behavior of alcoholics often appears to be antisocial in nature, while persons with ASP may also have alcoholism (Schuckit, 1973). A better separation of the pathways into each disorder may be useful in making a differential diagnosis between alcoholism without ASP and the combination of alcoholism and ASP. It is also possible that specific symptoms or groups of symptoms may occur more frequently in one disorder. Knowledge of such a clustering of symptoms would be useful in the diagnostic process.

This study found that men and women alcoholics, with or without ASP, frequently experience a wide variety of behavior problems prior to age 12. Similar findings have been reported in other studies (Hale, Hesselbrock, & Hesselbrock, 1982; Robins, 1966). These behaviors, which had formerly been considered to characterize the general minimal brain dysfunction/hyperactivity syndrome (Tarter *et al.*, 1977; Wender, personal communication, 1983) include, for example, daydreaming, impulsivity, getting into things, and the like.

Only a few such behaviors were found in this study to distinguish ASP from non-ASP alcoholics. These behaviors seem to fall into four relatively independent categories: inattention, impulsivity, conduct problems, and hyperactivity (Lahey, Green, & Forehand, 1980). Although no gender differences were found for these categories, differences due to ASP were noted for all categories. An examination of other behaviorally specific variables occurring before age 15 (e.g., truancy, vandalism, etc.) also indicated some differences in childhood and adolescence between ASP and non-ASP alcoholics. ASP alcoholics, regardless of gender, had a greater number of problems in school and were more delinquent than non-ASP alcoholics. Loeber and Dishion (1983), in a review of the literature, have shown the sturdiness of these two predictions of future delinquency, whether the data have been gathered prospectively or retrospectively. This study extends their findings past juvenile delinquency into adult ASP (with associated alcoholism).

One of the difficulties with the childhood data presented in this study is the large number of variables examined. Given the number of childhood variables analyzed and the number of differences found, it is cumbersome to gather and synthesize this amount of information for diagnostic purposes. The results of this study suggest that childhood aggression, school problems, and delinquency are the most useful behaviors for distinguishing ASP alcoholics from non-ASP alcoholics, with ASP alcoholics reporting a higher frequency of these behaviors. The childhood problems of hyperactivity and impulsivity were not useful discriminators of ASP and non-ASP alcoholics, even though these problems were frequently reported. However, symptoms alone do not necessarily indicate disease. Although subjects reported a relatively high frequency of hyperactivity symptoms, no data were available on whether they had actually been diagnosed as "hyperactive" or treated for this condition. Recent studies of diagnosed and treated "hyperactives" by August et al. (1983), Hechtman, Weiss, and Perlman (1984), and Millman (1979), however, supported the findings of this study. When a more restricted definition of "hyperactivity" is used, the adult outcome is more favorable than previously thought. While the "pure" hyperactivies may continue to have problems with inattention and impulsivity as young adults, it is the children with hyperactivity, conduct problems, and aggressivity who have the poorer adult outcomes of substance abuse and antisocial behavior. In this study, hyperactivity and impulsivity were frequently found in both the ASP and non-ASP alcoholics. When conduct disorder and school problems were also present, this adult outcome tended to include an early onset of alcoholism in association with ASP.

Childhood conduct disorder and school problems did not predict the total number (severity?) of DSM-III alcohol symptoms in adulthood, but were positively related to the total number of DSM-III ASP symptoms reported on the NIMH-DIS. Other studies (Robins, 1966; Robins & Ratcliff, 1979) have also demonstrated the continuation of childhood antisocial behavior into adulthood. Behaviors more proximal (i.e., occurring in adolescence) to the adult ASP symptoms were the best predictors of adult behavior. The relationship was strongest for job problems, vagrancy, violence, and criminal activities (see Table 5-5)—behaviors that reflect the ASP life style. The relationship was weakest for predicting poor personal relationships and lying.

A variety of adult antisocial behaviors were examined in this sample of ASP and non-ASP alcoholics. The behaviors most frequently reported included job troubles, criminal activities, traffic problems, vagrancy, violence, and lying. Patients with ASP, regardless of gender, reported engaging in these acts at a higher rate than non-ASP patients. Furthermore, female alcoholic patients with ASP generally were more frequently involved in these problem areas than non-ASP alcoholic men. These findings are consistent with the additional diagnosis of ASP. Similar findings have been reported by Cadoret, Troughton, and Widmer (1984). In their study, they also found that ASP alcoholics tended to report a few more alcoholic symptoms (e.g., disorderly conduct, fighting while intoxicated) than non-ASP alcoholics, but these symptoms may be reflecting the underlying sociopathy in the ASP alcoholics. The data from this study and that of Cadoret *et al.* indicate the extent of clinical heterogeneity in the population of alcoholics, and give further support to the notion of distinguishing ASP alcoholics from non-ASP alcoholics.

CONCLUSION

In summary, this study has found that ASP and non-ASP alcoholics can be distinguished, to some extent, on the basis of childhood behavior patterns. Although both ASP and non-ASP alcoholics reported a variety of childhood behavior problems and in high frequency, childhood aggression and school problems seemed to identify both men and women ASP alcoholics. These two childhood problem behaviors were also good predictors of similar types of behaviors in adulthood (e.g., job problems, aggressiveness, etc.). Finally, the types of behaviors that were found to predict adult ASP disorder also characterized the alcoholics with ASP and distinguished these patients from the alcoholics without ASP. ASP alcoholics had a higher frequently of job troubles, violent behavior, vagrancy, and the like. It is not clear whether these problems were "caused" by alcohol abuse or just exacerbated by chronic alcohol use.

ACKNOWLEDGMENT

This work was supported by the National Institute on Alcohol Abuse and Alcoholism (Grant No. 5 P50 AA03510 07).

REFERENCES

American Psychiatric Association. (1980). *Diagnostic and statistical manual of mental disorders* (3rd ed.). Washington, DC: Author.

August, G. J., Stewart, M. A., & Holmes, C. S. (1983). A four year follow-up of hyperactive boys with and without conduct disorder. *British Journal of Psychiatry, 143,* 192–198.

Cadoret, R., Troughton, E., & Widmer, R. (1984). Clinical differences between antisocial and primary alcoholics. *Comprehensive Psychiatry, 25,* 1–8.

Cahalan, D., & Room, R. (1974). *Problem drinking among American men.* New Brunswick, NJ: Rutgers University Center for Alcohol Studies.

De Obaldia, R., Parsons, O. A., & Yohman, R. (1983). Minimal brain dysfunction symptoms claimed by primary and secondary alcoholics: Relation to cognitive functioning. *International Journal of Neuroscience, 20,* 173–182.

Hale, M., Hesselbrock, M. N., & Hesselbrock, V. M. (1982). Childhood deviance and sociopathy in alcoholism. *Journal of Psychiatric Treatment and Evaluation, 4,* 33–37.

Hechtman, L., Weiss, G., & Perlman, T. (1984). Hyperactives as young adults: Past and current substance abuse and antisocial behavior. *American Journal of Orthopsychiatry, 54,* 415–425.

Hesselbrock, M. N., Babor, T. F., Hesselbrock, V. M., Meyer, R. E., & Workman, K. L. (1983). "Never believe an alcoholic?": On validity of self-report measures of alcohol dependence and related constructs. *International Journal of the Addictions, 18,* 593–609.

Hesselbrock, M. N., Choquette, K., Margoles, S., & Keener, J. J. (1984). *Comparison of the DSM-III alcohol abuse/dependence criteria with empirically derived scales of alcohol related symptomatology.* Unpublished manuscript, University of Connecticut Health Center.

Hesselbrock, M. N., Hesselbrock, V. M., Babor, T. F., Stabenau, J. R., Meyer, R. E., & Weidenman, M. A. (1984). Antisocial behavior, psychopathology and problem drinking in the natural history of alcoholism. In D. W. Goodwin, K. T. VanDusen, & S. A. Mednick (Eds.), *Longitudinal research in alcoholism* (pp. 197–214). Boston: Kluwer-Nijhoff.

Hesselbrock, M. N., Meyer, R. E., & Keener, J. K. (1985). Psychopathology in hospitalized alcoholics. *Archives of General Psychiatry, 42,* 1050–1055.

Kellam, S. G., Stevenson, D. L., & Rubin, B. R. (1983). How specific are the early predictors of teenage drug use? In L. Harris (Ed.), *Problems of drug dependence* (NIDA Research Monograph Series No. 43, pp. 329–334). Washington, DC: U.S. Government Printing Office.

Lahey, B. B., Green, K. D., & Forehand, R. (1980). On the independence of rating of hyperactivity, conduct problems and attention deficit in children: A multiple regression analysis. *Journal of Consulting and Clinical Psychology, 18,* 566–573.

Lewis, C. E., Rice, J., & Helzer, J. E. (1983). Diagnostic interactions: Alcoholism and antisocial personality. *Journal of Nervous and Mental Disease, 171,* 105–113.

Loeber, R., & Dishion, T. (1983). Early predictors of male delinquency: A review. *Psychological Bulletin, 94,* 68–99.

McCord, W., & McCord, J. (1960). *Origins of alcoholism.* Stanford, CA: Stanford University Press.

Millman, D. H. (1979). Minimal brain dysfunction in childhood: Outcome in late adolescence and early adult years. *Journal of Clinical Psychiatry, 40,* 371–380.

Robins, L. N. (1966). *Deviant children grown up: A social and psychiatric study of sociopathic personality*. Baltimore: Williams & Wilkins.

Robins, L. N. (1978). Sturdy childhood predictors of adult outcomes: Replications from longitudinal studies (Paul Hock Award Lecture, American Psychopathological Association, 1978). *Psychological Medicine, 8*, 611–622.

Robins, L. N. (1979). Longitudinal methods in the study of normal and pathological development. In K. P. Kisker, J. E. Meyer, C. Muller, & E. Stromgren (Eds.), *Psychiatrie der Gegenwart* (Vol. 1, pp. 677–684). Berlin: Springer-Verlag.

Robins, L. N., Helzer, J. E., Croughan, J., & Ratcliff, K. S. (1981). National Institute of Mental Health Diagnostic Interview Schedule: History, characteristics and validity. *Archives of General Psychiatry, 38*, 381–389.

Robins, L. N., Helzer, J. E., Croughan, J., Spitzer, R., & Bennett, F. (1979). *The National Institute of Mental Health Diagnostic Interview Schedule*. Rockville, MD: National Institute of Mental Health.

Robins, L. N., Murphy, G. E., & Breckenridge, M. B. (1968). Drinking behavior of young urban Negro men. *Quarterly Journal of Studies on Alcohol, 29*, 657–684.

Robins, L. N., Murphy, G. E., Woodruff, R. A., & King, L. J. (1971). The adult psychiatric status of black school boys. *Archives of General Psychiatry, 24*, 338–345.

Robins, L. N., & Ratcliff, K. S. (1979). Risk factors in the continuation of childhood antisocial behavior into adulthood. *International Journal of Mental Health, 7*, 526–530.

Schuckit, M. A. (1973). Alcoholism and sociopathy—diagnostic confusion. *Quarterly Journal of Studies on Alcohol, 34*, 157.

Tarter, R. E., McBride, H., Buonpane, N., Dorothea, R. N., & Schneider, N. (1977). Differentiation of alcoholics: Childhood history and drinking pattern. *Archives of General Psychiatry, 34*, 761–768.

Wender, P. H. (1971). *Minimal brain dysfunction in children*. New York: Wiley.

III

Psychopathology as a Modifier of Treatment Response, Outcome, Symptom Picture, and Course

6

"Psychiatric Severity" as a Predictor of Outcome from Substance Abuse Treatments

A. THOMAS MCLELLAN

In 1979 (McLellan, 1979), I reported the development of a new, multidimensional clinical research instrument for substance-abusing patients, called the Addiction Severity Index (ASI). The design of the ASI is based upon the premise that addiction to either alcohol or street drugs must be considered in the context of those additional treatment problems that may have contributed to and/or resulted from the chemical abuse. The objective of the ASI is to produce a "problem severity profile" of each patient through an analysis of seven areas commonly affected in drug- or alcohol-abusing patients. These include alcohol use, drug use, medical condition, employment, legal problems, family relations, and psychiatric status. My colleagues' and my experience has suggested that these problems combine in a variety of complex ways to create particular treatment needs in each patient. Furthermore, we feel that if these problems are not addressed along with the chemical dependence in a substance abuse treatment, they can leave the patient susceptible to relapse, readdiction, and return to treatment.

In each of the seven ASI areas, objective questions are asked measuring the number, frequency, and duration of problem symptoms in the patient's lifetime and in the past 30 days. The patient also supplies a subjective report of the recent (past 30 days) severity and importance of each problem area. The interviewer assimilates the two types of information to produce seven global ratings reflecting problem severity in each area. These 10-point (0 = "no problem," 9 = extreme problem") ratings have been shown to provide reliable and valid estimates of problem severity for both alcohol- and drug-dependent patients. The individual objective items offer a comprehensive basis for assessment at treatment admission and at subsequent evaluation periods (see McLellan, Luborsky, O'Brien, & Woody, 1980).

Using this instrument in a 4-year design, we have found that the nature and severity of these associated treatment problems are important predictors of patient outcome from both alcohol and drug abuse treatments. They may also be used prospectively at the time of admission to "match" patients to the most appropriate treatment. In particular, our results indicate that a global estimate of a patient's psychiatric symptomatology (i.e., his or her "psychiatric severity") is the single best overall predictor of outcome across patient types, treatment methods, and outcome measures. The data to be presented relevant to this issue are organized in two parts. In the first part, I present the design and results of our 4-year prediction study. These results show the importance of our global "psychiatric severity" measure in predicting treatment outcome. In the second part, I present a series of subsequent studies targeting the most psychiatrically impaired sample of our substance-abusing patients. We have attempted to determine the most effective and appropriate of the available treatment options for this important subgroup of substance abusers.

PSYCHIATRIC SEVERITY AS A PREDICTOR OF TREATMENT OUTCOME

GENERAL PROCEDURE

The 4-year outcome prediction project was carried out using a three-stage design (McLellan, Druley, O'Brien, & Kron, 1980). In Stage I, extensive patient background and 6-month follow-up data were collected on all patients who were admitted to the six programs within the treatment network during calendar year 1978. In Stage II, these initial data were analyzed to determine the nature and extent of patients' improvements within each program and the specific patient factors that were most predictive of optimum improvement within each program. In Stage III, the efficacy of these predictive factors was tested by assigning a 10-

month (1980) sample of newly admitted patients to the six programs, using the predictors to "match" patients to the most appropriate treatment. During-treatment improvement and posttreatment (6-month) outcomes were compared between those patients who *were* admitted to the program predicted to be appropriate ("matched" patients) and those patients who were admitted to a program that was not predicted to be appropriate ("mismatched" patients). Results and major conclusions are presented below for each stage of the project.

TREATMENT PROGRAMS

The substance abuse treatment network of the Veterans Administration (VA) in the Philadelphia area consisted of four inpatient (two alcohol, one drug, one combined) therapeutic community programs at the Coatesville VA Medical Center, plus outpatient alcohol and drug abuse clinics at the Philadelphia VA Medical Center. This treatment network has enjoyed cooperative referral arrangements since 1975. Once admitted to substance abuse treatment at either hospital within the network, patients are assigned to one of the six rehabilitation programs on the basis of their personal requests, the clinical judgment of the admitting staff, administrative considerations such as bed census or patient visit criteria, and simple chance.

The following are brief descriptions of the programs; for more complete information, see Gottheil, McLellan, and Druley (1979).

1. The Alcohol Treatment Unit (ATU) is a 60-day therapeutic community based on the principles of Alcoholics Anonymous (AA). The staff conducts small-group therapy four times weekly.
2. Fixed Interval Drinking Decisions (FIDD) is a research program designed to examine and treat alcoholism in the presence of alcohol. The 6-week treatment cycle consists of two 1-week alcohol-free periods and a 4-week drinking-decision phase in which two ounces of 80-proof alcohol are available, and the patients have the opportunity to decide whether to drink. Group and individual therapies are offered daily.
3. Combined Treatment (CMB) is a short-term (45-day) program that delivers intensive addition management therapy to both alcoholics and drug addicts.

4. Therapeutic Community (TC) offers personal and social drug abuse treatment in a 60-day program designed to "habilitate" the patient to society using individual and group psychological therapy, educational and vocational counseling, and the social structure of a self-governing therapeutic community.

5. Alcohol Outpatient (AOP) is a variable-length treatment program that concentrates on the medical, psychological, and social problems of outpatient alcoholics. Therapeutic goals include alcohol abstinence through referral to AA and the concurrent reduction of medical and psychological problems associated with alcoholism.

6. Methadone Maintenance (MM) offers methadone maintenance, in combination with a full program of psychiatric and social work counseling. Chemotherapeutic and individual therapy interventions are used to treat associated psychological problems of these patients.

STAGES I AND II

Subjects

All male veterans who presented for alcohol or drug abuse treatment at either the Coatesville or Philadelphia VA Medical Centers during 1978 were eligible for Stage I of the study. There were no significant differences in demographic or background characterstics between patients in the two hospitals, and approximately 90% of all subjects were Philadelphia residents. There were no treatment admission criteria other than eligibility for veterans' benefits.

We initially evaluated 1035 male veterans who were admitted to alcohol ($n = 671$) or drug abuse ($n = 364$) rehabilitation programs at the Coatesville or Philadelphia VA Medical Centers during 1978. Since the aims of the study were confined to patients who had been effectively engaged in the treatment process, we did not follow patients who dropped out of treatment prior to 5 inpatient days or five outpatient visits. We were able to contact approximately 85% of the remaining 879 patients 6 months after admission to treatment, and complete data were therefore available on 742 subjects (460 alcoholics and 282 drug addicts).

Table 6-1 summarizes the pretreatment characteristics of the study population, divided into alcoholics and drug addicts. Immediately no-

TABLE 6-1   Background Characteristics at Admission

Characteristics	Alcoholics		Drug addicts	Total
Demographic factors				
Age	46	**	31	40
% white	60	**	47	56
% black	39		52	43
Years education	11.2		11.7	11.4
Previous alcoholic and drug treatments	6		5	6
Medical problem severity[a]	3.0	*	2.2	2.7
% w/chronic medical problems	48	**	28	40
Medical hospitalizations	5	*	3	4
Employment problem severity[a]	4.1	*	5.2	4.6
% w/skill or trade	56	*	62	58
Longest period of employment (months)	69	**	36	59
Substance abuse problem severity	6.1		6.6	6.3
Years problematic alcohol use	13	**	3	10
Years opiate use	0.5	**	6	2
Years nonopiate use	1	**	4	2
Longest period of abstinence (months)	5		7	6
Legal problem severity	2.2	**	4.0	2.8
% awaiting charges	9	**	22	13
Months incarcerated	7	**	14	10
Family/social problem severity	3.9		4.2	4.0
% divorced, separated	43		36	40
% living alone	30	**	19	26
% friends w/alcohol or drug problems	27		25	26
Psychiatric problem severity	3.8		4.0	3.9
% having previous psychiatric treatment	16	**	8	13
% attempted suicide	17		17	17
Maudsley Neuroticism Scale	27		28	27
Beck Depression Inventory	17	*	14	16
IQ (age-connected)	103		101	102

Note. for alcoholics, $n = 460$; For drug addicts, $n = 282$; total $n = 742$.

[a] All severity ratings range from $0 =$ "No problem" to $9 =$ "Extreme problem."

$*p < .05.$

$**p < .01.$

ticeable are the distinct differences between the alcohol and drug populations in age ($t = 22.6$, $df = 877$, $p < .001$), and racial composition ($X^2 = 26.6$, $df = 1$, $p < .001$), while the groups were similar with respect to mean number of previous substance abuse treatments and years of education. In the remaining sections of the table, I have summarized the treatment problems for the total population and for each group by presenting the mean ASI problem severity ratings (see "Data

Collection"), as well as additional pertinent background characteristics to clarify the admission status of these patients.

These admission data indicate that the average patient started treatment with severe problems of alcohol or drug abuse, and also had moderately severe employment, family, and psychiatric problems. However, it is obvious that extreme differences existed at admission between the alcoholics and the drug addicts. The alcoholics presented with more severe medical problems, while the drug addicts showed more severe legal and employment problems.

Data Collection

Admission and Follow-up Data.

The admission and follow-up evaluations were based upon data from the ASI (McLellan, 1979; McLellan, Luborsky, O'Brien, & Woody, 1980). The ASI is a structured, 30- to 40-minute, clinical research interview designed to assess problem severity in seven areas commonly affected by addiction: alcohol use, drug use, medical condition, employment, legal problems, family relations, and psychiatric problems. In each of the areas, as noted above, objective questions measuring the number, extent, and duration of problem symptoms in the patient's lifetime are asked, and the patient also supplies a subjective report of the recent (past 30 days) severity and importance of each problem area. The interviewer assimilates the two types of information to produce a rating (0–9) of the patient's "need for treatment" in each area. These 10-point ratings have been shown to provide reliable and valid general estimates of problem severity for both alcoholics and drug addicts (McLellan *et al.*, 1985; McLellan, Luborsky, O'Brien, & Woody, 1980).

Follow-Up.

All follow-up evaluations were done through repeat ASI interviews by an independent research technician 6 months following treatment admission. No information from secondary sources was used, and all data were closely monitored to preserve confidentiality. The validity of the follow-up data was checked through built-in consistency checks within the ASI and through spot checks on subsamples of the outpatient population, by assessing the ASI data against urinalysis, pharmacy, and criminal justice system records. We found less than 5% inconsistency. Similar findings have been reported by many other investigators studying the validity of patients' self-reports. Since the fixed, 6-month follow-up interval produced unequal times between treatment discharge and the follow-up interview, we examined the relationships between time out of treatment and outcome status on all criterion measures. No significant correlations were found for any of the groups (all p's > .10), and there were no differences among the inpatient programs with regard to time out of treatment.

Developing Appropriate and Reliable Measures of Outcome.

We felt it was important to develop general measures of outcome in each of the seven problem areas, since assessments based solely on single-item criteria (e.g., days of drug use) offer meager and inherently unreliable estimates of posttreatment status (Nunally, 1967). We therefore constructed composite outcome measures based on combinations of objective items from each of the ASI areas. In this method, which has been used by Mintz and Luborsky in their studies of outcome from psychotherapy (Mintz, Luborsky, & Cristoph, 1979), several of the objective items within each ASI area were intercorrelated to eliminate unrelated items, and the remaining items were standardized, summed, and tested for conjoint reliability using Cronbach's formula (Cronbach & Furby, 1970). In this manner, seven composite criteria were constructed from sets of the ASI objective items, producing highly reliable (.73 or higher) general measures of outcome.

With regard to the number of outcome measures to be used in the analyses, we had originally hoped to be able to factor the seven composites into fewer measures of general improvement. However, an examination of the relationships between these measures (see McLellan, Luborsky, Woody, & O'Brien, 1981) indicated that there were very low intercorrelations between the criterion measures, both for the total population and for the alcohol and drug abuse samples individually. The lack of intercorrelation suggested that the outcome measures were tapping independent aspects of the outcome status, and that it would be important to examine each criterion separately.

What Factors Predicted Response to Alcohol and Drug Abuse Treatments?

We were primarily interested in what type of pretreatment information would predict outcome and in whether certain "types" of patients appeared to have better outcomes in certain programs. However, we knew that the treatment programs and the patients in them were quite different at the outset of treatment; thus it would not be meaningful to compare outcome results directly. We therefore required a statistical procedure that would allow us to account for this pretreatment variation and still detect outcome differences among programs and among patient–program combinations. To this end, we employed the stepwise multiple-regression procedure (Dixon & Brown, 1979).

The multiple-regression analysis permitted us to sequentially enter independent (predictor) variables that we considered important in determining outcome as measured by each of our composite scores. For each of these independent variables, the regression analysis performed two important functions. First, it tested whether the specific independent variable explained a significant ($p < .01$) proportion of outcome variance. Stated differently, the procedure was able to determine whether patients who differed on demographic, admission status, or during-treatment variables (e.g., age, race, years drinking, ASI psychiatric severity score) had significantly different scores on the outcome measure. Second, the regression procedure removed that portion of outcome variance accounted for by all of these variables. In this manner, it was possible to adjust (control) for pre-existing differences in demographic and admission status factors before testing for significant effects due to treatment programs and patient–program matches.

Table 6-2 describes the variables used in the regression equations and the order in which they were entered. Thus, the four demographic variables were entered first, followed by the pretreatment ASI severity scores (depicting the admission status of the patients), and then by the during-treatment measures of days in treatment and type of discharge. Therefore, the criterion measures were adjusted for differences in each of these variables prior to tests for differences among programs and patient × program interactions.

Specific tests for outcome differences between programs were accomplished in the standard manner, by assigning a bivariate (0, 1) variable to each treatment program and then entering each of these vari-

TABLE 6-2 Accounting for Outcome: Stepwise Multiple Regression

Type of independent variable (in order of entry)	Variables
1. Demographic	Age (years) Education (years) Race (0 = black, 1 = white) Previous treatments (number)
2. Admission status (ASI ratings)	Medical Employment Legal Family Psychiatric Substance abuse
3. During-treatment	Days in treatment Type of discharge (0 = favorable, 1 = unfavorable)
4. Treatment program	Variable for each treatment program
5. Interactions	Demographic × program variables Admission status × program variables

ables into regression analysis. Patient–program interaction effects were tested by multiplying each program variable with each demographic and admission status variable, and entering these product variables into the last stage of the analysis.

Thus, in summary, it was possible to determine whether a patient characteristic such as age was a significant determinant of outcome alone, regardless of treatment program, by entering the age variable early in the analysis. Similarly, it was possible to determine whether treatment in a particular program such as the ATU was associated with significantly better outcome by entering the ATU program variable after the demographic and admission status variables had been entered and adjusted for. Finally, it was possible to determine whether older patients had better outcomes when they were treated in the ATU (patient–program interaction) by entering that product variable after all other factors had been adjusted for.

Regression analyses were calculated separately for the alcoholic ($n = 460$) and drug addict ($n = 282$) samples (see "Subjects") on each of the seven follow-up criteria. An examination of the overall results from these first analyses indicated virtually no evidence of significant patient–program interactions in either sample. In short, these initial findings were quite comparable to results of previous national reports (Armor, Polich, & Stambul, 1978; Simpson, Savage, Lloyd, & Sells,

1978) showing no differences in outcome among different treatments or among different patient–program combinations.

Psychiatric Severity as Outcome Predictor

However, the results did show a clear and significant ($p < .01$) relationship between all of the outcome measures and the patients' pretreatment ASI psychiatric severity score. The correlations between admission psychiatric severity and the 6-month outcome measures were calculated for both the alcoholic and drug addict samples. Significant relatinships were seen on five of the seven measures for the alcoholics, and on six of the seven criteria for the drug addicts. In every case, *greater* pretreatment psychiatric severity was related to *poorer* 6-month outcome, and this variable alone accounted for an average of 10% of the outcome variance across the seven criteria.

Detailed Description of the ASI Psychiatric Severity Scales.

The 10-point ASI rating of psychiatric severity is made without regard for drug use, family problems, employment difficulties, or other problems, which are assessed separately. In the case of psychiatric severity, some of the more prominent items question each patient's experience with "significant periods of" depression, anxiety, confusion, persecution or paranoia, inability to concentrate, inability to control violent tendencies, and so on. It should be clear that this is a very basic, global estimate of symptom severity, psychopathology, or psychological health–sickness. It most resembles the Health–Sickness Rating Scale (Luborsky & Bachrach, 1974), which has now been adapted to the Global Assessment Scale and as such is included in the Schedule for Affective Disorders and Schizophrenia (SADS) (Endicott, Spitzer, & Fleiss, 1976). We have intercorrelated these measures in several studies, and the coefficients are uniformly .70 or above. We have previously published evidence for the high reliability of the ASI psychiatric severity rating (McLellan, Luborsky, O'Brien, & Woody, 1985), and we have since confirmed this at three different treatment sites and with 12 raters (McLellan *et al.*, 1985). Further, we have correlated the ASI psychiatric severity scale with standardized psychological tests, producing the following coefficients: Maudsley Neuroticism Scale, .69; Beck Depression Inventory, .71; total score on the Hopkins Symptom Checklist, .81; and a measure of cognitive impairment or brain damage, .62, but not IQ, .13. In sum, there is evidence that the ASI psychiatric severity scale is a reliable and valid, *global* estimate of the severity of psychopathology, *but does not designate specific psychiatric diagnosis.*

The strength and pervasiveness of the relationships in the present data suggested the possibility of further dividing the alcoholic and drug addict samples into low, middle, and high groups, based upon their pretreatment psychiatric severity scores, under the assumption that qualitatively different results might appear. To this end, we selected the mean value on the psychiatric severity scale, plus and minus one standard deviation, as the score range for the middle group in each sample. The low groups had psychiatric severity scores that were more than one standard deviation below the mean, and the high groups had severity scores more than one standard deviation above the mean. The middle group comprised 60–70% of the patient population, while the low and high groups comprised 15–20% each (McLellan, Luborsky, Woody, Druley, & O'Brien, 1983; Woody *et al.*, 1983). Patients who were rated in the low group were generally asymptomatic or had slight problems of anxiety or minor depression in their past. Middle-severity patients might have had recent symptoms of depression, anxiety, or cognitive confusion, but no clear history of recurring symptoms. Patients in the high group generally reported suicidal ideation, though disorder, and/ or cognitive confusion. Again, it is important to note that the designations were made on the basis of severity, not diagnosis or specific symptom patterns.

Interpretation of Regression Analyses.

Since seven regression analyses were computed for each of these six groups, there were obviously a large number of individual predictors for specific criteria. In order to present these results in a clear and interpretable fashion, I have summarized the regression results for the two low groups in Table 6-3, for the two high groups in Table 6-4, and for the two middle groups in Table 6-5. In these tables, the leftmost column indicates the category of independent (predictor) variables and the order in which they were entered into the equations. The variables that are shown were included only if they were significant ($p < .01$) predictors on *at least three* of the seven criteria. This is not to suggest that these were the only important variables, just that they were among

TABLE 6-3   Outcome Predictors in Patients with Low Psychiatric Severity

Type of variable	Alcoholics (n = 102)		Drug addicts (n = 68)	
	Variable	R	Variable	R
Demographic	No. of previous treatments	.32	—	—
Admission severity	Medical severity	.33	Drug use severity	.30
	Employment severity	.28	Employment severity	.30
During-treatment	Days in treatment	−.20	Days in treatment	−.28
Treatment program	—	—	—	—
Interactions	Legal severity × FIDD	.28	Employment severity × MM	.28
Mean outcome variance explained	34%		32%	

TABLE 6-4   Outcome Predictors in Patients with High Psychiatric Severity

Type of variable	Alcoholics (n = 82)		Drug addicts (n = 53)	
	Variable	R	Variable	R
Demographic	Age	.30	—	—
Admission severity	—	—	Drug use severity	−.26
During-treatment	—	—	—	—
Treatment program	CMB	.36	CMB	.44
	AOP	.37		
Interactions	—	—	—	—
Mean outcome variance explained	48%		54%	

the most salient and generally robust. The average zero-order correlation between the predictor variable and these criterion measures is presented in the R column for each sample. Since higher scores on the outcome criteria are indicative of greater problem severity, positive correlations indicate that *higher* scores on the predictor variable were related to *worse* outcomes. Thus, in the example of the low/alcoholic group (Table 6-3), the number of previous treatments was significantly (+.32) related to poorer posttreatment status on at least three outcome measures. Similarly, the number of days in treatment was significantly (−.20) related to better status on at least three outcome measures. The significant interaction between legal status and treatment in the FIDD

TABLE 6-5   Outcome Predictors in Patients with Midlevel Psychiatric Severity

Type of variable	Alcoholics (n = 276)		Drug addicts (n = 161)	
	Variable	R	Variable	R
Demographic	Age	.38		
	No. of previous treatments	.34	Race[b]	.37
			Age	− .27
Admission severity	Family severity	.28		
	Legal severity	.26	Employment severity	.36
During-treatment	Days in treatment	− .38	Days in treatment	− .35
	Type discharge[a]	− .26	Type discharge	− .27
Treatment program	FIDD	.25	CMB	.33
Interactions	Legal service × FIDD	.31	Family service × MM	.37
	Employment service × AOP	.30	Employment service × MM	.34
	Legal service × ATU	.28		
	Age × CMB	.25	Medical service × TC	.30
	Family service × AOP	.24	Drug use service × CMB	.28
	Family service × ATU	.24		
Mean outcome variance explained	44%		48%	

program ("Legal severity × FIDD") indicates that low/alcoholic patients with greater than average legal problems who were treated in the FIDD showed poorer results on at least three outcome measures than low/alcoholic patients with similar legal problems treated in the other alcohol programs.

Summary of Findings

When the alcoholic and drug addict samples were divided into six groups based upon the ASI psychiatric severity measure, several specific relationships emerged that had been masked in the ungrouped analyses. For example, the regression results for the low groups were generally similar to the results for the ungrouped data. That is, greater amounts of treatment were associated with better outcomes, but there were no significant differences in outcome between the different programs, and only a few significant patient–program matches. However, an examination of the outcome results indicated that these low-group patients showed the best posttreatment status and the most significant amount of improvement on virtually all measures. These data led us to conclude that low-severity patients have the best treatment prognosis generally, and that they appear to improve significantly in *any* of the treatment programs to which they are assigned. The admission characteristics of these patients and the type of improvement shown are suggestive of the small group of alcoholic patients described in the Rand Corporation study (Armor *et al.*, 1978) who were able to return to "social drinking" following treatment. It may be that nonabstinent goals are possible for some members of this more intact group of patients. From a practical perspective, we have recommended that the majority of these low-severity patients be treated in an outpatient setting, since this is the most economical and seemingly equally effective alternative. Despite this general conclusion, the data indicate (consistent with our clinical experience) that even with the generally favorable prognosis for this group, patients with significant family and/or employment problems should be treated in an inpatient setting.

The results of our analyses in the high groups also showed few significant differences in outcome among programs and no significant patient–program matches. However, unlike the low groups, the high-severity patients did not show better outcome with more treatment. These Stage I data and our clinical experience indicated that *none* of the programs currently available within our treatment network were effective with these individuals. Interestingly, although treatment outcome could not realistically be called satisfactory, the MM program appeared to have the most positive impact on the high-severity drug patients, possibly due to the regulatory and weak antipsychotic effects of methadone.

Once the high and low groups (which comprised approximately 40% of the total population) were separated from the remaining (middle) population, it was possible to discern significant differences in outcome associated with specific treatments, and especially associated with specific treatments (i.e., specific patient–programs matches). For example, middle patients (both alcoholics and drug addicts) with more severe family and/or employment problems had poorer outcomes in outpatient treatment. These findings are consistent with our clinical experience and suggest that while severe alcohol or drug use, and even medical or legal problems, may be dealt with effectively in an outpatient setting, family and employment problems appear to be clear contraindications for outpatient treatment. Finally, two of the inpatient alcohol abuse treatment programs showed evidence of poorer outcomes with clients having more serious legal problems. We have suggested that these clients be transferred to the CMB program or (in some cases) the AOP program, which did not show poorer outcome with these patients.

Clinical Implications

The present data, as well as other reports (Armor *et al.*, 1978; DeLeon, 1984; Simpson *et al.*, 1978), indicate the importance of making independent pretreatment assessments of patient status in several areas commonly affected by addiction. These addiction-related problem severity measures were the most significant predictors of outcome in all groups. The fact that patients with greater pretreatment psychiatric severity showed the poorest outcome is not surprising. A great deal of research has indicated that it is the best and most reliable predictor of treatment outcome in psychotherapy (Luborsky, Mintz, & Auerbach, 1980), and in substance abuse treatment (DeLeon, 1984; Meyer, 1983). What is remarkable is that alcohol and drug abuse severity were *not* generally important in predicting outcome. In fact, pretreatment psychiatric severity was a better predictor of posttreatment drinking than was pretreatment drinking. This finding in particular suggests why previous predictive studies, which have used brief data collection instruments concentrating on demographic and substance abuse variables, have not demonstrated meaningful outcome prediction.

Finally, the demonstration of significant differences in outcome as a function of interactions between patient factors and treatment programs suggests that different forms of substance abuse treatment, like other medical treatments, have specific as well as general effects. Further, the data illustrate how the specific effects of the treatment programs may combine with the particular treatment needs of the patient to produce favorable outcomes, as well as contraindications.

As a test of the validity and utility of these predictors in normal clinical practice, those factors that were statistically significant predictors of outcome in this study were utilized as determinants of treatment assignment in Stage III of the project. Thus, we were able to determine whether these factors were generalizable enough to be of practical value in producing improved treatment effectiveness for the six-program treatment network.

Stage III

The data and analyses from Stages I and II, respectively, of the project formed the basis for several hypotheses regarding the most effective and efficient method for matching substance abuse patients to appropriate treatments. These hypotheses were tested using a new sample of patients admitted to treatment during 1980 to the same programs.

Subjects

Subjects were all male veterans who applied for substance abuse re-habilitation treatment at the Philadelphia or Coatesville VA Medical Centers during the months from February through October 1980. As in the retrospective stage of the project, all patients who completed a minimum of 5 inpatient days or five outpatient visits were considered eligible for the study.

We initially interviewed 649 patients (238 alcoholic and 411 drug-dependent). Approximately 15% of each group dropped out of treatment prior to the eligibility criterion. Follow-up efforts were successful with 94% of eligible subjects, leaving 466 subjects (178 alcoholic, 298 drug-dependent) with complete data.

Programs

The same six programs that were studied in 1978 were again studied in 1980. There were obviously changes in personnel during this period, with three of the six programs changing their directors. However, no program changed either its basic orientation to treatment or its program length.

Data Collection Procedure

Admission and follow-up data were recorded on all subjects by independent research technicians, using the ASI in the same manner as previously described.

All follow-ups were completed 6 months ($\pm$ 2 weeks) following treatment admission by an independent research technician in the same manner as described in Stage I. Of the attempted follow-ups, 94% were successful, and the completion rates were not different between the alcohol and drug abuse samples or among the six treatment programs (all p's > .10).

Results

Matched and mismatched patients were compared using a range of ASI criteria. Comparisons of improvement from admission to follow-up (paired t tests), as well as adjusted comparisons of 6-month outcome (analysis of covariance), were calculated on all 19 criteria (7 composite scores, 12 single-item measures).

Alcohol-Dependent Patients.

Comparisons of improvement from admission to follow-up (Table 6-6) indicate that both groups showed similar types of improvement, predominantly in the areas of employment and alcohol use. However, the matched patients also showed some evidence of significant ($p < .05$) improvement in the areas of medical and psychiatric status, while the mismatched patients did not. Analyses of 6-month outcome status variables for the two groups, adjusted for pretreatment differences in age, number of prior treatments, and the admission criterion score, are presented in the final column of Table 6-6. As can be seen, the matched patients showed significantly better outcomes (accounting for pretreatment differences) in the areas of drug use, legal status, family relations, and psychological function. In addition, 16 of the 19 comparisons showed better status in the matched patients, although only 8 comparisons were statistically significant.

Thus, the data indicate generally better adjustment to treatment, somewhat more improvement, and better 6-month outcomes in the matched alcohol-dependent patients than in the mismatched group.

Drug-Dependent Patients.

Measures of improvement from admission to follow-up on the 19 criterion variables indicated significant and pervasive improvement in the areas of alcohol and drug use, legal status, and family relations for both groups and additional improvements in psychiatric status for the mismatched group (Table 6-7). Thus, the mismatched drug abuse patients showed somewhat more improvement (12 vs. 11) than the matched

TABLE 6-6 Comparisons of Admission to 6-month Performance of Matched and Mismatched Alcohol-Dependent Patients

Criteria[a]	Matched patients ($n = 81$)		Mismatched patients ($n = 97$)		ANCOVA[b] on follow-up
	Admission	Follow-up	Admission	Follow-up	
Medical factor	22 *	11	18	14	.10
% days medical problems	65	36	56	40	
Employment factor	−20	−15	−14	−14	
% time worked	16 **	27	13 **	32	
Money earned/day	13.37	10.83	5.14	8.65	
Welfare income/ day	1.38 *	0.84	2.80 *	1.32	.10
Alcohol use factor	29 **	9	26 **	10	
% days any drinking	69 **	29	60 **	28	
% days intoxicated	60 **	19	50 **	17	
Drug use factor	0	0	1	2	**
% days opiate use	0	0	6	2	
% days nonopiate use	2	2	4	4	*
Legal factor	5	1	10	3	.10
% days of crime	3	0	2	0	
Illegal income/day	0.22	0	2.59	0	
Family factor	12	7	17	12	**
% days of family problems	4	6	16	10	
Psychiatric factor	140 *	91	199	175	*
% days of psychiatric problems	42 *	27	54	52	.10

[a] All criteria were measured during the 30-day period preceding admission and the 6-month follow-up. Higher factor scores indicate greater problem severity.

[b] Covariates in the analysis were age, number of prior alcohol or drug abuse treatments, and the admission criterion score.

*$p < .05$.

**$p < .01$.

group, largely in family relations and psychiatric status, although both groups showed considerable improvement. However, when the 6-month outcome status of these two groups was compared using analysis-of-covariance procedures to adjust for pretreatment differences, the matched drug abuse group showed generally better outcome. In fact, the matched group had better outcomes on all 19 variables, significantly so in the areas of medical status, employment, drug use, illegal income, and psychiatric function. Thus, as in the alcohol-dependent sample, the comparisons indicated better within-treatment and posttreatment adjustment in the matched drug-dependent patients.

TABLE 6-7 Comparisons of Admission to 6-month Performance of Matched and Mismatched Drug-Dependent Patients

Criteria[a]	Matched patients (n = 116)			Mismatched patients (n = 182)			ANCOVA[b] on follow-up
	Admission		Follow-up	Admission		Follow-up	
Medical factor	8		6	21		10	*
% days of medical problems	19		18	57		30	*
Employment factor	−20		−16	−11		−11	**
% days worked	41		42	23		27	**
Money earned/day	20.77		17.99	7.43		9.03	*
Welfare income/day	0.97		1.20	2.06		2.00	
Alcohol use factor	5	**	3	7	**	4	
% days any drinking	39	**	25	39	**	26	
% days intoxicated	15	*	7	14	**	9	
Drug use factor	14	**	4	16	**	7	*
% days opiate use	72	**	10	61	**	20	.10
% days nonopiate use	19	**	4	34		27	*
Legal Factor	6	**	2	10	**	3	
% days of crime	24	**	7	33	**	8	
Illegal income/day	12.49	**	2.56	20.12	**	4.81	**
Family factor	11	**	7	14	**	10	*
% days of family problems	5		5	20	**	10	
Psychiatric factor	110	*	78	223	**	131	*
% days of psychiatric problems	21		17	59	**	36	*

[a] All criteria were measured during the 30-day period preceding admission and the 6-month follow-up. Higher factor scores indicate greater problem severity.

[b] Covariates in the analysis were age, number of prior alcohol or drug abuse treatments, and the admission criterion score.

*$p < .05$.

**$p < .01$.

Further Analysis without High-Severity Patients.

Although these analyses were quite encouraging in both patient samples, it was possible that the results might be accounted for by differences in the proportion of patients with serious psychiatric symptomatology at admission—the high-psychiatric-severity group that we had identified in the 1978 analyses. The results of our 1978 analyses suggested that these high-severity patients responded poorly to all of the available alcohol or drug abuse treatments (see also Armor *et al.*, 1978; Simpson *et al.*, 1978). Thus, in our treatment assignment strategy, we considered these high-severity patients to be unsuited for *any* program and there were no "matched" patients in the high-psychiatric severity groups.

Therefore, in an attempt to provide a more fine-grained analysis of the treatment assignment issue, we eliminated all high-psychiatric-severity patients and reanalyzed the data in both the alcohol- and drug-dependent samples, divided into matched and mismatched groups.

Analyses of improvement from admission to the 6-month follow-up point showed generally widespread improvement among both matched and mismatched groups in each subsample. Major improvements for the alcohol-dependent subsamples were seen in the areas of alcohol use and employment. Generally, these groups had low initial levels of drug use or criminality. Thus the only areas that might have been expected to show more significant change were medical condition, family relations, and psychiatric function. Major improvements for the drug-dependent subsamples were in the areas of drug use, illegal activity, and sometimes alcohol use. There was less evidence for significant improvement in medical condition, family relations, psychiatric function, and (surprisingly) employment. In all of the subsamples, there were more improvements at generally higher levels of significance in the matched patients.

Analyses of covariance on the 6-month follow-up data, using age, number of previous alcohol/drug abuse treatments, and the admission criterion score to adjust for pretreatment differences, yielded evidence for significantly better outcomes among the matched patients in all subsamples *except* the middle/alcoholic group. Although 10 of the 19 comparisons showed better outcome among the matched patients in this subsample, there were two significantly better outcomes for the mismatched patients and only two significantly better outcomes for the matched patients. Comparisons in all other subsamples yielded almost uniformly better outcomes (generally significantly so) for the matched patients.

Therefore, we must conclude that even without the potentially magnifying effects of high-psychiatric-severity patients, there was considerable evidence for significantly better during-treatment performance and posttreatment adjustment in the matched patients than in their mismatched counterparts.

SUMMARY AND DISCUSSION OF STAGES I, II, AND III

An evaluation of treatment effectiveness in male veteran substance abuse patients was conducted in six treatment programs from two cooperating medical centers. The evaluation study was conducted in three stages over 40 months. In Stage I, all patients admitted to the six programs were evaluated comprehensively at the start of treatment and again, 6 months later, using an instrument developed and tested during this project (see McLellan, Luborsky, O'Brien, & Woody, 1980).

The comprehensive evaluation instrument used in the study allowed us to identify one major predictive factor that was well related to treatment outcome in most of the seven criterion areas. This predictive factor was a 10-point interviewer rating of global psychiatric severity at admission to treatment. This psychiatric severity rating was based upon patients' reports of past and present psychiatric symptoms. The alcohol and drug abuse samples were stratified into low-, middle-, and high-severity groups, and the outcome data were reanalyzed. Results showed evidence of outcome differences among the treatment programs and evidence of significant outcome differences associated with patient–program matching, especially among the middle-severity patients. The results provided the basis for a decision strategy to match incoming alcohol and drug patients to the most appropriate treatment program within the six-program network.

In Stage III of the study, the early data were used to generate *a priori* predictions for each patient regarding appropriate (matched) and inappropriate (mismatched) treatment program assignments. Admission staff were not apprised of the matching strategy; thus Stage III patients were assigned to treatments in the same manner as in Stage I, permitting an experimental test of the matching strategy by comparing the treatment response in matched and mismatched patients. Results of these comparisons indicated generally superior performance during treatment and better 6-month outcomes in the matched patients than in their mismatched counterparts. Furthermore, these results were consistent across the majority of subsamples and all of the treatment programs examined.

Limitations of the Study

Prior to a detailed discussion and interpretation of these results, it is important to examine the design and methodological limitations of the study. The first stage of the design was explicitly nonexperimental, since the patients were not assigned to the treatment programs. Furthermore, it could be argued that since there were no explicit hypotheses suggested or tested, the procedure was simply a "fishing expedition." An experimental design is appropriate for investigating a few key variables in a situation where it is possible to control external variation. In the present study, we were not sure which variables were potentially the most important in determining treatment outcome. Moreover, we felt that strictly experimental procedures were inappropriate for wide general use in evaluation studies of this type (see Bale, Van Stone, Kuldau & Miller, 1980; Gottheil, McLellan, & Druley, 1981), questionable on ethical grounds, and impractical to implement. The lack of experimental procedures was partially compensated for by the statistical procedures, which adjusted the treatment programs for differences in patient characteristics. We also added rigor to the analysis by using a range of outcome criteria and two types of predictive analyses. It was recognized that these statistical adjustments would not entirely compensate for the rigor of an experimental design; yet we felt that they provided the advantage of a methodology that could be widely applied by other treatment networks without disrupting normal clinical function.

With regard to the methods used to analyze the data, several points are relevant. First, the reliability of the admission and follow-up self-reports of the patients were spot-checked by requesting urine samples and pay stubs, and by checking criminal records. We are satisifed that there was no general tendency for patients to falsify these self-reports, although there was naturally an error rate (less than 10% variance across items), due to difficulties in comprehension and recall. Furthermore, several other investigators have examined this issue with essentially the same conclusions (Ball, 1972; Sobel & Sobell, 1975).

Conclusions

Three project findings suggest several implications with regard to the delivery of health services to alcohol- and drug-dependent patients. First, the data from both the 1978 and 1980 patient cohorts and for both the alcohol- and drug-dependent samples clearly indicated that substance abuse rehabilitation was effective even without modification of treatment assignment procedures. The impact of this finding was given added weight by the consistency in the type, magnitude, and distribution of improvements shown in these cohorts from 1978 to 1980.

A second major finding from the project results is that the effectiveness of this six-program treatment network was improved by more than 37% (across all outcome criteria) by matching patients to the most appropriate treatment program within the treatment network. We were able to determine the patient background and admission status variables that were predictive of optimum outcome in each treatment program within the network. The practical value of these empirically based predictive factors was tested in a new patient cohort, treated 2 years later in the same network. Patients who were assigned and admitted to a program, based upon the predictive factors (matched patients), had significantly better adjustment and performance during treatment, showed more significant improvements, and had generally better 6-month outcomes than patients who were treated in the same programs but had been predicted to have a different treatment assignment (mismatched patients).

The third major finding from the project was that a truly comprehensive patient assessment at admission, probing potential problem areas such as employment, physical health, legal status, family relations, and especially psychiatric function, is absolutely necessary to the process of matching patients and treatments. We feel certain that a key reason for the historical lack of success at predicting outcome and matching patients to treatments lies in the previous focus upon patient demographic factors and quantitative measures of alcohol and drug use as the major predictive factors. The data presented here and by other authors (Luborsky *et al.*, 1980) suggests that patient demographic factors, even when combined with a full range of measures on alcohol and drug use patterns, provide relatively little information regarding treatment responsiveness and/or posttreatment adjustment. Apparently, the use of alcohol and/or street drugs is one of the few things that this otherwise diverse population has in common, thus reducing the value of substance use itself as a differential predictor. It was only after the strong relationship between admission psychiatric status and posttreatment outcome was noticed that we were able to develop the predictive strategy discussed. It should be noted that admission psychiatric severity was a better predictor of posttreatment alcohol/drug use than was alcohol/drug use at the time of admission.

In this regard, the relationship between the severity of patients' pretreatment psychiatric problems and their response to substance abuse treatment had clear implications for the most appropriate and clinically effective match of patients and treatments. For example, low-severity patients (i.e., patients whose psychiatric severity score at admission was more than one standard deviation below the population mean) showed the best outcomes from treatment, regardless of the program to which they were assigned. Because of this, these patients were most suited to the less expensive outpatient programs, at a savings of more than $53 per patient per day, or an average of more than $3000 per patient over the normal course of treatment. The clear contraindications to outpatient treatment for these low-severity patients were significant problems in employment and/or family relations. Such contraindications are quite logical and consistent with clinical observation. When outpatient treatment is hindered by these problems, targeted referral to employment development agencies (inpatient or outpatient) or to family counseling services has been attempted. We have not as yet determined whether these services can be effectively and economically provided by the outpatient programs, or whether they should continue to be provided by targeted referral. This will be the subject of future investigations.

On the basis of findings from the 1978 data, we concluded that high-psychiatric-severity patients, both alcohol- and drug-dependent, had the least improvement and the poorest outcomes, regardless of the program in which they were treated. This conclusion was also borne out in the 1980 data. In the case of the high-severity/alcohol-dependent sample, no rehabilitation program was found to be effective with the majority of special problems found in this group. We have studied this group of patients (McLellan, Erdlen, & O'Brien, 1981) and have recommended that they be detoxified and stabilized, then referred to inpatient psychiatric treatment. This suggestion is not based upon the demonstrated effectiveness of our psychiatric programs with these patients. Rather, it stems from the lack of effectiveness and the profound administrative problems associated with these patients in our alcohol treatment programs. These patients were more than twice as likely to return to hospitalization (often via the emergency room) as the other alcohol-dependent patients during the 6-month follow-up interval.

While the high-severity/drug-dependent patients had the poorest outcomes of all treated drug abuse patients, a series of studies on this group has suggested some potential treatment solutions. The results of these studies and their clinical implications are discussed in the next major section of this chapter.

DETERMINING APPROPRIATE TREATMENTS FOR THE HIGH-PSYCHIATRIC-SEVERITY DRUG ABUSER

CHOOSING THE BEST ALTERNATIVE: TC OR MM

Despite the disappointing results of our available treatments for the high-severity group of drug abusers, we were left with the day-to-day decision of what to do with the 15–20% of our drug abuse patients who fall into this group. Staff from both the MM and TC programs recognized their limitations with these patients, and treatment in the inpatient psychiatric units was virtually prohibited by the admitting staffs of those units. Given the limited practical alternatives available, we felt it would be important to compare the effectiveness of our two programs with the high-severity patients, and specifically to examine the issue of treatment duration. We reasoned that this type of patient might respond more slowly to treatment, and might, therefore, require a more extended treatment plan than the conventional 60-day program presently available in our TC program.

Thus, we compared rates of improvement on the ASI criteria of drug use, employment, and criminality for 118 patients admitted to the TC program and 154 patients admitted to the MM program during 1980. Each of these samples was divided into low-, middle- and high-severity groups in the previously described manner, using the admission score from the ASI psychiatric severity scale. The percent improvement scores were calculated for the three criteria by subtracting the ASI follow-up criterion score from its coresponding admission score and then dividing the result by the admission score. The result was a measure of percent improvement from admission to 6-month follow-up on each of the three criteria.

The Total Sample

Figure 6-1 depicts the relationship between percent improvement on the three criteria and days in treatment for the total sample of patients treated in the TC (left panel) and the MM (right panel) programs. The plotted lines are linear regressions, which represent the best linear estimate of percent improvement, based upon knowledge of the number of days in treatment. It is important to note that these regression lines are *idealized and are not exact measures of patient improvement* at all points along the line. We have analyzed these data in many ways and have developed several methods of depicting the results. All analyses have revealed essentially the same results, and we feel that they are best represented using these linear regressions.

In the Figure 6-1 plot, the solid line in the center of the two panels indicates no change from admission to 6-month follow-up, while the area above the line indicates improvement and the area below the line indicates worsening. In these plots, the approximate midpoint of the line indicates the mean percent improvement for the groups, while the slope of the line indicates the extent to which more days of treatment were associated with greater percent improvement.

As can be seen, there were general similarities among the functions for both programs. For all measures in each program, there was a direct relationship between time spent in treatment and amount of positive change. Patients who dropped out of treatment early showed less improvement (or worsening, on some measures) than patients who stayed in treatment longer. Clearly, there were some differences in the functions and in the absolute amounts of improvement shown. For both programs, the drug use measure showed the most immediate changes and the greatest absolute amount of improvement. Change in employment was less immediate and showed less total improvement, but equal treatment durations produced greater changes in patient improvement. This is illustrated by the steeper slope of the function and suggests that comparable amounts of treatment had quantitatively different effects on the outcome measures. Legal status showed significant worsening in TC patients with treatments of less than 30 days, but with extended treatment (up to 90 days), there was significant positive change. Similar effects were seen for the MM patients on the legal status measure.

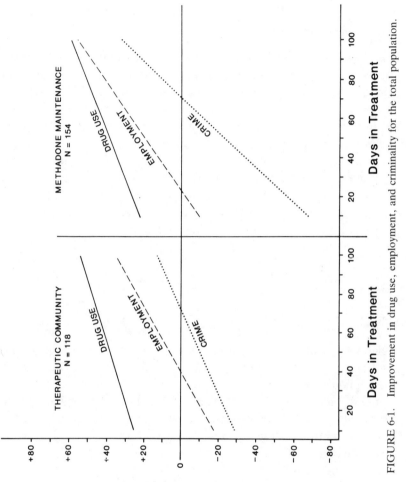

FIGURE 6-1. Improvement in drug use, employment, and criminality for the total population.

123

Thus, these initial analyses of the total samples indicated that while there were differences among the measures in the latency, rate, and absolute amounts of improvement, greater lengths of treatment in either program were associated with greater amounts of improvement.

Low-Severity Patients

Figure 6-2 presents the regression plots illustrating the relationships between treatment duration and percent improvement on the three outcome measures for low-severity patients treated in the TC ($n = 29$) and the MM ($n = 38$) programs. It is apparent that the nature of these plots is different from those seen in Figure 6-1. Although there was, again, a direct relation between treatment duration and percent improvement in both treatment modalities, the plots for these low-severity patients indicate that there were more immediate improvements with less treatment. Furthermore, the majority of plots are flatter, indicating that longer treatments were not associated with dramatic improvements. However, the absolute levels of improvement were generally higher, across the three measures, than those depicted in Figure 6-1.

Middle-Severity Patients

Figure 6-3 presents the same relationships for middle-severity patients treated in the TC ($n = 52$) and the MM ($n = 86$) programs. The relationships presented here are again similar between the programs, and are quite comparable to those seen in Figure 6-1. The plots for these middle patients are steeper on all measures than those for the low patients, indicating a greater effect of treatment. Further, the plots for the legal status and employment measures in the TC patients, and for the legal status and drug use measures in the MM patients, indicate that shorter treatment durations were associated with worse status at 6 months than at admission.

High-Severity Patients

Figure 6-4 presents the same relationships for high severity patients treated in the TC ($n = 28$) and the MM ($n = 30$) programs. As can be seen, there were *qualitative differences* in the percent improvement functions between the treatment programs. The functions for the MM

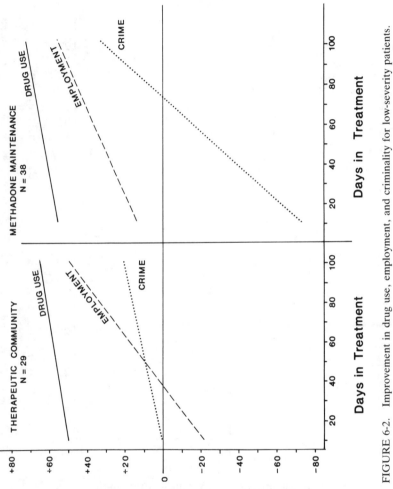

FIGURE 6-2. Improvement in drug use, employment, and criminality for low-severity patients.

125

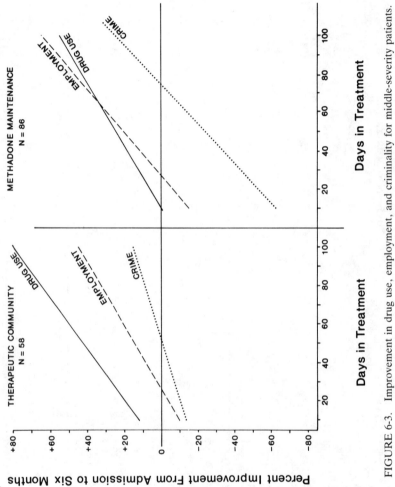

FIGURE 6-3. Improvement in drug use, employment, and criminality for middle-severity patients.

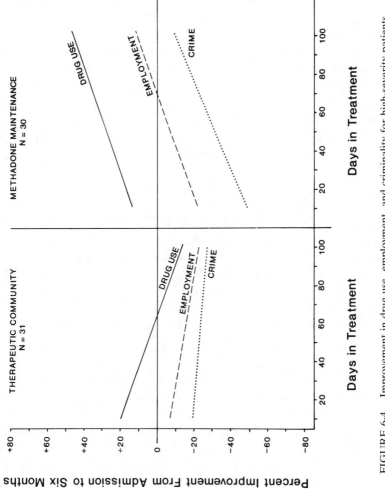

FIGURE 6-4. Improvement in drug use, employment, and criminality for high-severity patients.

127

patients are similar to those shown in Figure 6-2, with relatively flat slopes, indicative of an attenuated treatment duration effect. However, the absolute levels of improvement shown were substantially lower than those in the other severity groups, at all treatment durations. In fact, the employment measure did not show a net improvement until after 70 days of treatment, and the legal status measure never showed a net improvement.

The percent improvement functions for the high-severity TC patients were unlike those seen in any other group for either program. For each measure, there was a negative relation between time in treatment and percent improvement, especially in the measures of drug use and criminality. These plots indicated that high-severity patients who stayed in TC treatment for longer durations showed less improvement (in fact, worsening) than those who stayed shorter amounts of time.

Conclusions

Two conclusions can be derived from these results. First, treatment was effective across the majority of patients and outcome measures. We have previously reported on the effectiveness of drug abuse treatment in an earlier sample (McLellan, Woody, Luborsky, & O'Brien, 1982), and these data indicate that treatment continues to be associated with significant positive changes. Further, there was a clear and direct relationship between treatment duration and amount of improvement, with those patients who remained in treatment longest showing the most improvement and the best outcomes.

The second conclusion from these results is that psychiatric severity was an important predictor of treatment response generally and of differential treatment response in the more psychiatrically impaired drug abuse patients. Results of these and previous analyses (Laporte, McLellan, & O'Brien, 1981; McLellan, Erdlen, & O'Brien, 1981; McLellan et al., 1983) indicate that patients with few psychiatric problems at admission showed the greatest improvement and the best outcomes, while patients with the highest levels of pretreatment psychiatric problems showed the least improvement and the poorest outcomes. The additional finding from these data was that the psychiatric severity measure was also a predictor of a differential treatment response. Specifically, in the case of high-severity patients, longer treatment durations were associated with some additional improvement in the MM program, but this was not the case when they were treated in the TC program. High-severity patients who stayed in the TC program for longer durations had less improvement than similar patients who stayed for shorter periods of time.

It is our opinion that the TC program was counterproductive for these high-severity patients, and that the explanation for this effect lies in the particular therapeutic techniques of the TC modality. Like most other drug-free therapeutic communities, our program was based upon the Synanon model (Biase, 1972) and was implemented in 1971 for the primary purpose of treating heroin addicts. The goals of the program are quite clear: the total elimination of all drugs, including marijuana, and the responsible use of alcohol. Therefore, there is a general sanction against the use of psychotropic medications during treatment, although some antidepressant medications have been prescribed. Therapy is conducted by paraprofessional and ex-addict counselors three to five times per week, and the usual method is group encounter. The primary agent of therapeutic change is, as in most TC programs, the community itself. The self-governing community sets rigorous behavioral guidelines, polices its members strictly, and metes out punishments to offenders; these usually incude public admission of guilt, followed by an embarrassing penance.

Evaluations of this particular TC program, as well as other, more general evaluations of the TC modality, indicate that these techniques are generally quite effective, especially for the more intact opiate abuser. However, in the case of the more impaired polydrug abuser, we have reason to believe that these techniques are particularly contraindicated. Our experience indicates that high-severity patients are often younger, generally use fewer opiate but more nonopiate drugs, and have fewer social and personal supports than the patients for which this modality was originally designed. For these patients, the stresses of community living, the absence of potentially appropriate medication, and particularly the group encounter therapy may be countertherapeutic. In this regard, it is interesting to note that we have not found this negative relationship between treatment duration and percent improvement among the high-severity alcoholic patients treated in the ATU, although it too is a therapeutic community. Consistent with our explanation, it is significant that the ATU does not employ group encounter techniques, does not mete out embarrassing punishments, and does approve the more liberal use of psychotropic medications during treatment.

Optimizing Treatment within the MM Modality

The results of our comparative study had indicated that, relative to the TC program, the MM program was potentially more effective with the high-severity drug abuse patients. However, we recognized that even this level of performance was less than satisfactory. We therefore attempted to determine whether additional services might be added to our existing program that might provide special benefit to these patients.

The Psychotherapy Study: Subjects, Treatments, Hypotheses

To this end, we began a study designed to measure the potential benefits of adding professional psychotherapy to existing drug counseling services within the MM program. In this study, recently admitted opiate-dependent veterans were randomly assigned to receive either supportive–expressive psychotherapy plus counseling, cognitive–behavioral psychotherapy plus counseling, or drug counseling alone (see Woody *et al.*, 1983). All therapy was provided by trained, supervised professionals on a weekly basis over a 24-week period. Drug counseling was provided by rehabilitation workers with bachelor's degrees who had an average of 8 years' experience in the drug abuse field.

Our working hypothesis was that the psychotherapy would be able to reduce drug use and improve overall patient functioning by diminishing the intensity of the psychiatric symptoms. To test this hypothesis, we examined data on the first 62 patients to complete therapy and divided them into four groups, based on ASI ratings of psychiatric severity that were obtained at intake; we felt that this provided a valid estimate of general psychological status. On this basis, we selected two extreme groups: those showing high levels of symptoms ($n = 21$) and those showing low levels of psychiatric symptoms ($n = 21$). A total of 42 patients were included in these two groups, excluding 20 patients who were in the midrange. We selected only the extremes, since we felt that this method would give us the best chance to test our hypothesis.

We then subdivided these groups on the basis of their treatment assignment into high-severity/counseling ($n = 10$), high-severity/therapy ($n = 11$), low-severity/counseling ($n = 11$), and low-severity/therapy ($n = 10$). A summary of the psychological test results for these four groups is presented in Table 6-8. As seen, the groups were distinctly different in terms of the amount of psychopathology.

TABLE 6-8   Psychological Status of the Four Groups at the Start of the Survey

	High-severity/counseling	Low-severity/counseling	High-severity/therapy	Low-severity/therapy
n	10	11	11	10
Beck Depression Inventory	18	10	21	9
Maudsley Neuroticism Scale	41	24	37	20
Shipley IQ	100	102	96	104
Shipley CQ	80	87	80	94
ASI psychiatric severity	5.1	2.7	5.6	2.3

Pre- to Posttreatment Improvement

We examined pre- to posttherapy improvement for patients in each group using the ASI. The ASI severity scores and other related items are presented in Table 6-9. As seen, the high-severity/counseling group showed improvement only in areas clearly related to drug use. One might expect this, since the patients were on methadone. The low-severity/counseling group demonstrated significant improvement in several areas, indicating that the counselors had a distinctly greater impact on this group than on the high-severity patients. Conversely, the high-severity/therapy group demonstrated significant improvement in several areas, equal to that seen in the low-severity counseling group. The low-severity/therapy group had made considerable improvement, perhaps of greater magnitude than that of the low-severity/counseling group.

Drug Treatment Results

The mean methadone doses for each group are seen in Figure 6-5. There was a significantly ($p < .01$) higher mean methadone dose for the high-severity/counseling patients than for any of the other three groups. The low-severity/therapy group received a significantly ($p < .05$) lower dose than any of the other three groups, and the high-severity/therapy and low-severity/counseling groups received comparable intermediate dosages. The mean dosage of the high-severity/counseling group was significantly ($p < .05$) greater than the other groups in both a statistical and clinical sense. Urine drug screening results are seen in Figure 6-6. The high-severity/counseling group had significantly ($p < .05$) more drug-positive urines than either of the other three groups, which had about the same frequency of positive urines.

TABLE 6-9 Pre- to Posttherapy (7-Months) Improvement

Criteria	High-severity/ counseling			Low-severity/ counseling			High-severity/ therapy			Low-severity/ therapy		
Medical severity	3.1		2.4	1.7		3.2	2.5		3.5	1.8		0.7
Days medical problems	4		2	2		4	3		3	1		1
Employment severity	4.5		4.6	5.1	*	3.2	3.8		3.0	3.9	*	2.7
Days worked	9		11	10		13	7		10	9		13
Money earned	272		306	242	*	380	309	*	482	318	**	523
Abuse severity	5.7	*	3.8	3.8	**	1.4	4.9	*	3.0	4.0	**	1.4
Days drunk	4		2	2		1	3		2	2		0
Days opiate use	6		3	10	**	2	5		2	8	*	3
Days nonopiate use	10		8	4		2	7	*	3	3		1
Money for drugs	430	**	190	164	**	47	344	**	65	188	**	8
Legal severity	3.1		3.0	4.5	*	3.1	2.8	*	0.7	2.0	*	0.8
Days crime	6		3	10		4	5		0.8	1		0.4
Illegal income	216		181	506	*	300	186	**	43	166	**	10
Psychiatric severity	5.1		4.8	2.7		1.8	5.6	*	3.0	2.5	*	1.0
Days psychiatric problems	17		13	8		3	15		8	4	*	1

* = p < .05.

** = p < .01.

132

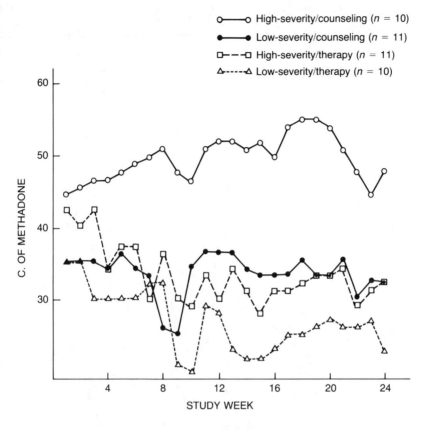

FIGURE 6-5. Mean methadone dosage by group.

Comments on the MM Study

Prior to discussing the potential role of psychotherapy with these patients, it is important to mention a design limitation in this project. Patients treated in the therapy groups saw a helping person (therapist or counselor) an average of 23 times, whereas those in the counseling-alone group saw their counselors an average of 17 times. Thus, the patients in the therapy groups spent about 30% more time with a helping person. This design was deliberate and was instituted to determine whether the addition of professional therapy to counseling services would provide extra benefits. This question was the major practical issue addressed by the project. We never considered it reasonable that therapists could be

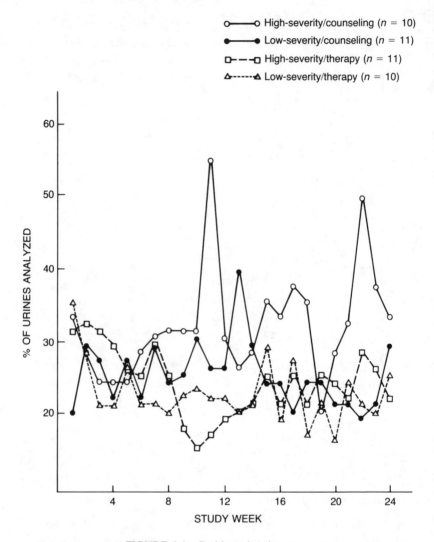

FIGURE 6-6. Positive urines by group.

used to replace counselors. However, we do think it may be practical and even cost-effective for psychotherapy to supplement the important role of counselors with certain patients.

Despite the design limitations, the results of this study offered convincing evidence that traditional drug abuse counseling was able to provide significant benefit to the low-severity patients. In fact, the overall results for the low-severity/counseling patients were comparable to those for the low-severity/therapy patients. However, the data also indicated that counseling alone was only marginally effective with the high-severity patients, despite the use of significantly greater average doses of methadone. The supplemental therapy did provide significant benefit to the high-severity patients, especially in the areas of drug abuse, legal status, and psychiatric function. It is important to note that these improvements were brought about while concurrently lowering the average methadone dose—an important consideration for therapists concerned about producing high levels of physiological tolerance in patients.

Given the favorable results of adding psychotherapy to drug counseling for these patients, we find it interesting to speculate about why the psychotherapy allowed for a reduction in drug use without the need to elevate the methadone. One important factor in this regard was the development of an important relationship between patient and therapist. Authors in the field have theorized that drug dependence is a substitute for important personal relationships. However, we think that the benefits shown were more than simply the results of a relationship. Our observations suggest that the benefits of therapy were a result of the ability to form a relationship, combined with special knowledge and skill about how to use it. We have noticed that many of the counselors form good patient relationships, but have trouble managing them, especially with the very disturbed patients. It is also important to remember that, like other patients who have been treated with psychotherapy, the high-severity patients had significant psychiatric problems especially in the areas of depression and anxiety. To the extent that drug use is an attempt to medicate these problems, and to the degree that psychotherapy can reduce them, psychotherapy can reduce drug use indirectly.

GENERAL SUMMARY AND CONCLUSIONS

The present chapter has reviewed a 7-year program of research at the Philadelphia VA Medical Center investigating the psychiatric factors in determining response to drug abuse treatment. This body of research suggests five conclusions:

1. The severity of a substance abuse patient's psychiatric condition at treatment admission is the single best predictor of response to treatment (see DeLeon, 1984; Luborsky *et al.*, 1980; McLellan *et al.*, 1983;

Meyer, 1983). The psychiatrically severe substance abuser shows less improvement during treatment and much poorer outcome following treatment than other patients, regardless of treatment modality (Mc-Lellan, Erdlen, & O'Brien, 1981; McLellan *et al.*, 1982).

I should reiterate here that we have used the term "psychiatric severity" to indicate the seriousness of a patient's overall psychiatric impairment, without regard to specific diagnosis. We have determined psychiatric severity from a structured interview designed to assess the number and intensity of psychiatric symptoms (the ASI), and we have also calculated a measure of psychiatric severity from a standardized combination of widely used psychological tests (e.g., the Beck Depression Inventory, the Hopkins Symptom Checklist—90 Item, and the Maudsley Personality Inventory). Clearly, this severity measure is not meant to take the place of a psychiatric diagnosis. However, we and others have found that a global estimate of overall severity can be easily and reliably judged by a nonprofessional, and can offer a useful supplemental estimate of the potential type and amount of intervention needed.

2. The psychiatrically severe substance abuser (i.e., the patient with clear and concurrent problems of addiction and one or more other psychiatric disorders) represents approximately 15–30% of our primary psychiatric and primary drug-dependent patient populations (see Atterman, Erdlen, & McLellan, 1980; Crowley, Chesluk, Dilts, & Hart, 1974; Hekiman & Gershon, 1968; McLellan, Druley, & Carson, 1978).

3. The psychiatrically severe substance abuser may be reliably identified and evaluated by trained technicians using a brief, structured interview (see McLellan, 1979; McLellan, Luborsky, O'Brien, & Woody, 1980).

4. Given the available drug abuse treatment options, our data indicate that MM is more effective than inpatient, drug-free, TC treatment. This may be due in part to the stabilizing effect of the methadone schedule, in part to the antidepressant and antipsychotic effects of methadone, and in part to the probable contraindication of encounter therapy and patient self-governance interventions used by TCs.

5. While MM combined with regular counseling and a full program of medical and social services appears to produce some minor benefits for high-psychiatric-severity drug abuse patients, this is usually at great cost of staff time and energy. Furthermore, even these results are less than satisfactory. We have found that these patients in particular are

easier to manage and can show significant improvement when professional, weekly psychotherapy sessions are added to the existing program of services. For these patients, the addition of professional psychotherapy over a 6-month period has been associated with significant reductions in drug abuse, illegal activity, and psychiatric symptoms (see Woody *et al.*, 1983).

We conclude that brief psychological assessment of drug-dependent patients at admission may be useful in differentiating those patients who are likely to show sustained benefit from traditional counseling and those who are not. The present data indicate that, despite the modest improvements shown by these high-severity drug abusers, their 6-month outcomes suggest that they are likely candidates for recidivism and rehospitalization. We must, therefore, conclude that primary drug abuse counseling and rehabiliation, as offered in conventional MM or TC settings, is not by itself adequate to bring about enough change to make self-support likely, even for relatively short periods. Drug-dependent patients with more severe psychological problems require more focused and independent interventions to address their psychopathology directly through appropriate medication and psychotherapy. Drug abuse rehabilitation programs may serve as a valuable first step in the extended treatment of these patients. By stabilizing the drug abuse and improving general adjustment, they may provide the necessary prerequisites for effective assessment and subsequent treatment of the psychiatric problems found in this growing population of patients.

ACKNOWLEDGMENT

This work was supported by the National Institute on Drug Abuse (Grant No. DA02554).

REFERENCES

Alterman, A. I., Erdlen, F., & McLellan, A. T. (1980). Alcoholic schizophrenics. In E. Gottheil *et al.* (Eds.), *Substance abuse and psychiatric illness* (pp. 141–169). New York: Pergamon Press.

Armor, D. J., Polich, J. M., & Stambul, H. B. (1978). *Alcoholism and treatment.* Santa Monica, CA: Rand Corporation.

Bale, R., VanStone, W., Kuldau, J., & Miller R. (1980). Therapeutic communities versus methadone maintenance. *Archives of General Psychiatry, 37,* 1434–1449.

Ball, J. C. (1972). The reliability and validity of interview data obtained from 59 narcotic addicts. *American Journal of Sociology, 72*, 26–40.

Biase, D. J. (1972). Phoenix Houses: Therapeutic communities for drug addicts. In L. Kemp (Ed.), *Drug abuse: Current concepts and research* (pp. 210–230). Springfield, IL: Charles C. Thomas.

Cronbach, L. J., & Furby, L. (1970). How should we measure "change"—or should we? *Psychological Bulletin, 74*, 187–198.

Crowley, R. J., Chesluk, D., Dilts, S., & Hart, R. (1974). Drug and alcohol among psychiatric admissions. *Archives of General Psychiatry, 30*, 172–177.

DeLeon, G. (1984). *The therapeutic community: Study of effectiveness* (NIDA Treatment Research Monograph , DHHS Publication No. ADM 84-1286). Washington, DC: U.S. Government Printing Office.

Dixon, W. J., & Brown, M. D. (Eds.). (1979). *BMDP-79: Biomedical computer programs*. Los Angeles: University of California Press.

Endicott, J., Spitzer, R. L., & Fleiss, J. L. (1976). The Global Assessment Scale: A procedure for measuring overall severity of psychiatric disturbance. *Archives of General Psychiatry, 33*, 766–771.

Gottheil, E., McLellan, A. T., & Druley, K. A. (Eds.). (1979). *Addiction research and treatment: Converging trends*. New York: Pergamon-Maxwell.

Gottheil, E., McLellan, A. T., & Druley, K. A. (1981). Reasonable and unreasonable standards in evaluation of substance abuse treatments. In E. Gottheil, A. T. McLellan, & K. A. Druley (Eds.), *Matching patient needs and treatment methods in substance abuse* (pp. 371–388). New York: Pergamon Press.

Hekimon, L. J., & Gershon, S. (1968). Characteristics of drug abusers admitted to a psychiatric hospital. *Journal of the American Medical Association, 205*, 119–126.

Laporte, D., McLellan, A. T., & O'Brien, C. P. (1981). Treatment response in psychiatrically impaired drug abusers. *Comprehensive Psychiatry, 22*, 411–419.

Luborsky, L., & Bachrach, H. (1974). Eighteen experiences with Health–Sickness Rating Scale. *Archives of General Psychiatry, 31*, 292–304.

Luborsky, L., Mintz, J., & Auerbach, A. (1980). Predicting the outcomes of psychotherapy: Findings of the Penn Psychotherapy Project. *Archives of General Psychiatry, 37*, 471–481.

McLellan, A. T. (1979, June). *The Addiction Severity Index*. Paper presented at the meeting of the Committee on Problems of Drug Dependence, Philadelphia.

McLellan, A. T., Druley, K. A., & Carson, J. E. (1978). Evaluation of substance abuse problems in a psychiatric hospital. *Journal of Clinical Psychiatry, 39*, 425–430.

McLellan, A. T., Druley, K. A., O'Brien, C. P., & Kron, R. (1980). Matching substance abuse patients to appropriate treatments: The Addiction Severity Index. *Drug and Alcohol Dependence, 5*, 189–195.

McLellan, A. T., Erdlen, F. R., & O'Brien, C. P. (1981). Psychological severity and response to alcoholism rehabilitation. *Drug and Alcohol Dependence, 8*, 23–35.

McLellan, A. T., Luborsky, L., Cacciola, J., Griffith, J. E., Evans, F., & Barr, H. (1985). New data from the Addiction Severity Index: Reliability and validity in three centers. *Journal of Nervous and Mental Disease, 173*, 412–423.

McLellan, A. T., Luborsky, L., O'Brien, C. P., & Woody, G. E. (1980). An improved evaluation instrument for substance abuse patients: The Addiction Severity Index. *Journal of Nervous and Mental Disease, 168*, 26–33.

McLellan, A. T., Luborsky, L., Woody, G. E., & O'Brien, C. P. (1981). Are the "addiction-related" problems of substance abusers really related? *Journal of Nervous and Mental Disease, 169*, 68–74.

McLellan, A. T., Luborsky, L., Woody, G. E., Druley, K. A., & O'Brien, C. P. (1983). Predicting response to drug and alcohol treatments: Role of psychiatric severity. *Archives of General Psychiatry, 40*, 620–625.

McLellan, A. T., Woody, G. E., Luborsky, L., & O'Brien, C. P. (1982). Is treatment for substance abuse effective? *Journal of the American Medical Association, 247*, 1423–1427.

Meyer, R. (1983, May). *Sociopathy as a negative predictor of treatment for alcohol abuse.* Paper presented at the annual meeting of the American Psychiatric Association, New York.

Mintz, J., Luborsky, L., & Cristoph, P. (1979). Measuring the outcomes of psychotherapy: Findings of the Penn Psychotherapy Project. *Journal of Consulting and Clinical Psychology, 47*, 319–334.

Nunally, J. (1967). *Psychometric theory.* New York: McGraw-Hill.

Simpson, D. D., Savage, L. J., Lloyd, M. R., & Sells, S. B. (1978). *Evaluation of drug abuse treatments based on first year follow-up* (NIDA Research Monograph, DHHS Publication No. 78–411). Washington, DC: U.S. Government Printing Office.

Sobel, L. C., & Sobell, M. B. (1975). Outpatient alcoholics give valid self-reports. *Journal of Nervous and Mental Disease, 161*, 32–42.

Woody, G. E., Luborsky, L., McLellan, A. T., O'Brien, C. P., Beck, A. T., Blaine, J., Herman, I., & Hole, A. (1983). Psychotherapy for opiate addicts: Does it help? *Archives of General Psychiatry, 40*, 639–645.

7

Psychiatric Disorders in Opiate Addicts: Preliminary Findings on the Course and Interaction with Program Type

BRUCE J. ROUNSAVILLE
HERBERT D. KLEBER

REASONS FOR PRIOR DE-EMPHASIS OF PSYCHOPATHOLOGY IN TREATMENT

Although there are numerous theories of drug abuse that emphasize societal factors, family influences, and the pharmacological properties of the drugs themselves (Lettieri, Sayers, & Pearson, 1980), there is a long history to the idea that opiate addiction is a behavioral manifestation of underlying psychological disturbance (Blatt, McDonald, Sugarman, & Wilbur, 1984; Khantzian, 1976; Krystal & Raskin, 1970; Yorke, 1970). Empirical support for the importance of psychopathology in opiate addiction is provided by a large literature demonstrating that rates of psychological symptoms and deviant personality traits are higher in addicts than in comparison groups (Blatt *et al.*, in press; Craig, 1979a, 1979b).

Despite widespread recognition that psychopathology is common in opiate addicts, treatment efforts frequently ignore or de-emphasize psychological issues for two principal reasons. First, reliable and valid means for detecting psychopathology have been unavailable or excessively expensive and time-consuming. The bulk of empirical studies of psychopathology in opiate addicts have utilized symptom or personality scales that have limited utility in a clinical setting. Although results of this "dimensional approach" may tell the clinician that a client has a high score on a particular dimension (e.g., depression), no information is provided regarding how this symptom fits with a constellation of other positive and negative findings that might allow a clinician to decide whether or not to treat the symptoms (e.g., begin a course of pharmacotherapy with tricyclic antidepressants). An alternative "categorical" approach to detecting psychopathology can be used to evaluate the subject for the presence or absence of various psychological syndromes, which are defined as comprising meaningful groupings of symptoms that have a known prognosis and treatment (Weissman & Klerman, 1978). This approach to diagnosis, which is based on a medical tradition, has had limited utility in the treatment of psychopathology in opiate addicts, because methods for obtaining psychiatric diagnosis have emphasized lengthy interviews by psychiatrists and have been characterized by poor reliability (Beck, Ward, Mendelson, Mock, & Erbaugh, 1962; Spitzer & Fleiss, 1974). However, in the past 15 years, specified criteria have been available for diagnosing psychiatric disorders (American Psychiatric Association, 1980; Feighner, Robins, & Guze, 1972; Spitzer, Endicott, & Robins, 1978) and structured interview schedules such as the Schedule for Affective Disorders and Schizophrenia (SADS; Endicott & Spitzer, 1978) and the Diagnostic Interview Schedule (DIS; Robins, Helzer, Croughan, & Ratcliff, 1981) have been developed that would enable non-MD raters to reliably categorize opiate addicts (Rounsaville, Cacciola, Weissman, & Kleber, 1981; Rounsaville, Rosenberger, Wilber, Weissman, & Kleber, 1980).

A second major reason for limited emphasis on psychopathology in managing opiate addicts has been the unavailability of specific and effective treatments. Until the widespread use of phenothiazines as pharmacotherapy for psychotic disorders, antidepressants for depressive disorders, and lithium preparations for bipolar illness, the most typical treatment offered for a variety of disorders was long-term psychotherapy. Prior to the widespread use of methadone maintenance, psychotherapy for opiate addicts had discouraging results characterized by very high dropout rates (Brill, 1977; Nyswander, Winick, Bernstein, Brill, & Kaufer, 1958). However, more recent findings have supported the efficacy of psychotherapy when offered in the context of methadone and narcotic antagonist programs (Rounsaville & Kleber, 1985a). The findings of Woody and associates (Woody *et al.*, 1983; see also chapter by Woody, O'Brien, McLellan, & Luborsky, this volume) underscore the importance of psychopathology in relationship to the value of psychotherapy for opiate addicts, by demonstrating that it has the greatest efficacy for those with moderate to severe ratings of global psychopathology. Thus, there now appear to be effective and comparatively specific pharmacological and psychological treatments to be offered to opiate addicts with significant psychopathology.

RATES AND CHARACTERISTICS OF PSYCHIATRIC DISORDERS IN OPIATE ADDICTS

Our past research has indicated that opiate addicts seeking treatment (Rounsaville, Weissman, Kleber, & Wilber, 1982), as well as untreated addicts in the community (Rounsaville & Kleber, 1985), have high rates of treatable psychiatric disorders. Using a structured interview schedule, the SADS—Lifetime Version (SADS-L; Endicott & Spitzer, 1978) and the highly specified Research Diagnostic Criteria (RDC; Spitzer *et al.*, 1978), we found that 70.3% of a sample of 533 opiate addicts seeking treatment had a current psychiatric disorder, and 86.9% met diagnostic criteria for at least one psychiatric disorder other than drug abuse at some time in their lives. The specific disorders for which rates were substantially higher in addicts than in participants in a community survey in the same city (Weissman, Myers, & Harding, 1978) were major and minor depression, chronic minor mood disorders (intermittent depression, labile personality, cyclothymic personality), alcoholism, antisocial personality, phobias, and generalized anxiety disorder. The great majority of psychiatric disorders were accounted for by three diagnoses: major depression, antisocial personality, and alcoholism. Further evaluation of opiate addicts with these three diagnoses suggested that they were distinguished from the general treated population in numerous ways.

Major depression was the most frequently diagnosed psychiatric disorder in treated opiate addicts, with 23.8% found to be currently depressed and 53.9% with a lifetime diagnosis. Depression in opiate addicts had a number of characteristics (Rounsaville, Weissman, & Kleber, 1983):

1. Most addicts who became depressed had their first major episode only after they had developed a substance abuse problem.

2. Depressive episodes in opiate addicts were characterized by comparatively mild symptomatology.
3. The symptoms complained of by depressed opiate addicts did not appear to conform to a pattern that might be easily explained by sedative effects of opiates or other sedatives, or by withdrawal effects from opiates or other drugs.
4. There was a substantial but complex relationship between drug use and depression, with higher levels associated with heavier drug use prior to seeking treatment.
5. Depression in opiate addicts was associated with other personality pathology.
6. A comparison of addicts in the community and those seeking treatment showed that depression and problems in social functioning may provide some motivation for seeking treatment.
7. Depression seemed to be associated with high levels of stressful events and other indices of social crisis, and to be relieved when crisis situations were past.

Alcoholism was a second very common additional disorder in treated opiate addicts, of whom 13.7% met RDC criteria for a current episode and 34.5% had a lifetime diagnosis. Several features were found to characterize alcoholism in opiate addicts (Rounsaville, Weissman, & Kleber, 1982b):

1. Regarding the sequence of alcoholism and opiate addiction, most alcoholic addicts had alcohol problems before developing a drug use disorder and seeking treatment.
2. Entrance into treatment did not appear to lead to either increased or decreased alcohol abuse; and alcohol abuse while in treatment usually took place in those who had a history of alcohol problems.
3. When compared with nonalcoholic addicts, alcoholic addicts had fewer assets and more liabilities, including a more disruptive childhood history, heavier history of legal problems and polydrug abuse, more severe problems with social functioning, and higher rates of psychiatric disorders.

Regarding antisocial personality in opiate addicts, two mutually exclusive types were identified: (1) primary antisocial addicts, comprising 27.2% of the sample, and consisting of those with a history of antisocial activities that are independent of the need to obtain drugs; and (2) secondary antisocial addicts, comprising of 27.7% of the sample, whose antisocial behavior was found to be directly related to drug use. Both types of antisocial addicts were distinguished from those without this disorder by having a history of heavier drug use and greater evidence of criminal activity. However, the primary antisocial addicts were distinguished from both secondary antisocial addicts and nonantisocial addicts by having greater evidence of childhood disruptions and more severe additional psychopathology (Rounsaville, Eyre, Weissman, & Kleber, 1983). It is of interest that antisocial personality disorder was found to coexist with affective disorders, anxiety disorders, and/or alcoholism in this population. The prevalence of antisocial personality disorder was higher when criteria from the *Diagnostic and Statistical Manual of Mental Disorders*, third edition (DSM-III; American Psychiatric Association, 1980) were employed, compared with when RDC criteria were applied.

PROGNOSTIC SIGNIFICANCE OF PSYCHIATRIC DISORDERS IN OPIATE ADDICTS

As well as being found in a large number of opiate addicts, psychopathology appears to be of substantial prognostic significance. McLellan and his colleagues (McLellan, Luborsky, Woody, O'Brien, & Druley, 1983; see also chapter by McLellan, this volume) have found that severity of the drug abuse patient's psychiatric condition at treatment admission is the single best predictor of response to drug abuse treatment, accounting for an average of 10–12% of outcome variance. Addicts with severe psychiatric impairment comprised 18.5% of one sample of veteran addicts seeking treatment; the impaired group had less improvement during treatment and much poorer outcome following treatment than other patients, regardless of the treatment modality. We (Rounsaville & Kleber, 1984; Rounsaville, Weissman, & Kleber, 1982a) conducted 6- and 30-month follow-up evaluations of a sample of opiate addicts seeking treatment. We determined that being in a depressive episode was predictive of poorer occupational functioning, poorer control of illicit drug use, and more psychological symptoms during the first 6 months following treatment seeking, as well as of poorer psychosocial functioning, more medical problems, and poorer current adjustment measured 2.5 years following entrance into treatment. Antisocial personality was associated with more legal problems 6 months following entrance to treatment, and with poorer psychosocial functioning, greater difficulty with legal occupational functioning, and poorer current functioning at the 2.5-year follow-up time.

COURSE OF PSYCHIATRIC DISORDERS AND
PATIENT–PROGRAM MATCHING

In the study reported in this chapter, we have re-evaluated a sample of opiate addicts 2.5 years after they were first categorized according to psychiatric diagnosis as they applied for treatment at a drug dependence unit in New Haven, Connecticut. At follow-up evaluations, we have assessed the subjects' intercurrent functioning during the 2.5 years, and the amount and type of treatment they have received. In addition, diagnostic evaluations have been repeated. At this writing, the study is ongoing, and we here present preliminary findings gathered on a partial sample. For this presentation, we focus on two issues:

1. Do opiate addicts appear to recover from psychiatric disorders over time?
2. Do opiate addicts with differing psychiatric disorders have a differential response to type of treatment offered?

Do Opiate Addicts Appear to Recover from Psychiatric Disorders over Time?

In our earlier 6-month follow-up study, we found that rates of current depression dropped from 20% to 12% during the time following entrance into treatment, and a corresponding reduction in mean depressive symptoms was detected (Rounsaville, Weissman, Wilber, Crits-Christoph, & Kleber, 1982). During the same time period, the rate of current alcoholism went from 6% to 14%, and the rate of antisocial personality disorder climbed from 22% to 31% (Rounsaville *et al.*, 1981). These fluctuations in rates of disorders may have reflected changes in the course of addiction in our sample, although unreliability of the diagnostic procedures may also have accounted for the changes. In the current study, a greater number of subjects and a longer term of follow-up may allow us to evaluate more thoroughly the factors associated with changes in psychopathology in opiate addicts, such as staying depressed, recovering from depression, or becoming depressed.

Knowledge of the course of psychiatric disorders over time in opiate addicts can provide a greater indication of the clinical significance of psychiatric disorders in this group.

Do Opiate Addicts with Differing Psychiatric Disorders Have a Differential Response to Types of Treatments Offered?

The issue of patient–program matching has been a lively one, because of the desire to maximize the efficacy of scarce treatment resources. Data from experimental studies with random patient assignment are unavailable, largely because such projects are infeasible to carry out (Bale *et al.*, 1980). Despite this, two reports have evaluated patient–program matching of drug abusers in a naturalistic setting. In a follow-up study of 1812 male opiate addicts, Simpson and Savage (1981–1982) developed a profile of the "typical" clients assigned to three types of treatment programs: methadone maintenance (MM), therapeutic community (TC), and outpatient drug-free (DF) programs. They found that clients assigned to the different programs were substantially different, with the MM clients being older, more likely to have been married, more likely to have family dependents and an employment history, and likely to have a longer history of opiate use. The TC and DF clients were comparatively similar, except that the DF clients were younger and had correspondingly fewer years of criminal history and drug use, and less legal pressure. Despite Simpson and Savage's finding that patient–program matching was taking place on clinical grounds, they did not find that the addicts with profiles that were typical of each type of program received differentially greater benefit from being assigned to that program. Hence, the typical MM client (e.g., older, married, etc.) had no more favorable outcome if assigned to MM than to DF or TC treatment.

In the only study of patient–program matching that evaluated psychological characteristics, McLellan and colleagues (McLellan, Luborsky, O'Brien, & Woody, 1980; see also chapter by McLellan, this volume) found that patients with high ratings of psychological problems on the Addiction Severity Index (ASI) had the poorest outcomes, regardless of program type, and that patients with low severity did well across programs. A more recent report (McLellan, Woody, Evans, & O'Brien, 1983) indicates that those with high psychiatric severity did not receive improved benefit with increased length of stay in a TC, but did profit from longer treatment on MM. For those drug abusers in a sample of 292 patients with a middle range of severity of psychological problems, MM programs showed significantly better outcome with the opiate–stimulant abusers. TCs showed a better outcome with the opiate–depressant abusers, and there were no differences with the opiate-only group. McLellan and his colleagues have hypothesized that methadone may act to reduce mania and paranoia produced by the stimulant drugs, and that the regulatory and weak antipsychotic effects of the methadone may be particularly beneficial to the opiate–stimulant users. On the other hand, methadone and sedative hypnotic drugs produce synergistic effects, which may make it difficult for opiate–sedative users to reduce their drug use and to concentrate upon other aspects of their rehabilitation.

Thus, the two existing studies of patient–program matching have yielded mixed results, although the client characteristics considered in the matching were quite different across the studies. To date, there have been no attempts to evaluate the importance of specific psychiatric disorders in relationship to treatment success in different types of drug abuse programs.

THE PRESENT STUDY

METHODS

Setting and Sample

Subjects for this study were opiate-addicted applicants for treatment at the Screening and Evaluation section of the Drug Dependence Unit (DDU) of the Connecticut Mental Health Center, associated with the Yale School of Medicine's Department of Psychiatry, in New Haven, Connecticut. This unit serves an urban and suburban population of approximately 400,000 people. The Screening section is the mode of entry for several modalities of treatment offered to clients with a problem of drug abuse. Following screening, clients may be referred to (1) an MM program; (2) an inpatient detoxification unit; (3) a naltrexone program; (4) a brief treatment and evaluation program; (5) a residential adult TC; or (6) a residential adolescent TC.

Timing of Interviews

In this study, we have attempted to locate and recontact 361 subjects who were first evaluated 2.5 years prior to the second interview. For the current presentation of preliminary findings, data have been derived from interviews completed on 197 of these subjects. Interviewing is continuing on the remainder of the sample.

Interviews

There were eight raters, with master's or bachelor's degrees and previous experience in psychiatric interviewing. Under the supervision of a psychiatrist, the raters received extensive training for use of the SADS and RDC. Training included observation of interviews and ratings, coratings, and interviewing with a supervisor present. In order to conduct interviews for this study, it was required that the rater complete five consecutive conjoint interviews on which RDC diagnoses were in complete agreement with those of a more experienced rater. After training, reliability was periodically spot-checked.

Of the eight interviewers, five participated in the original evaluation made when subjects were entering treatment. Three different interviewers and one of the original interviewers performed the evaluations in the follow-up study. Follow-up ratings were performed by different interviewers from those completing the initial ratings and were performed by interviewers who were blind to the initial diagnoses.

Assessments

Psychiatric Diagnosis.

Information for making diagnostic judgments was collected on the SADS-L (Endicott & Spitzer, 1978).

Based on the information collected on the SADS-L, the subjects were classified according to the RDC (Spitzer *et al.*, 1978). Diagnoses on the RDC are made both for the current time period and for lifetime, with the exception of several diagnoses that are considered lifetime diagnoses only, regardless of whether or not the subject is currently manifesting symptoms of the disorder. These lifetime-only disorders are the personality disorders (depressive, labile, schizotypal features, cyclothymic, Briquet syndrome, antisocial) and the bipolar disorders. Psychiatric disorders that cannot be categorized due to limitation of information or absence of diagnostic criteria are listed as "other." In the current study, diagnostic concordance was evaluated on the lifetime diagnoses.

Other Assessments.

Information regarding addicts' course of drug use, employment, social functioning, and legal involvement was obtained with a structured questionnaire. Overall functioning was assessed using the Global Assessment Scale (Endicott, Spitzer, Fleiss, & Cohen, 1976).

Severity of current drug-related problems was assessed using the ASI (McLellan *et al.*, 1980). The ASI is a structured clinical interview designed to evaluate the extent to which the addict has problems in the areas of medical health, employment, substance abuse, illegal behavior or legal problems, social functioning, and psychological symptoms. The interviewer obtains both objective information (e.g., number of hospitalizations) and subjective information (e.g., "How much have you been troubled by medical problems over the past 30 days?") in each problem area, and makes an overall rating on a 10-point scale (scale range of 0–9), the higher ratings indicating greater impairment. In addition, the interviewer rates the level of confidence he or she feels about the accuracy of the information obtained. Questions on the ASI cover two time periods: the previous 30 days and lifetime history.

Depressive symptoms were assessed using the Beck Depression Inventory (BDI; Beck & Beck, 1972). This is a 13-item self-report of depressive symptoms, which has been validated using comparisons with previously established methods of diagnosing depression and is reported to discriminate between anxiety and depression.

RESULTS

Outcome in Opiate Addicts 2.5 Years after Seeking Treatment

In Table 7-1, selected aspects of treatment outcome are presented. As shown there, only 42% of the addicts avoided being arrested after seeking treatment, but most of those arrested were arrested only once or twice. Regarding employment, 43% were employed most or all of the time. A substantial majority (63%) received more than 6 months of treatment, while 16% received evaluation only and 20% remained in treatment the entire time. At the follow-up evaluation, 74% had no significant depressive symptoms as measured by the BDI. Finally, there was a range of performance in regard to continued regular illicit opiate use, with 28% reporting no use after seeking treatment, 22% describing use less than half of the time, 31% describing use more than half of the

TABLE 7-1 Aspects of Treatment Outcome for 197 Opiate Addicts 2.5 Years Following Entrance into Treatment

Aspects	*n*	%
Legal: Number of arrests		
0	82	42
1–2	88	45
3 and up	27	13
Employment: Months employed		
None	45	23
1–15	67	34
16–29	39	20
30	46	23
Drug treatment: Months receiving any drug treatment		
0	32	16
1–6	42	21
7–18	60	31
18–29	24	12
30	39	20
Current depression: Beck Depression Inventory score		
0–8 (not depressed)	146	74
9–15 (mild–moderate)	35	18
16–27 (moderate–severe)	16	8
Opiate use: % time out of institutions using opiates		
0%	56	28
1–50%	44	22
51–99%	62	31
100%	35	19

time, and 19% describing continual opiate use during the entire 2.5 years. Thus, in most dimensions there was a considerable range of outcomes, with a substantial minority doing very well, the greatest number having moderate problems, and a substantial minority doing very poorly.

Factor Analysis of Treatment Outcome Measures in Opiate Addicts

In order to evaluate the predictive significance of diagnoses of psychiatric disorders at entrance to treatment, it is essential to define relevant outcome measures. To take into account a variety of aspects of treatment outcome, and to define a manageable number of outcome variables, we performed a factor analysis on 15 measures of clinical status and intervening behavior, assessed at the 2.5-year follow-up evaluation. The variables were these: number of arrests; number of months in prison; number of months employed; number of months in a drug treatment program; percentage of noninstitutionalized time using opiates; the mean Global Assessment Scale over 2.5 years; overall social functioning over 2.5 years; ASI medical problems; ASI employment problems; ASI substance abuse problems; ASI legal problems; ASI family/social problems; ASI psychiatric problems; and BDI. Using the principal-components method of factor analysis and the varimax rotation, five factors were obtained with eigenvalues of greater than 1, and these accounted for 62% of the variance in outcomes. The five factors were most heavily loaded on by the variables shown in Table 7-2, and were labeled "psychosocial," "treatment/abstinence for opiates," "medical disability," "current functioning," and "legal/employment."

Relationship between Psychiatric Disorders Diagnosed as Current at Intake and 2.5-Year Follow-up Evaluations

We compared rates of current diagnoses and overlap between current diagnoses made at entrance to treatment and the 2.5-year follow-up evaluation to answer the following questions: (1) Were the rates of current psychiatric disorders changing over time? (2) Of the addicts with current psychiatric disorders at the follow-up evaluation, how many represented new cases? and (3) Of the addicts with current psychiatric disorders at onset of treatment, how many would be improved and no longer in an episode at follow-up evaluation? The results of the cross-

TABLE 7-2   Factor Analysis of Treatment Outcome Measures in 197 Opiate Addicts

Principal components	Factor loading	% variance explained by factor
Factor 1: Psychosocial		22
Overall social functioning	.70	
Global Assessment Scale	.71	
Beck Depression Inventory	.55	
% time using opiates	.52	
Factor 2: Treatment/abstinence from opiates		16
Number of months of drug treatment	−.86	
% time using opiates	.57	
Factor 3: Medical disability		9
Number of months disabled	.85	
ASI medical problems	.80	
Factor 4: Current functioning		8
ASI family/social problems	.78	
ASI substance abuse problems	.75	
ASI psychiatric problems	.67	
ASI employment problems	.51	
Factor 5: Legal/employment		7
Months employed	−.77	
Months in prison	.69	
ASI legal problems	.51	

tabulation between RDC diagnoses made at treatment entrance and at the 2.5-year re-evaluation are presented in Table 7-3.

Comparison of Rates over Time.

Regarding the comparison of overall rates of current psychiatric disorders and the two evaluations, there was remarkable stability in all categories except major depression. At the 2.5-year follow-up evaluation, the rates of current major depression had dropped from 21% to 10%. For alcoholism, anxiety disorders, antisocial personality, and no diagnosis, the rates varied very little across the two evaluation periods.

New Cases at Follow-up Evaluation.

Regarding the development of new cases of disorders over the 2.5-year period following treatment seeking, there was considerable variability across diagnoses. Over all, the categories, 11% developed a disorder that had not been diagnosed at the initial rating. For alcoholism and depression, most of those currently in episodes at the follow-up interview had been previously diagnosed, and there was an incidence of only 3% of new cases for each of the disorders. For anxiety disorders, the overall rates were low, but the majority of those diagnosed at follow-up were new cases. Interestingly, for antisocial personality (which is considered to characterize an individual's stable, adult functioning), there was considerable fluctuation, with 13% newly meeting criteria for the disorder.

Improved and/or Lost Diagnoses.

The final question pertained to improvement in disorders over time. This varied considerably across disorders. For depression, the majority of those depressed at entrance to treatment were no longer in an episode at the follow-up evaluation. Conversely, there was neither a large increase nor a decrease in current alcoholism, with current alcoholics usually staying in that status at the follow-up evaluation. With anxiety disorders, approximately as many improved as developed new disorders. This pattern of approximately equal numbers losing and gaining a diagnosis was also found with antisocial personality; 14% of the sample no longer qualified for the diagnosis after having received it at onset of treatment. Across all categories, 15% were newly found to qualify for no diagnosis at the re-evaluation.

TABLE 7-3   Relationship of Psychiatric Disorders Present at Onset of Treatment to Disorders Present at 2.5-Year Follow-Up

Status of disorder	Major depression	Alcoholism	Any anxiety disorder	Antisocial personality	Any psychiatric disorder
Present at follow-up					
New cases	3%	3%	4%	13%	11%
Old cases (previously diagnosed)	7%	7%	2%	10%	69%
Not present at follow-up					
Present at intake	14%	3%	5%	14%	15%
Not present either time	76%	87%	89%	63%	5%
Total present at follow-up	10%	10%	6%	23%	80%
Total present at intake	21%	10%	7%	24%	84%

Correlates for Diagnosis and Diagnostic Change in Opiate
Addicts

What accounted for the diagnostic changes detected over time—either
in rates, as with the diagnosis of depression, or in those receiving the
diagnosis, as with antisocial personality, alcoholism, or any diagnosis?
Two kinds of changes took place: (1) Those with disorders at entrance
to treatment recovered or lost the diagnoses at follow-up; and (2) those
without a diagnosis at entrance to treatment received a new diagnosis
at outcome. To assist us in assessing the two kinds of changes, we had
ratings available from entrance into treatment and the 2.5-year follow-
up evaluation. Regarding recovery or loss of a diagnosis, it would be
important to detect features at entrance to treatment that might distinguish those who recovered from those who did not. At the 2.5-year
follow-up, it would be important to note whether those no longer in an
episode continued to have residual evidence of impairment from the
original episode. Regarding those who were newly diagnosed, it would
be of value to detect factors that could be noted at onset of treatment
that might predict the development of a disorder. At the follow-up
evaluation, it would be important to note whether new cases were distinguishable from those with previously diagnosed episodes.

To examine correlates and predictors of change in diagnostic status,
four groups were created in a 2 × 2 design for each diagnosis: those
who had a present disorder at both ratings; those who received a new
diagnosis at follow-up but had not met criteria previously; those whose
disorder was diagnosed at entrance to treatment but not at the follow-
up rating; and those who did not receive a current diagnosis at either
time. This analysis was only performed for the three most common
diagnoses: major depression, alcoholism, and antisocial personality. The
four groups were compared with two-way analyses of variance (ANO-
VAs), which yielded three types of comparisons: a main effect for presence of a disorder at entrance to treatment, indicating how those initially
diagnosed differed from those without an initial diagnosis; a main effect
for diagnosis at follow-up, indicating how those with a current diagnosis
at that time differed from those without that diagnosis; and an interaction effect, indicating whether those whose diagnostic status changed
were significantly different from those whose diagnostic status did not
change. The results of these ANOVAs are presented in Tables 7-4 and
7-5.

TABLE 7-4   Comparison of Longitudinal Diagnosis Status to Ratings Made at Intake

Diagnosis	BDI	ANOVA 1	2	3	MPI Neuroticism	ANOVA 1	2	3	SAS Mean	ANOVA 1	2	3
Major Depression		***	**	n.s.		**	n.s.	n.s.		**	n.s.	n.s.
Not present either time	7.5				23.7				2.1			
Newly diagnosed	12.0				21.1				2.3			
Diagnosis lost	14.0				34.2				2.6			
Present both times	17.4				37.0				2.7			
Alcoholism		n.s.	**	n.s.		n.s.	*	n.s.		***	n.s.	n.s.
Not present either time	61.0				26.3				1.3			
Newly diagnosed	85.4				32.7				0.0			
Diagnosis lost	48.3				20.3				11.8			
Present both times	78.2				30.0				12.1			
Antisocial personality		**	n.s.	n.s.		*	n.s.	n.s.		n.s.	n.s.	n.s.
Not present either time	2.6				2.2				26.7			
Newly diagnosed	3.1				2.2				25.7			
Diagnosis lost	3.9				2.3				26.1			
Present both times	3.7				2.4				26.9			

Note. Significance of two-way ANOVA: 1 = main effect for diagnosis at entrance; 2 = main effect for diagnosis at follow-up; 3 = interaction effect of Time 1 × Time 2.

*$p < .05$.

**$p < .01$.

***p .0001.

As shown in Table 7-4, the diagnoses made at entrance to treatment were significantly correlated with corresponding measures of symptoms and other aspects of functioning. Thus, currently depressed addicts had higher levels of BDI-rated depressive symptoms, Maudsley Personality Inventory (MPI)-rated neuroticism, and (SAS)-rated overall impairment in social functioning; currently alcoholic addicts had higher MAST scores (not displayed); and antisocial addicts had a heavier arrest record (not displayed) and poorer SAS-measured social functioning. There were no significant interactions, indicating that those who gained or lost diagnoses were not significantly distinguishable from each other. However, for major depression and alcoholism, there was some indication at entrance to treatment that those who would subsequently develop the diagnosis were similar to those already diagnosed. For example, the average BDI score of those who gained a diagnosis for depression was higher than that for those who never met criteria for the disorder and

TABLE 7-5 Comparison of Longitudinal Diagnosis Status to Other Aspects of Addiction Course at 2.5-Year Follow-Up

Diagnosis	Factor 1: Psychosocial[a] (range = -6.3-9.4)	ANOVA 1 2 3	Factor 2: Treatment/ abstinence[b] (range = -4.1-5.5)	ANOVA 1 2 3	Factor 3: Medical disability[a] (range = -2.6-7.7)	ANOVA 1 2 3	Factor 4: Current functioning[a] (range = -5.1-8.8)	ANOVA 1 2 3	Factor 5: Legal/ employment (range = -2.9-7.0)	ANOVA 1 2 3
Major depression		n.s. * n.s.		n.s. n.s. n.s.		n.s. *** **		n.s. ** **		n.s. n.s. n.s.
Not present at either time	-.51		-.10		-.40		-.53		-.08	
Newly diagnosed	1.64		1.24		2.74		2.96		-.14	
Diagnosis lost	.89		-.06		.26		.55		.14	
Present both times	1.11		-.21		.63		.78		-.26	
Antisocial personality		* *** n.s.		n.s. n.s. *		n.s. n.s. *		n.s. *** n.s		n.s. *** n.s.
Not present at either time	-.68		.14		.01		-.56		-.55	
Newly diagnosed	1.16		-.77		-.13		1.14		1.24	
Diagnosis lost	.04		-.25		-.61		-.26		.35	
Present both times	2.12		.50		.74		1.99		.85	

Alcoholism					
Not present at either time	-.18	.01	-.09	-.13	-.08
Newly diagnosed	1.24	-.60	-.09	1.10	.73
Diagnosis lost	.16	.02	.74	-.39	-.48
Present both times	.66	.51	.35	.69	.25
	n.s. n.s. n.s.	n.s. n.s. n.s.	n.s. n.s. n.s.	n.s. n.s. n.s.	n.s. n.s. n.s.

Note. Significance of two-way ANOVA: 1 = main effect for diagnosis at entrance; 2 = main effect for diagnosis at follow-up; 3 = interaction effect of Time 1 × Time 2.

[a]A higher score indicates poorer functioning.

[b]A higher score indicates better outcome.

*p < .05.

**p < .01.

***p < .0001.

nearly as high as for those who were in current episodes. With alcoholics, although the MAST scores of those who were to be newly diagnosed alcoholics were very low (mean = 0), they had a comparatively heavy history of opiate use and comparatively high scores on the MPI Neuroticism Scale, possibly indicating future difficulty in remaining drug-free even if opiates were given up.

Table 7-5 presents the comparison of diagnoses made at the two rating times to ratings of functioning during the 2.5 years following entrance to treatment. As shown there, the most significant associations were between diagnoses made at the follow-up evaluations and other ratings made at that time. Thus, current depression was related to the longitudinal psychosocial factor, the medical disability factor, and the current functioning factor. Likewise, antisocial personality at follow-up was related to the longitudinal psychosocial factor, the current functioning factor and the legal/employment factor. In contrast, current alcoholism was not correlated with any of the factors but it was significantly correlated with individual measures, such as the ASI substance abuse severity scale and the mean Global Assessment Scale rating for the follow-up period. Significant interactions were noted for major depression, such that newly diagnosed depressives had the highest ratings of medical disability and impaired current functioning. For antisocial addicts, significant interaction effects suggested that those who were diagnosed as antisocial at both rating periods were more likely to remain in treatment and off illicit opiates, and more likely to have medical disabilities.

Overall, the findings in Tables 7-4 and 7-5 appear to indicate that current RDC diagnoses most strongly reflect addicts' functioning during the time preceding the diagnostic interview, even when, as is the case with antisocial personality, the diagnosis is intended to characterize an individual's functioning over the entire adult lifetime.

Relationship of Diagnosis to Success in Treatment

In Table 7-6, we present treatment outcome as measured by the five outcome factors in clients in different diagnostic categories receiving three types of treatment: (1) MM, (2) TC, and (3) DF. To evaluate the effects of diagnosis on outcome, of treatment type on outcome, and of the interaction between diagnosis and treatment type, a two-way ANOVA was performed. This ANOVA yielded three types of comparisons:

a main effect across diagnostic types, a main effect across treatment types, and an interaction between diagnosis and treatment type. If significant diagnosis–program matching was taking place, significant interactions would be anticipated. The three types of effects are described separately.

Diagnosis Differences.

For each of the four categories evaluated, there was a significant relationship between diagnosis at onset of the treatment and treatment outcome measured 2.5 years later. Depressed opiate addicts had generally poorer psychosocial functioning over the 2.5 years, were more likely to have disabling medical problems, and had generally poorer current functioning at the 2.5-year follow-up evaluation. Antisocial addicts had poorer psychosocial functioning over the 2.5 years and greater legal/employment problems during the same time. Alcoholic addicts had poorer psychosocial functioning over the 2.5 years, were more likely to remain in treatment and abstinence from illicit opiates, and were more likely to have disabling medical problems. Addicts with no psychiatric diagnosis at onset of treatment had better psychosocial functioning over the 2.5 years and better general current functioning at the time of the 2.5-year follow-up interview.

Program Differences.

The major effect of the treatment types was on Factor 2, which combined retention in treatment and abstinence from illicit opiates. For this factor, the MM and TC treatments had significantly better outcome than the DF treatment.

Diagnosis–Program Interactions.

In regard to medical disability as an outcome, it was found that both depressed and alcoholic addicts in the TC treatment were more likely to be medically disabled during the follow-up period. In regard to abstinence from opiates and remaining in treatment, alcoholic addicts in the TC had more favorable outcome than those in other modalities and had more favorable outcomes than nonalcoholics in the TC.

TABLE 7-6 Relationship of Psychiatric Diagnosis to Treatment Outcome in Opiate Addicts in Different Treatment Settings

Diagnosis	Treatment type	Factor 1: Psychosocial[a] (range = -6.3–9.4)	ANOVA 1	ANOVA 2	ANOVA 3	Factor 2: Treatment/ abstinence[b] (range = -.41–5.5)	ANOVA 1	ANOVA 2	ANOVA 3	Factor 3: Medical disability[a] (range = -2.6–7.7)	ANOVA 1	ANOVA 2	ANOVA 3	Factor 4: Current functioning[a] (range = -5.1–8.8)	ANOVA 1	ANOVA 2	ANOVA 3	Factor 5: legal/ employment[a] (range = -2.9–7.0)	ANOVA 1	ANOVA 2	ANOVA 3
Major depression																					
Yes	MM	.18	*	n.s.		.72	*	***	n.s.	.22	**	n.s.	*	.41	**	n.s.		-.34	n.s.	n.s.	n.s.
	TC	1.38				1.27				1.02				.91				.12			
	DF	.13				-1.57				.24				.27				.42			
No	MM	-.03				.55				.06				.03				-.08			
	TC	.40				-.41				-1.04				-.60				.26			
	DF	-1.11				-1.67				-.78				-1.53				.02			
Antisocial personality																					
Yes	MM	.97	*	n.s.	n.s.	.63	n.s.	***	n.s.	-0.8	n.s.	n.s.	n.s.	.97	n.s.	n.s.	n.s.	.19	**	n.s.	n.s.
	TC	1.17				.72				.80				.81				.42			
	DF	.43				-1.80				-.68				-.26				1.50			
No	MM	-.36				.64				.21				.00				-.34			
	TC	.64				.09				-.62				-.31				.11			
	DF	-.84				-1.57				-.22				-.86				-.18			

	* n.s.n.s.	* *** *	* n.s. *	n.s.n.s.n.s.	n.s.n.s.n.s.
Alcoholism					
Yes MM	.02	.56	.00	.22	-.27
TC	1.45	1.49	.95	1.00	.27
DF	.55	-1.60	.22	-.48	.67
No MM	-.06	.67	.21	.26	-.21
TC	.34	-.56	-.99	-.66	.15
DF	-.84	-1.63	-.46	-.79	.07
	* n.s.n.s.	n.s. ***n.s.	n.s.n.s.n.s.	* n.s.n.s.	n.s.n.s.n.s.
No diagnosis					
Yes MM	-1.43	.20	-.68	-1.21	-.54
TC	.05	-.44	-.79	-1.43	.00
DF	-1.21	-1.97	-.72	-.81	.74
No MM	.16	.71	.27	.45	-.16
TC	.96	.44	-.06	.35	.25
DF	-.41	-1.55	-.23	-.71	.07

Note. Significance of two-way ANOVA: 1 = significance of diagnostic difference; 2 = significance of program difference; 3 = diagnosis × program interaction.

[a] A higher score indicates poorer functioning.

[b] A higher score indicates better outcome.

*p < .05.

**p < .01.

***p < .0001.

161

DISCUSSION

Course of Psychiatric Disorders in Opiate Addicts

In this follow-up re-evaluation of opiate addicts 2.5 years following entrance into treatment, we found that the sample remained heterogeneous regarding the presence or absence of psychiatric disorders, and that major depression, antisocial personality, and alcoholism remained the most commonly made additional diagnoses. Overall rates of disorders were highly stable, with rates of nonopiate diagnosis of 84% at entrance to treatment and 80% at 2.5-year follow-up. Within the overall stability of diagnostic rates, there was variability in patterns for the course of major depression, antisocial personality, and alcoholism, and these disorders are discussed separately.

Major Depression.

Major depression was the only disorder for which current rates dropped substantially at the follow-up re-evaluation, moving from 21% at entrance to treatment to 10% at the follow-up evaluation. This replicated previous findings showing improvement of depression at a 6-month follow-up, but did not represent an improvement beyond the 12% rate noted at that time (Rounsaville, Weissman, Wilber, Crits-Cristoph, & Kleber, 1982). Thus, entrance into treatment seems to represent a high point in an addict's tendency to become depressed, and being in a current episode may provide some of the incentive for seeking treatment. This point has been further reinforced by our comparison of addicts seeking treatment with untreated addicts in the community (Rounsaville & Kleber, 1985b). The rate of 10% depressed may represent a baseline level for this population, but this remains substantially higher than the rate of about 4% for current major depression as reported from community samples (Myers *et al.*, 1984; Weissman, Myers, & Harding, 1978). It is noteworthy that most of the addicts found to be currently depressed at the follow-up evaluation were those who had been found to be previously depressed at entrance to treatment, and that the rate of new cases was only 3%. Receiving a diagnosis of depression at either time period was most closely associated with other measures of current or recent social and psychological functioning, although those who went on to become new cases at follow-up had higher levels of depressive symptoms than continued nondepressives, even at entrance into treatment.

Antisocial Personality.

Although rates of antisocial personality were highly stable in our sample (24% at intake, 23% at follow-up), there was considerable fluctuation in the addicts who received the diagnosis: 14% lost the diagnosis at follow-up and 13% were newly diagnosed. In that the diagnosis is intended to characterize a personality style that endures through an individual's entire adult life, this finding may indicate either poor execution by the raters or a weakness of the RDC system for making this diagnosis with opiate addicts. However, it may also indicate some genuine recovery or worsening in antisocial tendencies in those whose diagnoses changed. In order to qualify for the RDC diagnosis of antisocial personality, an individual needs to fulfill four major criteria: (1) evidence of major role irresponsibility (e.g., failure to work when expected); (2) childhood history of antisocial behavior; (3) adult history of repeated antisocial acts; and (4) evidence of impaired ability to form sustained intimate relationships. At the initial evaluation, opiate addicts who received this diagnosis had evidence of greater legal involvement and poorer social functioning, while those who were later to receive the diagnosis were not different from those who did not receive the diagnosis in these areas. Moreover, at the follow-up evaluation, those who were newly diagnosed appeared to have had comparatively severe problems with longitudinal psychosocial functioning, current functioning, and arrests and employment during the intervening 2.5 years. Conversely, those who lost the diagnosis had comparatively low ratings in these areas, which are directly related to the first, third, and fourth criteria. Hence, the fluctuation in the individuals receiving the diagnosis appears to have followed from changes in behavior during the 2.5 years intervening between the two ratings. Moreover, it would appear that antisocial addicts are not unchangeable with treatment. Although those with an initial diagnosis of antisocial personality as a group had poorer psychosocial functioning and greater legal/employment problems during the subsequent 2.5 years, they did not differ from nonantisocial addicts in retention in treatment and abstinence from illicit opiates, and many were found no longer to qualify for an antisocial diagnosis at follow-up evaluation. This finding underscores the importance for using a multidimensional approach to evaluation of treatment outcome (Rounsaville, Weissman, & Kleber, 1982a), because it allows clinicians to assess the strengths as well as the weaknesses of a subpopulation of addicts. Although treatment outcomes for antisocial opiate addicts was poorer in some areas (e.g., legal/employment), it was not different in others (e.g., abstinence from illicit opiates). This suggests that the diagnosis and behavior of these addicts were not due just to the need to support a narcotic habit, since they continued to be impaired in the legal arena even when not using drugs. An old distinction between the "criminal addict" and "addict criminal" seems to be borne out.

Alcoholism.

The rates of current alcoholism were highly stable across evaluations. Moreover, the number of newly symptomatic alcoholics was small (3%) and exactly balanced by the number of those whose alcoholism improved. This finding replicates that of our 6-month follow-up evaluation, indicating no large increase in alcoholism (Rounsaville, Weissman, & Kleber, 1982b), and lends further evidence against the suggestion that opiate addicts do not resolve their drug problems but simply substitute alcoholism for opiate addiction. In our sample, 19% reported complete abstinence from illicit opiates during the 2.5 years following entrance into treatment, and 31% reported being opiate-free more than half of the time. However, there was no corresponding increase in alcoholism rates.

As with other diagnoses, concurrent evaluations made at the time of each rating support the diagnosis of current alcoholism. However, at entrance into treatment, it was also found that the small group who were later to develop alcoholism had a history of comparatively heavy opiate use and ratings of high neuroticism as measured by the MPI. Hence, the group who became alcoholic showed some indication of their vulnerability at entrance into treatment.

Evidence for Patient–Program Matching

As we have reported elsewhere, addicts with additional psychiatric disorders had poorer treatment outcome measured 2.5 years following entrance to treatment in selected areas (Rounsaville & Kleber, 1984). Thus, out of five areas of outcome assessed, addicts with major depression had poorer outcome in three; addicts with antisocial personality in two; addicts with alcoholism in two; and those with any diagnosis in two. Despite this, we found little evidence for patient–program matching. For example, depressed addicts and antisocial addicts had greater evidence of medical disability when they received TC treatment. However, this is more likely to be an indication of differential referral practices regarding residential treatment, with the most disabled individuals being offered this type of service. One suggestive finding was that alcoholic addicts were more likely to stay in treatment and be opiate-free in TC treatment and had a better outcome in this area than nonalcoholic addicts in TC treatment. This may correspond to the findings of McLellan, Woody, Evans, and O'Brien (1983) that abusers of both opiates and sedatives were more successfully treated in TC than in MM programs.

In evaluating our failure to find strong evidence for patient–program matching as related to addicts with different types of psychiatric disorders, the lack of random assignment must be taken into account. Because addicts are assigned to the different treatment modalities on the basis of preconceived clinical judgments about the treatment most likely to be of use to them, it is difficult to know whether our failure to find a matching effect represents the process or the presence of a selection bias. To illustrate how the selection bias might effect evidence for patient–program matching, one could consider the hypothesis that TC programs are better than MM programs for antisocial addicts. Even if this were true, if counselors assigned only the most severely antisocial cases to TCs, then their comparatively poor prognosis might mask the potential of TCs to change relatively moderate cases. To some extent, selection bias can be taken into account statistically by controlling for initial ratings of clinical severity. In the current study, on our partial sample, this more sophisticated analysis was not performed, although we intend to examine the issue more intensively with the complete data set.

CONCLUSION

By demonstrating the stability of rates and prognostic significance of psychiatric disorders, this follow-up evaluation of opiate addicts lends further weight to our previous research suggesting the importance of psychopathology in this population. However, it must be noted that the current report covers findings derived from only slightly more than half of the sample that is targeted to be evaluated. Those remaining to be tested include a mixture of those whose initial assessments came later and those who have proven more difficult to find because they have lost touch with treatment or relocated. Those who remain to be evaluated may be very different from the group on which the current report is based: Either they may have succeeded in giving up drugs to such an extent that they have had no further contact with treatment, or they may have continued drug abuse after giving up on treatment. Thus, definitive conclusions regarding the findings of this project must be postponed until the full sample is assessed.

ACKNOWLEDGMENT

Support for this work was provided by Grant No. RO1-DA03090 and Research Scientist Development Award No. KO2 DA00089 to Bruce J. Rounsaville from the National Institute on Drug Abuse.

REFERENCES

American Psychiatric Association. (1980). *Diagnostic and statistical manual of mental disorders* (3rd ed.). Washington, DC: Author.

Bale, R. N., Van Stone, W. W., Kuldau, J. N., Engelsing, T. M. J., Elashoff, R. M., & Zarcone, V. P. (1980). Therapeutic communities versus methadone maintenance: A prospective controlled study of narcotic addiction treatment. Design and one year follow-up. *Archives of General Psychiatry, 37,* 179–193.

Beck, A. T., & Beck, R. W. (1972). Screening depressed patients in family practices: A rapid technique. *Postgraduate Medicine, 52,* 1181–1185.

Beck, A. T., Ward, C. H., Mendelson, M., Mock, J. E., & Erbaugh, J. K. (1962). Reliability of psychiatric diagnosis: A study of consistency in clinical judgments and ratings. *American Journal of Psychiatry, 119,* 351–357.

Blatt, S. J., McDonald, C., Sugarman, A., & Wilbur, C. (1984). Psychodynamic theories of opiate addiction: New directions for research. *Clinical Psychology Review, 4,* 159–189.

Brill, L. (1977). The treatment of drug abuse: Evolution of a perspective. *American Journal of Psychiatry, 134,* 157–160.

Craig, R. J. (1979a). Personality characteristics of heroin addicts: A review of the empirical literature with critique—Part I. *International Journal of the Addictions, 14,* 513–532.

Craig, R. J. (1979b). Personality characteristics of heroin addicts: A review of the empirical literature with critique—Part II. *International Journal of the Addictions, 14,* 607–626.

Endicott, J., & Spitzer, R. L. (1978). A diagnostic interview: The Schedule for Affective Disorders and Schizophrenia. *Archives of General Psychiatry, 37,* 837–844.

Endicott, J., Spitzer, R. L., Fleiss, J. L., & Cohen, J. (1976). The Global Assessment Scale: A procedure for measuring overall severity of psychiatric disorder. *Archives of General Psychiatry, 33,* 766–771.

Feighner, J. P., Robins, E., & Guze, S. B. (1972). Diagnostic criteria for use in psychiatric research. *Archives of General Psychiatry, 26*, 57–71.

Khantzian, E. J. (1976). The ego, the self and opiate addiction: Theoretical and treatment considerations. *International Review of Psychoanalysis, 5*, 189–198.

Krystal, H., & Raskin, H. A. (1970). *Drug dependence aspects of ego function.* Detroit: Wayne State University Press.

Lettieri, D. J., Sayers, M., & Pearson, H. W. (1980). *Theories on drug abuse* (National Institute on Drug Abuse Research Monograph 30, DHHS Publication No. ADM 80-96). Rockville, MD: U.S. Government Printing Office.

McLellan, A. T., Luborsky, L., O'Brien, C. P., & Woody, G. E. (1980). An improved diagnostic evaluation instrument for substance abuse patients: The Addiction Severity Index. *Journal of Nervous and Mental Disease, 168*, 26–33.

McLellan, A. T., Luborsky, L., Woody, G. E., O'Brien, C. P., & Druley, K. A. (1983). Predicting response to alcohol and drug abuse treatments: Role of psychiatric severity. *Archives of General Psychiatry, 40*, 620–625.

McLellan, A. T., Woody, G. E., Evans, B., & O'Brien, C. P. (1983). Methadone versus therapeutic community in treatment of mixed abusers: Role of psychiatric symptoms. *Annals of the New York Academy of Sciences, 398*, 104–126.

Myers, J. K., Weissman, M. M., Tischler, G. L., Leaf, P. J., Overschel, H., Anthony, J. C., Boyd, J. H., Burke, J. D., Kramer, M., & Stoltzman, R. (1984). Six month prevalence of psychiatric disorders in three communities: 1980–1982. *Archives of General Psychiatry, 41*, 959–967.

Nyswander, M., Winick, C., Bernstein, A., Brill, I., & Kaufer, G. (1958). The treatment of drug addicts as voluntary outpatients: A progress report. *American Journal of Orthopsychiatry, 28*, 714–727.

Robins, L. N., Helzer, J. E., Croughan, J., & Ratcliff, K. S. (1981). The NIMH Diagnostic Interview Schedule: Its history, characteristics, and validity. *Archives of General Psychiatry, 38*, 381–389.

Rounsaville, B. J., Cacciola, J., Weissman, M. M., & Kleber, H. D. (1981). Diagnostic concordance in a follow-up of opiate addicts. *Journal of Psychiatric Research, 16*, 191–201.

Rounsaville, B. J., Eyre, S., Weissman, M. M., & Kleber, H. D. (1983). The antisocial opiate addict. *Advances in Alcohol and Substance Abuse, 2*(4), 29–42.

Rounsaville, B. J., & Kleber, H. D. (1984). Psychiatric disorders and the course of opiate addictions: Preliminary findings on predictive significance and diagnostic stability. In S. M. Mirin (Ed.), *Substance abuse and psychopathology* (pp. 133–151). Washington, DC: American Psychiatric Press.

Rounsaville, B. J., & Kleber, H. D. (1985a). Psychotherapy/counseling for opiate addicts: Strategies for use in different treatment settings. *International Journal of the Addictions, 20*, 869–896.

Rounsaville, B. J., & Kleber, H. D. (1985b). Untreated opiate addicts: How do they differ from those seeking treatment? *Archives of General Psychiatry, 42*, 1072–1077.

Rounsaville, B. J., Rosenberger, P. H., Wilber, C. H., Weissman, M. M., & Kleber, H. D. (1980). A comparison of the SADS/RDC and the DSM-III: Diagnosing drug abusers. *Journal of Nervous and Mental Disease, 168*, 90–97.

Rounsaville, B. J., Weissman, M. M., & Kleber, H. D. (1982a). Predictors of treatment outcome in opiate addicts: Evidence for the multidimensionality of addicts' problems. *Comprehensive Psychiatry, 23*, 462–478.

Rounsaville, B. J., Weissman, M. M., & Kleber, H. D. (1982b). The significance of alcoholism in treated opiate addicts. *Journal of Nervous and Mental Disease, 170*, 479–488.

Rounsaville, B. J., Weissman, M. M., & Kleber, H. D. (1983). An evaluation of depression in opiate addicts. *Research in Community and Mental Health, 3*, 257–289.

Rounsaville, B. J., Weissman, M. M., Kleber, H. D., & Wilber, C. H. (1982). Heterogeneity of psychiatric diagnosis in treated opiate addicts. *Archives of General Psychiatry, 39*, 161–166.

Rounsaville, B. J., Weissman, M. M., Wilber, C. H., Crits-Cristoph, K., & Kleber, H. D. (1982). Diagnosis and symptoms of depression in opiate addicts: Course and relationship to treatment outcome. *Archives of General Psychiatry, 39*, 151–156.

Simpson, D. D., & Savage, L. J. (1981–1982). Client types in different drug abuse treatments: Comparisons of follow-up outcomes. *American Journal of Drug and Alcohol Abuse, 8*, 401–418.

Spitzer, R. L., Endicott, J., & Robins, E. (1978). Research Diagnostic Criteria: Rationale and reliability. *Archives of General Psychiatry, 35*, 773–782.

Spitzer, R. L., & Fleiss, J. L. (1974). A re-analysis of the reliability of psychiatric diagnosis. *British Journal of Psychiatry, 125*, 341–350.

Weissman, M. M., & Klerman, G. L. (1978). Epidemiology of mental disorders: Emerging trends in the United States. *Archives of General Psychiatry, 35*, 705–712.

Weissman, M. M., Myers, J. K., & Harding, P. S. (1978). Psychiatric disorders in a United States urban community: 1975–1976. *American Journal of Psychiatry, 135*, 459–462.

Woody, G. E., Luborsky, L., McLellan, A. T., O'Brien, C. P., Beck, A. T., Blaine, J., Herman, I., & Hole, A. (1983). Psychotherapy for opiate addicts: Does it help? *Archives of General Psychiatry, 40*, 639–645.

Yorke, C. (1970). A critical review of some psychoanalytic literature on drug addiction. *British Journal of Medical Psychology, 43*, 141–159.

8

Psychotherapy as an Adjunct to Methadone Treatment

GEORGE E. WOODY
LESTER LUBORSKY
A. THOMAS MCLELLAN
CHARLES P. O'BRIEN

OVERVIEW OF PSYCHIATRIC DISORDERS OF METHADONE-MAINTAINED ADDICTS

The efficacy of psychotherapy for addiction, and the relationship of psychiatric illness to addiction, have both been topics of long-standing interest to clinicians. These two topics are closely related, and it is difficult to discuss the role of psychotherapy in treating methadone-maintained addicts without first commenting on the kinds of psychiatric disorders that they experience. This is the case because psychotherapy generally addresses the addiction indirectly, via the associated or underlying psychiatric disorders. Thus, while psychopathology in addictive disorders is discussed throughout this volume, a brief overview of the psychiatric disorders seen in methadone-maintained addicts is offered in this chapter to provide an introduction to the specific indications for psychotherapy in the methadone-maintained patient.

Some writers have questioned whether the psychiatric illnesses found in addicts are caused by the addiction, precede it, or occur concomitantly with but independently from it. Probably what we observe by the time the patient appears for treatment is the result of a complex of biological and situational factors; some exist prior to the drug abuse, others develop as a consequence of the addiction, and still others are independent phenomena. Most of the psychiatric disorders observed in addicts occur after the addiction begins and are by definition secondary disorders. It is very difficult to determine what proportion of these disorders may have emerged in the absence of the addiction, or which were present before it. Many addicts begin compulsive drug use in their late teens or early 20s, and this early age of onset further complicates the primary–secondary issue. Nevertheless, the fact remains that addicts have many psychiatric disorders, and that these disorders resemble the psychiatric illnesses that are seen in nonaddicts. As described elsewhere in this volume by Rounsaville and Kleber, the most prevalent forms of psychiatric disorder found in their studies of opioid addicts in New Haven have been affective disorders, antisocial personality disorder, and alcoholism (Rounsaville; Weissman, Kleber, & Wilber, 1982).

The drugs that are self-administered by addicts are some of the most potent mood-altering drugs available, and these drugs directly affect the patients' psychological status. The drugs used may either reduce, exacerbate, or cause concurrent psychiatric disorders. The influence that drugs play on psychopathology appears to be a consequence of their pharmacological effects. For example, stimulants often cause paranoid disorders; sedative–hypnotics may cause depression; and opiates have antianxiety and antipsychotic properties (McLellan, Woody, & O'Brien, 1979). As Khantzian and Schneider (this volume) and others (Khantzian, Mack, & Schatzberg, 1974; Wurmser, 1979) describe, some types of drug abuse may begin or be continued as a form of self-medication to treat anxiety, depression, or other psychiatric disorders. Descriptions of narcotic use to relieve depression and other types of psychic distress are found in psychoanalytic case studies (Hartmann, 1969) and in literary accounts, such as De Quincey's *Confessions of an English Opium-Eater* (1821/1907).

> I was necessarily ignorant of the whole art and mystery of opium-taking; and what I took I took under every disadvantage. But I took it; and in an hour, Oh heavens! what a revulsion! what a resurrection, from its lowest depths of the inner spirit! what an apocalypse of the world within me. That my pains have vanished was now a trifle in my eyes; this negative effect was swallowed up on the immensity of those positive effects which had opened before me, in the abyss of divine enjoyment thus suddenly revealed. Here was a panacea, for all human woes; here was the secret of happiness, about which philosophers had disputed for so many ages, at

once discovered; happiness might now be bought for a penny, and carried in the waistcoat pocket; portable ecstasies might be hand corked up in a pint-bottle; and peace of mind could be sent down by the mail. (p. 179)

This description is interesting, particularly since it was written in the 19th century but yet reflects some present-day observations and theories. It appears to picture drug use as an attempt to achieve euphoria, as well as to relieve depression, anxiety, and other dysphoric experiences. This interface between mood states and drugs provides a theoretical basis for the use of psychotherapy as an adjunct to methadone treatment.

Theoretically, depression, anxiety/stress, and some of the other psychiatric problems that are described by De Quincey and that have been documented to exist in clinical psychiatric studies of addicts should respond to psychotherapy, as well as to the potent mind-altering drugs that patients regularly self-administer. Successful treatment of these problems by psychological means may improve the overall effectiveness of drug treatment programs, since the psychiatric problems are, in many cases, related to the drug use and also to other disabilities such as vocational performance (McLellan, Luborsky, Woody, Druley, & O'Brien, 1983).

REVIEW OF THE LITERATURE AND DESCRIPTION OF TREATMENT TYPES

Early Clinical Reports about Psychotherapy with Addicts

One of the first studies that examined the efficacy of professional psychotherapy with addicts was that done by Nyswander, Winick, Bernstein, Brill, and Kaufer, reported in 1958. This study advertised professional psychotherapy as being available to any interested addicts in New York City. Only 70 persons responded by contacting the clinic, and only 13 of these became regularly engaged in therapy. These engaged patients had an average of 35 appointments with psychotherapists over a period of approximately 1 year. They were compared to a control group of 22 minimally treated patients who kept an average of 8 appointments. Although the engaged patients showed more benefits than the minimally treated patients, the investigators concluded that the role of psychotherapy was minimal, because so few applied for it and because only a small proportion of those who applied actually became engaged. This study, taken together with case reports that emphasized the extreme difficulties encountered when trying to treat addicts with psychotherapy (Fenichel, 1945; Glover, 1932; Rado, 1933; Savitt, 1963), seems to have influenced the way many clinicians and researchers have conceived of the role that psychotherapy may play in addiction treatment programs. Essentially, these collective experiences appear to have stimulated efforts to look elsewhere for effective treatments.

THE INTRODUCTION OF METHADONE MAINTENANCE AND PARAPROFESSIONAL DRUG COUNSELING

One of the most significant results of the search for other treatments was the development of methadone maintenance. This occurred shortly after the publication of Nyswander *et al.*'s study of psychotherapy, and it introduced a new era in drug abuse treatment. This era was marked by a rapid expansion of drug treatment programs, and it saw the emergence of many ideas and debates regarding how best to treat addicts within this newly developed and greatly expanded treatment network. It was marked by the involvement of many "helpers" with opiate addicts. In terms of their backgrounds, they spanned a wide range, from highly trained medical professionals such as psychiatrists and psychiatric nurses, to social workers, minimally trained paraprofessionals, and ex-addicts. Most of the day-to-day clinical contact with addicts who were treated with methadone was carried out by the paraprofessionals. With the assistance of medical supervision, and the guidance of regulatory agencies such as the Food and Drug Administration and the Drug Enforcement Administration, a specific form of psychological treatment was developed that has become known as "drug counseling" (DC). This is currently the standard form of psychological treatment available in most methadone programs.

DESCRIPTION OF PARAPROFESSIONAL DC

DC is a goal-directed therapy with special emphasis on the delivery of concrete services. The counselor is the person at the clinic who helps the patient identify specific problems in the areas of drug use, physical health, interpersonal relationships, family interaction, and vocational or educational goals. As problems are identified, the counselor, with the assistance of a supervisor, begins to develop a treatment plan that is reviewed on a regular basis. This plan provides some structure for the content of the counseling sessions.

In addition, the counselor monitors the patient's progress and compliance with the treatment plan. For example, he or she checks the patient's weekly drug screening urinalysis to determine patterns of illicit drug use. Likewise, he or she monitors the patient's progress and the dosage of methadone; in this way, the counselor is able to determine the advisability of detoxification or of medication increases or decreases. The counselor also monitors the patient's vocational rehabilitation efforts.

DC also entails liaison functions. The counselor is frequently asked to intervene between the patient and numerous legal and community service agencies, such as public assistance, probation, the courts, and so on. He or she also keeps the patient informed of program rules, services, privileges, and policy changes. Similarly, the counselor provides the initial screening interviews when the patient is asking to be medicated for complaints such as insomnia, depression, or anxiety.

A final aspect of DC is active and direct intervention in crisis situations such as the development of extreme rage, acute depression, or loss of a place to live. Here the counselor often implements a combination of environmental manipulation (e.g., hospitalization, talking with the family to encourage limit setting), suppression of affect by tranquilization, and helping the patient initiate positive action that will reduce the conflict.

The counselor is also likely to be involved in discussing the rules of the larger program. For example, the rules encourage patients to maintain clean urines and remain in school or employment by rewarding those who are eligible with a reduced schedule of medication visits to the clinic. They discourage antisocial or aggressive behavior by providing for suspension of patients who deal in drugs, fight, or directly threaten staff members.

A typical counseling situation might begin when a counselor meets with a patient, reviews the clinic chart, and observes that the urine tests show opiates. The counselor questions the patient regarding what has been happening and how he or she is feeling. The patient says that the methadone dose is not yet high enough, that he or she is having withdrawal symptoms beginning late in the day, and that he or she has been using heroin. The counselor then arranges for the patient to meet with a program physician, who evaluates the need for an increase in methadone dose. At the same time, the patient mentions that he or she has a court appearance in 2 weeks and requests a note for the judge saying that he or she is participating in a treatment program. The counselor has the patient sign a release of information form, prepares a note, and then gives it to the patient to take to his or her lawyer. These techniques and duties have been summarized in a counseling manual (Woody, Stockdale, & Hargrove, 1977).

As seen in this brief description of paraprofessional counseling, the focus is primarily external. This external focus differentiates DC from psychotherapy. Psychotherapy attempts to identify and alter internal psychic processes that are creating or contributing to difficulties that the patient is experiencing. There are many types of psychotherapy currently in use. Two that are widely used, and with which we are especially familiar, are supportive–expressive (SE) and cognitive–behavioral (CB) therapy.

DESCRIPTION OF TWO COMMON FORMS OF PROFESSIONAL PSYCHOTHERAPY: SE AND CB

SE is an analytically oriented, focal psychotherapy modeled after that described by Malan (1963) and Sifneos (1972) and after a form of therapy used for many years at the Menninger Foundation in Topeka, Kansas (Wallerstein, Robbins, Sargent, & Luborsky, 1956). Its techniques have been summarized in a treatment manual (Luborsky, 1976). The two main types of techniques used are supportive and expressive, as the name implies. The expressive techniques aim to help the patient identify and work through problematic relationship themes. The therapist identifies these (transference) themes via the relationship with the patient and via parallels with what the patient says about other important relationships, such as those with the parents, spouse, or other family members. Special attention is paid to the meanings that the patient attaches to the drug dependence. For example, some patients may deny having any problems. They keep appointments with their therapists out of "curiosity" or because they think they "ought to," but they maintain that things are going well in spite of unemployment, an unstable living situation, or the like. When they have particular problems—say, with their spouses—they may refuse to discuss them, miss several sessions, and use drugs; they may then ask their counselors to have their methadone dose increased. In such cases, the therapists identify the patients' denial as it appears in the transference, in the problematic relationships, and in the drug use. The therapists work with the patients, aiming to diminish the denial and to examine the way the patients feel and respond to these situations. If the therapists are successful, treatment should help these patients address their problems more directly, and thus increase the likelihood of finding better solutions to life's problems than using drugs.

CB therapy is an active, directive, time-limited system of psychotherapy that focuses on uncovering and understanding the relationship and influence of automatic thoughts and underlying assumptions on problematic feelings and behaviors. The therapy, developed by Aaron T. Beck, has been shown to be effective for treating certain kinds of depression (Beck, 1976). Beck and his colleagues have found that depressed patients subscribe to a system of negatively biased thoughts, attitudes, and beliefs that lead to a consistently distorted perception of themselves (e.g., as worthless), the future (e.g., as hopeless), and the world around them (e.g., as dangerous). Beck has found that significant improvement in mood can result when a patient learns systematically to correct these exaggerated thoughts so that they more accurately reflect reality. For example, treatment may begin with a person who is withdrawn and depressed, and who continually feels worthless and unable to succeed at anything. A CB therapist, once he or she identifies these specific negative beliefs and the more general dysfunctional underlying assumptions from which they derive, develops a cognitive formulation of the patient and his problems. The therapist and the patient then collaborate to correct these beliefs by applying a variety of techniques that have as their goal a more accurate perception of objective reality. Techniques used include recording and analyzing specific automatic thoughts, running experiments to test them out, role playing, and a variety of other cognitive and behavioral methods.

During CB therapy with addicts, for example, some patients might tell their therapists that they cannot feel normal without drugs and that therefore they never intend to stop using them. The therapists and patients together test this belief by examining existing evidence (e.g., experiences in which the patients actually felt good without using illicit substances) and generating new evidence (e.g., having the patient's attend a party while not under the influence of drugs). Similar procedures are used for a variety of distorted beliefs, so that by the end of a successful course of therapy, the patients can themselves correct inaccurate beliefs and substitute a number of more functional thoughts and constructive coping mechanisms. This treatment has been described in many publications, including a CB treatment manual that has been adapted for use with opiate addicts (Beck & Emery, 1977).

RE-EMERGENCE OF INTEREST IN PROFESSIONAL PSYCHOTHERAPY WITH ADDICTS

The era that began with the development of methadone maintenance saw the re-emergence of thinking regarding the possible contribution of psychopathology to addiction, and of the positive influence that professional psychotherapy might contribute to outcome. This new emphasis on the importance of psychiatric factors and the possible role that psychotherapy might play as an adjunct to methadone treatment has been best described by Wurmser (1979) and Khantzian and colleagues (Khantzian *et al.*, 1974; see also chapter by Khantzian & Schneider, this volume). Both Wurmser and Khantzian's group spent considerable time treating opiate addicts, with many of their patients being on methadone. They and others observed that many patients had significant psychiatric disorders (a finding later confirmed by Rounsaville and Kleber and others, as described in this volume); that these disorders contributed to their drug use; and, furthermore, that some of these very disturbed patients were being treated primarily by paraprofessional counselors who, by definition, have relatively little formal training in psychiatric diagnosis and treatment. These observations raised questions about the staffing patterns that were being used in methadone programs. Prominent among the questions raised were these: How well do the methadone treatment programs really work? Does DC add anything to methadone maintenance alone? And, if the methadone programs are reasonably effective, can highly trained professionals add anything to paraprofessional counseling?

During this period, a number of clinical studies were completed that re-examined the efficacy of professional psychotherapy with addicts;

TABLE 8-1 Box Scores of Psychotherapy Studies with Random Assignment and Controls

Authors	Therapy type	Result
Willett, 1973 (*n* = 18)	Group	Rx better
LaRosa, Lipsius, & LaRosa, 1974 (*n* = 42)	Individual	Rx better
Abrams, 1979 (*n* = 15)	Group	Rx better
Connett, 1980 (*n* = 19)	Group	No difference
Resnick, Washton, Stone-Washton, 1981 (*n* = 66)	Individual	Rx better
Stanton, Todd, and Associates, 1982 (*n* = 42)	Family	Rx better
Rounsaville, Glazer, Wilber, *et al.*, 1983 (*n* = 72)	Individual	No difference
Woody *et al.*, 1983 (*n* = 110)	Individual	Rx better

these are summarized in Table 8-1. All the studies except that of Resnick, Washton, Stone-Washton, (1981) (who treated naltrexone patients) were done with methadone-maintained addicts. All of these studies employed random assignment, and six of the eight showed that patients receiving professional psychotherapy did better than those receiving counseling alone. Five of these studies had a number of methodological problems. Among the problems were small sample size, lack of definition of the psychopathology being treated, lack of definition of the treatments provided, lack of documentation that the proposed treatments were delivered as intended, and use of a very narrow range of outcome measures. Three of the studies—those done by Stanton, Todd, and Associates (1982), Rounsaville, Glazer, Wilber, Weissman & Kleber *et al.* (1983), and Woody *et al.* (1983)—avoided many of the design problems that were found in the earlier studies.

Stanton *et al.*'s study examined the efficacy of structural family therapy when added to routine counseling services. It was the first well-designed study of a specific psychotherapy with an addict population. The treatment methods used were well described, several control groups were employed, and a moderately broad range of outcome measures was used. This study found good evidence for the efficacy of structural family therapy with this population. The results were published in several papers and also in a book (Stanton *et al.*, 1982).

Though Stanton *et al.*'s study explored the efficacy of one specific type of therapy for methadone-maintained addicts, it did not examine the efficacy of any of the more widely used forms of individual psychotherapy, such as those described earlier. These questions were addressed in subsequent years by two major studies, which, taken together, are by far the best-designed and most comprehensive ever done to examine the efficacy of psychotherapy for methadone-maintained opiate addicts. Each project had a diagnostic section in addition to a psychotherapy study. The results of the diagnostic studies were generally consistent and have been summarized earlier in the chapter.

The two psychotherapy studies, however, had differing results. The study completed by Rounsaville *et al.* (1983) at the New Haven–Yale program examined interpersonal psychotherapy when added to routine counseling and group therapy services in a methadone treatment program. No differences in outcome were found between the two groups, though both showed improvement. This study was characterized by a low rate of participation, as well as by a high dropout rate by those patients who did agree to participate. The study done by Woody *et al.* (1983) at the Philadelphia Veterans Administration (VA) Medical Center–University of Pennsylvania (hereafter referred to as the VA–Penn study) also found that all treatment groups improved, but that the patients who received additional psychotherapy made more gains than did those in the counseling alone group. This study engaged a significantly larger proportion of the methadone clinic population than the New Haven–Yale study, and also had a lower dropout rate.

A somewhat related project was done at about the same time by Herrington, Benzer, Jacobson, and Harkins (1983) in Wisconsin. This work examined the progress and outcome of 40 physicians enrolled in an alcohol and drug dependence treatment program. This report was not a prospective study, and it did not use methadone maintenance. It also did not employ random assignment or a control group, but it did obtain follow-up on a reasonably large number of subjects for an extended period of time (27 subjects were followed up for 1 to 2 or more years), and it carefully documented and described the various aspects of the treatment program. Several factors were felt by the authors to be important for recovery. First was consistent participation in the overall program, which was a 2-year, three-phase program that started with inpatient detoxification and then moved into outpatient and re-entry activities. Also included were regular urine testing, prompt return to meaningful employment, and family involvement in the patients' treatment and individual psychotherapy. This report was very positive in its evaluation of psychotherapy, as reflected in the following statement:

> Insight oriented and expressive supportive psychotherapy effectively augments and enhances the other elements of treatment. Although initially resistant to psychotherapy, many of our patients later acknowledged it to be one of the most significant events in their recovery process. (Herrington *et al.*, 1983, p. 2256)

THE VA–PENN STUDY

The VA–Penn study found similarly positive results, and much of the remainder of this chapter consists of a presentation of data from that project. This approach is taken because the VA–Penn study is the largest and most comprehensive project done to date that examines the efficacy of professional psychotherapy when used as an adjunct to methadone treatment. The number of subjects (all male veterans) who were studied in this project provides data not only on the general question of overall efficacy, but also on the question of who among this population might be best served by the additional psychotherapy.

TREATMENTS AND THERAPISTS

The treatments studied were DC alone, DC plus SE, and DC plus CB, as described earlier in this chapter. The major purpose was to see whether there is any evidence that professional psychotherapy adds anything to paraprofessional counseling services for methadone-maintained patients.

Each treatment was described in a manual, and these manuals were used for training and ongoing supervision of counselors and therapists. The entire study took approximately 4½ years to complete. The psychotherapy was offered for 6 months, and patients were evaluated at intake, at 1 month, at 7 months (1 month after therapy ended), and at 1 year. Eighteen counselors and nine therapists participated. There were five SE and four CB therapists. All therapists except two had either an MD or a PhD and at least 2 years of clinical experience since completing training. One CB therapist had no formal degree, but had 7 years' experience as a CB therapist. One SE therapist was completing a PhD program, but had 3 years of clinical experience during one portion of training. All therapists had some experience with addicts or alcoholics, and five had worked in either alcohol or other drug abuse treatment programs for 1 or more years. Care was taken in selecting only therapists who were both experienced in their particular techniques and also interested in treating drug addicts. The therapists were chosen by the supervisor of each therapy, who was Lester Luborsky for the SE therapists and Aaron T. Beck for the CB therapists. The DC counselors had worked in the drug treatment program for an average of 3 years and were familiar with counseling techniques and clinic procedures. About half had bachelor's degrees, and most had learned counseling procedures via on-the-job training. Some had also been trained as hospital corpsmen while on military duty.

DESIGN OF THE STUDY

The design of the study was as follows: The project was fully described to prospective patients, and those who were interested were randomly assigned to one of the three treatment conditions upon signing the consent form and completing an extensive intake procedure. Patients were given a brief explanation of the kind of treatment they would receive after random assignment, in the manner described by Orne and Wender (1968). This explanation was given on the assumption that most patients had little knowledge of what was expected in psychotherapy and that a brief explanation would facilitate the treatment process. Following this, the principal investigator or a member of the research staff introduced each patient to his therapist or counselor and encouraged him to keep all the scheduled appointments.

Patients who completed the intake procedure were required to complete three appointments with their counselor and an additional three appointments with their therapist (if they were assigned to SE or CB). These initial appointments had to be completed within the first 6 weeks; if patients failed to complete the appointments, they were considered nonengaged and dropped from the study. Approximately 80% of patients who completed intake kept these initial appointments. The demographic status of the patients in each of the treatment groups is shown in Table 8-2, and a summary of their lifetime psychiatric diagnoses (based on the Research Diagnostic Criteria [RDC]) is given in Table 8-3.

TABLE 8-2   Background Status of 110 Male Opiate-Dependent Psychotherapy Subjects

Demographic variables	Treatment group		
	SE ($n = 32$)	CB ($n = 39$)	DC ($n = 39$)
Age (years)	31 + 6	29 + 6	29 + 5
Race (%)			
Black	59	67	59
White	41	33	41
Education (years)	12	13	12
Marital status (%)			
Married	37	28	36
Divorced, separated*	25	49	28
Never married	38	23	36
Living with parents	28	31	28
Living alone*	12	13	23
Criminal convictions	4	3	3
Months incarcerated	13	14	11
Problem drinking (years)	1	2	2
Regular drug use (years)			
Heroin*	7	10	11
Methadone hydrochloride	2	2	2
Depressants	2	2	2
Stimulants	2	1	1
Prior drug treatments	4	3	4

*$p < .01$ by analysis of variance and paired t test.

RESULTS

Overall Results

The overall results have been published in detail elsewhere (Woody *et al.*, 1983) and are summarized as follows: Of patients meeting the study criteria, 60% expressed an interest in participating, and 60% of these actually became engaged. Of 150 patients who started in the project, 121 completed the intake procedure and their initial appointments. Complete 7-month data were available on 110 of these subjects. Patients receiving the additional psychotherapy showed more and greater gains then those receiving DC alone, and with less use of prescribed and self-administered medications.

This result was interesting, but did not readily lend itself to any practical application. Essentially, we could not imagine a situation where all interested methadone-maintained opiate addicts might be given ad-

TABLE 8-3 Lifetime Research Diagnostic Criteria Diagnoses

	Treatment group						
Diagnosis	SE		CB		DC		Total
Drug use disorder	32	(100)	39	(100)	39	(100)	110	(100)
Affective disorders							
Major depressive disorder	13	(41)	14	(36)	20	(51)	47	(43)
Minor depressive disorder*	0	(0)	1	(3)	7	(18)	8	(7)
Intermittent depressive disorder	7	(22)	3	(7)	3	(7)	13	(12)
Labile personality	2	(6)	6	(15)	2	(5)	10	(9)
Cyclothymic personality	5	(16)	3	(8)	3	(8)	11	(10)
Hypomanic disorder**	7	(23)	2	(5)	12	(30)	21	(19)
Manic disorder	0	(0)	0	(0)	1	(3)	1	(1)
Bipolar II	4	(13)	1	(3)	6	(15)	11	(10)
Anxiety disorders							
Generalized anxiety	1	(3)	1	(3)	1	(3)	3	(3)
Panic disorder	0	(0)	0	(0)	0	(0)	0	(0)
Phobic disorder	3	(9)	0	(0)	1	(3)	4	(4)
Obsessive–compulsive disorder	1	(3)	0	(0)	1	(3)	2	(2)
Alcoholism	7	(22)	9	(24)	10	(26)	26	(24)
Antisocial personality	6	(19)	6	(15)	4	(10)	16	(15)
Schizotypal features	2	(6)	1	(3)	3	(8)	6	(6)
Other psychiatric disorders	1	(3)	0	(0)	0	(0)	1	(1)

Note. Numbers outside parentheses represent n's; numbers inside parentheses are percentages.

*$p < .05$.

**$p < .01$ by analysis of variance.

ditional professional psychotherapy. We undertook further analyses to see whether we could identify more precisely where the psychotherapy effect might be located, and how it might be used practically.

Examination of Patient Subgroups According to Psychiatric Severity

We examined subgroups of the overall sample in an attempt to find those subjects who benefited the most and the least from the additional treatments. Our rationale for the first series of these examinations was as follows: Clinical observations suggest that some proportion of drug taking in almost all addicts is an attempt to self-medicate discomfort associated with life stress or psychiatric symptoms. However, there is reason to believe that this attempt at self-medication may account for a much greater proportion of drug taking in those addicts with clinically significant levels of psychiatric symptoms. This in turn suggests that while the addition of professional psychotherapy may be generally useful in drug abuse treatments, it may be particularly important for that group of patients with additional serious psychiatric illness. Furthermore, since psychotherapy services are usually expensive and of limited availability, it is important from a practical perspective to identify subgroups of the patient population who can be most responsive to additional psychotherapy.

We therefore used the pretreatment psychiatric severity ratings that were determined by use of a number of clinical tests at the start of the study to evaluate the baseline psychiatric status of the patients. We combined all of these scores into a single composite that was highly correlated with the individual measures and generally indicative of the patients' global psychiatric status. Patients were divided into thirds according to their global psychiatric status rating. The third with the lowest scores was termed the low-severity group; the middle third was termed the middle-severity group; and the most disturbed group of patients, the upper third, was termed the high-severity group. Initial severity scores in all three groups were comparable for each treatment condition.

An examination of the three low-severity groups indicated substantial improvement in several measures in all treatment conditions. There was some indication that the SE/low-severity and DC/low-severity patients had more improvement and better outcome than the CB/low-severity patients in employment, but analyses of the 7-month outcome measures indicated no significant ($p > .10$) differences across the three treatments.

Middle-severity patients showed substantial positive change in all three treatment conditions, although the psychotherapy groups showed more changes in the psychological test measures. However, unlike the results with the low-severity patients, the 7-month comparisons indicated significant between-groups differences in 10 of the 16 comparisons, with the DC-only group showing the worst outcome on 7 of these. Thus, while all groups showed a number of significant improvements, the psychotherapy groups showed generally better outcomes in these middle-severity patients.

An examination of the three high-severity groups showed very different results. The high-severity patients from both therapy groups (SE and CB) showed a number of significant improvements in most of the outcome measures, but especially in employment, legal, and psychiatric status. In contrast, the high-severity patients in the DC-only group showed very little improvement generally, and significant ($p < .05$) change only in the drug use measures. Comparisons of the adjusted (analysis of covariance) 7-month scores indicated that the DC/high-severity patients had significantly poorer ($p = \le .05$) outcomes on 9 of the 16 comparisons.

In addition to the 7-month data, we also examined the standard clinical records of methadone doses, prescriptions for ancillary psychotropic medications, and urinalysis reports for patients in each of the treatment subgroups. These three measures are routinely and regularly collected on all patients during treatment, and we have found them to be sensitive indicators of treatment response.

Results of analyses of variance on these measures indicated significant differences among the severity groups on methadone doses and prescriptions for psychotropic medications. High-severity patients, regardless of treatment condition, had higher mean doses of methadone, a higher proportion of drug-positive urines, and a higher frequency of psychotropic drug prescriptions ($p \le .05$) than low- or middle-severity patients, who did not differ from each other ($p > .10$). Comparisons across therapy conditions yielded significant main effects on the variables of methadone dose ($p < .001$). Treatment ($\times$) severity interaction effects were significant for all three variables ($p < .01$). There were no significant differences in these variables among the three treatment conditions for the low-severity patients ($p > .10$). However, as in the analyses of earlier data, comparisons for the middle-severity and especially the high-severity patients yielded much different results. The middle- and high-severity DC patients had significantly higher mean methadone doses ($p < .01$), a significantly higher proportion of drug-positive urines ($p < .05$), and a significantly higher frequency of prescriptions for psychotropic medications ($p < .01$) than patients in either of the psychotherapy groups. The two psychotherapy groups did not differ from each other on any measure ($p > .10$).

Three main findings were evident from these results. First, and not surprisingly, patients with high levels of psychiatric symptoms had less satisfactory pretreatment adjustment in all areas of functioning than other patients. This finding is consistent with earlier work (McLellan *et al.*, 1983; Luborsky, Crits-Cristoph, Auerbach, & Mintz, in press), and it applies regardless of treatment group assignment. Second, the high-severity patients did not respond nearly as well to any of the treatments as did the middle- or low-severity patients. Their response to DC alone was especially problematic.

Our third and the most novel finding was the relationship between the patients' psychiatric severity and the specific treatments that were used. The additional psychotherapy altered the typical relationship between psychiatric severity and outcome. The high-severity patients who received the additional therapy showed improvement in many areas, while the DC/high-severity DC group improved only in drug use. Further, these high-severity therapy patients were able to make their gains with lower doses of methadone, less prescribed psychotropic medication, and less illicit drug use than the DC/high-severity patients. A more complete description of these results is available elsewhere (Woody, McLellan, Luborsky, O'Brien, Blaine, *et al.*, 1984).

Examination of Outcome by Therapist

We next turned to an examination of outcome by therapist. We had formed the impression that some therapists consistently effected better outcomes than others. This study offered a particularly good opportunity to examine differences in therapists' performance, for three reasons. First, the therapists were trained and regularly supervised using manuals that explicitly defined and described the techniques employed in the performance of each therapy. These manuals provided specific criteria that could be used by independent raters to derive reliable, valid, and discriminable evaluations of the nature and content of the three therapies (Luborsky, Woody, McLellan, & O'Brien, 1982). Second, each therapist's sessions were tape-recorded throughout the course of the study. These taped sessions provided a representative sample of each therapist's performance during therapy and could be used by independent raters to evaluate the extent to which the therapists conformed to the particular techniques of their therapy as defined by the manuals. Finally, objective data on several measures of patients' status were collected at the start of the study and again at the 7-month follow-up. This provided a comprehensive range of measures upon which to evaluate patients' improvement and outcome.

Our initial step in comparing the effectiveness of the therapists was to calculate the mean percentage of change from the start of the study

to the 7-month evaluation point for all patients in each therapist's caseload. This improvement rate was calculated on seven outcome measures
from the Addiction Severity Index (ASI). The ASI is a clinical research
interview, designed to assess problem severity in seven areas of functioning commonly impaired in drug-dependent patients: medical, em-
ployment/support, drug abuse, alcohol abuse, legal, family/social, and
psychiatric. In each of these areas, both objective and subjective questions are asked to measure the number, extent, and duration of problem
symptoms in the patient's lifetime and in the past 30 days. Sets of
objective and subjective items from each of the problem areas are standardized and summed to produce composite or factor scores that provide
reliable and valid general estimates of problem severity at each evaluation point (McLellan, Luborsky, O'Brien, & Woody, 1980). It is important to note that the ASI interviews were done by independent technicians who were not part of the treatment staff and were not aware of
patients' group assignments. Table 8-4 shows the percent change from
pretreatment status (positive or negative) for different therapists'
caseloads. Three therapists (or counselors, in the case of DC) were
selected from each treatment group.

The differences in patient improvement rates among the therapists
are obvious from Table 8-4. This was true in all treatment groups and
on most of the seven outcome measures. One-way analyses of variance
on the percent change scores indicated a significant ($p \leq .05$) between-
therapists effect on all measures. Further, the range in these performance measures was quite dramatic. For example, the patients of Therapist A showed an average improvement in psychological status from
the start to the 7-month point of more than 100%, while Therapist E's
patients showed only a 19% change and Therapist C's showed 4% worsening.

As an additional measure of the magnitude of change shown by
each therapist's caseload, measures of effect size were calculated for
each of the seven change measures and then averaged to produce a
single score (last column, Table 7-4). These effect-size measures have
limitations with regard to their generalizability, but they do offer an
additional means of comparing therapist efficacy. As can be seen, the
average effect sizes for the nine therapists parallel the data on percent
change, with Therapist A showing by far the largest effect, Therapists
B, D, E, and F showing moderate changes, and Therapist C, along with
Counselors G, H, and I, showing the smallest changes.

TABLE 8-4 Percent Change from Start of Treatment to 7-Month Follow-up, According to Type of Therapist/Counselor

Therapists/counselors	n	Drug use	Employment status	Legal status	Psychiatric status	Beck Depression Inventory	SCL-90	Maudsley Neuroticism Scale	Average effect size[a]
SE therapists									
A	10	34	32	20	102	58	44	64	.74
B	8	33	34	17	49	37	46	59	.59
C	8	-14	12	7	-4	8	-2	13	.19
CB therapists									
D	11	61	19	17	34	36	39	44	.53
E	10	70	22	13	19	24	30	30	.44
F	9	48	10	11	14	14	21	33	.46
DC counselors									
G	9	51	8	13	1	4	9	-1	.20
H	6	46	-4	6	2	-3	11	3	.13
I	7	66	17	7	15	14	15	17	.27

Note. All criteria were measured during the 30 days before treatment start and before 7-month follow-up. Factor scores represent composites of several items indicative of patient status in that area. Percent change was calculated against the treatment-start baseline.

[a] Within-therapist effect size was averaged across all seven criteria. Effect-size calculation for each criterion was pretreatment mean minus posttreatment mean, divided by pretreatment standard deviation. Small change = .2, moderate change = .5, large change = .8. (See Luborsky, Crits-Cristoph, Auerbach, & Mintz, in press.)

187

Thus, we found that the choice of therapist was an important determinant of outcome. Further analyses of the therapist data indicated that those who obtained the best results formed the most positive relationships with their patients, and also conformed the most closely to their specified techniques. Our impression is that a positive, helping relationship provides a necessary foundation from which the psychological techniques can be usefully applied. The absence of a positive relationship makes it very difficult for the techniques of the psychotherapy to be meaningfully applied. These results are described in greater detail in another paper (Luborsky, McLellan, Woody, O'Brien, 1985).

Examination of Outcome by Diagnostic Groupings

We then turned to an analysis of outcome by diagnostic groupings. To accomplish this, we compared treatment outcome for psychotherapy patients who fell into three RDC categories: opiate dependence only; opiate dependence and depression; and opiate dependence and anti-social personality (ASP) disorder. Both therapy groups were combined in this analysis in order to achieve a sufficient number of subjects in each category.

Patients in each of the first two categories improved considerably, with the largest therapy effect being in those with depression. However, there was no significant effect of psychotherapy in patients with only ASP, except that drug use was reduced. These findings are supportive of the idea expressed by many others that psychotherapy is not helpful for people with only sociopathy (Shamsie, 1981). These findings are summarized in Table 8-5.

In a subsequent analysis, we examined outcome of patients with a *Diagnostic and Statistical Manual of Mental Disorders*, third edition (DSM-III) diagnosis of opiate dependence and ASP disorder only, and compared them with patients who had opiate dependence plus an additional psychiatric disorder. Here, the group of patients with another psychiatric disorder showed significant gains, mainly in the areas of psychiatric status and employment. Thus, some patients with sociopathy appear to be therapy-amenable (Adams, 1961), and these are those with symptoms of other psychiatric disorders such as depression or anxiety. However, the disabilities associated with the core characteristics of ASP disorder are probably less amenable to change, even in this more re-

TABLE 8-5 Effectiveness of Therapy for Three Diagnostic Groups (RDC Diagnoses)

Criteria	Opiate abuse only (n = 28)		Opiate abuse and depression (n = 14)		Opiate abuse and ASP (n = 10)	
	Start	7-month	Start	7-month	Start	7-month
Drug use factor	199	106	187**	26	154*	118
Days opiates	8*	4	6	3	6*	5
Days nonopiates	4	2	2	1	4	3
Employment	129**	48	148	86	133	129
Days working	9	13	4*	8	6	7
Money earned	417*	535	334	391	151	211
Legal status	217*	121	209*	109	255	186
Crime days	7*	3	5*	2	5	3
Illegal income	248*	106	227*	75	291	226
Psychiatric status	167*	122	232**	109	189	159
Beck Depression Inventory	10*	6	15**	10	12	12
SADS Depression	17	17	28	22	23	21
SADS Anxiety	17	15	22	22	21	20
Maudsley Neuroticism	20	17	32**	20	25	23
SCL-90	138*	123	165*	151	160	155
Global Assessment Scale	66	75	47**	70	63	71
Psychiatric severity[a]	2.1	1.8	5.8*	2.9	4.6	3.8

Note. All criteria were measured drug 30 days prior to study start and at 7-month follow-up. Higher scores indicate greater severity.

[a] This was a global rating of severity by an interviewer on a scale of 0–9.

*p < .05.

**p < .01.

sponsive subgroup. These findings are also described in more detail in another paper (Woody, McLellan, Luborsky, & O'Brien, 1985).

ADMINISTRATIVE PROCEDURES

This review of the literature, and the description of the VA–Penn study in particular, could make the application of psychotherapy to a methadone program sound easier than it actually is. We encountered many difficulties with the VA–Penn project, and some of these were anticipated during the planning stage. Before beginning the study, we gave considerable thought to the administrative procedures that might be used in a psychotherapy study with this population. We had participated in the family therapy study done by Stanton and colleagues in 1976 (see Stanton *et al.*, 1982), and that experience taught us that there are special conditions under which therapy has the best chance to work. On the basis of Stanton *et al.*'s study, we expected three problems to occur: (1) missed appointments by patients; (2) competition between counselors and therapists; and (3) loss of morale by therapists in response to the nature of the addicts' problems.

We implemented the following procedures from the start of the study, in a largely successful attempt to combat these problems:

1. The program director administered the psychotherapy study as an integral part of the ongoing treatment services.
2. The therapists had part-time offices in the treatment facility, and efforts were made to ensure that they felt they were a part of the treatment program. This close linkage between the therapists and the program reduced the chances that therapists would feel disengaged, or that they would be perceived as irrelevant by the patients.
3. Attention was paid to facilitating coordination and cooperation between therapists and counselors, especially at the beginning of the project.
4. Attention was paid to patient compliance. Patients were reminded promptly if they missed appointments. Missed appointments were considered reflections of difficult social conditions or transference phenomena that should be addressed in therapy.
5. Patients were started in therapy shortly after they entered the program, because we felt that doing this would probably increase the chances for successful engagement.
6. Attention was paid to hiring only therapists who were interested in drug addicts and who felt comfortable with them.
7. Ongoing supervision of therapists was provided by a senior clinician who was skilled in the particular form of treatment that the therapists were to provide.

In addition to these administrative procedures, therapists were hired by time blocks so that they were paid whether patients kept or missed appointments, and counselors were paid $2 per patient for filling out weekly treatment report forms that were part of the data collection process.

These methods were necessary to carry out this study, and their absence in the New Haven–Yale project may have accounted for the much lower participation and compliance of their patients in the psychotherapy program.

OVERVIEW AND PRACTICAL IMPLICATIONS

The practical applications that emerge from this work are of general interest. The overall data, both from the VA–Penn project and the work of others, indicate that professional psychotherapy can be helpful with this population, provided they become engaged in it. This engagement is possible when the patients are in a residential program, when they keep regular appointments after detoxification, or when they are actively addicted but undergo the stabilizing influence of methadone maintenance treatment. The VA–Penn data indicate that there are certain subgroups of methadone-maintained patients who may be good (or poor) candidates for supplemental professional psychotherapy. The best candidates are those with significant psychiatric problems, designated here as the high-severity patients. The traditional poor outcome for these patients can be improved upon by the addition of competent and interested professional psychotherapists to the ongoing treatment services. These psychotherapists must be fully integrated into the overall program, and must have the ability to get along with other staff members. When therapists are integrated in this manner, we find that the counselors look to them for help with their most difficult patients. If therapy works, the successful management of these troublesome high-severity patients can reduce stress on the entire staff, in addition to providing direct benefits to the individual patients. Cost-effectiveness arguments can be made on the basis of the additional gains that can be achieved with a group of patients who make very little progress with the standard treatment, and usually at considerable expenditure of staff time.

Little mention has yet been made of group therapy. No major controlled studies have been done on group therapy with methadone-maintained patients. One of the studies cited earlier used groups and found evidence for positive results (Abrams, 1979), while another found no differences in outcome between group therapy and DC alone (Connett, 1980). Group therapy is widely used in residential programs. It appears to be used less extensively in most outpatient programs, though it has the potential to be a more cost-effective way of delivering professional treatment than individual therapy. Our impression is that it can be helpful; however, we have encountered serious practical problems in trying to establish it as a viable modality. Effective group therapy requires regular attendance by all members. Frequent absences seriously interfere with the group process and make meaningful therapy difficult. Unacceptable levels of attendance have been our greatest problem in trying to start meaningful groups. We have found that individual therapy is more easily adapted to methadone patients. These patients are not good at keeping regular appointments to begin with, and they also are subjected to a large number of schedule changes. Examples are patients doing shift work whose schedule changes periodically, or people who must appear in court or at social agencies at frequent and unpredictable intervals. This combination of impaired self-discipline with changing social circumstances has contributed to our problems in carrying out group therapy.

There also may be an inordinately high level of resistance to group therapy in a methadone-maintained population. Almost all of our patients have committed serious crimes. Effective therapy requires a high level of disclosure, and the issues of confidentiality in a group setting are much more complicated than in individual therapy. Patients cannot be certain who they are telling about their behavior in group therapy, or what the group members may do with their disclosures. This kind of problem may contribute to difficulties in carrying out meaningful group therapy, especially in an outpatient program. Another issue that has been problematic has been the tendency of some groups either to turn into gripe sessions, or to attempt to use group pressure to accomplish dubious goals (e.g., as dispensing travel money, prescribing diazepam, or providing more take-home methadone doses). This is not nearly as serious a problem as poor attendance, but it can create diversions and, when combined with irregular attendance, can be difficult to redirect into a therapeutic process. Thus, our feeling is that group therapy *can* work; however, individual therapy has been easier to implement in an outpatient setting.

We realize that some of this chapter is lopsided and slanted toward our own work, but this imbalance also indicates that the number of psychotherapy studies with addicts is small. We find reason to believe, from literature reviews and from our own work and experience, that professional psychotherapy can be helpful with substance abuse patients in general, and as a supplement to DC for specific kinds of patients in methadone treatment. The VA–Penn study is the only one to date that provides sufficient data to evaluate the issue of efficacy in detail. The results of this study suggest that the general question, "Is psychotherapy helpful?," should be broken down into components including "Under what conditions?," "Provided by what therapists?," and "For what specific types of patients?" We think that it is important to attempt to replicate the results so far obtained in other clinics, using a similar wide range of measures. A review of the few controlled studies and of our own experience generates a positive feeling about the contribution that professional psychotherapy can make as an adjunct to methadone treatment, provided it is applied in a way that gives it the best chance to work. Not enough data are available at this point to permit us to say definitely, "Yes, it really does work," but we hope that more data will be provided in future years.

REFERENCES

Abrams, J. (1979). A cognitive behavioral versus nondirective group treatment program for opioid addicted persons: An adjunct to methadone maintenance. *International Journal of the Addictions, 14*, 503–511.

Adams, E. (1961). *Effectiveness of interview therapy with older youth authority wards: An interview evaluation of the PICD project* (Research Report No. 20). Sacramento: California Youth Authority.

Beck, A. T. (1976). *Cognitive therapy and the emotional disorders*. New York: International Universities Press.

Beck, A. T., & Emery, G. D. (1977). *Individual treatment manual for cognitive behavioral psychotherapy for drug abuse*. Unpublished manuscript. (Available from Girard Bank Building, 5th Floor, 36th and Walnut Streets, Philadelphia, PA 19104)

Connett, G. (1980). Comparison of progress of patients with professional and paraprofessional counselors in a methadone maintenance program. *International Journal of the Addictions, 15*, 585–589.

De Quincey, T. (1907). *Confessions of an English opium-eater*. London: Dent. (Original work published 1821)

Fenichel, O. (1945). Drug addiction. In *The psychoanalytic theory of neurosis* (pp. 375–386). New York: Norton.

Glover, E. (1932). On the aetiology of drug addiction. *International Journal of Psychotherapy, 13*, 298–328.

Hartmann, D. (1969). A study of drug-taking adolescents. In R. S. Eissler, A. Freud, H. Hartmann, S. Lustman, & M. Kris (Eds.), *The psychoanalytic study of the child* (Vol. 24, pp. 384–398). New York: International Universities Press.

Herrington, R. E., Benzer, D. G., Jacobson, G. R., & Harkins, M. K. 1982. Treating substance-use disorders among physicians. *Journal of the American Medical Association, 247*, 2253–2257.

Khantzian, E. J., Mack, J. E., & Schatzberg, A. F. (1974). Heroin use as an attempt to cope: Clinical observations. *American Journal of Psychiatry, 131*, 160–164.

LaRosa, J. C., Lipsius, J. H., & LaRosa, J. H. (1974). Experiences with a combination of group therapy and methadone maintenance in the treatment of heroin addiction. *International Journal of the Addictions, 9*, 605–617.

Luborsky, L. (1976). *A general manual for supportive–expressive psychoanalytically oriented psychotherapy*. Unpublished manuscript. (Available from Piersal Building, Room 203, Hospital of University of Pennsylvania, 36th and Spruce Streets, Philadelphia, PA 19104.)

Luborsky, L., McLellan, A. T., Woody, G. E., O'Brien, C. P., & Auerbach, A. (1985) (in press). Therapist success and its determinants. *Archives of General Psychiatry*, 42:602–611.

Luborsky, L., Crits-Cristoph, P., Auerbach, A., & Mintz, J., (in press). *Psychotherapy: Who will benefit and how?* New York: Basic Books.

Luborsky, L., Woody, G. E., McLellan, A. T., & O'Brien, C. P. (1982). Can independent judges recognize different psychotherapies?: An experience with manual-guided therapies. *Journal of Consulting and Clinical Psychology, 50*, 49–62.

Malan, D. (1963). *A study of brief psychotherapy*. Philadelphia: J. B. Lippincott.

McLellan, A. T., Luborsky, L., O'Brien, C. P., & Woody, G. E. (1980). An improved diagnostic instrument for substance abuse patients: The Addiction Severity Index. *Journal of Nervous and Mental Disease, 168*, 26–33.

McLellan, A. T., Luborsky, L., Woody, G. E., Druley, K. A., & O'Brien, C. P. (1983). Predicting response to alcohol and drug abuse treatments: Role of psychiatric severity. *Archives of General Psychiatry, 40*, 620–625.

McLellan, A. T., Woody, G. E., & O'Brien, C. P. (1979). Development of psychiatric illness in drug abusers: Role of drug preference. *New England Journal of Medicine, 301*, 1310–1314.

Nyswander, M., Winick, C., Bernstein, A., Brill, I., & Kaufer, G. (1958). The treatment of drug addicts as voluntary outpatients: A progress report. *American Journal of Orthopsychiatry, 28*, 714–729.

Orne, M., & Wender, P. (1968). Anticipatory socialization for psychotherapy: Method and rationale. *American Journal of Psychiatry, 124*, 88–98.

Rado, S. (1933). The psychoanalysis of pharmacothymia. *Psychoanalytic Quarterly, 2*, 1–23.

Resnick, R. B., Washton, A. M., Stone-Washton, N. (1981). Psychotherapy and naltrexone in opioid dependence. In L. Harris (Ed.), *Problems of drug dependence* (NIDA Research Monograph 34, DHHS Publication No. ASM 81-1058, pp. 109–115). Washington, DC: U.S. Government Printing Office.

Rounsaville, B. J., Glazer, W., Wilber, C. H., Weissman, M M., & Kleber, H.D. (1983). Short-term interpersonal psychotherapy in methadone-maintained opiate addicts. *Archives of General Psychiatry, 40*, 629–636.

Rounsaville, B. J., Weissman, M. M., Kleber, H. D., & Wilber, C. H. (1982). The heterogeneity of psychiatric diagnosis in treated opiate addicts. *Archives of General Psychiatry, 39*, 161–166.

Savitt, R. A. (1963). Psychoanalytic studies on addiction: Ego structure in narcotic addiction. *Psychoanalytic Quarterly, 32*, 42–57.

Shamsie, S. J. (1981). Antisocial adolescents: Our treatments do not work—where do we go from here? *Canadian Journal of Psychiatry, 26*, 357–364.

Sifneos, P. (1972). *Short-term psychotherapy and emotional crisis*. Cambridge, MA: Harvard University Press.

Stanton, M. D., Todd, T. C., & Associates. (1982). *The family therapy of drug abuse and addiction.* New York: Guilford Press.

Wallerstein, R., Robins, L., Sargent, H., & Luborsky, L. (1956). The Psychotherapy Research Project of the Menninger Foundation. *Bulletin of the Menninger Clinic, 20,* 221–280.

Willett, E. A. (1973). Group therapy in a methadone treatment program: An evaluation of changes in interpersonal behavior. *International Journal of the Addictions, 8,* 33–39.

Woody, G. E., Luborsky, L., McLellan, A. T., O'Brien, C. P., Beck, A. T., Blaine, J., Herman, I., & Hole, A. (1983). Psychotherapy for opiate addicts: Does it help? *Archives of General Psychiatry, 40,* 639–645.

Woody, G. E., McLellan, A. T., Luborsky, L., & O'Brien, C. P. (1985). Sociopathy and psychotherapy outcome. *Archives of General Psychiatry, 42,* 1081–1086.

Woody, G. E., McLellan, A. T., Luborsky, L., O'Brien, C. P., Blaine, J., Fox, S., Herman, I., & Beck, A. T. (1984). Severity of psychiatric symptoms as a predictor of benefits from psychotherapy: The Veterans Administration–Penn study. *American Journal of Psychiatry, 141,* 1172–1177.

Woody, G. E., Stockdale, D., & Hargove, E. (1977). *A manual for drug counseling.* Unpublished manuscript. (Available from G. E. Woody, Drug Dependence Treatment Unit [158], Philadelphia Veterans Administration Hospital, 39th Street and Woodland Avenue., Philadelphia, PA 19104.)

Wurmser, L. (1979). *The hidden dimension: Psychopathology of compulsive drug use.* New York: Jason Aronson.

IV

Psychopathology of Intoxications

9

The Relevance of Laboratory Studies in Animals and Humans to an Understanding of the Relationship between Addictive Disorders and Psychopathology

STEVEN M. MIRIN

Theoretical formulations about the causes of substance abuse have traditionally been based on data gathered in a particular setting by an individual or a group of individuals from a single scientific discipline. Thus, the sociologist may view substance abuse as a by-product of poverty, social disruption, and/or the adverse influence of one's peer group, while the psychoanalyst may emphasize the role of developmental factors, parenting, and the role of underlying psychopathology. Using principles derived from studies of classical and operant conditioning, behavioral psychologists have focused on those aspects of the internal or external environment that "reinforce" drug-taking behavior. Ultimately, however, understanding the effects of heroin, cocaine, and other drugs of abuse on human behavior is a task that will require the careful application of a multidisciplinary approach.

Until recently, most of our information about the drug experience in humans has come from descriptive accounts of users, which, while clinically interesting, are difficult to interpret. Under all circumstances, drug effects are mediated not only by pharmacological factors (e.g., dose, age, route of administration), but a host of individual and environmental variables as well. In an attempt to control and make sense of the tremendous number of variables that have an impact on the drug experience, a number of investigators have studied the effects of various drugs of abuse in a laboratory or research ward environment. Most of these studies have entailed administration of opiates, central nervous system (CNS) depressants, stimulants, cannabis, or hallucinogens to individuals who themselves have had a range of prior drug experiences. While most of these studies have focused on acute drug effects, some have also examined the sequelae of chronic drug administration. This chapter reviews a small portion of the vast literature these studies have generated, focusing on those areas relevant to the abuse potential of these agents in humans. Data from animal studies are also cited where they shed light on the ability of these drugs to shape human behavior. Before I embark on such a review, however, a few comments on methodological issues are in order.

INTERPRETING THE RESULTS OF LABORATORY STUDIES

ANIMAL STUDIES

Studies of drug effects in animals offer several important advantages, the most obvious of which is that experiments that would be dangerous and/or unethical in human beings can be carried out in animals. Such studies may involve the administration of potentially toxic doses of a drug; the use of drug combinations that may produce severe drug interactions; installation of drugs into the bloodstream, the cerebral ventricles, or brain tissue itself; and the observation of drug effects given in conjunction with the placement of chemically or electrically induced brain lesions. Studies of drug effects carried out in some animal species, particularly rodents, also allow for the implementation of research designs that require large numbers of experimental subjects, while in less plentiful but hardier species (e.g., subhuman primates), one can assess the effects of acute or chronic drug administration in the same subject over long periods of time under conditions in which other variables (e.g., physical, environmental, dietary) are controlled for.

Though the study of the effects of abused drugs in animals has added a great deal to our understanding of how such drugs affect behavior, there are conceptual and methodological issues raised by reliance on animal data alone. Most importantly, animals lack the capacity to apprise us of their expectations of the drug experience or the way in which a given drug affects their perceptual ability, cognitive function, or mood. Thus, the effects of drugs on these variables must be inferred from the observation and measurement of derivative behaviors, such as an animal's ability to respond to various stimuli, learn simple or complex tasks, or interact with peers, during periods of drug intoxication or withdrawal. Species and strain differences, about which we know relatively little, also affect the behavioral response to exogenously administered drugs. Finally, subtle changes in the experimental setting and design also influence the effects of psychoactive drugs on animal behavior. For example, the effects of marijuana on fighting behavior in laboratory rats are profoundly influenced by cage size, the number of same-sex peers present in the cage during the period of drug intoxication, the relative availability of sexual partners, and the time elapsed since the animals' last meal (Carlini & Masur, 1969).

Studies in Humans

As in the case of animal studies, laboratory studies of drug effects in humans must take into account drug-related variables such as dosage, route, and frequency of administration; blood and brain levels achieved; the rate of drug metabolism; and the possible development of metabolic and/or pharmacodynamic tolerance. Additionally, interpretation of findings from human studies is further complicated by the need to account for the expectations of the user, his or her prior drug experience, the psychological substrate upon which drug effects are superimposed, and the planned or unplanned influence(s) of the experimental setting itself.

Finally, since stimulus–response relationships exist in a temporal framework, events that precede or follow drug administration clearly influence drug response (Dews, 1984). These so-called "schedule" effects may be a planned part of the experimental paradigm, or they may occur spontaneously and unexpectedly. Regardless of how they arise, schedule effects may contribute to a drug's ability to act as an extremely potent reinforcer in one situation but not in another. This is particularly true in studies of chronic drug administration, in which subjects may develop tolerance and/or physical dependence on the drugs administered. Thus, at the beginning of such experiments we may be measuring drug effects in a naive and/or drug-free individual; however, later in the same study, we are observing the acute effects of a particular drug superimposed on a substrate of chronic use. Thus, not only are acute effects different from chronic effects, but acute effects seen early in a cycle of drug administration may be far different from those that occur in the context of chronic use.

Despite these methodological difficulties, laboratory studies in both animals and humans have contributed a great deal to our understanding of how abused drugs affect cognition, mood, and behavior. In addition, these studies have introduced and helped to clarify important concepts such as drug reinforcement and craving. This may be best illustrated by reviewing some of the studies carried out on the effects of opiate drugs in animals and humans.

THE OPIATES

REINFORCING EFFECTS

Animal Studies

Opiate self-administration has been extensively studied in a number of animal species. Like other drugs of abuse, the opiates appear to function as primary reinforcers in animal models of addiction (Weeks, 1969; Woods & Schuster, 1968), meaning that they strengthen and maintain those behaviors that immediately precede their use. Moreover, their relative potency in this regard appears to be directly correlated with their abuse potential in humans (Schuster & Villareal, 1968). The reinforcing properties of this class of drugs have been demonstrated in a variety of animal species. For example, monkeys can eventually learn to prefer an opiate-containing solution to regular tap water in a free-choice situation and then gradually to escalate the dose consumed over time (Claghorn, Ordy, & Nagy, 1965). These animals can also learn to perform operant work (e.g., bar pressing) for injections of drugs like morphine and codeine (Downs & Woods, 1974; Woods & Schuster, 1968).

Once an animal becomes physically dependent, opiate drugs also serve as *secondary* reinforcers, in that they function to relieve real or anticipated abstinence symptoms. Thus, rats exposed to a series of daily morphine injections eventually learn to prefer a previously aversive morphine solution to tap water (Wikler & Prescor, 1967). Prolonged exposure to morphine and/or the development of physical dependence is crucial in the development of this preference. Physically dependent animals will also perform operant work (for opiates) to avoid experiencing abstinence symptoms; under such circumstances, the operant "price" of earned injections may be raised to very high levels (Woods & Schuster, 1968). Moreover, lowering the dose per injection will result in a compensatory increase in the number of injections (Weeks & Collins, 1968). The parallels between these data and what one observes in human opiate abusers are quite striking (see below).

A number of lines of evidence suggest that the primary reinforcing properties of opiate drugs are attributable to the direct pharmacological effect of these agents on those brain areas responsible for the mediation of pleasure or "reward" (Olds & Milner, 1954; Stein, 1968). These brain areas (e.g., portions of the hypothalamus) are rich in neurons that use norepinephrine as a chemical neurotransmitter and whose activity appears to be stimulated by intraventricular administration of drugs like morphine (Esposito & Kornetsky, 1977); this, in turn, may be integrally related to the pleasurable subjective effects of such drugs. Consistent with this finding, drugs that inhibit norepinephrine synthesis (e.g., alpha-methyltyrosine) will inhibit the development of morphine-seeking behavior in some laboratory animals (W. M. Davis & Smith, 1972; W. M. Davis, Smith, & Khalsa, 1975).

Data from animal studies also suggest that, in addition to the primary and secondary reinforcing properties of the opiates, drug-seeking behavior may also be elicited by conditioned stimuli. For example, W. M. Davis and Smith (1972) reported that rats previously made dependent on morphine and subsequently detoxified would work for saline injections in the presence of environmental cues previously associated with morphine administration. An explanation for this finding may be found in the earlier work of Wikler and Pescor (1967), who found that detoxified rats would manifest "wet dog shakes" and other signs of opioid withdrawal in environments in which they had previously experienced episodes of drug intoxication and/or withdrawal. Wikler, Martin, Prescor, and Eades (1963) also found that rats experiencing these so-called "conditioned abstinence" phenomena quickly learned to prefer an otherwise aversive solution of etonitazene, a powerful opioid, to tap water. In a more recent study, Carnathan, Meyer, and Cochin (1977) found that rats would continue to work for conditioned opiate-associated reinforcers for as long as 6 weeks after their last drug experience. Interestingly, these authors also reported a positive correlation between the length of prior opiate dependence and the animals' willingness to work for this type of secondary reinforcement—a finding that may have clinical implications for the treatment of opiate abuse in humans.

Studies in Humans

Many of the early studies on the effects of opiate drugs in humans were carried out at the Addiction Research Center of the U.S. Public Health Service Hospital in Lexington, Kentucky. In one such study, Martin and Fraser (1961) compared the physiological and subjective effects of heroin and morphine given intravenously, and found that addicts prefered heroin despite the fact that the two drugs had comparable durations of action and produced comparable levels of euphoria when administered in this fashion. In suggesting that side effects (e.g., epigastric sensations, paresthesias) related to heroin use might have served as discriminative stimuli in former heroin users, these authors introduced the notion that, even in humans, conditioning factors may affect the subjective response to opiate drugs.

In general, most laboratory studies of opiate use in humans have employed fixed-dose, fixed-interval schedules of drug self-administration, which bear little resemblance to the pattern of opiate use observed in more natural settings (e.g., on the street). There have been a number of studies, however, in which subjects have been allowed to titrate their own drug dosage within specified limits. One of the earliest was carried out by Wikler (1952), who allowed a single ex-addict to self-administer morphine over a 120-day period. In this subject, chronic morphine administration was accompanied by diminished hunger, reduced fear of pain, and decreased sexual interest. With the onset of physical dependence, opiate administration also served to stave off abstinence symptoms. Thus, in this individual, morphine served initially as a primary, and subsequently as a secondary (i.e., negative), reinforcer.

BLOCKADE OF OPIATE REINFORCEMENT

Reminiscent of the animal studies described earlier, some studies of opiate self-administration in humans have attempted to quantitate the reinforcing effects of these drugs by requiring subjects to perform some form of operant work in order to receive the drug. This methodology also allows for the assessment of treatments whose efficacy depends on the successful blockade of opiate reinforcement (e.g., methadone, narcotic antagonists). In one such study, Martin *et al.* (1973) allowed addicts being treated with methadone to work for 4-mg injections of hydromorphine hydrochloride (Dilaudid). In most subjects, operant work output for Dilaudid was decreased once the daily dose of methadone exceeded 50 mg per day. Some, however, continued to work for Dilaudid injections even while being maintained on 100 mg of methadone per day. One possible explanation for this phenomenon might be incomplete cross-tolerance, so that subjects were still able to experience the reinforcing properties of Dilaudid. Alternatively, conditioned responding to the ritual of intravenous drug use may have also played a role (see above).

Narcotic antagonists are drugs that competitively inhibit the effects of opiates at functionally important receptor sites in the brain and elsewhere. Patients pretreated with adequate doses of these drugs are unable to experience the subjective (i.e., reinforcing) effects of subsequently administered opiates (Martin *et al.*, 1973; Meyer, Mirin, Altman, & McNamee, 1976; O'Brien & Greenstein, 1976; Resnick, Volavka, Freedman, & Thomas, 1974). The theoretical base for the use of narcotic antagonists in the treatment of opiate addiction lies in the contention of Wikler (1965, 1968) that for most addicts, compulsive opiate use constitutes an attempt to reduce the pain of pharmacologically induced or classically conditioned abstinence symptoms. The latter may be readily elicited by exposure to exteroceptive stimuli (i.e., cues) associated with previous episodes of opiate self-administration and/or withdrawal. These might include being in the presence of opiates, observing an individual "shooting up," or merely being in a neighborhood in which opiate drugs were previously consumed. Such stimuli, in combination with internal cues (e.g., feeling tense, depressed, or bored), are postulated to trigger an increase in drug craving, which is usually followed by drug-seeking behavior. Data from animal studies (Schuster & Villareal, 1968) suggest that in animals experiencing pharmacologically induced or conditioned abstinence symptoms, failure to experience anticipated opiate reinforcement customarily leads to a brief increase in drug-seeking behavior; this is followed by a gradual decline and eventual extinction of such behavior, accompanied by signs of increased anger and frustration. By the same token, Wikler (1971) theorized that pretreatment with drugs that block opiate reinforcement (i.e., narcotic antagonists) might eventually lead to the extinction of abstinence-induced drug self-administration in humans.

In a series of studies carried out by our group (Meyer & Mirin, 1979), detoxified opiate addicts were allowed self-regulated access to increasing doses of intravenous heroin in order to test the efficacy of a narcotic antagonist (naltrexone) in reducing opiate use under nonblind and double-blind conditions. In these studies, most antagonist-treated (i.e., blocked) subjects appeared to realize quickly that heroin was essentially unavailable to them, and, therefore, ceased challenging antagonist blockade after only a few trials ($x = 4.3$). There was, however, a subgroup of subjects who persisted in challenging antagonist blockade ($x = 15.9$ trials). These individuals also reported persistently elevated levels of drug craving and appeared to respond to each injection of "blocked" heroin with subjective signs of opiate intoxication (i.e., pupillary constriction and a drop in respiratory rate). Extinction of these classically conditioned autonomic effects coincided with these subjects' eventual decision to cease challenging antagonist blockade. The decision itself, however, appeared to be the result of a process of cognitive labeling in which subjects sooner or later decided that they were receiving a narcotic antagonist (as opposed to placebo), and that therefore they were precluded from getting "high." This recognition was usually accompanied by the development of an irritable dysphoria, which may be the human equivalent of the increased aggressivity seen in animal models of extinction. Other investigators (O'Brien, O'Brien, Mintz, & Brady, 1975) have reported similar findings in opiate addicts self-administering saline.

Effects of Opiates on Sociability and Mood

Given the clinical folklore regarding the efficacy of drugs such as heroin in enhancing sociability and elevating mood, laboratory studies of these effects (of opiates) are quite illuminating. For example, Fraser, Jones, Rosenberg, & Thompson *et al.* (1963) studied the effects of acute and chronic heroin use in subjects who received the drug in graduated doses up to a maximum of 95 mg per day for 19 days, after which they were maintained on this dose for an additional 40 days. They found that, although the initial phases of heroin administration were accompanied by increased physical activity and sociability, this effect was soon replaced by increasing lethargy and social withdrawal. Similarly, Haertzen and Hooks (1969), using a variety of self-report measures, found that during the initial phases of heroin use, subjects displayed increased motor activity, slept less and engaged in more interpersonal contact. However, as heroin use continued and dosage increased, these same individuals became increasingly dysphoric and displayed decreased motivation for physical, mental, and social activity.

In our own studies (Mirin, Meyer, & McNamee, 1975, 1976), the initial response to unblocked heroin use was psychomotor excitation and elevated mood. As heroin use continued and subjects became more intoxicated, however, the euphorigenic effects of the drug were less apparent, while the degree of manifest psychopathology (as measured by both psychiatric rating scales and subject self-reports) increased. Indeed, subjects were clearly more depressed, confused, suspicious, hostile, and uncooperative, while their own self-reports confirmed their feeling more angry and worried. Of note is that while chronic heroin use was accompanied by increased psychopathology, acute administration of the drug provided some brief euphoria and tension relief. As heroin use continued, however, there was evidence of the development of tolerance to these acute effects. In general, our findings were consistent with a tension reduction model of opiate reinforcement.

CRAVING FOR OPIATES

Opiate addicts frequently report that relapse occurs in response to the sudden onset of drug "craving," which they describe as an uncomfortable tension state accompanied by an urge to self-administer their drug of choice. Increased craving most frequently occurs in the context of opiate withdrawal; however, in drug-free ex-addicts, craving may increase following exposure to stimuli that signal drug availability (see above). These stimuli, in turn, engender an approach–avoidance conflict (i.e., whether to use drugs or not), sometimes accompanied by signs and symptoms of conditioned abstinence.

Since craving is a highly subjective phenomenon, present primarily under conditions in which addicts expect to obtain opiates, it is an elusive concept to study. Nonetheless, there have been several laboratory studies of opiate self-administration in which craving has been observed and quantitated (Meyer, McNamee, Mirin, & Attman, 1974a, 1974b). In our work (Meyer, Mirin, Altman, & McNamee, 1976), opiate addicts allowed nonblind access to increasing doses of intravenous heroin manifested a marked rise in subjective feelings of craving, as measured by their own quantitative self-reports. Moreover, craving scores remained high throughout the period of heroin availability and dropped only after subjects were detoxified with decreasing doses of methadone. Interestingly, craving scores in these subjects fell only slightly in response to each dose of heroin, despite their becoming overtly intoxicated.

In a subsequent double-blind study of heroin self-administration (Meyer & Mirin, 1979), subjects were pretreated with either a narcotic antagonist (naltrexone) or placebo prior to being allowed access to heroin. In placebo-treated individuals (who were getting "high"), craving scores followed the same pattern seen in our earlier nonblind studies, although overall craving levels were somewhat lower in these subjects. In contrast, subjects who were pretreated with naltrexone reported a dramatic decrease in craving even while heroin was available. As mentioned previously, however, two distinct subgroups of blocked subjects could be discerned: those who reported a sharp drop in craving immediately after the first dose of "blocked" heroin and who challenged narcotic antagonist blockade only briefly, and those who showed no significant drop in craving after the first dose of "blocked" heroin and who persisted in challenging antagonist blockade. Among the latter, extinction of conditioned autonomic responding to blocked heroin was accompanied by a fall in drug craving. Of further note is that those antagonist-treated subjects who manifested conditioned autonomic effects and elevated craving in response to blocked heroin did poorly (relative to other blocked subjects) with respect to their willingness to continue in antagonist treatment on an outpatient basis.

Thus, it appears that in a laboratory setting, measurement of the craving in response to blocked heroin may help to identify those individuals who are particularly sensitive to discriminative stimuli that signal drug availability and trigger conditioned abstinence responses, and that those individuals are at increased risk for relapse upon return to the community. The data also suggest that if addicts are allowed regular and controlled access to heroin (i.e., under a program of heroin maintenance), the pharmcological effects of heroin may also serve as a discriminative stimulus, and thus craving may remain elevated in such patients despite their experiencing opiate reinforcement. Indeed, the most important variables related to relapse in opiate addicts are the perception of drug availability and the associated increase in craving that this perception engenders.

ALCOHOL

Of the CNS depressants abused by humans, the most readily available, and most problematic from a public health standpoint, is alcohol.As a result, there has been a substantial research effort to better define the subjective and behavioral effects of this drug in humans. The literature in this area is voluminous, but only selected aspects of it can be considered here. For the most part, the emphasis in this section is on those laboratory studies designed to explore the reinforcing effects of alcohol and its role in altering sociability, mood, feelings of anxiety, tension, and aggression. Data from animal studies are cited where relevant to these general issues.

REINFORCING EFFECTS

As in the case of the opiates, alcohol appears to function as a primary reinforcer in animal models of drug self-administration. Thus, rhesus monkeys allowed unlimited access to intravenous doses of alcohol will initiate and maintain a pattern of drug self-administration over several weeks, with occasional periods of self-initiated abstinence (Deneau, Yanagita, & Seevers, 1969). Similar findings have been reported with other CNS depressants, such as pentobarbital (Goldberg, Hoffmeister, Schlichting, & Wuttke, 1971), diazepam, and chlordiazepoxide (Yanagita & Takahashi, 1973). Once animals become physically dependent on alcohol, they will perform the operant work necessary to maintain their level of drug intake over extended periods of time. Moreover, during such periods, decreasing the dose per injection will increase the rate of drug self-administration (Woods, Ikomi, & Winger, 1971). Finally, in alcohol-dependent monkeys given time-limited access to the drug, initial episodes of drug taking are quite frequent, after which they become somewhat irregular, perhaps due to the sedative effects of the drug (Woods *et al.,* 1971). This pattern of alcohol use is not unlike that seen in human alcohol abusers, where the goal is rapid intoxication followed by sporadic use designed to maintain blood alcohol levels sufficient to remain intoxicated.

EFFECTS ON SOCIABILITY

The effects of alcohol on sociability and mood in humans have also been explored in laboratory studies. For example, in a series of studies, Mendelson and colleagues (Mendelson, 1964; Mendelson, Mello, & Solomon, 1968) allowed groups of alcoholic subjects to engage in chronic drinking in a research ward setting. In these individuals, alcohol intoxication altered power relationships within the group, but did not increase sociability. On the other hand, increased interpersonal stress was often followed by a decrease in alcohol consumption on the unit. Using a similar experimental paradigm, Nathan, Titler, Lowenstein, Solomon, and Rossi (1970) required alcoholic subjects to perform operant work to obtain "purchase points," which then could be used to purchase either alcohol or time out of social isolation. The majority of these alcoholic subjects spent all their points on alcohol, and the amount of drinking was roughly the same during periods of socialization and isolation. The introduction of a bar and bartender into this experimental setting (Nathan, O'Brien, & Lowenstein, 1971) produced a brief increase in attempts at socialization, but subjects still spent the majority of their accumulated "purchase points" for alcohol. Finally, Bigelow, Liebson, and Griffiths (1974) found that brief periods of social isolation actually suppressed drinking behavior on their ward, especially when the television set and reading materials were removed. Thus, in a research ward setting, drinking does not increase socialization. Conversely, socialization per se will not reduce alcohol consumption, but under certain circumstances, isolation will. These findings suggest that for alcoholics, at least, human interaction is neither a substitute nor a stimulus for drinking behavior. Rather, it appears that experiencing drug effects is the primary motivation for alcohol consumption. It is this distinction (among others) that may separate alcoholics from social drinkers.

EFFECTS ON MOOD

In natural settings, the acute effects of alcohol on mood are quite variable and not easy to predict. Clearly these effects are influenced by a host of factors, including the dose of alcohol consumed, the rate of absorption, the blood alcohol level achieved, the setting in which the drug is taken, the expectations of the user, and his or her underlying mood state. Prior drug experience and conditioned responding may also play a role. In addition, the euphorigenic effects of alcohol seem more apparent in group drinking situations, while solitary drinking appears to facilitate the development of dysphoria.

In laboratory studies designed to assess changes in mood related to alcohol consumption, both alcoholic and nonalcoholic drinkers have shown acute dose-related effects of intoxication, with a characteristic transition from elation and hyperactivity at low doses to depression and psychomotor retardation at higher doses (Alterman, Gottheil, & Crawford, 1975; Nagarajan, Gross, Kissin, & Best, 1973; Warren & Raynes, 1972). Not surprisingly, alcoholic subjects in these studies have characteristically required higher doses than nonalcoholic subjects in order to demonstrate such effects, probably as a consequence of both metbolic and behavioral tolerance.

Attempts to assess mood changes in alcoholic and nonalcoholic subjects during periods of chronic intoxication have also been carried out by a number of investigators (D. Davis, 1971; Mello & Mendelson, 1972; Nathan & O'Brien, 1971. Most have found that both social drinkers and chronic alcoholics will experience anxiety and depression during sustained periods of chronic use, although acute doses may continue to produce either brief episodes of euphoria or a temporary amelioration of the negative affects associated with chronic intoxication. The similarity of these findings to data derived from studies of acute and chronic administration of opiate drugs should be noted (Mirin, Meyer, & McNamee, 1975).

Effects on Tension and Anxiety

The role of alcohol as a reducer of tension and/or anxiety has also been explored in a research ward setting. For example, Steffen, Nathan, and Taylor (1974) studied four alcoholic subjects over a 12-day period of drinking and found that subjective reports of stress were generally correlated with blood alcohol levels. These authors interpreted this finding as corroborating the positive correlation between the internal perception of stress and increased craving for alcohol. On the other hand, Higgins and Marlatt (1975) found that alcoholics put in a stressful situation (e.g., being threatened with electric shock) did not increase their alcohol consumption over baseline levels. In reviewing the literature on the relationship between alcohol use and tension reduction, Cappell and Herman (1972) found that experimental stressors do not substantially increase alcohol consumption in either alcoholics or controls, but that alcoholics invariably consume more alcohol than controls under both stressful and nonstressful circumstances. Finally, under certain conditions, it appears that stress may be followed by a decrease in alcohol consumption, particularly in social drinkers. These authors concluded that tension reduction is not a primary reinforcing effect of alcohol.

EFFECTS ON AGGRESSIVITY

The apparent role of alcohol in facilitating homicide, suicide, and other types of violent behavior has been amply documented using a variety of epidemiological techniques (Goodwin, 1973; Tinklenberg, 1973). This has led, naturally enough, to laboratory studies designed to explore the role of alcohol in facilitating the expression of aggressive behavior in both animals and humans. Among other findings, such studies have revealed that mice given alcohol tend to become more sexually aggressive (Cutler & Mackintosh, 1975), engage in more "exploratory" behavior, and make more attempts to expand their territory at the expense of their peers (Chance, Mackintosh, & Dixon, 1973). Similarly, studies in human subjects have also found that hostile and aggressive behavior is more evident during periods of either acute or chronic intoxication (Mendelson & Mello, 1974; R. C. Smith, Parker, & Noble, 1975; Steinglass & Wolin, 1974; S. P. Taylor & Gammon, 1975), regardless of whether subjects are alcoholics or nonalcoholics. Thus, S. P. Taylor and Gammon (1975) studied 40 subjects who were told that they would be allowed to deliver electric shocks of varying intensity to their "opponents" in a competitive reaction-time task. In this experimental paradigm, aggressivity, as measured by shock intensity, was inhibited by concurrent administration of low doses of alcohol. On the other hand, high-dose alcohol use facilitated aggressive behavior, with competitors being willing to deliver more intense shocks to their opponents.

Since behavior during alcohol intoxication is, in part, learned, some investigators have attempted to control for the effects of expectancy when studying the relationship between alcohol use and aggressive behavior. One way of doing so is to introduce a placebo control condition. In this context, Lang, Goeckner, Adesso, and Marlatt (1975) used the shock administration paradigm described above (S. P. Taylor & Gammon, 1975) and found that aggressivity, as measured by the intensity and duration of electrical shock, was greater in those subjects who *thought* they were consuming alcohol, regardless of whether they actually received alcohol or placebo. This was thought to demonstrate the role of social learning in the expression of alcohol-facilitated aggression. In a subsequent study, Marlatt, Kosturn, and Lang (1975) extended these findings by reporting that subjects who were provoked (e.g., by insults), but who were denied the opportunity to retaliate, tended to consume more alcohol than those who were allowed to engage in aggressive behavior (e.g., shock administration).

Yet another perspective on the interaction between alcohol use and aggressive behavior stems from research findings, in both animals and humans, of a presumptive relationship between these two variables and the secretion of the male sex hormone testosterone. Studies in subhuman primates (Rose, Gordon, & Bernstein, 1972; Rose, Haladay, & Bernstein, 1971) have revealed that being the recipient of aggression and/or losing status within one's social group can be associated with a decline in plasma testosterone secretion. In subsequent studies, these investigators found a decrement in plasma testosterone in men experiencing the stress of officer candidate school or anticipating combat (Kruez, Rose, & Jennings, 1972). Data linking increased plasma testosterone levels with either a past history or current propensity for aggressive behavior, however, are less convincing.

The relationship among alcohol use, aggression, and sex hormone secretion was explored by Mendelson and Mello (1974), who found plasma testosterone levels to be suppressed in men during a period of chronic drinking, with recovery following alcohol withdrawal. However, no particular relationship was demonstrated between testosterone levels and aggressive behavior in these subjects. Mendelson and his colleagues (Mendelson, Ellingboe, & Kuehnle, 1976; Mendelson, Mello, & Ellingboe, 1977) also studied the acute effect of alcohol administrtion on the release of both testosterone and luteinizing hormone (LH). Since both hormones are released in episodic bursts (from the testes and pituitary, respectively), hormone levels were measured at 20-minute intervals over a 6-hour period before and after alcohol administration. In this study, an increase in blood alcohol was accompanied by a fall in plasma testosterone, presumably as a result of alcohol's direct toxic effect on the Leydig cells of the testes. This, in turn, was followed by a rise in LH secretion, presumably as part of the feedback response to a drop in plasma testosterone.

In searching for a psychoendocrine link between sex hormone levels and alcohol-induced aggressivity, one might speculate that it is this secondary rise of LH that is associated with increased anger and aggression in people who drink. This hypothesis gains support from the observation that acute administration of opiate drugs, which is usually followed by euphoria, tension relief, and decreased aggressivity, is accompanied by suppression of both testosterone and LH, an effect mediated by the effect of opiates on central hypothalamic mechanisms (Mirin, Mendelson, Ellingboe, & Meyer, 1976).

In summary, alcohol intoxication appears to facilitate aggressive behavior in a research ward setting. This effect is particularly evident at high blood alcohol levels and is enhanced under conditions of increased interpersonal stress. These data are consistent with clinical descriptions of the role of alcohol consumption in enhancing aggressivity in more natural settings, and may be due to a variety of factors, including the following: a direct stimulatory effect of alcohol on those limbic structures that mediate the expression of aggressive drives; inhibition of the cortical structures that inhibit these limbic centers; and/or the drug's effect on neuroendocrine mechanisms (e.g., the hypothalamic–pituitary–gonadal axis), which, in turn, may affect those brain areas involved in the regulation of aggressive instincts and behavior. No doubt, all of these effects are themselves influenced by social learning accrued from prior drinking experiences and a host of individual psychological and biological variables about which we know relatively little.

CNS STIMULANTS

In humans, CNS stimulants, such as amphetamine, methamphetamine, and cocaine, generally act to enhance alertness, suppress appetite, and reduce sleep and combat fatigue (Martin, Sloan, Sapira, & Jasinski, 1971) In many nontolerant individuals, they also produce euphoria. In laboratory animals, administration of these agents will stimulate locomotor activity, suppress appetite, and enhance both spontaneous and operant behavior (Randrup & Munkvad, 1972; Wallach, 1974).

REINFORCING EFFECTS

Central Mechanisms

Laboratory studies in both animals and humans reveal much about the CNS mechanisms that function in the regulation of mood. Such studies also shed light on the role of particular brain neurotransmitters in the mediation of "reward" or pleasure. In the brain, the CNS stimulants act to facilitate the release of catecholamines (i.e., norepinephrine and dopamine) from presynaptic neurons (Carlsson, 1970; C. B. Smith, 1963). They also increase the availability of these neurotransmitters at functionally important postsynpatic receptor sites in the brain by blocking the re-uptake of catecholamines by presynaptic neurons (K. M. Taylor & Snyder, 1971) and by inhibiting the enzyme monoamine oxidase (MAO), thus interfering with the intercellular breakdown of catecholamines (Burn & Rand, 1958). In addition, some central nervous system stimulants and/or their metabolites appear to act as so-called "false" neurotransmitters at catecholaminergic synapses (Brodie, Cho, & Gessa, 1970).

Studies in Laboratory Animals

Animal studies provide substantial evidence that CNS stimulants like amphetamine, methamphetamine, and cocaine act as primary reinforcers in the rat, monkey, and other animal species (Deneau *et al.,* 1969; W. M. Davis & Smith, 1972). Consequently, such animals will perform operant work (e.g., lever pressing) for intravenous injections of these drugs. Moreover, once a pattern of drug self-administration is established, these animals will work even harder to prevent the total daily dose from being decreased; this suggests that the drugs act as secondary (or negative) reinforcers as well.

   Drugs that interfere with the synthesis, storage, or release of norepinephrine from presynaptic neurons have been shown to interfere with stimulant self-administration behavior in animals (Stein, 1964; Wallach, Rotrosen, & Gershon, 1973; Wise, Berger, & Stein, 1973). Similarly, drugs that inhibit dopamine-beta-hydroxylase, the enzyme that converts dopamine to norepinephrine, also interfere with amphetamine use in animal models of drug self-administration (Wise & Stein, 1970). Both findings suggest that the power of stimulant drugs as primary reinforcers is dependent upon the effects of these agents on brain catecholamine systems.

Data from electrophysiological studies also shed light on the mechanisms by which the CNS stimulants function as primary reinforcers in animals (and perhaps humans). Advances in stereotactic technology now make it possible to implant stimulating electrodes in rat brain areas thought to be involved in the mediation of reward or pleasure. Animals so prepared will perform operant work to receive electrical stimulation to these brain areas, which, interestingly, are rich in catecholamine neurotransmitters, particularly norepinephrine (Stein, 1968). Administration of CNS stimulants such as amphetamine or methamphetamine will enhance the rate of electrical self-stimulation in these animals (Philips, Brooke, & Fibiger, 1975).

Finally, though the reinforcing properties of the CNS stimulants appear to be mediated primarily by their effects on noradrenergic neurons, there are data to suggest that dopaminergic neurons may also play a role here. For example, 6-hydroxydopamine is a compound that, when taken up by catecholamine-containing neurons, will destroy these neurons (G. Jonsson, Malmfors, & Sachs, 1975). Intracisternal or intraventricular injections of 6-hydroxydopamine into areas containing dopaminergic neurons have been shown to partially block the effects of amphetamine on brain self-stimulation in laboratory animals (A. S. Hollister, Breese, & Cooper, 1974). In contrast, destruction of neuronal tracts containing norepinephrine-secreting neurons does not produce this result (Cooper, Cott, & Breese, 1974). These data suggest that at least some dopaminergic neurons may form part of a generalized arousal system whose activity may be modified by administration of CNS stimulants.

In summary, laboratory studies in a variety of animal species suggest that CNS stimulants facilitate both the release of norepinephrine and dopamine from CNS neurons, and electrical self-stimulation behavior. These actions may underlie the ability of these agents to alter mood and behavior and to function as primary reinforcers. They may also contribute to the potential for abuse of these drugs in humans.

Studies in Humans

In humans, moderate doses of CNS stimulants will suppress appetite, elevate mood, relieve fatigue, and induce a certain degree of hyperactivity (Martin *et al.*, 1971). As in laboratory animals, these effects are thought to be mediated by the effects of CNS stimulants on brain catecholamines (i.e., norepinephrine and dopamine) (Carr & Moore, 1969; Glowinski, Axelrod, & Iversen, 1966; Schildkraut, 1970).

Well-controlled laboratory studies of the acute effects of stimulants in humans are relatively scarce. Most have entailed administration of amphetamine or methamphetamine to experienced users. In one such study, Bell and colleagues (Bell, 1973) administered intravenous methamphetamine hydrochloride, in doses ranging from 55 to 640 mg per day, to 14 subjects who had been previously dependent on methamphetamine sulfate. Most subjects developed a typical amphetamine psychosis (see below), similar to that seen during their prior bouts of methamphetamine use. Onset of psychosis was relatively sudden, usually within an hour of receiving methamphetamine, and in most instances was present for 24–48 hours. In two subjects, the psychotic episode lasted at least 6 days. Similar results were obtained by Angrist and Gershon (1970), who administered high doses of methamphetamine to four subjects over a 2- to 3-day period, L. E. Jonsson and Sjostrom (1970) also observed psychotic reactions in 15 intravenous methamphetamine users given oral amphetamine in a laboratory setting.

The Sequelae of Chronic Use

Animal Studies

Studies of the effects of chronic stimulant use in laboratory animals (e.g., the cat) reveal an increase in alerting responses and arousal, followed by the development of stereotyped patterns of behavior (Wallach, 1974; Wallach & Gershon, 1972). The latter may include side-to-side movements of the head and eyes, investigative sniffing, and occasionally repetitive grooming. In general, these animals appear to be responding to internal stimuli that some have speculated may be the feline equivalent of auditory or visual hallucinations.

The development of stereotyped behaviors in animals receiving CNS stimulants is influenced by the intrinsic characteristics of the animal. Thus, in subhuman primates, some investigators have noted the development of picking behavior, which is reminiscent of the parasitosis seen during chronic amphetamine use in humans. Animals with a past history of chronic stimulant use, even those that have remained drug-free for 6 months or more, may also respond to single doses of a stimulant drug with re-emergence of their characteristic stimulant-induced stereotypy (Wallach, 1974). In other instances, stereotypy can occur after the first dose in previously naive users and persist for as long as drug administration continues (Wallach, 1974; Wallach & Gershon, 1972).

Though the precise mechanism of stereotypic behavior is unknown, electrical stimulation of the amygdala in drug-free animals can produce many of the behavioral responses observed during chronic amphetamine use, including sniffing, searching behavior, fearfulness, and increased aggressivity (Fangel & Kaada, 1960; Kaada, Andersen, & Jansen, 1954). This finding suggests that some of these effects may be mediated through limbic system structures, particularly those areas that subserve attention and arousal.

In animal studies, chronic administration of CNS stimulants is accompanied by the development of tolerance to the appetite suppressant effects of these drugs, but not to the production of stereotyped behavior. Some have suggested that tolerance development is due to the neuronal synthesis and release of p-hydroxynorephedrine from noradrenergic neurons, a compound that may function as a false neurotransmitter in the brain (i.e., a transmitter that is ineffective in stimulating noradrenergic postsynaptic receptors) (Brodie et al., 1970). The lack of development of tolerance to stereotyped behavior may be explained by the fact that this action of the CNS stimulants may be mediated by dopaminergic neurons that do not synthesize p-hydroxynorepinephrine. Further support for this hypothesis comes from the finding that in some animal species, chronic amphetamine use is accompanied by a decrease in both brain dopamine and homovanillic acid, the major dopamine metabolite in the brain (Moore & Thornburg, 1973), and that stimulant-induced stereotypy can be inhibited by prior administration of drugs that interfere with the effects of dopamine at postsynaptic receptor sites (e.g., phenothiazines) (Bunney, Walters, Roth, & Aghajanian, 1973). In contrast, drugs that antagonize the effects of norepinephrine in the brain and/or periphery (e.g., reserpine, propranolol) have no effect on stimulant-induced stereotypic behavior.

Studies in Humans

In humans, chronic administration of high doses of CNS stimulants (e.g., amphetamines, cocaine) frequently produce a well-defined toxic psychosis that is often difficult to distinguish from paranoid schizophrenia (Ellinwood, 1967, 1969). This syndrome, presumably due to chronic stimulation of dopaminergic pathways in the brain (see above), is characterized by suspiciousness; hypervigilance; visual, auditory, olfactory, and tactile hallucinations; paranoid delusions; ideas of reference; distortions in body image; hyperactivity; lability of mood; and occasional violence. In addition, as in animal models, stereotyped compulsive, ritualized behavior (e.g., sorting, counting, taking things apart) is also seen. Unlike patients with functional psychoses, patients with stimulant-induced psychoses have a relatively high incidence of visual hallucinations and display affect appropriate to the external circumstances (Chapman, 1954). In contrast to patients with other organic toxic psychoses, however, there is a relative absence of disorientation and confusion in these patients.

Laboratory studies of chronic stimulant use in humans, though scarce, provide valuable insight into the mode of action of these drugs as well as their effects on behavior and mood. In one such study, Griffith, Cavanaugh, and Held (1970) administered large doses of amphetamine to six supposedly normal individuals, all of whom had some prior experience with amphetamines. Within 5 days, five of the six subjects developed a typical paranoid psychosis. Whether the rapidity of onset of the psychosis was related to the fact that these subjects had prior drug experience is unclear. However, in clinical settings, it has been reported that even a single dose taken by an experienced user may precipitate psychotic behavior. The similarities between these phenomena and the stereotypy observed in animal studies of chronic stimulant use have caused some to hypothesize that the underlying mechanisms may be similar (i.e., excess dopaminergic activity).

Clinical experience with chronic amphetamine users, particularly those who develop amphetamine psychosis, has fostered speculation about the premorbid personality characteristics of such individuals. However, attempts to define the demographic or psychological characteristics of those stimulant abusers who are prone to develop psychosis have generally failed to distinguish between predrug and drug-induced psychopathology. For example, Ellinwood (1967) studied a group of 25 patients who had taken large doses of amphetamines for 3 months or more, comparing those who had developed psychotic thinking with those who had not. Both groups scored relatively high on the schizophrenic, psychasthenic, psychopathic deviant, and hysterical subscales of the Minnesota Multiphasic Personality Inventory (MMPI), compared to a control group of persons who did not abuse stimulants, but the two subgroups (i.e., psychotic and nonpsychotic) of amphetamine abusers could not be distinguished from each other on the basis of their MMPI profiles. Amphetamine users were also found to be more eccentric, bizarre, and sociopathic, compared to the general addict population of the U.S. Public Health Service Hospital in Lexington, Kentucky, where the study was carried out.

STUDIES OF STIMULANT WITHDRAWAL

Abrupt cessation of chronic amphetamine use is frequently followed by a characteristic abstinence syndrome, characterized by low mood, lethargy, fatigue, bulimia, hypersomnia, and excessive rapid eye movement (REM) sleep. The depressive component of this syndrome has been generally attributed to the depletion of brain catecholamines, specifically norepinephrine, which occurs during chronic stimulant abuse (Schildkraut, Watson, Draskoczy, & Hartman, 1971). The presence of one or more false neurotransmitters (see above) may also play a role.

Laboratory studies of stimulant withdrawal are relatively rare. Watson, Hartmann, and Schildkraut (1972) studied four chronic, high-dose amphetamine users who were abruptly withdrawn from the drug; they measured changes in affective state, sleep patterns, and 24-hour urinary excretion of 3-methoxy-4-hydroxyphenylglycol (MHPG), purportedly the major metabolite of norepinephrine originating in the brain (Schildkraut, 1970). In all subjects, amphetamine withdrawal was followed by the development of depressed mood, which was maximal 48–72 hours after the last dose, though one subject experienced persistent depression for months. Withdrawal was also accompanied by an increase in total sleep time, REM sleep, and REM density (i.e., the number of REMs occurring within each REM period). Urinary MHPG, which was elevated above normal levels during chronic amphetamine administration, fell dramatically in the 48 hours after the drug was stopped, remained low during the 4-day period of withdrawal-related depression, and returned to normal levels thereafter.

In a study carried out by our group (Meyer & Mirin, 1976), changes in mood, catecholamine metabolism, sleep, and behavior were explored in two chronic amphetamine users hospitalized in a research ward setting. All subjects were maintained on dextroamphetamine sulfate, 60 mg/day (a dose consistent with their daily intake prior to hospitalization).

After 7 days on dextroamphetamine, *both* subjects were switched to placebo. After an 18-day drug-free period, they received a 20-mg oral dose of dextroamphetamine; 4 days later, they received a second such dose—this time after pretreatment with fluphenazine, 1.5 mg intramuscularly.

In this study, amphetamine withdrawal was accompanied by a marked rise in depressive symptomatology, as reflected in the subjects' scores on the Hamilton Depression Rating Scale and the Mania–Depression Scale. Depressive symptoms peaked within 2–3 days and then diminished sharply. In contrast to the Watson *et al.* (1972) study, amphetamine withdrawal was accompanied by a transient increase in MHPG excretion, which persisted for 4–5 days and then returned to prewithdrawal levels.

When the subjects were switched to placebo, all-night sleep tracings revealed a sharp increase in both the number of REM periods and overall REM time, as well as a decrease in REM latency (i.e., the time between sleep onset and the first REM period). Subsequent administration of 20 mg of dextroamphetamine reversed these sleep findings dramatically—an effect that was blocked by pretreatment with fluphenazine. Fluphenazine also blocked the increase in peripheral sympathetic activity produced by dextroamphetamine, as well as the drug's euphorigenic effects.

Data from these studies suggest that the depression following stimulant withdrawal is accompanied by alterations in the synthesis, release and/or metabolism of brain catecholamines, and that these changes may be similar to those seen in certain subtypes of naturally occurring, biologically based, depressive disorders. In most instances, these changes are a consequence of the withdrawal process itself and are transient. In some individuals, however, stimulant withdrawal may unmask a persistent underlying depression for which amphetamines and/or other CNS stimulants have been used in an attempt at self-treatment.

In an attempt to study this issue further, our group (Mirin, Weiss, Sollogub, & Michael, 1984a) evaluated a group of chronic stimulant abusers admitted to a drug treatment unit for other forms of psychopathology, with the help of clinical interviews, serial application of psychiatric rating scales, the collection of family pedigree data, and a battery of laboratory tests thought to be useful in the assessment of patients with affective disorder. Application of these measures in a group of 36 stimulant abusers (30 cocaine, 6 amphetamines) revealed that more than

50% were suffering from some form of underlying affective disorder, either unipolar depression (30.6%) or bipolar illness (22%), prior to, or concurrent with, their stimulant abuse problem. In addition, analysis of family pedigree data in these patients revealed a statistically significant increase in affective disorder in their first-degree relatives when compared to both the general population and a group of age-matched abusers of other drugs (i.e., opiates or CNS depressants) (Mirin, Weiss, Sollogub, & Michael, 1984b). Finally, in stimulant abusers who were suffering from "retarded" depressions, the 24-hour urinary excretion of MHPG was found to be low, relative to that of stimulant abusers who were not depressed. The persistence of these findings, even after patients had been drug-free for 4 weeks, suggests that in stimulant abusers with "retarded" depressions, the self-administration of drugs that produce transient increases in central noradrenergic activity is consistent with an attempt to self-treat an underlying affective disorder.

CANNABIS

Cannabis[1], a drug that has been used as an intoxicant for centuries, has also been the subject of extensive laboratory study in both animals and humans in the last two decades. For the purposes of this chapter, however, I will focus primarily on the acute and chronic effects of cannabis intoxication in humans as most relevant to a discussion of the abuse potential of this drug.

As in the case of other drugs, both objective and subjective responses to cannabis intoxication are shaped by pharmacological, individual, and environmental factors (L. E. Hollister, Overall, & Gerber, 1975). Dosage, route of administration, and prior drug experience clearly play a role, as do the expectations of the user and the setting in which the drug is consumed. In the laboratory, the interaction between research subjects and laboratory personnel, the presence or absence of other intoxicated individuals, and the laboratory environment itself also shape the subjective response to cannabis intoxication (Cappell & Kuchar, 1974). In general, the impact of environmental variables on the

[1]In this chapter, the generic term "cannabis" is used to denote marijuana and/or its more potent form, hashish. Studies of the effects of a specific form of cannabis (e.g., marijuana) or its active ingredient, Δ-9-tetrahydrocannabinol (THC), are noted in the text.

perception of drug effects appears to be greater when laboratory subjects are exposed to low and intermediate doses of the drug, compared to when higher doses are used.

ACUTE EFFECTS ON BRAIN FUNCTION AND PERFORMANCE

A number of investigators have explored the effects of acute and chronic cannabis intoxication on brain function and/or performance on a variety of psychomotor tasks. Studies of the acute effects of cannabis smoking on brain electrophysiology reveal characteristic electroencephalographic alterations, including slowing of alpha waves and enhanced slow-wave and spike activity from deeper (i.e., subcortical) structures (Fink, Volavka, Panagiotopoulos, & Stafanis, 1976; Heath, 1976). Increased alpha and slow-wave activity have also been reported following administration of large doses of marijuana or its major active ingredient, delta-9-tetrahydrocannabinol (THC) (Tassinari, Ambrosetto, & Gastaut, 1976; Tassinari, Peraita-Adrados, Ambrosetto, & Gastaut, 1974). Studies of cortical-evoked potentials recorded from scalp electrodes have yielded variable findings, but the positive wave seen at approximately 300 milliseconds after a standard applied stimulus (P300) appears to be decreased during acute cannabis intoxication. The relationshp between this finding and the effect of marijuana on attention remains unclear.

The acute effects of cannabis on psychomotor performance are dose-related and affected by prior drug history. In one of the earliest studies designed to look at these parameters in humans, our group (Meyer, Pillard, Shapiro, & Mirin, 1971) compared six heavy and six casual smokers of marijuana on a variety of subjective and performance measures in response to placebo, a fixed dose of marijuana, and a self-selected *ad libitum* dose. With regard to subjective effects, casual users had similar responses to both placebo and active drug, though their performance on a variety of psychomotor tasks was far more impaired when receiving either a fixed dose or a self-selected *ad lib* dose of the active drug. In contrast, heavy users were better able to distinguish between placebo and active drug and seemed more sensitive to the marijuana high. On the other hand, heavy users also demonstrated greater immunity to the disruptive effects of marijuanna on psychomotor performance, perhaps as a consequence of pre-existing behavioral tolerance. The degree of perceptual impairment was not marked in either group, a finding that may be attributed to the low doses used in this study.

Marijuana intoxication has also been shown to produce impairment of short-term memory, altered time sense, increased reaction time, and a decrement in perceptual–motor coordination (Moskowicz & Mc-Glothlin, 1974; Tinklenberg & Darley, 1976). Effects on memory appear to last for several hours after smoking, and some have suggested that the drug may affect the storage of new information in long-term memory (Gianutsos & Litwack, 1976). THC has been found to alter the rate, sequence, and goal-directedness of thinking processes, and to contribute to both temporal disorganization and the development of delusional ideation in previously normal subjects (Melges *et al.*, 1974). Subjects allowed to smoke the equivalent of 20 mg of THC over a 10-minute period may also develop profound difficulties in tracking information over time, as well as persecutory ideation (Melges *et al.*, 1974).

EFFECTS ON SOCIAL INTERACTION AND AGGRESSION

Regular users of cannabis cite the drug's facilitory effects on social interaction as an important reason for continued use. This is so, despite the fact that most nonintoxicated observers would agree that cannabis use in group settings frequently results in either incoherent attempts at conversation and/or increasing social withdrawal. Laboratory studies of the acute effects of the drug on social interaction have been carried out by a number of investigators (Babor, Mendelson, Greenberg, & Kuehnle, 1975; Jones & Benowiz, 1976; Salzman, Van der Kolk, & Shader, 1976). In one such study, Babor *et al.* (1975) found that both moderate and heavy marijuana users tended to interact less during periods of drug intoxication, while Galanter *et al.* (1974) reported that marijuana use failed to increase feelings of cohesiveness or produce any consistent changes in affect or insight in experienced users participating in group therapy sessions.

The effect of cannabis preparations on social behavior has also been linked to the drug's purported antihostility effect. The latter has been explored in a number of laboratory studies in both animals and humans. In mice, administration of cannabis resin produces a dose-related decrease in isolation-induced aggression, as well as a decrease in social interaction (Santos, Sampio, Fernandes, & Carlini, 1966; Siegel & Poole,

1969). On the other hand, cannabis has also been reported to induce fearfulness in a number of animal species, including the dog, rabbit, and monkey (Mechoulam, 1973), particularly following high-dose use.

In humans, acute marijuana intoxication is accompanied by a decrease in feelings of hostility (Tinklenberg, 1974), even after introduction of a frustrating stimulus. In our own studies (Mirin, Shapiro, Meyer, Pillard, & Fisher, 1971), we found that while heavy and casual users had similar "trait scores" on the Bass–Durkee Hostility Scale, heavy users were significantly more hostile as measured by the Psychiatric Outpatient Mood Scale (POMS) in response to a psychiatric interview designed to explore the subjects' motivation for drug use. Moreover, chronic users frequently tended to initiate drug use in response to feelings engendered by interpersonal conflict. These findings suggest that for some chronic users, the behavioral placidity and feelings of detachment induced by cannabis use may function to modify hostile tendencies, particularly as they occur in certain interpersonal situations.

THE EFFECTS OF CHRONIC USE

Motivation

The precise sequelae of chronic cannabis use have been a subject of debate in the clinical literature. In cultures in which there is considerably more chronic, high-dose use than in this country (e.g., Nepal, Jamaica), some controlled studies have concluded that such use may result in a "cannabis psychosis" (Sharma, 1975), while others have not (Rubin & Comitas, 1975). In this country, chronic heavy use has been associated with a greater prevalence of underlying psychopathology and a tendency to abuse other psychoactive drugs (Mirin *et al.*, 1971), as well as the development of an "amotivational syndrome" (Allen & West, 1968) in some individuals. However, some have suggested that the lack of motivation observed in chronic heavy users may be the result of either a pre-existing or a drug-induced depression (Halikas, 1974; Halikas, Goodwin, & Guze, 1971; Kupfer, Detre, Koral, & Fajans, 1973).

In an attempt to explore these issues in a laboratory setting, Mendelson, Kuehnle, Greenberg, and Mello (1976) studied 27 heavy and casual marijuana users who were allowed to work for marijuana cigarettes in a research ward environment. Each subject served as his or her own control through three successive phases: a 5-day baseline period;

21 days in which subjects could acquire and smoke marijuana cigarettes on a fixed-ratio, fixed-interval schedule; and a 5-day postsmoking period. In this study, both heavy and casual users increased their daily marijuana consumption over time, with heavy users doing so at a somewhat more rapid rate. In both groups, however, operant work output decreased as a function of the dose of marijuana consumed, though heavy users maintained a higher level of work output and smoked more of the drug than casual users.

Cognitive Functioning

Persistent reports of poor school performance in chronic cannabis users, especially with complex tasks that require sustained attention, have fostered attempts to better define the effects of such use on cognitive functioning. In one such study, Culver and King (1974) compared a group of chronic marijuana users with chronic users of hallucinogens and a non-drug-using control group with respect to their performance on a variety of tasks designed to assess brain functioning. During a 1-year period of prospective follow-up, casual or heavy use of marijuana did not appear to produce a deterioration in cognitive functioning, intelligence, or performance on tests of perceptual–motor ability. On the other hand, failure to find decrements in these areas may have been a consequence of the measures employed, the length of the follow-up period, or the subtlety of any impairments induced by the drug.

THE HALLUCINOGENS

As a class of compounds, the hallucinogens share the ability to induce toxic states in the user that mimic functional psychoses. In sufficient doses, the drugs produce perceptual distortions and changes in mood, usually without accompanying disturbance of memory or orientation. In addition, some of these drugs induce euphoria, experiences of depersonalization or *déjà vu*, hallucinations, generalized loss of body and ego boundaries, and emotional liability (Hoffman, 1961; L. E. Hollister & Hartman, 1962). Though some have claimed that the hallucinogenic drugs are psychedelic (i.e., mind-expanding), most investigators would agree that this is not the case. Rather, the hallucinogens appear to induce, in the user, exquisite sensitivity to relatively low levels of internal and external stimulation, rendering them highly vulnerable to sensory overload (Shulgin, 1964).

In the late 1960s and early 1970s, the above-described properties of the hallucinogens were assigned considerable personal and social value by a generation of young adults; this led to their frequent use and abuse. This phenomenon, in turn, triggered a spate of clinical and laboratory studies designed to elucidate the pharmacological properties of the hallucinogens and their effects on both animal and human behavior. While the literature on this subject is voluminous, only a brief and selective review is attempted here, with emphasis on those properties that contribute to the recreational abuse of these drugs.

ACUTE EFFECTS ON BRAIN FUNCTION

The "mind-altering" properties of the hallucinogens have naturally fostered attempts to elucidate the effects of these drugs on CNS functioning. In animals, the ability to record brain electrical activity through stereotactically implanted or scalp electrodes facilities this task. In one such study, Purpura (1956) studied the effects of the hallucinogen LSD on brain electrical activity in the cat, observing inhibition of both the primary sensory cortex and the nonspecific sensory system with corresponding excitation of the primary sensory pathways. Subsequent studies (Evarts, 1958) have revealed similar findings, while also suggesting that the drug tends to be concentrated in those subcortical structures that subserve vision—a finding consistent with the production of visual hallucinations.

In humans, LSD and other hallucinogens (e.g., psilocybin, mescaline) produce disturbances in the integration of sensory information, foster the development of perceptual distortions, and disrupt cognitive functioning. As in animals, these effects may be the result of a decrease in the cortical threshold for certain types of primary sensory input (e.g., auditory, visual Hill, Fischer, & Warshay, 1969), in turn producing a degree of hypersensitivity to low- to moderate-intensity stimulation.

MOTIVATION FOR USE

Though hallucinogens such as LSD have been subject to abuse, they are not known to function as primary reinforcers in animal models of drug self-administration. Also, while tolerance to the effects of hallucinogens apparently develops quite rapidly, there is no evidence that physical dependence develops as a consequence of chronic administration. In humans, daily use is quite rare. While some have reported that sex is more pleasurable under the influence of drugs like LSD, this effect is not regarded to be an important motivation for repetitive use.

Clinicians experienced in the treatment of substance abusers frequently maintain that predrug personality is an important influence on drug-using behavior, with respect to both drug of choice and the propensity to become a chronic user. Accordingly, a number of studies have sought to identify those personality characteristics that might render an individual more prone to repetitive use of these drugs. In this context, some have reported that the behavioral and subjective response to hallucinogenic drugs is enhanced in individuals who are highly suggestible or excitable, as well as individuals who are overly sensitive to external stimuli (Fischer, Marks, Hill, *et al.*, 1968). Based on these findings, one could postulate that, for some individuals, the hallucinogenic drug experience serves to augment a pre-existing propensity for stimulus-seeking behavior, and that drugs enhancing sensory input may be regarded as pleasurable or reinforcing by such individuals. Thus the drug may be sought out by introspective, withdrawn stimulus "reducers" (Silverman, 1969, 1971) in an attempt to break through the psychological, and perhaps neurophysiological, barriers to affective responsivity.

In some respects, this model of drug self-administration is analogous to the use of cocaine and other CNS stimulants by manic–depressive patients, who use such drugs not only as short-acting antidepressants during periods of depression, but also as enhancers of their "highs" during periods of hypomania or mania. Moreover, like stimulant abusers who experience affective flattening during drug withdrawal, repetative hallucinogen use may, in part, be an attempt to recapture the perceptual and affective intensity characteristic of the drug experience.

Potential Therapeutic Uses

Laboratory studies of the effects of hallucinogens in humans have gradually given way to clinical studies carried out in patients with infantile autism (Bender, 1966), psychopathic personality (Shagass & Bittle, 1967), and chronic pain (Kast & Collins, 1964). While early studies in autistic children reported increased awareness of the external environment, elevation of mood, and a decrease in stereotypic and self-destructive behavior, later and more carefully controlled studies yielded mixed results. Similarly, while some patients diagnosed as having psychopathic personality disorders reported the development of "insight" into their behavior, with a corresponding increase in motivation to change, long-term improvement failed to materialize (Shagass & Bittle, 1967).

The finding that LSD, and perhaps other hallucinogens, appear to increase tolerance for high-intensity stimulation has led to a number of clinical trials in which the analgesic properties of these drugs have been tested. In monkeys, intravenous LSD (up to 1 mg/kg) appeared to abolish the response to painful stimuli (Evarts, 1958), an effect possibly mediated by inhibition of those pathways carrying pain fibers to association areas of the cerebral cortex. In a study in humans, Kast (1966) reported a decrease in reported pain intensity in some severely ill terminal patients in the 10 days following a single LSD experience, though the drug experience itself was decidedly unpleasant for some patients. In another study, Kast and Collins (1964) gave 128 acutely ill medical patients up to 100 μg of LSD, which they reported provided more effective analgesia than either meperidine or hydromorophone.

SUMMARY

In the last 15 years, laboratory studies involving various drugs of abuse have contributed greatly to our understanding of the effects of these agents on the mood and behavior of those who use them. Such studies have been useful in testing hypotheses generated by clinical experience, and in objectifying and quantifying drug-related phenomena that would otherwise be highly subjective.

In this chapter, I have attempted to review some of the vast and growing literature such studies have generated. The focus here has been on studies that explore the effects of these drugs on brain function, which, in turn, contribute to their abuse potential in humans. Given the continued interest in this area, the next 15 years should provide clinicians and researchers with the opportunity to design even more sophisticated studies that will further elucidate the fatal attraction these drugs have for a substantial segment of our society.

REFERENCES

Allen, J. R., & West, L. J. (1968). Flight from violence: hippies and the green rebellion. *American Journal of Psychiatry, 125,* 364–374.

Alterman, A. I., Gottheil, E., & Crawford, H. D. (1975). Mood changes in an alcoholism treatment program based on drinking decisions. *American Journal of Psychiatry, 132,* 1032–1037.

Angrist, B. M., & Gershon, S. (1970). The phenomenology of experimentally induced amphetamine psychosis—preliminary observations. *Biological Psychiatry, 2,* 95–107.

Babor, T. F., Mendelson, J. H., Greenberg, I., & Kuehnle, J. C. (1975). Marijuana consumption and tolerance to physiological and subjective effects. *Archives of General Psychiatry, 32,* 1548–1552.

Bell, D. S. (1973). The experimental reproduction of amphetamine psychosis. *Archives of General Psychiatry, 29;* 35–40.

Bender, L. (1966). D-lysergic acid in the treatment of the biological features of childhood schizophrenia. *Diseases of the Nervous System, 27,* (Suppl.), 39–42.

Bigelow, G., Liebson, I., & Griffiths, R. (1974). Alcoholic drinking: Suppression by a brief time-out procedure. *Behavior Research and Therapy, 12,* 107–115.

Brodie, B. B., Cho, A. K., & Gessa, G. L. (1970). Possible role of p-hydroxynorephedrine in the depletion of norepinephrine induced by d-amphetamine and intolerance to this drug. In E. Costa & S. Garattini (Eds.), *Amphetamines and related compounds* (pp. 217–230) New York: Raven Press.

Bunney, B. S., Walters, J., Roth, R., & Aghajanian, G. (1973). Dopaminergic neutrons: Effects of antipsychotic drugs and amphetamine on single cell activity. *Journal of Pharmacology and Experimental Therapentics, 185,* 560–571.

Burn, J. H., & Rand, M. J. (1958). The action of sympathomimetic amines in animals treated with reserpine. *Journal of Physiology, 144,* 314–336.

Cappell, H., & Herman, P. C. (1972). Alcohol and tension reduction: A review. *Quarterly Journal of Studies on Alcohol, 33,* 33–64.

Cappell, H., & Kuchar, E. (1974). Pharmacologic and nonpharmacologic factors in marijuana intoxication. *Clinical Toxicolory, 7,* 315.

Carlini, E. A., & Masur, J. (1969). Development of aggressive behavior in rats by chronic administration of *Cannabis sativa* (marijuana). *Life Sciences, 8,* 607–620.

Carlsson, A. (1970). Amphetamine and brain catecholamines. In E. Costa & S. Garattini (Eds.), *Amphetamines and related compounds* (pp. 289–300). New York: Raven Press.

Carnathan, G., Meyer, R. E., & Cochin, J. (1977) Narcotic blockage, length of addiction and persistence of intravenous morphine self-administration in rats. *Psychopharmacology, 54,* 67–71.

Carr, L. A., & Moore, K. E. (1969). Norepinephrine: Release from brain by d-amphetamine *in vivo. Science, 164,* 322–323.

Chance, M. R. A., Mackintosh, J. H., & Dixon, A. K. (1973). The effects of ethyl alcohol on social encounters between mice. *Journal of Alcoholism, 8,* 90–93.

Chapman, A. H. (1954). Paranoid psychoses associated with amphetamine usage—a clinical note. *American Journal of Psychiatry, 111,* 43.

Claghorn, J. L., Ordy, J. M., & Nagy, A. (1965). Spontaneous opiate addiction in rhesus monkeys. *Science, 149,* 440–441.

Cooper, B. R., Cott, J. M., & Breese, G. R. (1974). Effects of catecholamine-depleting drugs and amphetamine on self-stimulation of brain following various 6-hydroxydopamine treatments. *Psychopharmacology, 37,* 235–248.

Culver, C. M., & King, F. W. (1974). Neuropsychological assessment of undergraduate marihuana and LSD users. *Archives of General Psychistry, 31,* 707–711.

Cutler, M. G., & Mackintosh, J. H. (1975). Effects of delta-9-tetrahydrocannabinol on social behaviour in the laboratory mouse and rat. *Psychopharmacology 44,* 287–289.

Davis D. (1971). Mood changes in alcoholic subjects with programmed and free-choice experimental drinking. In N. K. Mello & J. H. Mendelson (Eds.), *Recent advances in studies of alcoholism* (DHHS Publication No. HSM 71-9045, pp. 596–618). Washington, DC: U.S. Government Printing Office.

Davis, W. M., & Smith, S. G. (1972). Alpha-methyltyrosine to prevent self-administration of morphine and amphetamine. *Current Therapeutic Research 14,* 814–819.

Davis, W. M., Smith, S. G., & Khalsa, J. H. (1975). Noradrenergic role in the self-administration of morphone or amphetamine. *Pharmacology, Biochemistry and Behavior, 3,* 447–484.

Deneau, G. A., Yanagita, T., & Seevers, M. H. (1969). Self administration of psychoactive substances by the monkey. *Psychopharmacologia, 16,* 30–48.

Dews, P. B. (1984). Maintenance of behavior by "schedules": An unfamiliar contribution to maintenance of abuses. In G. Serban (Ed.), *The social and medical aspects of drug abuse,* pp. 59–66. New York: Spectrum.

Downs, D. A., & Woods, J. H. (1974). Codeline- and cocaine-reinforced responding in rhesus monkeys: Effects of dose on response rates under a fixed-ratio schedule. *Journal of Pharmacology and Experimental Therapeutics, 191,* 179–188.

Ellinwood, E. H., Jr. (1967). Amphetamine psychosis: I. Description of the individuals and process. *Journal of Nervous and Mental Diseases, 146,* 144–273.

Ellinwood, E. H., Jr. (1969). Amphetamine psychosis: III. A multidimensional process. *Seminars in Psychiatry, 1,* 208.

Esposito, R., & Kornetsky, C. (1977). Morphine lowering of self-stimulation thresholds: Lack of tolerance with long-term administration. *Science, 195,* 189–191.

Evarts, E. V. (1958). Neurophysiological correlates of pharmacologically induced behavioral disturbances in H. C. Solomon, S. Cobb, & W. Penfield. (Eds.), *The brain and human behavior* Baltimore: Williams & Wilkins.

Fangel, C., & Kaada, B. R. (1960). Behavior, attention and fear induced by cortical stimulation in the cat. *Electroencephalography and Clinical Neurophysiology, 12,* 575.

Fink, M., Volavka, J., Panagiotopoulos, C. P., & Stafanis, C. (1976). Quantitative EEG studies of marihuana, delta-9-THC and hashish in man. In S. Szara & M. Braude (Eds.), *Pharmacology of marihuana* (pp. 383–392). New York: Raven Press.

Fischer, R., Marks, P. A., Hill, R. M., *et al.* (1968). Personality structure as the main determinant of drug induced (model) psychoses. *Nature, 218,* 296–298.

Fraser, J. F., Jones, B. E., Rosenberg, D. E., Thompson, A. K. (1963). Effects of addiction to intravenous heroin on patterns of physical activity in man. *Clinical Pharmacology and Therapeutics, 4,* 188–196.

Galanter, M. Stillman, R., Wyatt, R. J., Vaughan, T. B., Weingartner, H., & Nurnberg, F. L. (1974). Marihuana and social behavior: A controlled study. *Archives of General Psychiatry, 30,* 518–521.

Gianutsos, R., & Litwack, A. R. (1976). Chronic marijuana smokers show reduced coding into long-term storage. *Bulletin of the Psychonomic Society, 7*(3), 277–279.

Glowinski, J., Axelrod, J., & Iversen, L. L. (1966). Regional studies of catecholamines in rat brains, 4: Effects of drugs on disposition and metabolism of H^3-norepinephrine and H^3-dopamine. *Journal of Pharmacology and Experimental Therapeutics, 153,* 30–41.

Goldberg, S. R., Hoffmeister, F., Schlichting, V., & Wuttke, W. (1971). A comparison of pentobarbital and cocaine self-administration in rhesus monkeys: Effects of dose and fixed ratio parameters. *Journal of Pharmacology and Experimental Therapeutics, 179,* 277–283.

Goodwin, D. W. (1973). Alcohol in suicide and homicide. *Quarterly Journal of Studies on Alcohol, 34,* 144–156.

Griffith, J. D. Cavanaugh J. H., & Held, J. (1970). Experimental psychosis induced by the administration of d-amphetamine. In E. Costa & S. Garratini (Eds.), *Amphetamines and related compounds* (pp. 897–904). New York: Raven Press.

Haertzen, C. A., & Hooks, N. T. (1969). Changes in personality and subjective experience associated with the chronic administration and withdrawal of opiates. *Journal of Nervous and Mental Disease, 148,* 606–614.

Halikas, J. A., Hoofein, F. E., & Guze, S. B. (1971). Marijuana effects: A survey of regular users. *Journal of the American Medical Association, 217,* 692–694.

Halikas, J. A. (1974). Marijuana use and psychiatric illness. In L. L. Miller (ed.), *Marijuana: Effects on human behavior.* New York: Academic Press.

Heath, R. G. (1976). Marihuana and delta-9-THC: Acute and chronic effects on brain function of monkeys. In S. Szara & M. Braude (Eds.), *Pharmacology of marihuana.* New York: Raven Press.

Higgins, R. L., & Marlatt, G. A. (1975). Fear of interpersonal evaluation as a determinant of alcohol consumption in male social drinkers. *Journal of Abnormal Psychology, 84,* 644–651.

Hill, R. M., Fischer, R., & Warshay D. (1969). Effects of psychodysleptic drug psilocybin on visual perception: Changes in brightness preference. *Experientia, 25,* 166–169.

Hoffman, A. (1961). Chemical, pharmacological and medical aspects of psychotomimetics. *Journal of Experimental Medicine, 5,* 31–51.

Hollister, A. S., Breese, G. R., & Cooper, B. R. (1974). Comparison of tyrosine hydroxylase and dopamine-b-hydroxylase inhibition with the effects of various 6-hydroxydopamine treatments on d-amphetamine-induced motor activity. *Psychopharmacology, 36,* 1–16.

Hollister, L. E., & Hartman, A.M. (1962). Mescaline, lysergic acid diethylamide and psilocybin: Comparison of clinical syndromes, effects on color perception and biochemical measures. *Comprehensive Psychiatry, 3,* 235–241.

Hollister, L. E., Overall, J. E., & Gerber, M. L. (1975). Marihuana and setting. *Archives of General Psychiatry, 32,* 798–801.

Jones, R. T., & Benowiz, N. (1976). The 30-day trip—clinical studies of cannabis tolerance and dependence. S. Szara & M. Braude (Eds.), *Pharmacology of marihuana.* New York: Raven Press.

Jonsson, G., Malmfors, T., & Sachs, C. (1975). 6-hydroxydopamine as a denervation tool in catecholamine research. In *Chemical tools in catecholamine research* New York: American Elsevier. (vol. 1).

Jonsson, L. E., & Sjostrom, K. (1970). A rating scale for evaluation of the clinical course and symptomatology in amphetamine psychosis. *British Journal of Psychiatry, 2,* 95–107.

Kaada, B. R., Andersen, P., & Jansen, J. (1954). Stimulation of the amygdaloid nuclear complex in unanesthetized cats. *Neurology* (Minneapolis), *4,* 48.

Kast, E. L. (1966). LSD and the dying patient. *Chicago Medical School Quarterly, 26,* 80–87.

Kast, E. L., & Collins, V. S. (1964). A study of lysergic acid diethylamide as an analgesic agent. *Current Researches in Anesthesia and Analyesia,* 285.

Kreuz, L. E., Rose, R. M., & Jennings, J. R. (1972). Suppression of plasma testosterone levels and psychological stress: A longitudinal study of young men in officer candidate school. *Archives of General Psychiatry, 26,* 479–482.

Kupfer, D. J., Detre, T., Koral, J., & Fajans, P. (1973). A comment on the "amotivational syndrome" in marijuana smokers. *American Journal of Psychiatry, 130,* 1319–1322.

Lang, A. R., Goeckner, D. J., Adesso, V. J., & Marlatt, G. A., (1975). Effects of alcohol on aggression in male social drinkers. *Journal Abnormal Psychology, 84,* 508–518.

Marlatt, G. A., Kosturn, C. F., & Lang, A. R. (1975). Provocation to anger and opportunity for retaliation as determinants of alcohol consumption in social drinkers. *Journal Abnormal Psychology, 84,* 652–659.

Martin, W. R., & Fraser, H. F. (1961). A comparative study of physiological and subjective effects of heroin and morphine administered intravenously in post-addicts. *Journal Pharmacology and Experimental Therapeutics, 133,* 338–399.

Martin, W. R., Jasinski, D. R., Haertzen, C. A., Kay, D. C., Jones, B. E., & Carpenter, R. W. (1973). Methadone—a reevaluation. *Archives of General Psychiatry, 28,* 286–295.

Martin, W. R., Sloan, J. W., Sapira, J. D., & Jasinski, D. R. (1971). Physiologic, subjective, and behavioral effects of amphetamine, methamphetamine, ephedrine, phenmetrazine, and methylphenidate in man. *Clinical Pharmacology and Therapeutics, 12,* 245–258.

Mechoulam, R. (1973). *Marihuana: Chemistry, pharmacology, metabolism and clinical effects.* London: Academic press.

Melges, F. T., Tinklenberg, J. R., Deardorff, C. M., Davies, N. H., Anderson, R. E., & Owen, C. A. (1974). Temporal disorganization and delusional-like ideation: Processes induced by hashish and alcohol. *Archives of General Psychiatry, 30,* 855–861.

Mello, N. K., & Mendelson, J. H. (1972). Drinking patterns during work-contingent and noncontingent alcohol acquisition. *Psychosomatic Medicine, 34,* 139–164.

Mendelson, J. H. (Ed.). (1964). Experimentally induced chronic intoxication and withdrawal in alcoholics. *Quarterly Journal of Studies on Alcoholic,* (Suppl. 2).

Mendelson, J. H., Ellingboe, J., & Kuehnle, J. C. (1976). Effects of alcohol and marihuana on plasma luteinizing hormone and testosterone. In *Proceedings of the Committee on Problems of Drug Dependence* (pp. 525–537). Washington, DC: National Academy of Sciences/National Research council.

Mendelson, J. H., Kuehnle, J. C., Greenberg, I., & Mello, N. (1976). Operant acquisition of marihuana in man. *Journal of Pharmacology and Experimental Therapeutics, 198,* 42–53.

Mendelson, J. H., & Mello, N. K. (1974). Alcohol, aggression and androgens. In S. H. Frazier (Ed.), *Aggression* (Proceedings of the Assocation for Research in Nervous and Mental Disease pp. 225–247). Baltimore: Williams & Wilkins.

Mendelson, J. H., Mello, N. K., & Ellingboe, J. (1977). Effects of alcohol on pituitary–gonadal hormones, sexual function, and aggression in human males. In *Psychopharmacology: A generation of progress.* New York: Raven Press.

Mendelson, J. H., Mello, N. K., & Solomon, P. (1968). Small group drinking behavior: An experimental study of chronic alcoholics. In A. Wikler (Ed.), *The addictive states* Association for Research in Nervous and Mental Disease, pp. 399–430). Baltimore: Williams & Wilkins.

Meyer, R. E., McNamee, H. B., Mirin, S. M., & Altman, J. L. (1974a). A research paradigm for the analysis and modification of heroin-seeking behavior in man: Affective changes. In *Proceedings of the Committee on Problems of Drug De-*

pendence (pp. 974–981). Washington, DC: National Academy of Science/National Research Council.

Meyer, R. E., McNamee, H. B., Mirin, S. M., & Altman, J. L. (1974b). A research paradigm for the analysis and modification of heroin-seeking behavior in man: Methodology and preliminary results. In *Proceedings of the Committee on Problems of Drug Dependence* (pp. 645–668). Washington, DC: National Academy of Science/National Research Council.

Meyer, R. E., & Mirin, S. M. (1979). *The heroin stimulus.* New York: Plenum Press.

Meyer, R. E., & Mirin, S. M. (1976). Unpublished raw data.

Meyer, R. E., Mirin, S. M., Altman, J. L., & McNamee, H. B. (1976). A behavioral paradigm for the evaluation of narcotic antagonists. *Archives of General Psychiatry, 33,* 371–377.

Meyer, R. E., Pillard, R. C., Shapiro, L., & Mirin, S. M. (1971). Administration of marihuana to heavy and casual users. *American Journal of Psychiatry, 128,* 198–203.

Mirin, S. M., Mendelson, J. H., Ellingboe, J., & Meyer, R. E. (1976). Acute effects of heroin and naltrexone on testosterone and gonadotropin secretion: Pilot study. *Psychoneuroendocrinology, 1,* 539–369.

Mirin, S. M., Meyer, E. E., and McNamee, H. B. (1975). Psychopathology and mood during heroin use: Acute versus chronic effects. In *Proceedings of the Committee on Problems of Drug Dependence* Washington, DC: (pp. 300–319). National Academy of Sciences/National Research Council.

Mirin, S. M., Meyer, R. E., & McNamee, H. B. (1976). Psychopathology and mood during heroin use: Acute versus chronic effects. *Archives of General Psychiatry, 33,* 1503–1508.

Mirin, S. M., Shapiro, L., Meyer, R. E., Pillard, R. C., & Fisher, S. (1971). Heavy versus casual use of marihuana: a redefinition of the problem. *American Journal of Psychiatry, 127,* 1134–1141.

Mirin, S. M., Meyer, R. E., & McNamee, H. B. (1976). Psychopathology and mood during heroin use: Acute versus chronic effects. *Archives of General Psychiatry, 33,* 1503–1508.

Mirin, S. M., Weiss, R. D., Sollogub, A., & Michael, J. (1984b). Psychopathology in the families of drug abusers. In S. M. Mirin, (Ed.), *Substance abuse and psychopathology* (pp. 79–106). Washington, DC: American Psychiatric Press.

Moore, K. E., and Thornburg, J. E. (1973). Importance of brain dopamine for the stimulant actions of amphetamine. In E. Usdin & S. H. Snyder (Eds.), *Frontiers in catecholamine research* (pp. 1031–1034). New York: Pergamon Press.

Moskowitz, H., & McGlothlin, W. (1974). Effects of marihuana on auditory signal detection. *Psychopharmacology, 40* (2), 137–145.

Nagarajan, M., Gross, M. M., Kissin, B., & Best, S. (1973). Affective changes during 6 days of experimental alcoholization and subsequent withdrawal. In M. M. Gross (Ed.), *Advances in experimental medicine and biology: Vol. 35. Alcohol intoxication and withdrawal: Experimental studies* (pp. 351–363). New York: Plenum.

Nathan, P. E., & O'Brien, J. S. (1971). An experimental analysis of the behavior of alcoholics and nonalcoholics during prolonged experimental drinking: A necessary precursor of behavior therapy? *Behavior Therapy, 2,* 455–476.

Nathan, P. E., O'Brien, J. S., & Lowenstein, L. M., (1971) Operant studies of chronic alcoholism: Interaction of alcohol and alcoholics. In M. K. Roach, W. M. McIssac, & P. J. Creaven (Eds.), *Biological aspects of alcohol* (pp. 341–370). Austin: University of Texas Press.

Nathan, P. E., Titler, N. A., Lowenstein, L. M., Solomon, P., & Rossi, A. M. (1970). Behavioral analysis of chronic alcoholism: Interaction of alcohol and human contact. *Archives of General Psychiatry, 22,* 419–430.

O'Brien, C. P., & Greenstein, R. (1976). Naltrexone in a behavioral treatment program. In D. Julius & P. Renault (Eds.), *Narcotic antagonists: Naltrexone* (National Institute on Drug Abuse Research Monograph Series No. 9, pp. 136–140). Washington, DC: U.S. Government Printing Office.

O'Brien, C. P., O'Brien, T. J., Mintz, J., & Brady, J. P. (1975). Conditioning of narcotic abstinence symptoms in human subjects. *Drug and Alcohol Dependence* 115–123.

Olds, J., & Milner, P. (1954). Positive reinforcement produced by electrical stimulation of septal area and other regions of the rat brain. *Journal of Comparative Psychology, 47,* 419–427.

Philips, A. G., Brooke, S. M., & Fibiger, H. C. (1975). Effects of amphetamine isomers and neuroleptics on self-stimulation from the nucleus accumbens and dorsal noradrenergic bundle. *Brain Research, 85,* 13–22.

Purpura, D. P. (1956). Electrophysiological analysis of psychotogenic drug action: I. Effect of LSD on specific afferent systems in the cat. *Archives of Neurology and Psychiatry, 75,* 122–131.

Randrup, H., & Munkvad, I. (1972). Correlation between specific effects of amphetamines on the brain and on behavior. In E H. Ellingwood & S. Cohen (Eds.), *Current concepts on amphetamine abuse* pp. 17–25. Washington, DC: U.S. Government Printing Office.

Resnick, P., Volavka, J., Freedman, A. M., & Thomas, M. (1974). Studies of EN1639A (naltrexone): A new narcotic antagonist. *American Journal of Psychiatry, 131,* 646–650.

Rose, R. M., Gordon, P. P., & Bernstein, I. S. (1972). Plasma testosterone levels in the male rhesus: Influences of sexual and social stimuli. *Science, 178,* 643–645.

Rose, R. M., Haladay, J. W., & Bernstein, I. S. (1971). Plasma testosterone, dominance rank and aggressive behaviour in male rhesus monkeys.*Nature, 231,* 366–368.

Rubin, V., & Comitas, L. (1975). *Ganga in Jamaica: A medical anthropological study of chronic marihuana use.* The Hague: Mouton.

Salzman, C., Van der Kolk, B. A., & Shader, R. I. (1976). Marijuana and hostility in a small-group setting. *American Journal of Psychiatry, 133,* 1029–1032.

Santos, M., Sampio, M. R. P., Fernandes, N. S., & Carlini, E. A. (1966). Effects of *Cannabis sativa* (marihuana) on the fighting behaviour of mice. *Psychopharmacology, 8,* 437–444.

Schildkraut, J. J. (1970a). Neurochemical studies of the effective disorders. *American Journal of Psychiatry 127:* 358–360.

Schildkraut, J. J. (1970b). Tranylcypromine: Effects on norepinephrine metabolism in rat brain. *American Journal of Psychiatry, 126,* 925–931.

Schildkraut, J. J., Watson, R., Draskoczy, P. R., & Hartman, E. (1971). Amphetamine withdrawal depression and MHPG excretion. *Lancet, 1,* 485–486.

Schuster, C. R., & Villareal, J. E. (1968). The experimental analysis of opioid dependence. In D. H. Efron (Ed.), *Psychophzomacology: A review of progress* (DHEW Publication No. PHS 1836, pp. 811–828). Washington, DC: U.S. Government Printing Office.

Shagass, C., Bittle, R. M. (1967). Therapeutic effects of LSD: A follow-up study. *Journal of Nervous and Mental Disease, 144,* 471–478.

Sharma, B. P. (1975). Cannabis and its users in Nepal. *British Journal of Psychiatry, 127,* 550–552.

Shulgin, A. T. (1964). 3—ethoxy-4,5-methylenedioxy amphetamine, a new psychotomimetic agent. *Nature, 201,* 1120–1121.

Siegel, R. K., & Poole, J. (1969). Psychedelic-induced social behaviour in mice: A preliminary report. *Psychological Reports, 25,* 704–706.

Silverman, J. (1969). The study of individual differences in the effects of LSD-25 on sensory–perceptual functioning. In *Proceedings of the Conference on Adverse Reactions to LSD* (DHEW Publication No. PHS 1810, pp. 14–20). Washington, DC: U.S.Government Printing Office.

Silverman, J. (1971). Research with psychedelics: Some biopsychological concepts and possible clinical applications. *Archives of General Psychiatry, 25,* 498–510.

Smith, C. B. (1963). Enhancement by reserpine and a-methyldopa of the effects of d-amphetamine upon the locomotor activity of mice. *Journal of Pharmacology and Experimental Therapeutics, 142,* 343–349.

Smith, R. C., Parker, E. S., & Noble, E. P. (1975). Alcohol and affect in dyadic social interation. *Psychosomatic Medicine, 37,* 25–40.

Steffen, J. J., Nathan, P. E., & Taylor, H. A. (1974). Tension-reducing effects of alcohol: Further evidence and some methodological considerations. *Journal of Abnormal Psychology, 83,* 542–547.

Stein, L. (1964). Self-stimulation of the brain and the central stimulant action of amphetamine. *Federation Proceedings, 23,* 836–850.

Stein, L. (1968). Chemistry of reward and punishment. In D. H. Efron (Ed.), *Psychopharmacology: A review of progress* (pp. 105–123). Washington, DC: U.S. Government Printing Office.

Steinglass, P., & Wolin, S. (1974). Explorations of a systems approach to alcoholism: Clinical observations of a simulated drinking gang. *Archives of General Psychiatry, 31,* 527–532.

Tassinari, C. A., Ambrosetto, G., & Gastaut, H. (1976). Clinical and polygraphic studies during wakefulness and sleep of high doses of marihuana and delta 9-THC in man. In S. Szara & M. Braude (Eds.), *Pharmacology of marijuana.* New York: Raven Press.

Tassinari, C. A., Peraita-Adrados, M. R., Ambrosetto, G., & Gastaut, H. (1974). Effects of marihuana and delta-9-THC at high doses in man: A polygraphic study. *Electroencephalography and Clinical Neurophysiology, 36*(1), 94.

Taylor, K. M., & Snyder, S. H. (1971). Differential effects of d- and 1-amphetamine on behavior and on catecholamine disposition in dopamine and norepinephrine containing neurons of rat brain. *Brain Research, 28,* 295–309.

Taylor, S. P., & Gammon, C. B. (1975). Effects of type and dose of alcohol on human physical aggression. *Journal of Personality and Social Psychology, 32,* 169–175.

Tinklenberg, J. R. (1973). Alcohol and violence. In P. Bourne & R. Fox (Eds.), *Alcoholism: Progress in research and treatment* (pp. 195–210). New York: Academic Press.

Tinklenberg, J. R. (1974). Marijuana and human aggression. In L. L. Miller (Ed.), *Marijuana: effects on human behavior* pp. 339–357. New York: Academic Press.

Tinklenberg, J. R., & Darley, C. F. (1976). A model of marihuana's cognitive effects. In S. Szara & M. Braude (Eds.), *Pharmacology of marihuana.* New York: Raven Press.

Wallach, M. B. (1974). Drug-induced sterotyped behavior: Similarities and differences. In E. Usdin (Ed.), *Neuropsychopharmacology of monoamines and their regulatory enzymes* (pp. 241–260). New York: Raven Press.

Wallach, M. B., & Gershon, S. (1972). The induction and antagonism of central nervous system stimulant-induced stereotyped behavior in the cat. *European Journal of Pharmacology, 18,* 22–26.

Wallach, M. B., Rotrosen, J., & Gershon, S. (1973). A neuropsychopharmacological study of phenmetrazine in several animal species. *Neuropharmacology, 12,* 541–548.

Warren, G. H., & Raynes, A. E. (1972). Mood changes during three conditions of alcohol intake. *Quarterly Journal of Studies on Alcohol, 33,* 979–989.

Watson, R., Hartmann, E., & Schildkraut, J. J. (1972) Amphetamine withdrawal: Affective state, sleep patterns, and MHPG excretion. *American Journal of Psychiatry, 129,* 39–45.

Weeks, J. R., & Collins, R. J. (1968). Patterns of intravenous self-injection by morphine-addicted rats. In A. Wikler (Ed.), *The addictive states.* Baltimore: Williams & Wilkins.

Weeks, J. R. (1969). Self-maintained morphine addiction—a method for chronic programmed intravenous injection in unrestrained rats. *Federation Proceedings, Federation of the American Society for Experimential Biology, 20,* 397.

Wikler, A. (1952). A psychodynamic study of a patient during experimental self-regulated readdiction to morphine. *Psychiatric Quarterly, 26,* 270–293.

Wikler, A. (1965). Conditioning factors in opiate addiction and relapse. In D. M. Wilmer & G. G. Kassebaum (Eds.), *Narcotics* (pp. 85–100). New York: McGraw-Hill.

Wikler, A. (1968). Interaction of physical dependence and classical and operant conditioning on the genesis of relapse In A. Wikler (Ed.), *The addictive states* (pp. 280–287). Baltimore: Williams & Wilkins.

Wikler, A. (1971). Requirements for extinction of relapse-facilitating variables and for rehabilitation in a narcotic antagonist treatment program. In M. C. Braude, L. S. Harris, E. L. May, J. P. Smith, J. E. Villarreal (Eds.), (pp. 399–414). New York: Raven Press.

Wikler, A., Martin, W. R., Pescor, F. T., & Eades, C. A. (1963). Factors regulating oral consumption of an opioid (etonitazine) by morphine-addicted rats. *Psychopharmacology 5,* 55–76.

Wikler, A., & Prescor, F. T. (1967). Classical conditioning of a morphine abstinence phenomenon, reinforcement of opiod-drinking behavior and "relapse" in morphine-addicted rats. *Psychopharmacology, 10,* 255–284.

Wise, C. D., Berger, B. D., & Stein, L. (1973). Evidence of a-noradrenergic reward receptors and serotonergic punishment receptors in the rat brain. *Biological Psychiatry, 6,* 3–22.

Wise, C. D., & Stein, L. (1970). Amphetamine: Facilitation of behavior by augmented release of norepinephrine from the medial forebrain bundle. In E. Costa & S. Garattin (Eds.), *Amphetamines and related compounds* (pp. 463–485). New York: Raven Press.

Woods, J. H., Ikomi, F., & Winger, G. (1971). The reinforcing property of ethanol. In M. K. Roach, W. M. McIsaac, & P. J. Creaven (eds.), *Biological aspects of alcohol* (pp. 371–388). Austin: University of Texas Press.

Woods, J. H., & Schuster, C. R. (1968). Reinforcement properties of morphine, cocaine, and SPA as a function of unit dose. *International Journal of the Addictions, 3,* 231–237.

Yanagita, T., & Takahashi, S. (1973). Dependence liability of several sedative–hypnotic agents evaluated in monkeys. *Journal of Pharmacology and Experimental Therapeutics, 185,* 307–316.

10

Alcohol Idiosyncratic Intoxication and Other Alcohol-Related States of Acute Behavioral Disinhibition

JACOB H. JACOBY
MARC GALANTER

The *Diagnostic and Statistical Manual of Mental Disorders,* third edition (DSM-III; American Psychiatric Association, 1980) has contributed to the continuing debate over the frequently described but rarely seen disorder commonly known as "pathological intoxication." It has done so by defining the criteria of this disorder in a manner that now lends itself to empirical observation under the diagnosis of "alcohol idiosyncratic intoxication" (henceforth referred to as AII). It thus implies that there is a spectrum of behaviors that might reasonably be anticipated from an individual in a state of inebriation; it also suggests that drinking may lead to behavior far beyond what one has come to anticipate from the inebriate, and that this behavior is often provoked by much less alcohol than one might expect.

Specifically, DSM-III lists the following as diagnostic criteria for AII:

A. Marked behavioral change, e.g. aggressive or assaultive behavior that is due to the recent ingestion of an amount of alcohol insufficient to induce intoxication in most people.

B. The behavior is atypical of the person when not drinking.

C. Not due to any other physical or mental disorder. (American Psychiatric Association, 1980, p. 132)

AII is further characterized by DSM-III as frequently having among its essential features a subsequent amnesia for the period of intoxication. The behavior, as noted above, is atypical. During the episode, the individual seems out of contact with others. The change in behavior begins either while the individual is drinking, or shortly thereafter. The duration of the behavior is brief, terminating within hours. A small percentage of afflicted individuals have been reported to have temporal lobe spikes on their electroencephalograms (EEG). In addition, brain injury may also be associated with the syndrome, most commonly trauma and encephalitis. Individuals who are fatigued or who have a debilitating physical illness may also demonstrate a lower tolerance for alcohol and respond inappropriately to small amounts. DSM-III also knowledges that other exogenous agents, especially barbiturates and similar-acting substances, may also occasionally cause abrupt changes in behavior.

We begin with a review of the historical development of this disorder as described in DSM-III, and we contrast some of these aforementioned parameters with similar presentations seen in other psychiatric disorders.

HISTORY, CULTURE, AND LORE

The observation that an idiosyncratic reaction to alcohol may occur has been reported in the psychiatric literature (initially, the German literature) since the middle of the 19th century. Krafft-Ebing (1869) first described the condition and attributed to it acute delirium, hallucinations, and illusions of a depressive and persecutory nature, such that a destructive fit of rage might ensue. The occurrence of seizures was also noted. Factors that Krafft-Ebing thought might predispose an individual to such an abnormal response, or that might influence the manifestations of the reaction once initiated, included the premorbid emotional and physical state as well as genetic predisposition. Thus prior brain damage, toxic substances, heat stroke, physical exertion, excessive smoking, and sexual overactivity were all thought to be influential in this reaction to alcohol.

Thirty years later (1897), Krafft-Ebing further summarized his criteria for this pathological reaction. He now introduced the concept that onset of attacks could not be related to quantity of alcohol ingested, nor did such attacks necessarily appear at a time when other motoric manifestations of intoxication are apparent; rather, such fits could occur rapidly after ingestion of even "small" amounts of alcohol, or even after cessation of behavior more typically associated with drunkenness. He indicated that such activity, while of extraordinary strength, was generally coordinated or purposeful, and frequently displayed an irresistible desire for destruction. Associated amnesia was thought to occur for the entire period.

Over the course of almost the next half century, other writers contributed their own alternate descriptive criteria and psychodynamic formulations for the behavior they or others had observed.These contributions have been comprehensively discussed in one of the first reviews of this subject to appear in the English language (Banay, 1944).

Although this idiosyncratic reaction to alcohol has been discussed at length over the years, its formulation as a specific disease entity developed in an earlier and perhaps less critical era of psychiatry. Psychiatry itself hs undergone a change, with greater emphasis placed on diagnosis. Operational definitions of major psychiatric disorders have since been devised that enable different observers to standardize behavioral parameters more easily. It is true that, with a disorder that appears to be as rare as AII, review of case notes may be required to obtain a sufficient number of patients for meaningful analysis, and may be the most practical approach. Indeed, such a nosological approach represents a major foundation of all psychiatric disorders. (It should be noted, however, that as many as 8–9% of all first admissions in the New York State Hospital system were attributed to alcoholic psychosis [Banay, 1944, computing the data of Pollock, 1941], and that almost all first admissions for alcoholism with psychosis in the United States at the time of Banay's writing were diagnosed as pathological intoxication.)

While data on the present prevalence of AII are unavailable, it is our clinical impression that the actual rate of its occurrence must be very small. In fact, neither of us has seen a single episode of AII in our entire psychiatric experience; or, at the least, we are not sure that patients who were drunk and violent actually met DSM-III criteria for all. This discrepancy between our observations and those of earlier observers illustrates the need for more stringent criteria. In the absence of universally accepted inclusion criteria, diagnosis and prevalence will certainly vary as different criteria are applied or omitted.

While the astute reader may discern some hesitancy on our part to acknowledge the legitimate existence of AII, such doubts are not new to the literature. May and Ebaugh (1953) state that "there is no justification for continuing to believe in the existence of pathological intoxication as a special diagnostic category. It is a diagnostic catch-all, and difference of opinion as to its symptomatology may be attributed to failure to distinguish between the various reaction types." They based their conclusions on the inconsistencies and variations in clinical descriptions of the disorder, and on the difficulty in verifying the accuracy or reliability of informants in specific cases. Thus, for instance, it has been possible to attribute an idiosyncratic reaction to a chronic alcoholic who swears that he or she ingested only a "minimal amount" of alcohol (an amount that defies specific definition even in DSM-III) prior to engaging in a particularly violent encounter. In other instances, the reports of nonprofessional and less than impartial witnesses have been accepted. After reviewing several dozen cases of pathological intoxication, May and Ebaugh (1953) concluded that in none was there any reliable evidence that symptoms had arisen as a result of the ingestion of an amount of alcohol that would be expected to have no effect on the average individual!

Two more recent reviews (Coid, 1979; Hollender, 1979) also express skepticism as to the authenticity of such a behavioral entity. Hollender makes note of the similarity of pathological intoxication to two other states of acute behavioral disinhibition (i.e., an attack of *negi negi* and a case of a man who had gone berserk). *Negi negi* is a sometimes affliction of the Bena Bena tribe of Guinea. It has also been called "hysterical psychosis" (Langness, 1965) or "dissociative reaction" (Hollender, 1976). In the present case cited by Langness, an agitated young man charged a group of people with a club and had to be restrained by four tribesmen. His eyes were glazed and his skin was cold to the touch. His panting breathing was labored, and he did not appear aware of his surroundings. Amnesia is reported to be a concomitant of such attacks. Hollender (1979) further notes that the Bena Bena people do not view such individuals as offenders, but rather as victims of malevolent ghosts. Thus such episodes are soon forgotten, and the perpetrator escapes any stigma or public censure. In this particular instance, it was felt that the man had actually harbored resentment against his clansmen and his wives. However, since aggression against these members of the tribal society is strictly taboo, the man had no means of directly expressing his anger. Thus frustrated, he opted for an indirect expression of his resentment with an implicity sanctioned attack of *negi negi*. As a parallel occurrence in our own society, Hollender cites the case of a distraught man recently separated from his wife, who smashed his home furnishings immediately before riding off in a van; he subsequently crashed into a bridge abutment and died. Neither the tribesman nor the van driver were suspected by Hollender of alcohol use.

Such episodes of acute behavioral disinhibition are not limited to these two societies and are apparently found in a wide range of cultures. For example, two seemingly separate syndromes have been observed in Malaysia (Freedman, Kaplan, & Sadock, 1976). In *latah,* all ongoing activity stops precipitiously as a result of the subject's being startled, and a set of unusual and uncontrollable motor and verbal responses is initiated. In *amok,* a sudden, unprovoked outburst of wild rage is noted during which the subject runs madly about, sometimes in the possession of a weapon; this leads to a lethal and indiscriminate attack, which can frequently be terminated only by violent countermeasures. This outburst is generally preceded by a period of brooding or mild depression. After the attack, the person feels exhausted, has complete amnesia, and often commits suicide. Similar episodes have been noted in Africa. Freedman *et al.* observe, "It has been theorized that a culture that imposes heavy restrictions on adolescents and adulthood but allows children free rein to express their aggression may be especially prone. Loss of face and shame has been proposed as a determining factor" (1976). *Piblokto* is another and less violent example, found in Eskimos (predominantly women). It is characterized by attacks lasting 1–2 hours, during which the person screams, tears off her clothing, and destroys it. She may begin to thrash about the snow or ice while imitating the cry of a bird. Amnesia for this event is noted upon return to normality.

The question may be asked: Would our interpretation of these events have been altered had these people ingested even a small quantity of alcohol before the onset of their rampage? In fact, the answer to this question touches upon another theme that has been appreciated in the literature since the first description of AII by Krafft-Ebing. Even at this dawn of a newly-described disorder, mention was made that the fit of rage may be due to incidental or underlying emotional factors. Heilbronner (1901) observed that emotional changes, such as fright, anxiety, quarrels, or being the target of pranks, could bring on a pathological response to alcohol. Bonhoefer (1901) also stated that the rage reaction could be covering up a deep-seated anxiety. This concept of the prevalence of pre-existing psychopathology in AII received its most substantial elaboration from Binswanger (1935). He hypothesized that AII could be seen in repressed individuals who took alcohol to escape the dysphoria generated by their repression. Many such people were considered to be mentally defective, with less insight into their condition than "normally" endowed psychopaths and thus less able to control their emotional outbursts. Such dysphoric individuals might control themselves in an acceptable manner under most circumstances. However, with the disinhibition of alcohol, an outburst of repressed aggression might ensue, leading to acts of violence. While aggressive acts might be the most frequent manifestation of the pathological reaction, any repressed material might break through, leading to a variety of responses, such as burglary, exhibition, or the like. Binswanger concluded, *"One should not ascribe too great a role to alcohol. It is only one factor in a long succession of simultaneously necessary and chronologically well-arranged circumstances"* (1935; emphasis in original). Indeed, Jellinek (1942) believed that AII occurred primarily in psychopathic personalities who frequently did not need the stimulation of alcohol to engage in such unprovoked fits of rage. Most of Binswanger's patients fit this category.

SCIENCE AND SOCIOLOGY

The discussion of AII has focused thus far on case reports or empirical observation, and on the various interpretations of such behavior. Attempts have also been made to attribute a more organic etiology to this disorder. This work has been based on the apparent similarity of episodes of AII and certain seizure disorders. Thus, these studies have focused on possible abnormalities in the EEG in individuals presenting with AII. It should be noted at the onset that the search for an EEG relationship need not be relevant or necessary to verify the existence of AII as a specific entity; for example, most dissociative states, of which AII may be an instance, have not been equated with any specific EEG changes. Experimental attempts to validate the existence of AII have focused on two major questions: (1) Can the voluntary ingestion of alcohol, under controlled conditions, lead to the onset of an attack of AII? (2) Are there specific EEG changes associated with such attacks? It is on these two points that we focus our discussion, although an attempt is made to magnify the scope so as to put the specific behavioral manifestations of AII in a broader context.

ALCOHOL AND ACUTE STATES OF AGGRESSION

As the level of intoxication deepens, earlier feelings of exhiliration may yield to a progressive loss of restraint. At such a stage, a wide variety of expressed emotions and behaviors may prevail. Under most circumstances, this state is short-lived, and the individual passes to a deeper and more incapacitating level of intoxication, or to a lighter state more amenable to customary individual, social, and/or cultural constraints. Unfortunately, self-control is not the hallmark of the intoxicated individual; thus aggressive and antisocial acts are frequent concomitants in both victims and perpetrators of aggressive and antisocial activity. Both murderers and their victims are often intoxicated during the commission of the crimes (Goodwin, 1973; Haberman & Baden, 1974; Virkunen, 1974). Indeed, there appears to be a higher rate of alcoholism in both murderers and the murdered (Carney, Tosti, & Turchette, 1968; Costello & Schneider, 1974; Haberman & Bader, 1974; Lachman & Cravens, 1974). Such relationships also appear to exist in nonhomicidal crimes of aggression (Banay, 1942; Mayfield, 1976; Nicol, Gunn, Gristwood, Foggitt, & Watson, 1973; Shupe, 1954) and in suicide (Hagnell, Nyman, & Tunvig, 1973; James, Scott-Orr, & Crenrow, 1963). Most alcoholics are intoxicated when they make suicide attempts (Moore, 1939), whereas nonalcoholics are sober (Ringle & Rotter, 1957). Frequently such attempts occur at the onset of drinking, in the context of explosive behavior (Mayfield & Montgomery, 1972). Alcohol may also precipitate or exacerbate episodes of violence in individuals with a past history of violent behavior (Detre, Kupfer, & Taub, 1972; Guze & Cartwell, 1965).

While alcohol use certainly has its antisocial sequelae in our society, one should not assume that such behavior is universally observed. Edwards (1974) argues convincingly, "Learned expectation of the likely form which drug-related behavior will take may be an important way in which societies control behavior by suggestion. If the individual is told that the drug will probably make him aggressive, then the drug will probably do so; if he is told that it will make him sleepy, he will then probably experience sleepiness." One can alter the behavioral and physiological effects of a drug (an active drug or a placebo) by calling it a "stimulant" or a "depressant" (Frankenhaeuser, Jaerpe, Svan, & Wrangsjoe, 1963). On a more global level, then, societal influences may have the force of metacommunications that are acted out at the time of drug or alcohol ingestion (MacAndrew & Edgerton, 1969).

Such influences on behavior while intoxicated are demonstrated in the following two examples:

> The Abipones, in their whole deportment, preserve a decorum scarce credible to Europeans . . . they never break out into clamours, threats and reproaches, as is usual to certain people of Europe. These praises are justly due to the Abipones as long as they remain sober; but when intoxicated, they shake off the bridle of reason, become distracted, and quite unlike themselves. . . . It often happens that a contention between two (when intoxicated) implicates and incites them all, so that snatching up arms, and taking the part, some of one, some of the other, they furiously rush to attack and slay one another. (Dobrizhoffer, 1822)

> The behavioral patterns associated with drinking are so formalized as to constitute a secular ritual. Members of the group are seated in chairs in an approximate circle. The "sponsor" of the party pours a glassful (about 300cc) at the table, turns and walks to stand in front of whomever he wishes, nods and raises the glass slightly . . . drinks half of the glassful in a single quick draught, and hands it to the person he has toasted, who then repeats the toast and finishes the glass in one gulp. While the "sponsor" returns to his seat, the recipient of the toast goes to the table to refill the glass and to repeat the ritual. . . . By the fourth hour there is little conversation, many people stare dumbly at the ground except when toasted and a few who may have fallen asleep or "passed out" are left undisturbed. . . . Among the Camba drinking does not lead to expressions of aggression in verbal or physical form. . . . Neither is there a heightening of sexual activity; obscene joking and sexual overtures are rarely associated with drinking. (Heath, 1958)

EEG CORRELATES OF ALCOHOL AND AGGRESSION

The possibility of EEG changes was first raised by Krafft-Ebing (1897) when he noted that a convulsion could appear at the height of an attack of AII. He compared the similarity of this state to epileptoid excitement and inferred that epilepsy might play a role in the genesis of this reaction. During this era, attention was also being focused on the relationship of epilepsy to criminality (Lombroso, 1911). Most criminals were felt to have an "epileptoid" constitution, although not all epileptics were considered to be criminals. Violent crimes were thought to be particularly characteristic of the epileptic. Maudsley (1873, 1906) suggested that epilepsy should always be considered in aggressive crimes, and felt that crimes committed suddenly and in a "blind fury" were often due to some form of epileptic process. Subsequent studies have modified these earlier impressions. While epilepsy may be associated with a higher probability of imprisonment (Gudmundsson, 1966; Gunn & Fenton, 1971), Epileptics are not especially vulnerable to crimes of violence (Gunn & Bonn, 1971) unless under the influence of alcohol abuse (Alstrom, 1950; Juul-Jensen, 1964). However, EEG abnormalities have been found more frequently in murderers whose crime was motivated or without motivation, as compared to those whose crime was accidental (Hill & Pond, 1952).

Lishman (1978) points out that reduced control over aggression is a not uncommon occurrence after head injury. Such subjects may exhibit sudden explosions of violent behavior with only minor provocation. No irritability is noted between attacks. It is felt that such outbursts may represent a lowered threshold to the effects of alcohol, or an exaggeration of premorbid personality traits. Occasionally it may represent an epileptic phenomenon. Such violent outbursts have been attributed to temporal lobe damage in some patients and to psychogenic factors in others (Sweet, Ervin, & Mark, 1969). Lishman presents the following case study:

> A man of 21 had shown repeated episodes of markedly aggressive behaviour, chiefly directed towards the police, since a road traffic accident two and a half years earlier. These had led to repeated convictions and several brief periods of imprisonment. He had previously been a police cadet and there was ample evidence that his conduct prior to the injury had been entirely satisfactory. Detailed investigations failed to show any evidence of brain damage; full EEG studies revealed no abnormality, psychological testing indicated good intelligence without evidence of intellectual impairment, and prolonged fasting showed no evidence of hypoglycaemia. The injury itself had been mild, without neurological sequelae and with a post-traumatic amnesia of only twenty minutes.
>
> The great majority of aggressive outbursts occurred after excessive drinking had set in during a phase of severe depression following loss of a friend in the accident, and continued as the patient became progressively embittered and disgruntled at his failure to find a new career. He now found himself in a vicious circle as a result of repeated convictions, and much of his aggressive behaviour could be seen as bravado in attempts to regain his self-esteem. His hatred of the police force was overt, and he felt their rejection keenly. When drunk, encounters with the police led immediately to the release of explosive outbursts of violence. (Lishman, 1978, p. 230)

This clinical vignette can include "episodic dyscontrol syndrome," temporal lobe epilepsy, or AII in its differential diagnosis.

The term "episodic dyscontrol syndrome" refers to patients who exhibit violent behavior as the only overt symptom of brain disease (Bach-y-Rita, Lion, Climent, & Ervin, 1971; Maletzky, 1973; Mark & Ervin, 1970). There is no demonstrable psychosis or brain damage. Such behavior is similar to AII in several respects. Outbursts can last for minutes to hours; many persons claim amnesia for the attack or a feeling of complete loss of control. There are also feelings of remorse upon learning of the violent actions. It differs from AII in that alcohol is not attributed to its onset, and the episode is frequently preceded by an aura. Such attacks are apparently much more frequent than AII, with reported frequency varying from once a day to several episodes per year.

Bach-y-Rita *et al.* (1971) noted abnormal EEGs or a history of seizure-like states in many of their episodic dyscontrol patients. They were, however, impressed by the "interaction of environment and patient leading to affective changes and then to a seizure-like state of loss of control. This occurs typically when demands are placed on the ego with which the patient is incapable of coping." In their descriptions of different presentations of the disorder, one group was given the diagnosis of pathological intoxication because they "went wild" after several drinks, had amnesia, and appeared to be psychotic when out of control. This occurred early in the course of intoxication. Maletzky (1973) also noted a high incidence of abnormal EEGs in his patient population, with such abnormalities always occurring, but not limited to the temporal region. All 22 patients in this series had a history of increased frequency and severity of attacks under the influence of alcohol. The amount of alcohol varied greatly, but "no case could have been explained solely on the basis of pathological intoxication." In general it appears that a high proportion of persons with disturbed personalities, especially aggressive sociopaths, are known to have abnormal EEGs (Lishman, 1978). Such abnormalities frequently involve the temporal lobes (Williams, 1969).

It would appear from the discussion thus far that there is a relationship between temporal lobe dysfunction and violence and/or behavioral disinhibition. As a point of reference, it is helpful to realize that the terms "psychomotor seizures" and "temporal lobe epilepsy" are often used synonymously. While this is an oversimplification, it is largely correct (Pincus & Tucker, 1978). Automatisms are one manifestation of such seizures. They tend to be repetitive and inappropriate. Frequently they involve such oropharyngeal activities as lip smacking, chewing, gagging, retching, or swallowing, but complicated acts that seem to blend with normal behavior are also observed (closer screening may reveal stereotypic or automatic behavior, but this may be influenced by environmental factors). Fugue states have also been observed. Outbursts of aggressive behavior are extremely rare.

The characteristic abnormality in psychomotor seizures is an anterior temporal spike focus, but in the waking state at least half the patients have a normal EEG (Gibbs & Gibbs, 1952). Even nasopharyngeal leads will not reveal abnormalities in all patients. If a normal EEG does not rule out psychomotor epilepsy, neither can a diagnosis be made solely on the presence of an abnormal EEG, since 10–15% of the general population have abnormal recordings (Pincus & Tucker, 1978). Thus it is quite difficult to attribute the presence of a seizure as a causative factor in a behavioral disturbance solely because of an abnormal EEG. As Pincus and Tucker (1978) note,

> "Defining the limits of normality in the EEG is also a major problem. There is no doubt that spikes, spike waves, focal slowing with phase reversal, and paroxysmal activity during wakefulness are abnormal, but there remains a question about theta rhythms intermixed with a dominant alpha pattern, prolonged slowing after hyperventilation, or even 14 and 6 positive spikes, all of which are often seen in normal adolescents." (p. 45)

Furthermore, states of alcohol and drug intoxication and/or withdrawal may also influence the EEG (Isbell, Fraser, Wickler, Belleville, & Eisenman, 1955). Again, Pincus and Tucker (1978) note,

> [T]he EEG abnormalities seen in some "psychopathic" patients with a history of aggressive behavior may possibly be secondary to brain damage. Hostile behavior may often elicit hostile reactions, and head injuries are quite commonly sustained during fights by patients who habitually start them. Thus brain damage and EEG abnormalities may be the result, not the cause of the emotional disturbance. . . . *The diagnosis of brain damage, epilepsy or psychosis cannot be made on the basis of EEG criteria alone, and the meaning of EEG abnormalities in the absence of seizures cannot always be determined.* (p. 47; emphasis added)

One may also question the significance of EEG changes where they have been observed in studies of controlled alcohol intake. In the first such study (Greenblatt, Levin, & DiCori, 1944), alcohol induced abnormal EEGs in three of five subjects who had had previous attacks of AII. In Marinacci's (1963) study of 402 patients, 20% had some EEG abnormalities prior to alcohol exposure (64 borderline abnormalities, 16 moderate generalized slowings). Alcohol administration induced anterior temporal lobe spiking in 55 patients, whereas only 18 showed "psychomotor episodes." It is unclear whether those with baseline EEG changes were also those who showed alcohol-induced EEG changes. Skelton's (1970) subject showed a normal EEG before and after alcohol administration on one occasion, but showed evidence of generalized cortical irritability with paroxysmal slow activity arising from the frontal regions bilaterally following another episode of alcohol ingestion.

Bach-y-Rita, Lion, and Ervin (1970) did not observe any alcohol-induced EEG seizure activity in 10 patients suspected of a previous episode of AII (mild slowing and some increased-amplitude alpha rhythm occurred secondary to alcohol). Two other patients in this study with known temporal lobe epilepsy and implanted depth electrodes showed increased abnormal activity most visible in the amygdala after alcohol infusion. Changes were at times visible in nasopharyngeal leads and only occasionally at surface electrodes. Zakowska-Dabrowska and Stryzy-zewski (1969) could not correlate EEG changes with behavioral changes following alcohol administration. Before intoxication, 11 of 63 patients displayed abnormal EEGs. Afterward, 23 more patients displayed an abnormality. No abnormal EEGs were noted in 6 patients with AII. In Maletzky's (1976) study, 15 of his 22 subjects showed a generalized slowing and disorganization, with occasional sharp waves in the temporal or occipital regions. No consistant correlation with behavior was noted. Thus two patients with EEG abnormalities showed no behavioral abnormalities, while two with alcohol-induced psychotic behavior had normal EEGs. Thus "EEG's were varying and not helpful. The sharp waves seen were never organized sufficiently to suggest an epileptic attack" (Maletsky, 1976). It would appear that we can reasonably state that if a relationship between EEG activity and AII exists, it does not do so at the cortical level. We must await more refined and subcortical recording before we can come to a more definitive conclusion.

AII AND SEIZURE-RELATED INVOLUNTARY ACTIVITY

Much of our attention has thus far been directed at comparing and contrasting behavioral presentations of AII with various episodes of violence, and the possible EEG correlates of such outbursts. The question of whether violence can occur during seizures or "postictal automatisms" is an important medical–legal issue. While the incidence of unprovoked violent activity under the influence of a seizure or its immediate sequelae is generally accepted as a possibility, many think that this is a rare concurrence (Gunn & Bonn, 1971; Hill & Pond, 1952; Knox, 1968; Ounsted, 1969; Rodin, 1973). Gunn (1974) noted marked similarities in medical, social, and psychiatric factors in hospitalized epileptic patients and epileptic prisoners, except that the latter group showed a higher incidence of alcohol abuse. Roth (1968) felt that any risk of violent activity among epileptics is more likely a manifestation of the psychiatric complications of the disorder. Other investigators have been more impressed with the possibility that violent outbursts are a direct result of an electrical irregularity. Pathological aggression occurring in 7% to more than 50% of patients with temporal lobe epilepsy has been reported (Currie, 1971; Falconer & Taylor, 1970; Glaser, 1967; Serafetinides, 1965). Mark and Ervin (1970) found the incidence of epilepsy among violent prisoners to be 10 times greater than that of the general population. More than half of this group had "warning states" preceding their violent acts and sleep or drowsiness after the attack. A history of head injury or disease and ensuing unconsciousness was noted in more than 75% of these subjects. Similar observations have been made in violent children referred from juvenile court (Lewis, 1977). The fact that these individuals may be at a higher risk of alcohol abuse and/or dependence complicates our understanding of the relationship among these brain dysfunctions, alcohol use, and violence.

AII AND MEMORY LOSS

Function during periods of short-term memory loss is observed in alcoholic blackouts. It is also seen in certain seizure disorders, hysterical states, and posttraumatic states. It is also reported to be a concomitant of AII. Such types of amnesia are limited to certain circumscribed themes; if they were more global, there would be evidence of a disturbance of consciousness or cognitive functioning. Transition to the normal state is usually abrupt, and an unexplained journey is present in about 25% of such cases (Lishman, 1978; Pincus & Tucker, 1978). The duration of an amnestic response during an alcoholic "blackout" and in psychomotor epilepsy may last for hours or days, although in the latter case the response is rarely manifested solely as a behavioral disturbance. An hysterical amnesia can last longer than this and may not have any other neurological signs. Inconsistencies in the amnestic account may subsequently be noted. The occurrence of blackouts has been correlated with the severity and duration of alcoholism. While Jellinek (1952) reported that *changes* in blood alcohol levels may be more important than the actual blood alcohol levels themselves, others report seeing blackouts only after consumption of large amounts of ethanol (Goodwin, 1971). Of interest is the fact that nonalcoholics may also have a blackout after alcohol ingestion (Goodwin, Crane, & Guze, 1969). Present evidence suggests that these blackouts represent impaired consolidation of new information, rather than "repression" motivated by a desire to forget events that happened while drinking (Goodwin, 1971). The relationship of the amnestic period described for AII to other amnestic states is unknown at this time.

AII AS A PSYCHOTIC STATE

Various authors have referred to some of the behavioral manifestations of an episode of AII as a psychotic or "psychotic-like" state. These assumptions appear to be based on the excessive and uncontrollable rage associated with AII. Most likely, some presentations of AII are due to an acute and violent psychotic episode; however, whether such cases actually reflect a response to alcohol, to another drug, or to a brief reactive psychosis unrelated to the ingestion of any specific substance is unclear at this time. Laboratory studies of alcohol administration to various research patient/subject populations have not clarified this question. Thus, catatonic patients who drank 150–400 cc of 40% alcohol over 1–2 hours showed a transient increase in verbal communicaton, but no aggression (Kantorovich & Constantinovich, 1935); likewise, normal subjects given a 9.5–10% intravenous solution of 1 cc/kg absolute alcohol showed no aggression (Hartocollis, 1962; Newman, 1935).

When patients with a prior history of aggression or AII (distinctions have not been clearly defined, or have been defined differently by various authors) have been administered alcohol, conflicting results have been reported. Five patients with a previous history of AII did not show any behavioral changes after ingesting an unspecified amount of alcohol (Greenblatt *et al.*, 1944) nor did 10 such subjects infused with 150–300 cc of a 25% solution (Bach-y-Rita *et al.*, 1970). However, of 402 patients allowed to imbibe various doses of alcohol, 18 showed changes in mental status described as "psychomotor episodes" (Marinacci, 1963). Of 63 male offenders allowed to drink 100 ml of 45% ethanol in 3–5 minutes,

6 exhibited behavior consistent with AII (Zakowska-Dabrowska & Strzyzewski, 1969). Skelton (1970) presents the case of a responsible member of the community who had committed murder and other acts of destruction while in an intoxicated state (for all of which he had no subsequent memory). Within 30 minutes of being infused with 6 ounces of a 95% alcohol solution, and when drinking the same amount on another occasion, he became agitated but responded to reassurance.

In another study, 22 neurologically intact patients with a history of more than one violent or bizarre episode under the influence of alcohol, and an amnesia for such episodes, were infused with 400–1200 cc of 25% alcohol (Maletzky, 1976). Behavioral changes resembling a psychotic state were observed in 15 patients. It should be noted that Maletzky's subjects were exposed to the average alcohol content of 8–24 bottles of beer, infused at a rate of 200 cc per hour, whereas Bach-y-Rita et al.'s patients were infused with an equivalent of 3–6 cans of beer over a 30-minute period. Maletzky (1976) has argued that the different results may partially be explained by the different blood alcohol levels induced in the two populations. Thus, according to his definition, small amounts of alcohol and time of onset from exposure to alcohol are not valid criteria. He was unable to correlate blood alcohol concentrations with onset of behavior, other than to note that "subjects with extensive drinking histories could tolerate higher doses of alcohol with fewer behavioral changes and comparatively lower BAC's."

One must wonder to what extent environmental cues present in the laboratory setting contributed to the differences noted. As Boyatzis (1977) noted in a study of barroom aggression, "the amount of interpersonal aggression is probably a function of the level of aversive stimuli present, cues allowing or provoking aggressive behavior, nature of the clientele, and the reason why the bar is patronized." Edwards (1974) has also expressed wariness of certain suggestive influences presented to the experimental and more natural subjects.

SUBSTANCE-INDUCED IDIOSYNCRATIC INTOXICATION

Alcohol is not the only drug linked to violent behavior, nor is it the only agent for which an idiosyncratic reaction has been reported. Thus, for example, while alcohol is the drug most likely to be associated with serious assaultive and sexual offenses, secobarbital appears to be overrepresented in violent crimes proportionate to its actual abuse (Tinklenberg & Woodrow, 1974). Indeed, this barbiturate has the reputation among street users of increasing aggressiveness (Smith, 1972). Tinklenberg (Tinklenberg & Woodrow, 1974) notes that "part of the process seems to be diffuse irritability with indiscriminate violence. For example, if I were under the influence of secobarbital right now and I didn't like the way you asked a question, I might attack you or perhaps someone else in front of you. I would be inclined to act out my extreme irritability in an assaultive way!"

Amphetamines, psychedelic drugs, and marijuana have also been implicated in assaultive behavior, although for the most part marijuana is usually sedating and is associated with nonviolent behavior (Blum, 1969; Goode, 1972). Adverse reactions similar to AII have been reported for marijuana or LSD (i.e., a "bad trip"). These are associated with irrational, frenzied, poorly controlled behavior that may entail aggressive actions (George, 1970). Such reactions to marijuana do not occur in most individuals who have used the same dose in the same setting. While such reactions are infrequent, they generally occur in individuals with prior psychiatric disorders or multiple-substance abuse (Tinklenberg, 1974). Maletzky (1973) has also reported episodic attacks of violence under the influence of chlordiazepoxide and diazepam.

To speak of possible biochemical or neuropharmacological substrates or differences that may explain idiosyncratic drug reactions is premature, given our present state of knowledge. There are, however, precedents for drugs' unmasking a predisposition for certain disorders. Thus, for example, drugs that increase intrasynaptic catecholamine levels have led to the onset of an attack of Gilles de la Tourette syndrome in some patients (Golden, 1974; Meyerhoff & Snyder, 1973) and to choreiform movements in some patients at high risk for Huntington disease (Chase, Wexler, & Barbeau, 1979). The behavioral effects of alcohol are generally considered to be secondary to its axonal depressant or anesthetic effects, and not due to any specific receptor interaction. Perhaps some effects of alcohol do result from an interaction with specific neurotransmitters, or with a receptor specific for ethanol.

AII AND THE LAW

The difficulty that medicine and psychiatry have had in grappling with the potential existence of AII as a discrete clinical entity is at least matched by the difficulty that the legal profession has had in dealing with apportionment of responsibility for acts committed during a state of intoxication. Indeed, a sense of final resolution appears to be lacking in both instances. The historical development and more contemporary perspectives of this problem in American and British law are comprehensively reviewed elsewhere ("Alcohol Abuse and the Law," 1981; Fingarette & Hasse, 1979; Hobson, 1962) and are not dealt with here.

On the one hand, "in some fundamental and intuitive sense, it is evident that we do not expect the same emotional control or the same physical reactions from a person who is under the influence of alcohol as we do from a sober person. The incapacity, when severe enough may be summed up by what we wish to call "irrationality" (Fingarett & Hasse, 1979). On the other hand, "when a person voluntarily drinks, he should be held criminally responsible at least to the extent that, when originally sober, he voluntarily placed himself in a disabling condition— a condition in which he might harm persons or property, and a condition out of which much of the harm to persons and property does actually arise" (Fingarette & Hasse, 1979). Of course, in cases of AII, imbibers should be considered more innocent in their intent and actions if they have no prior history or experience to suggest that they have the potential to unleash such a catastrophic response to such a small amount of alcohol. They would appear to be more culpable if they drank an amount sufficient to raise blood alcohol concentration to levels that are known to impair judgment, or if their actions can be shown to have an element of secondary gain. Thus, while alcoholics have a certain responsibility for the damage they have inflicted because they voluntarily made themselves irrational (we will not dwell on the issue of alcoholism as an involuntary disease), AII defendants are technically neither alcoholics nor voluntary collaborators in their behavior.

To the courts, then, goes the difficult responsibility of determining whose violence was sufficiently unanticipated to merit a defense of intoxication. If no clear guidelines are set forth, then verdicts set forth by the jury will exhibit a wide range of discretion. Undoubtedly, this will lead to inconsistent and discriminatory results, and also to an increase of spurious claims by defendants hoping for a sympathetic jury. On the other hand, abolition of the defense of intoxication also appears unreasonable. Thus, as indicated in the *Harvard Law Review* ("Alcohol Abuse and the Law," 1981), we need a neutral approach that avoids the unfairness to the defendant of never allowing an intoxication defense, but does not sacrifice society's interest in protecting itself. Perhaps such pleas can "be screened by the judge to ensure that the jury could reasonably believe the defendant lacked the necessary intent" (1981).

How can psychiatry contribute to this decision? Unfortunately, not as much as we would like. We can, however, point out to our legal colleagues that the best predictor of episodic violent behavior is a history of violent behavior. This, in turn, is associated with upbringing in a family environment notable for marital discord, overt brutality or emotional indifference, and alcoholism. Many AII individuals fall into this spectrum. Yet there is a body of evidence to suggest that neurological factors contribute to antisocial behavior. We know also that "the type of personality fundamentally lacking in responsiveness to ordinary informal cues or more formal social control (psychopathy, sociopathy or any of its rephrasings) will probably exhibit the same unresponsiveness in intoxicated and drug-seeking behavior" (Edwards, 1974). Should this knowledge alter the legal perception of and disposition of a perpetrator who is himself or herself the victim of unfortunate life circumstances

It would appear as of this writing that a sizable body of knowledge, based on many observations, supports the existence of a form of behavior that is considered to be extremely aggressive and temporally related to alcohol consumption. There have also been numerous unsuccessful attempts to elicit such behaviors when alcohol has been administered in the laboratory. Reasonable arguments have been advanced to deny the existence of a rage reaction to alcohol that cannot be attributed to other, more likely factors. Among these has been the observation that data supporting the existence of AII have come from studies that have lacked appropriate controls. Yet a number of distinguished clinical observers have been impressed by the paradoxical and unexpected reactions of some individuals after self-reported alcohol consumption, and these authors have advanced the notion of a specific diagnostic entity (AII). From our vantage point, the jury has yet to return a verdict.

REFERENCES

Alcohol abuse and the law. (1981). *Harvard Law Review, 94*, 1660–1712.
Alstrom, C. H. (1950). A study of epilepsy in its clinical, social and genetic aspects. *Acta Psychiatrica et Neurologica Scandinavica, 63* (Suppl.), 5–284.

American Psychiatric Association. (1980). *Diagnostic and statistical manual of mental disorders* (3rd ed.). Washington, DC: Robert L. Spitzer, MD, Chairperson.

Bach-y-Rita, G., Lion, J. R., Climent, C. E., & Ervin, F. R. (1971). Episodic dyscontrol: A study of 130 violent patients. *American Journal of Psychiatry, 127,* 1473–1478.

Bach-y-Rita, G., Lion, J. R., & Ervin, F. R. (1970). Pathological intoxication: Clinical and electroencephalographic studies. *American Journal of Psychiatry, 126,* 698–703.

Banay, R. S. (1942). Alcoholism and crime. *Quarterly Journal of Studies on Alcohol, 2,* 686–716.

Banay, R. S. (1944). Pathologic reaction to alcohol: 1. Review of the literature and original case reports. *Quarterly Journal of Studies on Alcohol, 4,* 580–605.

Binswanger, H. (1935). Klimische und charakter ologische untersnchungen an patholo-gisch Beranschten. *Zeitschrift für die gesamte Neurologie und Psychiatrie, 152,* 703–707.

Blum, R. H. (1969). Crimes of violence (a staff report to the National Commission on the Causes and Prevention of Violence). In R. Mulvihill & M. M. Tumin (Eds.), (Vol. 13, pp. 1461–1523). Washington, DC: U.S. Government Printing Office.

Bonhoefer, K. (1901). *Die akuten Geisteskrankheiten der Gewohnheitstrinker.* Jena: G. Fischer.

Boyatzis, R. E. (1977). Alcohol and interpersonal aggression. In M. M. Gross (Ed.), *Alcohol intoxication and withdrawal (Vol. 3B,* pp. 345–375). New York: Plenum.

Carney, F. J., Tosti, A., & Turchette, A. (1968). *An analysis of convicted murderers in Massachusetts: 1943–1966* (mimeo). Boston: Massachusetts Department of Cor-rection.

Chase, T. N., Wexler, N. S., & Barbeau, A. (Eds.). (1979). *Advances in neurology: Vol. 23. Huntington's disease.* New York: Raven Press.

Coid, J. (1979). Mania *à potu:* A critical review of pathological intoxication. *Psychological Medicine, 9,* 709–719.

Costello, R. M., & Schneider, S. L. (1974). Mortality in an alcoholic cohort. *International Journal of the Addictions, 9,* 355–363.

Currie, S. (1971). Clinical course and prognosis of temporal lobe epilepsy. *Brain, 94,* 173–190.

Detre, T. P., Kupfer, D. J., & Taub, S. (1972). *The nosology of violence.* Paper presented at the *Neurological Symposium on the Neural Basis of Violence and Aggression,* Houston, TX.

Dobrizhoffer, M. (1822). *An account of the Abipones, an equestrian people of Paraguay* (3 vols.). London: John Murray.

Edwards, G. (1974). Drugs, drug dependence and the concept of plasticity. *Quarterly Journal of Studies on Alcohol, 35,* 176–195.

Falconer, M. A., & Taylor, D. C. (1970). Temporal lobe epilepsy: Clinical features, pathology, diagnosis and treatment. In J. H. Price (Ed.), *Modern trends in psy-chological medicine* (vol. 2). London: Butterworths.

Fingarette, H., & Hasse, A. F. (1979). *Mental disabilities and criminal responsibility.* Berkeley: University of California Press.

Frankenhaeuser, M., Jaerpe, G., Svan, H. & Wrangsjoe, T. (1963). Psychophysiological reactions to two different placebo treatments. *Scandinavian Journal of Psychology, 4,* 245–250.

Freedman, A. M., Kaplan, H. I., & Sadock, B. J. (1976). *Modern synopsis of compre-hensive textbook of psychiatry II.* Baltimore: Williams & Wilkins.

George, H. R. (1970). Two psychotic episodes associated with cannabis. *British Journal of Addiction, 65,* 119–121.

Gibbs, F. A., & Gibbs, E. C. (1952). *Atlas of electroencephalography* (Vol. 2). Reading, MA: Addison-Wesley.

Glaser, G. H. (1967). Limbic epilepsy in childhood. *Journal of Nervous and Mental Disease, 144,* 391–397.

Golden G. S. (1974). Gilles de la Tourette syndrome following methylphenidate administration. *Developmental Medicine and Child Neurology, 16,* 76–78.

Goode, E. (1972). In Marihuana: A signal of misunderstanding. In *Technical papers of the first report of the National Commission on Marijuana and Drug Abuse* (Vol. 1, pp. 446–469). Washington, DC: U.S. Government Printing Office.

Goodwin, D. W. (1971). Blackouts and alcohol-induced memory dysfunction. In *Recent advances in studies of alcoholism.* Washington, DC: U.S. Government Printing Office.

Goodwin, D. W. (1973). Alcohol in suicides and homicides. *Quarterly Journal of Studies on Alcohol, 34,* 144–156.

Goodwin, D. W., Crane, J. B., & Guze, S. B. (1969). Alcoholic "blackouts": A review and clinical study of 100 alcoholics. *American Journal of Psychiatry, 126,* 191–198.

Greenblatt, M. Levin, S. & DiCori, F. (1944). The elctroencephalogram associated with chronic alcoholism, alcoholic psychosis, and alcoholic convulsions. *Archives of Neurology and Psychiatry, 52,* 290–295.

Gudmundsson, G. (1966). Epilepsy in Iceland: A clinical and epidemiological investigation. *Acta Neurologica Scandinavica, 25* (Suppl.), 7–24.

Gunn, J. (1974). Social factors and epileptics in prison. *British Journal of Psychiatry, 124,* 509–517.

Gunn, J., & Bonn, J. (1971). Criminality and violence in epileptic prisoners. *British Journal of Psychiatry, 118,* 337–343.

Gunn, J., & Fenton, G. W. (1971). Epilepsy, automatism and crime. *Lancet, 1,* 1173–1176.

Guze, S. B., & Cartwell, D. P. (1965). Alcoholism, parole observations and criminal recidivism: Study of 116 parolees. *American Journal of Psychiatry, 122,* 436–439.

Haberman, P. W., & Baden, M. O. (1974). Alcoholism and violent death. *Quarterly Journal of Studies on Alcohol, 35,* 221–231.

Hagnell, D., Nyman, E., & Tunvig, K. (1973). Dangerous alcoholics: personality varieties in aggressive and suicidally inclined subjects. *Journal of Social Medicine, 1,* 125–131.

Hartocollis, P. (1962). Drunkenness and suggestion: An experiment with intravenous alcohol. *Quarterly Journal of Studies on Alcohol, 23,* 376–389.

Heath, O.B. (1958). Drinking patterns of the Bolivian Camba. *Quarterly Journal of Studies on Alcohol, 19,* 491–508.

Heilbronner, K. (1901). Ueber pathologische Rauschzustande. *Muenchener Medizinische Wochenschrift, 48,* 962–965, 1013–1016.

Hill, D., & Pond, D. A. (1952). Reflections on one hundred capital cases submitted to electroencephalography. *Journal of Mental Science, 98,* 23–43.

Hobson, J. A. (1962). Addiction and criminal responsibility. *Medicolegal Journal, 30,* 85–97.

Hollender, M. H. (1976). Hysteria: The culture-bound syndrome. *New Guinea Medicial Journal, 19,* 24–29.

Hollender, M. H. (1979). Pathological intoxication—is there such an entity? *Journal of Clinical Psychiatry, 40,* 424–426.

Isbell, H., Fraser, H. F., Wickler, A., Belleville, R. E., & Eisenman, A. J. (1955). An experimental study of aetiology of "rum fits" and delirium tremens. *Quarterly Journal of Studies on Alcohol, 16,* 1–33.

James. I. P., Scott-Orr, D. N., & Crenrow, D. H. (1963). Blood alcohol levels following attempted suicide. *Quarterly Journal of Studies on Alcohol, 24,* 14–32.

Jellinek, E. M. (1942). *Alcohol addiction and chronic alcoholism.* New Haven, CT: Yale University Press.

Jellinek, E. M. (1952). Phases of alcohol addiction. *Quarterly Journal of Studies on Alcohol, 13,* 673–684.

Juul-Jensen, P. (1964). Epilepsy: A clinical and social analysis of 1020 adult patients with epileptic seizures. *Acta Neurologica Scandinavica, 5,* 1–148.

Kantorovich, N. V., & Constantinovich, S. K. (1935). Effect of alcohol in catatonic syndromes: preliminary report. *American Journal of Psychiatry, 92,* 651–654.

Knox, S. J. (1968). Epileptic automatism and violence. *Medicine, Science and the Law, 8,* 96–104.

Krafft-Ebing, R. (1869). Ueber eine form des rausches, welche ges manie verlauft. *Deutsche Zeitschrift fuer die Staats-Arzneikunde, 27,* 444–460.

Krafft-Ebing, R. (1897). *Lehrbuch der Psychiatrie* (Vol. 4.) Stuttgart: Enke.

Lachman, J. A., & Cravens, J. M. (1969). The murderers—before and after. *Psychological Quarterly, 43,* 1–11.

Langness, L. L. (1965). Hysterical psychosis in the New Guinea Highlands: a Bena Bena example. *Psychiatry, 28,* 258–277.

Lewis, D. O. (1976). Delinquency, psychomotor epileptic symptomatology and paranoid symptomatology: A triad. *American Journal of Psychiatry, 133,* 1395–1398.

Lishman, W. A. (1978). *Organic psychiatry: The psychological consequences of cerebral disorder.* Oxford: Blackwell Scientific Publications.

Lombroso, C. (1911). *Crime: Its causes and remedies* (H. P. Horton, Trans.). Boston: Little, Brown.

MacAndrew, C., & Edgerton, R. B. (1969). *Drunken comportment: A social explanation.* Chicago: Aldine.

Maletzky, B. M. (1973). The episodic dyscontrol syndrome. *Diseases of the Nervous System, 34,* 178–185.

Maletzky, B. M. (1976). The diagnosis of pathological intoxication. *Journal of Studies on Alcohol, 37,* 1215–1228.

Marinacci, A. A. (1963). A special type of temporal lobe (psychomotor) seizures following ingestion of alcohol. *Bulletin of the Los Angeles Neurology Society, 28,* 241–250.

Mark, V. H., & Ervin, F. R. (1970). *Violence and the brain.* New York: Harper & Row.

Maudsley, H. (1873). *Body and mind.* London: Macmillan.

Maudsley, H. (1906). *Responsibility in mental disease.* London: Kegan Paul, Trench, Trubner.

May, P. R. A., & Ebaugh, F. C. (1953). Pathological intoxication, alcoholic hallucinosis and other reactions to alcohol: A clinical study. *Quarterly Journal of Studies on Alcohol, 14,* 200–227.

Mayfield, D. (1976). Alcoholism, alcohol intoxication and assaultive behavior. *Diseases of the Nervous System, 37,* 288–291.

Mayfield, D. G., & Montgomery, D. (1972). Alcoholism, alcohol intoxication and suicide attempts. *Archives of General Psychiatry, 27,* 349–353.

Meyerhoff, J. L., & Snyder, S. H. (1973). Catecholamine in Gilles de la Tourette's disease: A clinical study with amphetamine isomers. *Advances in Neurology, 1,* 123–134.

Moore, M. (1939). Alcoholism and attempted suicide: Report of 143 cases. *New England Journal of Medicine, 221,* 691–693.

Newman, H. W. (1935). Alcohol injected intravenously: Some psychological and psychopathological effects in man. *American Journal of Psychiatry, 91,* 1343–1352.

Nicol, A. R., Gunn, J. C., Gristwood, J., Foggitt, R. H., & Watson, J. P. (1973). The relationship of alcoholism to violent behaviour resulting in long-term imprisonment. *British Journal of Psychiatry, 123,* 97–51.

Ounsted, C. (1969). Aggression and epilepsy: rage in children with temporal lobe epilepsy. *Journal of Psychosomatic Research, 13,* 237–242.

Pincus, J. H., & Tucker, G. J. (1978). *Behavioral neurology.* (2nd ed.). New York: Oxford University Press.

Pollock, H. M. (1941). *Mental disease and social welfare.* Utica, NY: State Hospitals Press.

Ringle, E., & Rotter, H. (1957). Zum Problem des selbstmordversuches in Rousch. *Weiner Zeitschrift fur Nervenheilk and deren Grenzebiete, 13,* 406–416.

Rodin, E. A. (1973). Psychomotor epilepsy and aggressive behavior. *Archives of General Psychiatry, 28,* 210–213.

Roth, M. (1968). Cerebral disease and mental disorders of old age as causes of antisocial behavior. In A. V. S. Rueck & R. Porter (Eds.), *The mentally abnormal offender* (Ciba Foundation Symposium). London: Churchill.

Serafetinides, E. A. (1965). Aggressiveness in temporal lobe epileptics and its relation to cerebral dysfunction and environmental factors. *Epilepsia, 6,* 33–42.

Shupe, L. M. (1954). Alcohol and crime. *Journal of Criminal Law, Criminology and Police Science, 44,* 661–664.

Skelton, W. O. (1970). Alcohol, violent behavior, and the electroencephalogram. *Southern Medical Journal, 63,* 465–466.

Smith, R. C. (1972). Compulsive methamphetamine abuse and violence in the Haight–Ashbury district. In E. H. Ellinwood & S. Cohen (Eds.), *Current concepts on amphetamine abuse* (pp. 205–216). Washington, DC: U.S. Government Printing Office.

Sweet, W. H., Ervin, F., & Mark, V. H. (1969). The relationship of violent behavior to focal cerebral disease. In S. Garattini & E. B. Sigg (Eds.), *Aggressive behavior: Proceedings of the International Symposium on the Biology of Aggressive Behavior.* Amsterdam: Excerpta Medica.

Tinklenberg, J. (1974). Marijuana and human aggression. In I. I. Miller (Ed.), *Marijuana: Effects on human behavior* (pp. 339–357). New York: Academic Press.

Tinklenberg, J. R., & Woodrow, K. M. (1974). Drug use among youthful assaultive and sexual offenders. In S. H. Frazier (Ed.), *Aggression,* Research Publication No. 52, Association for Research in Nervous and Mental Disease (Baltimore: Williams and Wilkins), pp. 209–224.

Virkunen, M. (1974). Alcohol as a factor precipitating aggression and conflict behavior leading to suicide. *British Journal of Addiction, 64,* 149–154.

Williams, D. (1969). Neural factors related to habitual aggression: Consideration of the difference between those habitual aggressive and others who have committed crimes of violence. *Brain, 92,* 503–520.

Zakowska-Dabrowska, T., & Strzyzewski, W. (1969). Wartose eksperymentalnego podania alkoholu w diagnozie tzw upicia patalogicznego. *Psychiatria Polska, 3,* 565–570.

V

*Psychopathology as
Consequence of Use*

11

Neurophysiological and Neuropsychological Concomitants of Brain Dysfunction in Alcoholics

JAMES T. BECKER

RICHARD F. KAPLAN

The knowledge that chronic alcohol misuse has potential behavioral consequences, including dullness of thought and judgment and impairment of memory, goes back hundreds of years (Horvath, 1975). However, only recently has the prevalence of alcohol-related brain dysfunction in clinical populations of chronic alcoholics been realized. This was due, in part, to the fact that the cognitive deficits that are common to recently detoxified alcoholics are not always made manifest with standard clinical instruments. Much of what has been learned recently about brain dysfunction associated with alcohol abuse has been the result of the refinement of neuroradiological, neurophysiological, and neuropsychological techniques. In a recent review of this extensive literature, Porjesz and Begleiter (1983) describe several neuropathological conditions, including the loss of brain tissue and neurophysiological abnormalities, that have been reported in a significant proportion of abstinent alcoholics. In a complementary review of the literature on cognitive dysfunction in alcoholism, Ryan and Butters (1983) describe deficits in neurologically intact alcoholics that include impairment of visual–perceptual functions, abstract reasoning and problem solving, and learning and memory abilities. Despite this considerable literature describing the physiological and behavioral consequences associated with alcohol abuse and dependence, there has been relatively little information about brain dysfunction in the alcoholic as a factor in treatment and recovery. One area of recent research particularly relevant to the treatment of chronic alcoholics concerns the reversibility of neuroradiological, neurophysiological, and neuropsychological evidence of brain dysfunction that can occur with abstinence. It is apparent from several studies (Ryan & Butters, 1983; Zilm, Huszar, Carlen, Kaplan, & Wilkinson, 1980) that the cognitive impairment and electroencephalographic (EEG) abnormalities observed in the recently detoxified alcoholic are transient to a certain extent and recover in the first 3–6 weeks following the cessation of drinking. There is also evidence that some neuropsychological recovery continues to occur with prolonged abstinence (Brandt, Butters, Ryan, & Bayog, 1983). It should be noted, however, that there is some controversy as to whether short-term reversibility of brain dysfunction in recovering alcoholics represents actual recovery from nervous system pathology or is the end of a protracted withdrawal syndrome that extends beyond the acute detoxification period (Begleiter, 1981). For the sake of the present argument, we are not making this distinction, although the reader should be aware that the mechanisms underlying neurological and behavioral recovery of function are not well understood and may differ with respect to the time frame in which recovery occurs. What is significant, however, is that it is precisely during the period when cognitive dysfunction is most apparent (i.e., the weeks following the cessation of drinking) that the major therapeutic intervention process occurs.

THE SCOPE OF THE PROBLEM

As part of the study of the natural history of alcoholism at the University of Connecticut Alcohol Research Center (ARC), 244 alcoholic inpatients were evaluated using the Halstead–Reitan neuropsychological test battery. The only criteria for admission to the study was a current *Diagnostic and Statistical Manual of Mental Disorders*, third edition (DSM-III) diagnosis of alcohol dependence and no other current serious medical or psychiatric illness. An age-adjusted index of current cognitive functioning, the Brain-Age Quotient (BAQ), was computed from six Halstead and Wechsler Adult Intelligence Scale (WAIS) subtests for each patient (Schau & O'Leary, 1977). The BAQ is standardized to have a mean value of 100 and a standard deviation of 15. Thus, a BAQ score of 100 means that the person is performing at the average level for someone of that age. The BAQ has been shown to be sensitive to the neuropsychological consequences associated with alcoholism, because it includes measures of abstracting ability and adaptive functioning (Schau & O'Leary, 1977).

Although the average length of abstinence in the ARC population was approximately 17 days, well past the 3- to 5-day period of acute withdrawal, the median BAQ score was 84. These data suggest that more than half of the alcoholic inpatients who were healthy enough to be included in the study performed in the impaired range. These findings were consistent with those reported previously by Schau and O'Leary (1977), who showed that a group of 38 alcoholic inpatients abstinent between 9 and 14 days had significantly lower BAQ scores than a matched control group. The obvious question arising from these data is to what extent this impaired cognitive status affects treatment outcome. Although there are relatively few data that address these issues, those that do exist clearly suggest it is a factor. In a follow-up study, O'Leary, Donovan, Chaney, Walker, and Schau (1979) reported that high BAQ scores were predictive of completion of treatment, and also of continued abstinence 1 year after initial treatment. In a separate report (Walker, Donovan, Kivlahan, & O'Leary, 1983) 59% of those with BAQ scores greater than 92 (which is in the normal range) were abstinent 9 months following hospitalization, whereas only 39% of those alcoholics with BAQ scores of 92 or less were abstinent at the end of the same 9-month period. While these findings are in no way conclusive, their implications for therapeutic intervention in the treatment of alcoholism are clear, and thus merit both awareness on the part of clinicians and continued investigation by treatment researchers.

In the remainder of this chapter, we review the nature of the radiological, physiological, and behavioral changes known to occur in abstinent alcoholics, and we emphasize recovery of function.

THE NATURE OF THE PHYSIOLOGICAL IMPAIRMENT

The damage to the central nervous system (CNS) associated with chronic alcoholism has been studied extensively, using both neuroradiological and neurophysiological techniques. The present discussion focuses only on the highlights of this large body of research, with more emphasis on those data related to the reversibility of brain dysfunction consequent to alcohol misuse. The reader is referred to an excellent recent review for more detailed analysis (Porjesz & Begleiter, 1983).

FINDINGS WITH COMPUTERIZED TOMOGRAPHY

A majority of alcoholics appear to manifest some cortical atrophy on computerized tomography (CT) scan, while ventricular enlargement occurs in a smaller but still significant portion of this population (Porjesz & Begleiter, 1983). Although differences in CT scan methodology have made direct comparisons between studies difficult, a number of investigators have reached the following conclusions:

1. The widening of sulci in the cerebral cortex, sylvian fissures, and interhemispheric fissure, and enlargement of the ventricular system, have been shown to occur in alcoholic populations that do not necessarily show clinical signs of brain damage (Ron, Acker, Shaw, & Lishman, 1982; Wilkinson & Carlen, 1980) or clinically apparent liver disease (Carlen, 1981).
2. The incidence of abnormal brain morphology among alcoholics appears to be highly related to age (Bergman *et al.*, 1983; Ron, Acker, & Lishman, 1980; Wilkinson & Carlen, 1980); however, measurable radiological changes have been reported in samples of alcoholics below the age of 40 (Bergman, Borg, Hindmarsh, Idestrom, & Mutzell, 1980; Carlen *et al.*, 1981; Hudolin, 1980
3. There appears to be only a weak relationship between morphological brain damage in the alcoholic and years of problem drinking when the effects of age are partialed out (Bergman *et al.*, 1980; Lishman, Ron, & Acker, 1980; and Ron *et al.*, 1982; Wilkinson & Carlen, 1980).

The relationship between morphological brain changes in alcoholics and impaired neuropsychological functioning in the same individuals has not been clearly established. There appear to be only relatively low correlations between CT scan scores and an individual's performance on the Halstead–Reitan neuropsychological battery (Wilkinson & Caren, 1980). Wilkinson and Carlen (1980) commented that some of the alcoholics were able to function remarkably well despite some substantial brain atrophy. Other investigators attempting to correlate CT scan measures of brain atrophy with other indices of neuropsychological impairment have reported similar problems in establishing clear relationships (Bergman *et al.*, 1980; Ron *et al.*, 1980). Several explanations have been offered to account for the seemingly tenuous relationship between structural and behavioral impairments, including imprecise or improper measurement of brain atrophy; interindividual variation of premorbid functioning (which would make the amount of deficit attributable to alcohol abuse difficult to estimate); and the possibility that atrophy per se may be the incorrect correlate and that other factors such as biochemical or physiological variables have been overlooked (Carlen *et al.*, 1981). On the other hand, when more precise morphological measurements are coupled with the analysis of specific cognitive functions, stronger relationships between CNS and behavioral changes appear to exist (Gebhardt, Naesser, & Butters, 1984). By measuring CT scan density numbers, rather than just the size of fluid-filled spaces, there was a significant correlation between thalamic and third ventrical atrophy and long-term memory performance in 24 abstinent alcoholics.

The structural changes reported in abstinent alcoholics do not appear static, and the extent of normalization of the morphological abnormalities appears to depend, in part, on the length of sobriety maintained by alcoholics. Thus, cerebral atrophy was partially reversed in four of six chronic alcoholics who were able to maintain abstinence between 36 and 97 weeks (Carlen, Holgate, Wilkinson, & Rankin, 1978). There is also a significant relationship between sulcal and sylvian fissure widening and reported length of abstinence (Lishman *et al.*, 1980). In addition to length of abstinence, age appears to be a factor in the reversibility of morphological changes, in that reversibility appears greater in younger alcoholics than in their older counterparts (Carlen & Wilkinson, 1980). In a longitudinal study of brain morphology changes in alcoholics (Ron *et al.*, 1982), CT scans were administered to 56 of an original sample of 100 patients at times ranging from 30 weeks to approximately 3 years following the initial examination. The 16 patients who remained abstinent showed clear improvement of their CT scans at follow-up, whereas the 40 individuals who continued to drink showed little change. Nevertheless, the scans for all 56 people were considered abnormal. These various findings have led to the suggestion that "brain shrinkage" rather than "brain atrophy" be used to describe the phenomena, since there is little knowledge of the underlying pathology, and the former term does not assume more specific neuropathological lesions (Lishman et al., 1980).

EEG FINDINGS

The EEG has also been used extensively to study CNS changes associated with alcoholism. However, there are few unequivocal findings with respect to the nature and extent of EEG abnormalities among the different alcoholic populations studied. Some of the confusion can be attributed to methodological differences, use of various medications, length of the abstinence period, the types of abnormalities studied, and the inclusion of alcoholics with other psychiatric or neurological diagnoses, all of which can affect the EEG (Begleiter & Platz, 1972; Kelley & Reilly, 1983). In addition, until recently, investigators have used qualititative measures of EEG patterns. Although this type of measurement provides a descriptive basis for alcohol-related brain dysfunction, it has not proven very useful in terms of quantifying such important dimensions as severity of impairment. On the other hand, computer-assisted quantification of the EEG data, called "spectral analysis," has demonstrated the potential for examining the relationships among the EEG, cognitive function, detoxification, medications, and time course of recovery in alcoholics (Coger, Dymond, & Serafetinides, 1979; Coger, Dymond, Serafetinides, Lowenstam, & Pearson, 1978; Kaplan, Glueck, Hesselbrock, & Reed, 1984; Zilm et al., 1980). Utilizing these quantifiable measures of the EEG, Coger and his colleagues (Coger et al., 1978) studied two groups of alcoholics that differed in severity of cognitive impairment. The more severely neuropsychologically impaired patients also had significantly more high-frequency EEG activity in the 20- to 30-Hz range. In another study (Coger et al., 1979), alcoholics had higher levels of low-frequency activity than nonalcoholic control subjects. In addition to more high-frequency activity, EEG alpha rhythms were reduced in alcoholics, particularly in those with greater neurological impairment (Zilm et al., 1980). More importantly, however, those alcoholics whose neurological scores improved during recovery had *increases* in power in the alpha frequency band.

We have recently reported the results from the first phase of the University of Connecticut ARC longitudinal study of brain dysfunction in 56 alcoholic patients (Kaplan, Glueck, Hesselbrock, & Reed). Eight channels of bipolar EEG were recorded from parasaggital sites over the frontal, temporal, centroparietal, and occipital regions of the skull. The EEG was recorded and then analyzed off-line, using power-spectral density techniques. Alcoholics had significantly more low-frequency power in the 1- to 4-Hz (delta) range than the nonalcoholic comparison group in each region of the skull. Conversely, alcoholics had significantly less 9- to 12-Hz (alpha) power than the comparison group. These findings are illustrated in Figure 11-1.

Our findings were consistent with other quantitative studies of resting EEG in alcoholics (Coger *et al.*, 1979; Zilm *et al.*, 1980), in that our sample had significantly less EEG power in the normally dominant alpha

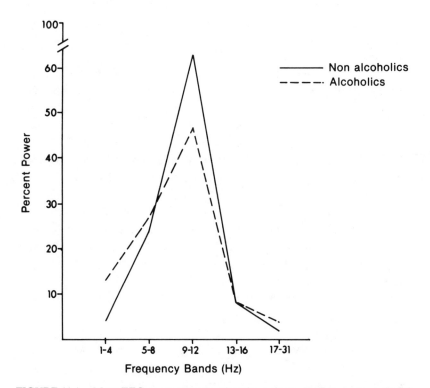

FIGURE 11-1.   Mean EEG percent power values from electrode placements on the left centroparietal region of the skull from alcoholics (*n* = 56) and a nonalcoholic comparison group (*n* = 29).

frequency band (9–12 Hz) and more EEG power in the low-frequency band (1–4 Hz) than comparable nonalcoholics. The alcoholic subjects were also given the Halstead–Reitan battery, and BAQ scores were derived from selected tests. We found that BAQ scores were negatively correlated with power in the delta band but positively correlated with power in the alpha frequencies. These data and those reported by Zilm *et al.* (1980) suggest that the relative absence of alpha activity, one of the most frequently described characteristics of alcoholics' EEG, may be indicative of diminished cognitive abilities. A preliminary analysis of the quantified EEG data from the second phase of our study, recorded approximately 1 year following the initial assessment, indicated reduced delta activity and an increase in alpha activity among those alcoholics who remained relatively abstinent. This clearly represents a trend toward normalization of the EEG with abstinence. Furthermore, at the 1-year follow-up, there was still a positive relationship between EEG normalization (decreases in delta power and increases in alpha power) and better performances on neuropsychological test performance, suggesting that cognitive recovery parallels EEG normalization (Kaplan *et al.*, 1984).

In a study currently in progress, we are examining the time course of EEG normalization and cognitive recovery during the weeks following the cessation of drinking (Kaplan & Becker, 1986). This has particular clinical relevance because much of the therapeutic intervention during inpatient alcohol treatment occurs within this time period. To examine this question, we are administering a series of EEGs and neuropsychological tests to recovering alcoholics at 6, 21, and 45 days following their last drink. A preliminary analysis of the available data appears to suggest that the normalization of the EEG may already be occurring as early as 21 days after the cessation of drinking. The data from one such subject in this study are presented in Figure 11-2. As can be seen, there were decreases in the amount of abnormal slow-wave activity and corresponding increases in 5- to 8-Hz and 9- to 12-Hz activity, a trend toward a more normal resting EEG pattern.

FINDINGS WITH EVOKED OR EVENT-RELATED POTENTIALS

Another neurophysiological method used in studying the functional integrity of the brain is that of the evoked potential (EP) or event-related potential (ERP). The EP or ERP is a record of the brain's electrophysiological activity made during repeated presentation of certain stim-

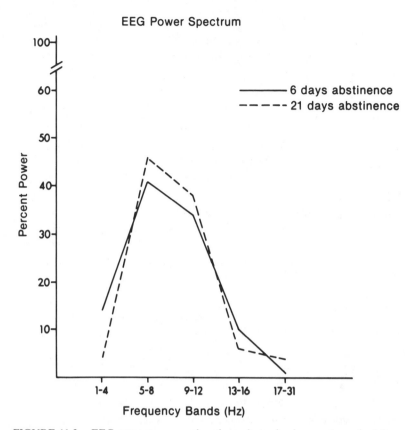

FIGURE 11-2.   EEG percent power values from electrode placements on the left centroparietal region of the skull from a 57-year-old male alcoholic at 6 days and 21 days of abstinence.

uli. The ERP technique uses computerized signal averaging to extract the brain's response to a repeated stimulus presentation. Background "noise" is canceled out. The resultant waveform is believed to represent the cognitive processing of the sensory information. The components of this waveform that occur soon after stimulus onset reflect the characteristics of the stimulus itself, while components that occur later appear to represent psychological factors such as stimulus recognition. ERPs have been extensively studied in abstinent alcoholics, and there is a consistent depression in the late-occurring components of this waveform, particularly in the P3 component (Begleiter, Porjesz, & Tenner, 1980; Porjesz & Begleiter, 1981, 1982). The P3 or P300 is particularly interesting, because it can be examined in an information-processing paradigm with the manipulation of the relevance of the stimulus modality. For example, the performance of abstinent alcoholic males was compared with that of nonalcoholic males on a task that required each subject to press a button only to the presentation of a particular visual stimulus. Responses were not to occur to other visual or to nonvisual stimuli. The nonalcoholics showed an enhanced P3 when the target was presented, suggesting that the stimulus had been identified and had taken on a particular salience to the brain. In contrast, the alcoholics' P3 component was significantly attenuated (Begleiter *et al.*, 1980).

Aberrant EPs and ERPs in alcoholics may become more normal during abstinence from alcohol. Auditory EPs that were attenuated in a group of alcoholic inpatients on the sixth or seventh day of abstinence increased in amplitude upon testing 20 days later (Salamy, Wright, & Faillace, 1980). However, alcoholics tested approximately 1 month after becoming sober and then again 3 months later showed only small improvements in EPs and then did not approach the EPs of comparable normal control subjects (Porjesz & Begleiter, 1983). This suggests that the functions tested by EPs may undergo a rapid recovery during the first few weeks of sobriety, but a slowing or cessation of change thereafter.

There is some evidence that the male children of alcoholic fathers, who are known to be at high risk for alcoholism because of a positive family history, show decrements in the P3 component of the ERP similar to those reported in abstinent alcoholic adults (Begleiter, Projesz, Bihari, & Kissin, 1984). Although this phenomena may represent a marker in individuals predisposed to the development of alcoholism, there has been, as yet, no mechanism proposed to explain the relationship of this finding to the development of alcoholism.

Together, the data emerging from both the neuroradiological and neurophysiological studies with recovering alcoholics suggest that there are transient changes in the neuropathological states commonly observed in the chronic alcoholic and that there is probably a relationship between reversibility of these brain dysfunctions and cognitive recovery.

THE NATURE OF THE BEHAVIORAL IMPAIRMENT

Individuals with long histories of alcohol abuse or alcoholism have significant impairments in cognitive function (see Ryan & Butters, 1983;

Parsons & Farr, Parsons & Leber, 1982, for reviews). These impairments encompass learning, memory, problem solving, abstraction, and perceptual functions, can affect both men and women (Fabian, Parsons & Silberstein, 1981) and can persist for many years after the cessation of drinking (Brandt *et al.*, 1983; Butters & Brandt, 1985).

LEARNING

The ability to learn new information and to associate previously unrelated stimuli can best be tested by the use of paired-associate learning tasks. For these tasks, individuals learn to make associations between two otherwise unrelated items (e.g., words such as "gate–native"). The number of associates that can be learned is an index of the patients' ability to store new information in long-term memory. The Symbol–Digit Paired-Associate (SDPA) learning task requires the subjects to learn to associate two-dimensional symbols, much like those from the Digit–Symbol test of the WAIS, with a single digit. The seven symbol–digit associates were presented to alcoholics and nonalcoholics during each of four trials, and the ability of the alcoholics to learn the associations was significantly impaired relative to that of the nonalcoholic controls (Ryan & Butters, 1980a, 1980b). A similar test can be used to examine the ability of individuals to learn to associate 10 pairs of words. Performance on this Verbal Paired-Associate (VPA) task by alcoholics has been found to be impaired relative to that of controls (Ryan & Butters, 1980a, 1980b; Ryan *et al.*, 1980), but may not be as severely affected as performance on the SDPA task (Brandt *et al.*, 1983).

The basis for the failure of alcoholics to perform well on paired-associates tasks may lie in an impairment in their ability actually to learn the associations between the stimuli, rather than difficulties in remembering the specific stimuli or recalling the associations, once they have been learned (Becker, Butters, Hermann, & D'Angelo, 1983b). Thus, when the number of associations learned is expressed as a function of the number of learning trials, the rate of acquisition of the associations by the alcoholics is significantly slower than that of controls. In spite of this impairment, alcoholics can recognize the specific stimuli that were used in a paired-associate task, and they can remember the learned associations after a 1-hour delay interval. This is important, since it suggests that memory is not totally disrupted in alcoholics, and that carefully structured therapy programs could take advantage of the relative strengths of the alcoholics' memory.

Another finding that is relevant to understanding alcoholics' learning defect is the observation that their learning performance can be improved if they are given specific mnemonics to aid learning. When specific instructions (and examples) on using mnemonic cues were given to alcoholic subjects, their performance on the VPA task improved dramatically (Ryan & Butters, 1980a). Left to their own devices, alcoholics appear to use relatively unsophisticated learning strategies and perform poorly. However, when instructed in the use of more elaborate learning schemes, their performance improves.

SHORT-TERM MEMORY

Separate and apart from the impaired ability to learn new information, alcoholics also have a significant impairment in both verbal and nonverbal short-term memory. Although early reports suggested that alcoholics' memory functions were normal, a clear impairment was uncovered when tests of sufficient difficulty were used (Ryan *et al.*, 1980). Thus, alcoholics generally perform relatively *well* on the Wechsler Memory Scale (WMS) and on tasks designed for use with severely amnestic patients. However, when short-term memory tasks are made more difficult (e.g., four- vs. three-word short-term memory test), a highly reliable performance impairment can be identified. For example, on the Benton Visual Retention Test (BVRT), subjects are shown cards with two-dimensional line drawings on them for either 5 (Form F) or 10 seconds (Form G). Either immediately (Form F) or 15 seconds later (Form G), the subjects are shown a choice card that has four designs drawn on it. The subjects' task is to choose the one of these four designs that has been presented as the stimulus to be remembered. Alcoholics were found to perform relatively well on Form F, which is the easier of the two tests, since there is no delay between presentation and tests. However, the performance of alcoholics was significantly impaired relative to that of controls on Form G, which has the 15-second delay between presentation and choice. This occurred in spite of the fact that the performance of both alcoholics and controls overall was improved relative to performance on Form F by the use of a 10-second stimulus exposure time (Ryan & Butters, 1980a, 1980b).

Short-term memory in alcoholics has also been assessed using a variation of the Brown-Peterson distractor task (Brown, 1958; Peterson & Peterson, 1959). For this task, the subjects are read a list of four words (e.g., "stain," "acid," "pear," "shed") followed by a three-digit number (e.g., "319"). In order to minimize rehearsal of the words during the retention interval, the subjects count backwards from the three-digit number by three's. Either 15 or 30 seconds later, they are told to stop counting and to recall as many of the stimulus words as possible. The performance of alcoholic patients was impaired relative to that of controls at both the 15- and 30-second delay intervals (Brandt *et al.*, 1983; Ryan & Butters, 1983).

Alcoholics with Korsakoff syndrome tend to make errors on this short-term task by recalling words from prior memory lists (Meudell, Butters, & Montgomery, 1978). Therefore, to the extent that there is a continuum of impairment between the alcoholics and the Korsakoff patients (Ryan & Butters, 1980a; Ryback, 1971), and the alcoholics share features of Korsakoff's syndrome, they should also be expected to make a large number of errors involving prior-item intrusion. Accordingly, we analyzed the alcoholics' performance on the four-word short-term memory test to determine the extent to which these subjects made prior-item intrusion errors. As in previous studies, these alcoholics were able to recall significantly fewer words after 15 or 30 seconds than nonalcoholic controls (see Figure 11-3). However, when the number of intrusion errors was expressed as a proportion of the total number of errors, the alcoholics made no more of this type of errors than did the controls. Thus, alcoholics *differ* from Korsakoff patients in terms of sensitivity to proactive interference.

CONCEPT FORMATION AND PROBLEM SOLVING

Some of the most sensitive indices of alcohol-induced cognitive dysfunction are those that test an individual's ability to solve problems and deal with abstract concepts. For example, the Category Test of the Halstead–Reitan battery requires subjects to detect a categorization rule and to apply this rule to problems of increasing complexity. The

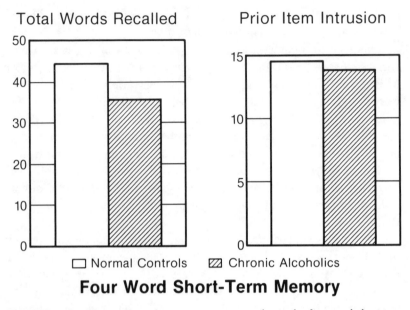

FIGURE 11-3. The number of correct responses made on the four-word short-term memory test by alcoholics and controls is shown on the left, and the proportion of those errors due to proactive interference is on the right.

performance of alcoholics has been shown to be impaired relative to that of controls on this task, and generally to fall in the "impaired" range (Jones & Parsons, 1971).

Another task that is sensitive to brain dysfunction in alcoholics is the Wisconsin Card-Sorting Task (WCST) (Grant & Berg, 1948). For this task, an individual is given a deck of cards with stimuli drawn on them that vary in terms of color, form, and number. The subject must sort the cards according to a rule established by the experimenter (i.e., color, form, or number), which he or she must infer from the examiner's responses to individual card sorts. After making 10 consecutive correct responses, the sorting principle is changed without warning. The subject must detect this change, identify the new rule, and begin responding accordingly. Alcoholics were found to be impaired in the performance of this task (Tarter, 1973, Tarter & Parsons, 1971a, 1971b; although not to the extent of patients with focal brain lesions (e.g., Milner, 1964).

Tarter and Parsons (1971a, 1971b) found that alcoholics did not have trouble acquiring the initial card-sorting rule (i.e., color) when performing the WCST, but made their errors when they switched to a *new* concept. This impairment could stem from two sources: either an inability to shift from the old sorting rule (i.e., perseverative errors), or a failure to maintain the new sorting rule. Analysis of the pattern of errors suggested that the alcoholics were as able as controls to shift away from the old rule; perseveration did not account for their poor performance. However, they *were* impaired in their ability to acquire the new rule. Specifically, after giving up the previously correct concept and identifying the new rule, the alcoholics were less likely to persist with the correct new strategy. They were more likely than controls to make errors even after strings of five or six correct responses. This inability to maintain a correct strategy was more apparent in alcoholics with longer drinking histories.

A more recent examination of the problem-solving abilities of alcoholics reinforced these previous findings and extended them significantly. On a modification of a test originally designed for use with children, alcoholics were found to be significantly impaired relative to controls in their ability to *create* a problem-solving strategy (Laine & Butters, 1982). Unlike the Category Test and the WCST, this test, a variation on the children's game, "20 Questions," requires subjects to generate their own strategy to solve a problem, rather than simply to detect an organizational principle. Subjects are shown a card with the pictures of 42 items (e.g., a saw, a house, a doll) on it, and are told to try to guess which one of the objects the experimenter was thinking of (see Figure 11-4). The subjects are told that they may ask any question they like, so long as it can be answered either "yes" or "no." They then begin to ask a series of questions until they guess the correct item.

Three question types have been defined for this task: constraint-seeking, hypothesis-scanning, and pseudoconstraint. Constraint-seeking questions are those that ask about more general organizational rules, and are useful in eliminating large numbers of alternatives regardless of the answer. Thus, "Is it a tool?" qualifies as a constraint-seeking question. Hypothesis-scanning questions are those that focus on specific items on the test card (e.g., "Is it the saw?") and are very inefficient questions, since an incorrect guess yields relatively little information. Finally, pseudoconstraint questions sound as if they might refer to a group of items (e.g., "Is it used to cut wood?"), but, in reality, refer only to a single item on the card.

The performance of alcoholics, alcoholics with Korsakoff's syn-

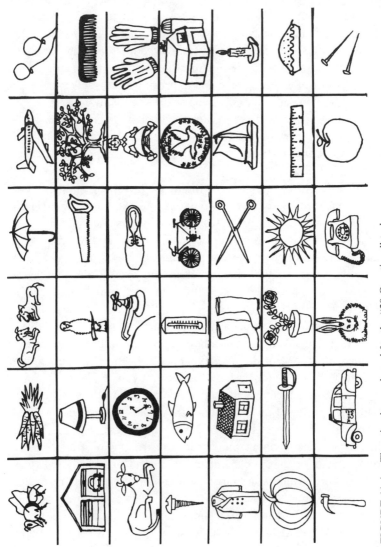

FIGURE 11-4.   The stimulus card used for the ''20 Questions'' task.

Source: From ''A Preliminary Analysis of the Problem-Solving Strategies of Detoxified Long-Term Alcoholics'' by M. Laine & N. Butters, *Drug and Alcohol Dependence, 10,* 235–242. Reprinted with permission.

drome, and nonalcoholic controls on this task was analyzed in terms of the types of questions that were asked (Becker, Butters, Rivoira, & Miliotis, in press). Nonalcoholic control subjects tended to ask constraint-seeking questions. That is, their questions focused on the more general organizational principles, and only became more specific when they had narrowed down the alternatives to a relatively small number. As can be seen in Figure 11-5, during the first five questions of the three trials, the controls asked an average of more than four constraint-seeking questions.

In contrast, the performance of the alcoholics differed significantly from that of the controls. They asked significantly fewer constraint-seeking questions and significantly more hypothesis-scanning questions. Like the alcoholics with Korsakoff's syndrome, the alcoholics asked fewer general questions, and focused more on specific attributes of the stimuli on the card.

The alcoholics' difficulty with the creation of a problem-solving strategy was further demonstrated when digits or letters were used as stimuli. As in the "20 Questions" task, subjects given this task are instructed to ask questions to guess the correct item (i.e., letter or digit).

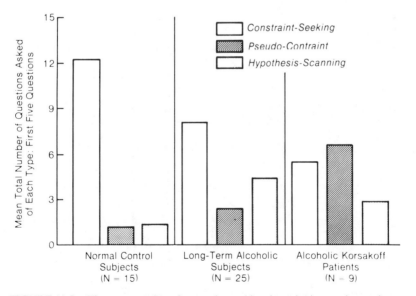

FIGURE 11-5.   The mean number of constraint-seeking, hypothesis-scanning, and pseudoconstraint questions asked during the first five questions of three trials.

As is not the case with the "20 Questions" task, however, there is no correct answer; the experimenter responds to each question in such a way as to maximize the number of stimuli that remain available. Thus, if the subject asks a question that would eliminate 6 items if answered "yes" and 12 items if answered "no," the experimenter says "yes," since this leaves the greatest number of stimuli available for the next question. By this contingency, subjects can never eliminate more than 50% of the items with any single question.

The results of the study employing the digit–letter task are shown in Figure 11-6 (Becker *et al.*, in press). It should be noted first that the nonalcoholic subjects eliminated, on average, approximately 40% of the alternatives with each question that they asked. In contrast, the alcoholics and the alcoholics with Korsakoff's syndrome were significantly poorer at eliminating alternatives than the controls. They asked questions that were less efficient at eliminating alternatives, and they did not appear to use the information from previous answers to guide their questions.

There appear to be two major impairments associated with these difficulties in problem solving. The first involves the relative concrete-

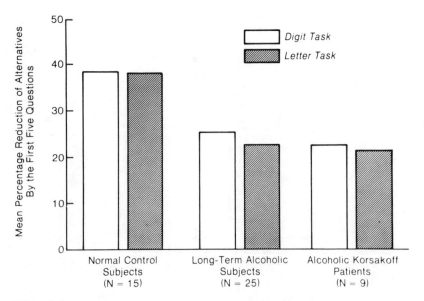

FIGURE 11-6. The mean proportion of stimuli eliminated with each question on the digit–letter task.

ness of the alcoholics' strategies, and may be related to the functions associated with general abstracting abilities. This was apparent on the "20 Questions" test when the alcoholics tended to focus on specific items rather than on a more general strategy. The second impairment, however, may arise from the alcoholics being abnormally insensitive to reinforcement contingencies. Thus, their failure to attempt to change their behavior based on lack of success (i.e., on the "20 Questions" task) may reflect not so much a lack of insight as an impaired ability to respond appropriately when they are not reinforced for their behavior. When alcoholics are faced with a lack of reinforcement for a response in an operant conditioning paradigm, they are less likely than controls to change their response in order to obtain a reinforcement (Oscar-Berman, Heyman, Bonner, & Ryder, 1980). This may be due to a fundamental abnormality in the alcoholics' response to reinforcement, rather than an insensitivity to the contingency (Oscar-Berman *et al.*, 1980). This abnormal response to reinforcement might also explain the alcoholics' failure to maintain correct response strategies for long series of trials on the WCST.

ECOLOGICALLY RELEVANT TESTS OF MEMORY DYSFUNCTION

Although the memory impairment in chronic alcoholics has been well documented for short- and long-term memory with verbal and nonverbal material (see Ryan & Butters, 1984, for review), the tests used to describe this dysfunction were all drawn from the laboratory. That is, these were tests taken from the domain of cognitive psychology (e.g., the Brown–Peterson distractor task) and then applied for use with alcoholics. Although they clearly delineated the alcoholics' memory problems, they did so without regard to the relevance of the behavior to the alcoholic. This problem takes on added significance when it is remembered that alcoholics do not rate cognitive dysfunction very high on a list of problems during sobriety (Griffin & Karp, 1981). Perhaps the memory impairment is overcome in the context of daily life, or perhaps it is an artifact of the laboratory testing situation.

Two recent experiments have addressed this issue. The first was an attempt to test the memory impairment of alcoholics using stimuli that were more ecologically relevant, and that were presented in a procedure more likely to be encountered in everyday life—learning to associate names with faces (Becker, Butters, Hermann, & D'Angelo, 1983a). The performance of a group of alcoholics was compared with that of non-alcoholic controls in their ability to learn and retain a set of 12 face–name associations. The subjects were first shown a set of 12 faces and told the name to be associated with it (e.g., "This is Mr. Taylor"). After all of the faces had been presented, they were shown again, but now the subject had to recall the correct name. All errors were corrected, but there were no additional instruction trials.

The performance of the alcoholics was significantly impaired relative to that of the controls (see Figure 11-7). They not only learned fewer of the associations, but also learned at a slower rate than the nonalcoholics. Subsequent testing of delayed recognition of the faces and names indicated that the learning deficit could not be attributed to

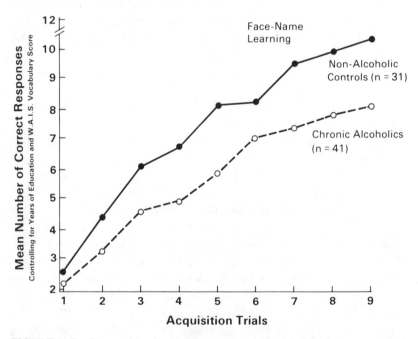

FIGURE 11-7.   The number of correct responses on each trial of the face–name paired-associate learning task.

Source: From "A Comparison of the Effects of Long-Term Alcohol Abuse and Aging on the Performance of Verbal and Nonverbal Divided Attention Tasks" by J. T. Becker, N. Butters, B. A. Hermann, & N. D'Angelo, *Alcoholism: Clinical and Experimental Research, 7,* 213–219. Reprinted with permission.

problems with perception of the faces. In addition, superior delayed recall by the alcoholics demonstrated that the associations, once learned, were not forgotten.

Recent evidence suggests that this test may, in fact, be very relevant to the demands placed on the alcoholic after treatment. When therapists were asked to rate alcoholics on a number of items relative to their treatment outcome, these ratings were highly correlated with performance on the face–name paired-associates learning task (Leber, Parsons, & Nichols, 1985). While the basis for this relationship is not clear, certainly this behavioral task is assessing some function related to the patients' ability to function during treatment for alcoholism.

A second study may be even more relevant to the demands placed on the alcoholic during recovery. In this study (Becker & Jaffe, 1984), the ability of alcoholics to remember information presented in an alcohol education class was compared with that of nonalcoholic inpatients and long-term abstinent alcoholics (i.e., Alcoholics Anonymous members). As a part of their regular treatment program, groups of alcoholic subjects were shown a film that dealt with the disease of alcoholism. This film was selected from the large number of films presented during treatment, based on the recommendation of experienced alcohol counselors who found it interesting and highly memorable. After the presentation of the film, the subjects were given two tests of their memory for the information presented in the film. The first, a test of recall, required the subjects to "fill in the blanks" (e.g., "According to the speaker, people drink for the effects of alcohol on the ___"). The second test, a test of recognition memory, was a multiple-choice test, and the subjects simply had to circle one of four possible answers.

Although the performance of the alcoholics was impaired overall relative to that of the nonalcoholic controls, this relationship changed as a function of the time since the alcoholics had entered into treatment. Thus, the performance of the alcoholics who had been in treatment for 1 week or less (Group 1) was impaired on both the recall and the recognition tests (see Figure 11-8). Those alcoholics who were not tested until 1 or 2 weeks following admission (Group 2) were impaired in the performance of the recall test, but not that of the recognition test. Finally, by the time the alcoholics had been in treatment for 3 weeks or longer (Group 3), their performance did not differ from that of inpatient nonalcoholics.

These data demonstrate that the memory impairment of alcoholics

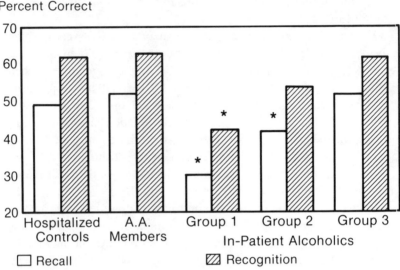

Memory for Treatment - Relevant Information

FIGURE 11-8. The performances of the inpatient alcoholics, outpatient alcoholics, and inpatient controls on the recall and recognition tests relating to the alcohol education film.

is evident even when tested in the context of their treatment program—-a highly ecologically relevant test. Other data gathered in this study may suggest the basis for this memory impairment, since some of the subjects were also given the Shipley Institute of Living Scale. This scale consists of two parts: a multiple-choice vocabulary test, and a completion test of abstraction ability (e.g., "A Z B Y C X D __"). The performance of the alcoholics on the recognition test was significantly correlated with that on the vocabulary test of the Shipley scale. This suggests that the recognition performance during the first week of sobriety may be related to a general cognitive disturbance. The performance on the recall test, on the other hand, was significantly correlated with that on the abstraction test, which suggests a different mechanism for the behavioral impairment related to functions of the frontal lobe system. Thus, the recovery of neuropsychological function during early abstinence may reflect two separate processes—one related to general cognitive function, and another to more specific frontal lobe functions.

RECOVERY OF FUNCTION

The performance of alcoholics on tests of cognitive function differs depending on the amount of time that has elapsed since they stopped drinking. These changes are most apparent during the first 4–6 weeks following detoxification, although some changes are evident even 5 years after the cessation of drinking (e.g., Cermak & Ryback, 1976; Claiborn & Greene, 1981; Eckhardt, Parker, Noble, Pautler & Gottschalk, 1979).

In order to properly evaluate recovery of function, it is necessary to separate the effects of time-dependent recovery (i.e., length of sobriety) from experience-dependent effects (i.e., how many times a patient has been tested). The former process is important because it suggests changes in behavior based on physiological responses. The latter process suggests that patients may learn to perform certain tasks well, and that if the learning can generalize to others measuring similar functions, then true remediation of impairment can be said to have occurred.

One way to separate the effects of practice from those of temporal recovery is to use a multiple-group testing procedure. For example, in the procedure used by Goldman and his associates (see Goldman, 1983, for review), three groups of alcoholics are tested following admission to a treatment program. The first group is tested three times (5, 15, and 25 days after admission); the second is tested only twice (15 and 25 days after admission). Finally, the third group is tested only 25 days after admission to the treatment program. This procedure allows for the assessment of time-dependent recovery by comparing the performance of the three groups of alcoholics at their respective *first* testings. Practice effects can be estimated by comparing the performance between the groups of subjects at the last test day. On this day, all of the subjects have been abstinent for 25 days, but they differ in the amount of practice they have had. Any between-group difference at this point will reflect improvement based on practice with the tests.

Two studies used this procedure to test the recovery of verbal and nonverbal cognitive functions (Ellenberg, Rosenbaum, Goldman, & Whitman, 1980; Sharp, Rosenbaum, Goldman, & Whitman, 1977). In the first study, the ability of alcoholics to learn the meanings of 10 words using the Synonyms Learning Test (SLT) was assessed. This procedure is useful because it controls for level of difficulty on an individual basis, and yet still tests the subjects' ability to learn complex verbal information (word meanings). The three groups of alcoholics were well matched for age and education, although the group of patients tested three times had abused alcohol for fewer years than the patients in the other groups. The results of this study demonstrate that even though the basic vocabulary skills of the alcoholics was normal at all testing (Mill Hill Vocabulary Test), the performances on the SLT differed as a function of length of abstinence. Specifically, the performance of the alcoholics tested after 5 days of sobriety was significantly poorer than that of the alcoholics tested for the first time 15 or 25 days after entering treatment. By the 15th day of treatment, all of the recovery of function appeared to have taken place, since there were no additional improvements in performance. Practice effects were not found to be significant, even in the group of subjects tested three times.

In a second study, the ability of alcoholics to perform verbal and nonverbal paired-associates learning tasks was evaluated. These tasks were selected because the level of performance in normals was equated between the verbal and nonverbal versions, and because norms had been established not only for normal performance, but for the performance of patients with focal brain lesions as well (Stark, 1961). As was found in the previous study, verbal abilities recovered quickly, returning to normal levels by day 15 of treatment. In contrast, overall performance on the visual–spatial version of this task did not recover as quickly. However, a subsequent analysis of the subjects' characteristics revealed that recovery of visual–spatial function depended to a large extent on length of problem drinking. Those alcoholics who had been drinking for less than 12 years performed the visual–spatial test as well at day 25 as the normative population. However, those alcoholics who had been drinking longer were performing as poorly after 25 days of sobriety as patients with focal right-hemisphere lesions. A similar pattern was seen with the verbal learning test, but the differences between the group of alcoholics were never significant. Thus, from these two studies, it is evident that recovery of function does occur soon after cessation of drinking. However, although these studies documented changes that occurred early in recovery, they did not address the question of the effects of long-term abstinence on performance.

Recently, a large cross-sectional study of recovering alcoholics was reported that specifically addressed the question of long-term abstinence (Brandt *et al.*, 1983). A total of 125 alcoholics were grouped according to their reported length of sobriety: short-term abstinence (1–2 months), long-term abstinence (12–36 months), or prolonged abstinence (> 60 months). The performance of these men was compared on tests of short-term memory, paired-associates learning, substitution (i.e., digit–symbol), and visual–perceptual function.

The results of this study demonstrated that recovery of function can occur over long periods of time, but that this recovery is not an "all-or-none" phenomenon. Specifically, verbal short-term memory (i.e., the Brown–Peterson task) returned to normal in the prolonged abstinence group, but did not differ between the short- and long-term abstinence groups. Similarly, recovery was also found on the test of nonverbal short-term memory (i.e., the BVRT). However, although BVRT performance improved, even that of the prolonged abstinence group did not return to normal. Recovery of function was also observed on tasks that required the rapid transcription of digits to symbols or symbols to digits (the digit–symbol and symbol–digit substitution tasks). The long-term abstinence group's performance was approximately midway between that of the short-term and prolonged abstinence groups.

The performance of the prolonged abstinence alcoholics did not show recovery of function on two tests. The first was the SDPA test. This test, as described earlier in this chapter, evaluates the ability of subjects to learn to associate a single-digit number with a two-dimensional line drawing. Similarly, the performance on the Embedded Figures Test, a test of perceptual processing, did not differ among the three groups of alcoholics.

These data, therefore, suggest that recovery of function may take place over a period of several years following the cessation of drinking. However, since this was a cross-sectional study, there are some difficulties in interpreting the data. Those alcoholics who were able to maintain sobriety for more than 5 years (the prolonged abstinence group) may have differed from those individuals who were abstinent for shorter periods of time on factors unrelated to alcoholism. Had the individuals in the prolonged abstinence group been tested within 1–3 months of their last drink (as had the short-term abstinence group), they might have performed significantly better than other alcoholics.

These data, and those of others (see Goldman, 1983), suggest that the cognitive functions of alcoholics may improve with abstinence, and that this improvement may continue for many years. Thus, these behavioral data confirm the electrophysiological changes that have been noted earlier in this chapter. There appears to be a biphasic recovery of function, with a rapid change early in sobriety (4–6 weeks) and a slower change occurring over years of continued abstinence.

These data also suggest that early intervention with alcoholics with cognitively demanding therapy may not be the most effective route to take. There are data that appear to show that neuropsychological test performance during the early phase of treatment predicts treatment outcome (Abbott & Gregson, 1981; Gregson & Taylor, 1977). These findings suggest that rehabilitation of the cognitive abnormalities in recovering alcoholics may enhance treatment outcome (Goldman, 1983) and perhaps should precede any more traditional therapeutic approaches.

Summary

The data presented in this chapter demonstrate that clear physiological and behavioral changes occur in individuals with long histories of alcohol abuse. The behavioral changes are pervasive, and they affect even those functions that are relevant to everyday life. Fortunately, abstinence from alcohol appears to result in recovery of function. Both electrophysiological and neuropsychological measures of brain function show significant improvement during the initial 2 months of sobriety. In addition, there may be a slower recovery process that endures for years with continued sobriety. These data suggest that early attempts at cognitively based therapy should be coupled with aggressive attempts at cognitive rehabilitation.

ACKNOWLEDGMENT

The writing of this chapter was supported in part by funds granted by the National Institute on Alcohol Abuse and Alcoholism to the University of Connecticut (AA5-20544, AA5-20461) and by the National Institute on Aging to the University of Pittsburgh (AG03705).

REFERENCES

Abbott, M. W., & Gregson, R. A. M. (1981). Cognitive dysfunction in the prediction of relapse in alcoholics. *Journal of Studies on Alcohol, 42*, 230–243.
Becker J. T., Butters, N., Hermann, B. A., & D'Angelo, N. (1983a). A comparison of the effects of long-term alcohol abuse and aging on the performance of verbal and

nonverbal divided attention tasks. *Alcoholism: Clinical and Experimental Research, 7,* 213–219.

Becker, J. T., Butters, N., Hermann, A., & D'Angelo, N. (1983b). Learning to associate names and faces: Impaired acquisition on an ecologically relevant memory task by male alcoholics. *Journal of Nervous and Mental Disease, 171,* 617–623.

Becker, J. T., Butters, N., Rivoira, P. & Miliotis, P. (in press). Asking the right questions: Problem solving in alcoholics and alcoholics with Korsakoff's syndrome. *Alcoholism: Clinical and Experimental Research.*

Becker, J. T., & Jaffe, J. H. (1984). Impaired memory for treatment-relevant information in inpatient men alcoholics. *Journal of Studies on Alcohol, 45,* 339–343.

Begleiter, H. (1981). Brain dysfunction and alcoholism: Problems and prospects. *Alcoholism: Clinical and Experimental Research, 5,* 264–265.

Begleiter, H., & Platz (1972). The effects of alcohol on the central nervous system in humans. In B. Kissin & H. Begleiter (Eds.), *The biology of alcoholism* (Vol. 2): *Physiology and behavior.* New York: Plenum Press.

Begleiter, H., Porjesz, B., Bihari, B., & Kissin, B. (1984). Event-relevant brain potential in boys at risk for alcoholism. *Science, 225,* 1493–1496.

Begleiter, H., Porjesz B., & Tenner, M. (1980). Neuroradiological and neurophysiological evidence of brain deficits in chronic alcoholics. *Acta Psychiatrica Scandinavica, 286,* 3–13.

Bergman, H., Axelsson, G., Idestrom, C. M., Borg, S., Hindmarsh, T., Makower, J., & Mutzell, S. (1983). Alcohol consumption, neuropyschological status and computer-tomographic findings in a random sample of men and women from the general population. *Pharmacology, Biochemistry and Behavior, 18,* 501–505.

Bergman, H., Borg, S., Hindmarsh, T., Idestrom, C., & Mutzell, S. (1980). Computed tomography of the brain and neuropsychological assessment of male alcoholic patients. In D. Richter (Ed.), *Addiction and brain damage* (pp. 201–214). Baltimore: University Park Press.

Brandt, J., Butters, N., Ryan, C., & Bayog, R. (1983). Cognitive loss and recovery in long-term alcohol abusers. *Archives of General Psychiatry, 40,* 435–442.

Brown, J. (1958). Some tests of the decay theory of immediate memory. *Quarterly Journal of Experimental Psychology, 10,* 12–21.

Butters, N., & Brandt, J. (1985). The continuity hypothesis: The relationship of long-term alcoholism to the Wernicke–Korsakoff syndrome. In M. Galanter (Ed.), *Recent developments in alcoholism* (Vol. 3, pp. 207–226). New York: Plenum Press.

Cala, L. A. (1983). CAT scan demonstration of alcohol-related brain damage in social drinkers. *Australian Alcohol/Drug Review, 2,* 81–83.

Carlen, P. (1981). Cerebral atrophy and functional deficits in alcoholics without clinically apparent liver disease. *Neurology, 31,* 377–385.

Carlen, P., Holgate, G., Wilkinson, D., & Rankin, J. (1978). Reversible cerebral atrophy in recently abstinent chronic alcoholics measured by computed tomography scans. *Science, 200,* 1076–1978.

Carlen, P., & Wilkinson, D. (1980). Alcoholic brain damage and reversible deficits. *Acta Psychiatrica Scandinavica, 62,* 103–118.

Cermak, L. S., & Ryback, R. S. (1976). Recovery of verbal short-term memory in alcoholics. *Journal of Studies on Alcohol, 37,* 46–52.

Claiborn, J. M., & Greene, R. L. (1981). Neuropsychological changes in recovering men alcoholics. *Journal of Studies on Alcohol, 42,* 757–765.

Coger, R., Dymond, A., & Serafetinides, E. (1979). Electroencephalographic similarities between chronic alcoholics and chronic, nonparanoid schizophrenics. *Archives of General Psychiatry, 36,* 91–94.

Coger, R., Dymond, A., Serafetinides, E., Lowenstam, I., & Pearson, D. (1978). EEG signs of brain impairment in alcoholism. *Biological Psychiatry*, *13*, 729–739.

Eckardt, M. J., Parker, E. S., Noble, E. P., Pautler, C. P., & Gottschalk, L. A. (1979). Changes in neuropsychological performance during treatment for alcoholism. *Biological Psychiatry*, *14*, 943–953.

Ellenberg, L., Rosenbaum, G., Goldman, M. S., & Whitman, R. D. (1980). Recoverability of psychological functioning following alcohol abuse: Lateralization effects. *Journal of Consulting and Clinical Psychology*, *48*, 503–510.

Fabian, M. S., Parsons, O. A., & Silberstein, J. A. (1981). Impaired perceptual–cognitive functioning in women alcoholics: Cross-validated findings. *Journal of Studies on Alcohol*, *42*, 217–229.

Gebhardt, C., Naesser, M., & Butters, N. (1984).Computerized measures of CT scans of alcoholics: Thalamic region related to memory. *Alcohol*, *1*, 133–140.

Goldman, M. S. (1983). Cognitive impairment in chronic alcoholics: Some cause for optimism. *American Psychologist*, *38*, 1045–1054.

Grant, D. A., & Berg, E. A. (1948). A behavorial analysis of degree of reinforcement and ease of shifting to new responses in a Weige-type card-sorting problem. *Journal of Experimental Psychology*, *38*, 404–411.

Gregson, R. A. M., & Taylor, G. M. (1977). Prediction of relapse in men alcoholics. *Journal of Studies on Alcohol*, *38*, 1749–1759.

Griffin, P. T., & Karp, R. (1981). The relative importance of mental dysfunction to chronic alcoholics. *Psychological Reports*, *48*, 543–546.

Horvath, T. (1975). Clinical spectrum and epidemiological features of alcoholic dementia. In J. Rankin (Ed.), *Alcohol, drugs and brain damage: Proceedings of a symposium, effects of chronic use of alcohol and other psychonetive drugs on cerebral functions* (pp. 1–19). Toronto: Addiction Research Foundation.

Hudolin, V. (1980). Impairments of nervous system in alcoholics. In D. Richter (Ed.), *Addiction and brain damage* (pp. 168–200). Baltimore: University Park Press.

Jones, B. M., & Parsons, O. (1971). Impaired abstracting ability in chronic alcoholics. *Archives of General Psychiatry*, *24*, 71–77.

Kaplan, R. F., & Becker J. T. (1986). *Neurophysiological and neuropsychological correlates of recovery from alcoholism*. Research in progress.

Kaplan, R. F., Glueck, B., Hesselbrock, M., & Reed, H. (1984). EEG abnormalities and cognitive dysfunction in alcoholism *INS Bulletin*, p. 20. (Abstract).

Kaplan R. F., Glueck, B., Hesselbrock, M., & Reed, H. (1985). Power and coherence analysis of the EEG in hospitalized alcoholics and non-alcoholic controls. *Journal of Studies on Alcohol*, *46*, 122–127.

Kelley, J., & Reilly, E. (1983). EEG alcohol, and alcoholism. In J. Hughes & W. Wilson (Eds.), *EEG and evoked potentials in psychiatry and behavioral neurology* (pp. 55–78). Boston: Butterworth Publishers.

Laine, M., & Butters, N. (1982). A preliminary analysis of the problem-solving strategies of detoxified long-term alcoholics. *Drug and Alcohol Dependence*, *10*, 235–242.

Leber, W. A., Parsons, O. A., & Nichols, N. (1985). Neuropsychological test results are related to men alcoholics therapeutic progress: A replication study. *Journal of Studies on Alcohol*, *46*, 116–121.

Lishman, W. A., Ron, M., & Acker, W. (1980). Computed tomography of the brain and psychometric assessment of alcoholic patients. In D. Richter (Ed.), *Addiction and brain damage* (pp. 215–227). Baltimore: University Park Press.

Meudell, P. R., Butters, N., & Montgomery, K. (1978). Role of rehearsal in the short-term memory performance of patients with Korsakoff's and Huntington's disease. *Neuropsychologia*, *16*, 507–510.

Milner, B. (1964). Some effects of frontal lobectomy in man. In J. Warren & K. Akert (Eds.), *The frontal granular cortex and behavior* (pp. 313–320). New York: McGraw-Hill.

O'Leary, M., Donovan, M., Chaney, E., Walker, R., & Schau, E. J. (1979). Application of discriminant analysis to level of performance of alcoholics and nonalcoholics on Wechsler–Bellevue and Halstead–Reitan subtests. *Journal of Clinical Psychology, 35*, 204–208.

Oscar-Berman, M., Heyman, G., Bonner, R., & Ryder, J. (1980) Human neuropsychology: Some differences between Korsakoff and normal operant performance. *Psychological Research, 41*, 235–247.

Parsons, O. A., & Farr, S. P. (1981). The neuropsychology of alcohol and drug use. In S. B. Filskou & T. J. Boll (Eds.), *Handbook of clinical neuropsychology* (pp. 320–365). New York: Wiley.

Parsons, O. A., & Leber, W. R. (1982). Premature aging, alcoholism, and recovery. In W. Gibson & M. F. Elias (Eds.), *Alcoholism and aging: Advances in research* (pp. 79–92). Boca Raton, FL: CRC Press.

Peterson, L. R., & Peterson, M. J. (1959). Short-term retention of individual verbal items. *Journal of Experimental Psychology, 58*, 193–198.

Porjesz, B., & Begleiter, H. (1981). Human evoked brain potentials and alcohol. *Alcoholism: Clinical and Experimental Research, 5*, 304–316.

Porjesz, B., & Begleiter, H. (1982). Evoked brain potential deficits in alcoholism and aging. *Alcoholism: Clinical and Experimental Research, 6*, 53–63.

Porjesz, B., & Begleiter, H. (1983). Brain dysfunction and alcohol. In *The pathogenesis of alcoholism* (pp. 415–475) New York: Plenum Press.

Ron, M. A. (1984, June). *The brain of alcoholics: An overview.* Paper presented at the NIAAA Conference on Neuropsychological Dysfunction in Alcoholics, Boston.

Ron, M. A., Acker, W., & Lishman, W. (1980). Morphological abnormalities in the brain of chronic alcoholics. *Acta Pyschiatrica Scandinavica, 286*, 41–47.

Ron, M. A., Acker, W., Shaw, G., & Lishman, W. (1982). Computerized tomography of the brain in chronic alcoholism. *Brain, 105*, 497–514.

Ryan, C., & Butters, N. (1980a). Further evidence for a continuum of impairment encompassing male alcoholic Korsakoff patients and chronic alcoholics. *Alcoholism: Clinical and Experimental Research, 4*, 190–198.

Ryan, C., & Butters, N. (1980b). Learning and memory impairments in young and old alcoholics: Evidence for the premature aging hypothesis. *Alcoholism: Clinical and Experimental Research, 4*, 288–293.

Ryan, C., & Butters, N. (1983). Cognitive deficits in alcoholics. In B. Kissin & H. Begleiter (Eds.), *The pathogenesis of alcoholism* (pp. 485–538). New York: Plenum Press.

Ryan, C., & Butters, N. (1984). Alcohol consumption and premature aging: A critical review. In M. Galanter (Ed.), *Recent advances in alcoholism* (Vol. 2). New York: Plenum Press.

Ryan, C., Butters, N., Montgomery, K., Adinolfi, A., & Didario, B. (1980). Memory deficits in chronic alcoholics: Continuities between the "intact" alcoholic and the alcoholic Korsakoff patient. In H. Begleiter (Ed.), *Biological effects of alcohol* (pp. 701–725). New York: Plenum Press.

Ryback, R. (1971). The continuum and specificity of the effects of alcohol on memory. *Quarterly Journal of Studies on Alcohol, 32*, 995–1016.

Salamy, J., Wright, J., & Faillace, L. (1980). Changes in average evoked responses during abstention in chronic alcoholics. *Journal of Nervous and Mental Disease, 168*, 19–25.

Schau, E. S., & O'Leary, M. R. (1977). Adaptive abilities of hospitalized alcoholics and matched controls: The Brain-Age Quotient. *Journal of Studies on Alcohol, 38*, 403–409.

Sharp, J. R., Rosenbaum, G., Goldman, M. S., & Whitman, R. D. (1977). Recoverability of psychological functioning following alcohol abuse: Acquisition of meaningful synonyms. *Journal of Consulting and Clinical Psychology, 45*, 1023–1028.

Stark, R. (1961). An investigation of unilateral cerebral pathology with equated verbal and visual–spatial tasks. *Journal of Abnormal and Social Psychology, 62*, 282–287.

Tarter, R. E. (1973). An analysis of cognitive deficits in chronic alcoholics. *Journal of Nervous and Mental Disease, 157*, 138–147.

Tarter, R. E., & Parsons, O. A. (1971a). Conceptual shifting in alcoholics. *Archives of General Psychiatry, 24*, 71–79.

Tarter, R. E., & Parsons, O. A. (1971b). Conceptual shifting in chronic alcoholics. *Journal of Abnormal Psychology, 77*, 71–75.

Walker, R. D., Donovan, D. M., Kivlahan, D., & O'Leary, M. R. (1983). Length of stay, neuropsychological performance and aftercare: Influences on alcohol treatment outcome. *Journal of Consulting and Clinical Psychology, 51*, 900–911.

Wilkinson, D. A., & Carlen, P. L. (1980). Relation of neuropsychological test performance in alcoholics to brain morphology measured by computed tomography. In H. Begleiter (Ed.), *Biological effects of alcohol* (pp. 693–699). New York: Plenum Press.

Zilm, D. H., Huszar, L., Carlen, P. L., Kaplan, H. L., & Wilkinson, D. A. (1980). EEG correlates of the alcohol-induced organic brain syndrome in man. *Clinical Toxicology, 16*, 345–358.

12

Alcoholism and Depression

JEROME H. JAFFE
DOMENIC A. CIRAULO

Few clinical phenomena are as well documented as the occurrence of depressive symptoms among men and women with alcoholism. This chapter briefly reviews some recent research findings on what these symptoms may represent, whether and when treatment is indicated, and what kinds of treatment seem useful. Although one might suspect that the course of alcoholism would be more malignant in those alcoholics prone to depression, some investigators report that alcoholics with depression seem to have a course similar to that of alcoholics without depression (Hesselbrock, Hesselbrock, Tennen, Meyer, & Workman, 1983; Woodruff, Guze, Clayton, & Carr, 1979). In comparing primary alcoholics with and without secondary depression, Schuckit (1983) found very few differences between the two groups in terms of course of illness or family histories of alcoholism or affective disorder. Other workers have found that alcoholics who develop depression may be more likely to seek treatment for their alcoholism because of their depressive symptoms (O'Sullivan, Daly, Carroll, Clare, & Cooney, 1979; O'Sullivan *et al.*, 1983; Woodruff, Guze, Clayton, & Carr, 1973).

Alcoholism is associated with higher suicide rates. From 5% to 27% of all deaths in alcoholics are due to suicide, as compared to about 1% in the general population; and 15–25% of all suicides are committed by alcoholics. This high rate of suicide is not necessarily associated with severe depressive symptoms. Berglund (1984) found that, while 47% of those who later committed suicide were rated as slightly depressed as compared to 33% of those who did not commit suicide, only 2% of the entire sample of hospitalized alcoholics were considered seriously depressed. Interestingly, a state labeled "irritability, dysphoria, and aggressiveness" was, like slight depression, far more common among those who later committed suicide, but the irritability/dysphoria characteristic was negatively correlated with the state of slight depression. In other studies (Beck, Steer, & McElroy, 1982), those subjects with primary depression and secondary alcoholism (usually women) were more likely to have made a serious suicidal gesture. It is reported that a considerable proportion of such suicides occur during early stages of acute or chronic intoxication (Mayfield & Montgomery, 1972). Further, alcoholics who make suicidal gestures often have histories of social loss in the weeks prior to the suicide or suicide attempt (Murphy, Armstrong, Hermele, Fischer, & Clendenin, 1979). Thus, the contributing factors to suicide may involve the depressigenic, toxic, and disinhibiting effects of alcohol; social losses; persistent symptoms of depression; and other characterological traits.

DEPRESSIVE SYMPTOMS: PREVALENCE

A substantial proportion (up to 98%) of alcoholics recently admitted to treatment programs report some of the same symptoms that are commonly reported by patients with depression (see Behar & Winokur, 1979; Hesselbrock, Hesselbrock, Tennen, Meyer, & Workman, 1983; Keeler, Taylor, & Miller, 1979). After a few days to several weeks, most of these patients report fewer symptoms (Freed, 1978; Hamm, Major, & Brown, 1979; Schuckit, 1979; Shaw, Donley, Morgan, & Robinson, 1975). The percentage of patients considered by clinicians to be "clinically depressed" will depend on the diagnostic criteria employed, the conceptual frameworks within which clinicians operate, and at what points in the cycle of alcohol use and withdrawal the patients are assessed.

The methods for determining the presence and significance of depressive symptoms include the use of self-evaluations such as the Zung Self-Rating Depression Scale, the Beck Depression Inventory (BDI), and the Raskin Depression Scale; subscales of broader symptom and personality scales, such as the Minnesota Multiphasic Personality Inventory (MMPI) and the Hopkins Symptom Checklist (SCL-90); clinician/observer ratings of depression (the Hamilton Depression Rating Scale); application of formal diagnostic criteria applied to material obtained in structured clinical interviews; and global diagnoses made after unstructured clinical interviews (for references, see Behar & Winokur, 1979; Freed, 1978; Hesselbrock *et al.*, 1983; Hesselbrock, Meyer, & Keener, 1985; Petty & Nasrallah, 1981). In some studies, these methods have been combined or are augmented by family history information and/or by biological tests, such as the dexamethasone suppression test (DST) (Dackis *et al.*, 1984; Khan *et al.*, 1984), or tests of thyroid function (Loosen, Wilson, Dews, & Tipermas, 1983). Some clinicians further categorize alcoholic patients with depressive symptomatology into those who meet formal diagnostic criteria for depression (e.g., those of the Diagnostic and Statistical Manual of Mental Disorders, third edition [DSM-III] or the Research Diagnostic Criteria [RDC]) prior to or independent of problems with alcohol use, and those who manifested alcoholism before the first onset of depressive symptomatology. These two groups are designated as primary depressives with secondary alcoholism, and primary alcoholics with secondary depression, respectively (see Cadoret, Troughton, & Widmar, 1984; Schuckit, 1979).

Studies by Keeler *et al.* (1979), Hesselbrock *et al.* (1983, 1985), and Cadoret *et al.* (1984) each illustrate different facets of the critical role of diagnostic criteria in determining the prevalence and significance of depression among alcoholic patients seeking treatment. Keeler *et al.* (1979) found that in a group of 35 recently detoxified alcoholic men, 8.6% were considered depressed on the basis of a clinical interview; 28% were considered depressed on the Hamilton Depression Rating Scale (using a cutoff score of 20 or more); 66% were rated as depressed using the Zung Self-Rating Depression Scale (using a cutoff score above 44); 43% were depressed when the criterion was an MMPI Depression Scale score greater than 70; and 71% would be considered depressed if the criterion were an elevated score on either the Zung or the MMPI. These workers endorsed the clinical interview as the appropriate method for determining which patients were candidates for treatment of their depression.

Hesselbrock *et al.* (1983) studied a larger and more diverse group of 185 men and 65 women who were also interviewed within a few days after admission to treatment. The findings were generally similar to those of Keeler *et al.* (1979), in that the self-administered scales emphasizing current symptoms categorized a significantly higher percentage of patients as depressed than did the clinical interview—in this case, the National Institute of Mental Health Diagnostic Interview Schedule (NIMH-DIS) administered by trained research assistants. In this study,

62% of patients were categorized by the MMPI as being depressed; 54% were categorized as depressed by the BDI; and 27% met the DSM-III criteria for one of the depressive disorders. Of the men who met DSM-III criteria for depression, 73% were also diagnosed as having antisocial personality (ASP). In this study, as in most others, females were more likely to have a diagnosable depressive disorder and less likely to have ASP as an additional diagnosis. In other studies, the percentage of alcoholics with primary depression appears to range from 3% to 46%, but is consistently found far more frequently among women than men (Beck *et al.*, 1982; Hesselbrock *et al.*, 1985; Schuckit, 1983; Winokur, Rimmer, & Reich, 1971).

Cadoret *et al.* (1984) also used the NIMH-DIS with a sample of 230 individuals 6 days after admission to an alcoholism treatment unit. In this study, the authors used the notion of primary and secondary disorders in order to form groups for comparison. Of the 230 patients, 8 were found to be drug abusers rather than alcoholics; 7% of the remaining 222 were found to be primary depressives (onset of depression before alcoholism); and 46% of the remaining 206 alcoholics were diagnosed as primary antisocial alcoholics. These antisocial alcoholics were then compared with 85 "pure primary" alcoholics (those remaining after the alcoholics with adult-onset antisocial behavior were excluded). The antisocial alcoholics reported far more depressive symptoms than the pure alcoholics, and a somewhat higher percentage of the former met DSM-III criteria for depressive disorders. However, the differences in the percentage of patients with formal diagnoses of depression did not fully reflect the differences in depressive symptomatology between the groups. The patients with ASP reported many more symptoms of depression and anxiety than those without, but their symptoms were often too transient (i.e., less than 2 weeks), or did not cluster in time so as to satisfy the DSM-III criteria for one of the depressive disorders. This study demonstrates that symptoms of dysphoria and depression can be prevalent in certain groups of alcoholic patients without leading to formal DSM-III diagnoses. Such studies force us to ask what role such symptoms (even when they do not cluster in time) may play in the genesis of alcoholism and the overall poor social functioning of the affected groups; they also lead us to wonder how patients ought to be grouped for purposes of treatment research.

Depressive symptoms are present in alcoholics in the community, as well as individuals entering treatment. In a community survey, Weissman and Myers (1980) found that 71% of 34 identified alcoholics were diagnosed as having at least one additional psychiatric disorder. Depression was the most common additional diagnosis: 44% had had major depression, 15% minor depression, 6% bipolar depression, and 18% depressive personality. In a national survey of adults in the United States, Midanik (1983) looked at the impact of varying the definition of "alcohol problem" on the incidence of depression among drinkers. She found that 3.6% of men and 3.8% of women who reported having an alcohol problem of any degree were found to have coexisting depression, when the latter was defined as a score of 16 or more on the Center for Epidemiological Studies Depression Scale. Among problem drinkers, 33% of women but only 17% of men had depressive symptoms. Among those who were considered alcoholic, using criteria of alcohol dependence and evidence of loss of control to make that diagnosis, 56.6% of women showed coexistent depression, as compared to 19% of men who met the criteria for both disorders.

PERSONALITY DISORDERS AND SYMPTOMS OF DEPRESSION AMONG ALCOHOLICS

As described above, currently used diagnostic schemes such as DSM-III do not yield mutually exclusive diagnoses. Alcoholics in treatment commonly receive multiple diagnoses, including major and minor depression, ASP, drug dependence, and/or phobia (as individual additional diagnoses or in combination) (Hesselbrock *et al.*, 1983). Some patients may meet criteria for borderline personality. Since depressive symptomatology is quite common in nonalcoholic individuals with borderline and/or antisocial personality (Cadoret *et al.*, 1984; Loranger & Tulis, 1985; Nace, Saxon, & Shore, 1983; Perry, 1985), the basis of depressive symptoms in those alcoholics with ASP or borderline personality disorder is difficult to determine. In any event, a very substantial proportion of alcoholics, whether in treatment or in the community, do meet criteria for one or more of the personality disorders, most commonly ASP (see Cadoret *et al.*, 1984; Hesselbrock *et al.*, 1985; Schuckit, 1983; Stabenau, 1984). While the reliability of diagnosing personality disorders has improved with the introduction of DSM-III, the reliability of diagnosis for all personality disorders is not equally good, and the distinctions between diagnoses are not always clear (Kass, Skodol, Charles,

Spitzer, & Williams, 1985). In two separate studies, there was more than a chance level of correlation between the traits that led to the diagnoses of histrionic, narcissistic, antisocial, and borderline personality disorders (Kass *et al.*, 1985; Stangl, Pfohl, Zimmerman, Bowers, & Corenthal, 1985). Each of these diagnoses has elements of dramatic, emotional, and erratic behaviors as well as depressive symptoms.

At one time, it was assumed that the depressive and dysphoric symptoms probably played a causal role in the genesis of excessive drinking, or that alcoholism and depression were manifestations of the same genetically transmitted vulnerability (Bohman, Cloninger, von Knorring, & Sigvardsson, 1984; Merikangas, Leckman, Prusoff, Pauls, & Weissman, 1985; Murray *et al.*, 1984; Schuckit, 1979). More recently there is some evidence that, by a process of assortative mating, some individuals inherit independent predispositions to alcoholism and/or personality disorders (Bohman *et al.*, 1984; Cadoret, O'Gorman, Troughton, & Heywood, 1985; Loranger & Tulis, 1985; Merikangas *et al.*, 1985; von Knorring, Cloninger, Bohman, & Sigvardsson, 1983). Loranger and Tulis (1985) suggest that it may be the impulsivity, rather than the affective instability common to these personality disorders, that leads to their association with high rates of alcoholism; they also suggest that the combination of impulsivity with irritability and aggression (more common in men) leads to ASP. The importance of childhood irritability and aggression as early markers for later alcoholism and ASP has likewise been emphasized by Lewis, Robins, and Rice (1985) (see also chapter by Michie Hesselbrock, this volume).

Finally, other data suggest that alcoholism results in consequent personality changes that may be confused with predisposing personality traits. Drake and Vaillant (1985) studied a cohort of men who were not obviously delinquent as adolescents. The nonalcoholic men with personality disorders showed evidence of maladaptive behavior in boyhood, while the alcoholic men did not differ significantly from those without personality disorders in terms of boyhood competence. The authors inferred from these and other observations that alcoholic men with personality disorders may exhibit extreme personality traits and impaired functioning "because of their drinking rather than because of the persistence of early adaptive problems" (p. 558). Schuckit (1983) has also emphasized the importance of differentiating antisocial behavior that is consequent to alcohol dependence from true ASP disorder.

Researchers attempting to categorize alcoholics with depressive symptoms for purposes of therapeutic trials face a number of difficulties in trying to create groups that are comparable in terms of the origins of depressive symptoms. This problem is made more vexing by uncertainties inherent in establishing diagnoses of coexisting personality disorders, and clarifying their temporal relationship to the onset of alcohol dependence.

PERSISTENCE OF SYMPTOMS AND THEIR SIGNIFICANCE

There is a consensus among clinicians that symptoms of depression in alcoholics are more frequent during the first few days after cessation of drug and alcohol intake and gradually decline to near-normal levels in most patients over a period of 1 or 2 weeks (Freed, 1978; Schuckit, 1979, 1983; Shaw *et al.*, 1975). This general observation has led some clinicians to the view that only a relatively few alcoholic patients who have severe and generally classic depressive symptoms require specific intervention (Keeler *et al.*, 1979; Schuckit, 1979, 1983). It has also led to the inference that the high level of symptomatology in recently admitted alcoholics is due in part to the toxic effects of alcohol and drugs, and therefore is best described as an organic affective disorder (Behar & Winokur, 1979; Schuckit, 1979, 1983). This conclusion may be supported indirectly by the finding that those alcoholics who become abstinent and remain so tend to report less depression than those who resume drinking (Freed, 1978; Hatsukami & Pickens, 1982).

Several studies suggest that some depressive symptoms appear to persist in some recovering alcoholic patients, even though these patients do not meet DSM-III criteria for an affective disorder and do not appear to be drinking. Pottenger *et al.* (1978) found that up to 59% of previously treated alcoholics had a clinically significant level (cutoff score of 7 or more) as measured by the Raskin Depression Scale. Behar, Winokur, and Berg (1984), in their cohort study of abstinent members of Alcoholics Anonymous (AA), reported that 15% had symptom clusters that met DSM-III criteria for depressive disorder. In our own work, we compared recently admitted alcoholics at a Veterans Administration (VA) hospital, veterans seeking care at an outpatient optometry clinic, and veterans at an AA group on a number of self-report scales measuring mood and depressive symptoms (the BDI and the Zung Self-Rating

Depression Scale). We recognized that these instruments were designed and validated to measure change in severity of depression in nonalcoholic populations experiencing classic affective disorders. It was our hypothesis that many alcoholics (both those with and those without personality disorders) may experience dysphoric and low levels of self-esteem that are not due to toxic effects and do not meet criteria for DSM-III major affective disorders. We also explored the use of scales developed by Haertzen, Martin, Ross, and Neidert (1980) to measure what were described as feelings of hypophoria, impulsivity, and sense of need, which are believed to be typical of addicts, alcoholics, and sociopaths. The questionnaire (the Psychopathic State Inventory) developed by Haertzen *et al.* (1980) has been further factor-analyzed by Cowan and coworkers (cited by Kay, 1980) into three subscales, which were labeled "defeated," "joyless," and "hypophoric," and which we refer to collectively as the "hypophoria scales." Over a period of more than 18 months, these instruments were routinely administered to patients newly admitted to an alcohol treatment service at a VA hospital. The instruments were readministered after 2 weeks of hospitalization and again prior to discharge. More than 180 subjects filled out forms on admission. The same instruments were also given to 25 members of AA who were abstinent for more than 6 months, and to 25 nonalcoholic, nonpsychiatric optometry outpatients. Various subgroups of inpatients and outpatients were also administered the NIMH-DIS, the Hamilton Depression Rating Scale, tests of cognitive function, and the DST.

Our objectives were to determine (1) whether alcoholics at a VA hospital, like the former addicts and alcoholics tested by Haertzen *et al.* (1980), had elevated hypophoria scores; (2) how the scores on these scales compared to those of control subjects; (3) whether these instruments measured the same phenomena measured by the BDI and the Zung scale; and (4) which scales, if any, were best suited to measure responses to our anticipated therapeutic interventions. We found, as others have (e.g., Shaw *et al.*, 1975), that for most recently admitted alcoholics, scores on the BDI declined substantially over the first few weeks of hospitalization (see below). It was our goal to identify a subgroup of patients whose symptoms persisted for more than 2 weeks, and who might therefore be candidates for controlled treatment studies. In order to decide on an appropriate cutoff score for our population, we looked at the scores of various control groups. The following findings of interest emerged from these studies.

First, we found that, while the BDI and the Zung scale correlated well with each other at initial and subsequent administration ($r \cong .70$), and while there was a significant initial correlation between these and the hypophoria scales ($r = .70$), the scores on the hypophoria scales did not decline over time, as did the BDI and Zung scores. This general stability is presented in Table 12-1, which also shows that the scores of alcoholics were significantly higher than those of nonalcoholic controls, and that abstinent AA members had scores falling between the other groups. Thus the hypophoria scales seemed to be tapping aspects of mood and self-regard that were distinct from those measured by the BDI and the Zung scale.

A second serendipitous finding was that, among alcoholics, scores on the BDI seemed to be significantly modified by repeated administration. Frequently, patients were taking laboratory tests or were otherwise unavailable to complete the BDI and other scales within the first days after admission, and sometimes an alcoholic patient had been transferred from a medical service. In some instances, the initial tests were not taken until the third week after admission (after which the tests would be readministered 2 weeks later and again prior to discharge). After dividing the subjects into three groups, based on how soon after admission they filled out the first test, we examined the test scores and found that in each group the scores declined with time and repeated administrations. However, initial scores on the first administration were almost the same, regardless of whether the questionnaire was completed during the first, second, or third week after admission. Our group (Becker, Jaffe, Ciraulo, 1985), and subsequently Choquette and Hesselbrock (1985), then undertook systematic trials that largely supported the finding of a significant practice effect for the BDI among alcoholics. Choquette and

TABLE 12-1   Mean Hypophoria Scores

Group	n	Mean hypophoria score
I: Inpatient alcoholics		
Abstinent 1 week	50	38.4
Abstinent 2 weeks	50	35.8
Abstinent 4–6 weeks	50	35.9
II: AA group	25	27.3
III: Nonalcoholic medical outpatients	25	20.5

Hesselbrock found that the Zung scale also exhibited this effect. The reactive qualities of such scales must be considered in designing therapeutic interventions.

A third general finding touches on the question of which alcoholics need or want treatment for dysphoria and mood disorder. We were concerned that selecting subjects for research on the basis of any cutoff score on the BDI or the Zung scale would be prejudging the question of how well these instruments measured disordered mood in alcoholics. We decided to compare the scores on these established instruments with a more direct approach, which asked subjects such questions as these: "How is your mood? Do you feel 'blue' or depressed? Do you feel that you don't get as much enjoyment from life as others do? Would you be interested in research treatment for the 'blues' or depression in alcoholics? Would you be willing to take a medically accepted drug to improve your mood? Would you be willing to take a new medication that is being tested?"

This questionnaire was given to more than 100 patients, and we found several of the expected correlations; that is, those who had high scores on the BDI were far more likely to report having the blues and being interested in treatment (82% of those with BDI scores above 15 wanted to take medication for the blues). We also found something else we had suspected: Many subjects with scores of 10 or lower on the BDI still reported having the blues; 62% with such scores were willing to take standard medication for the blues; and 47% were having sufficient discomfort to be willing to take a research drug and to give blood samples (Becker, Jaffe, & Ciraulo, 1985).

In sum, depressive symptoms are very common in alcoholic patients during the immediate period of abstinence. Some of the scales normally utilized to measure depressive symptoms in alcoholic patients may not be sensitive to persistent dysphoric mood states in these individuals. The diagnosis of major depressive disorder does not account for the presence of persistent dysphoric symptoms in most alcoholic patients. On the basis of current data, it is difficult to make a strong case that the persistent depressive or dysphoric symptoms frequently reported by alcoholics contribute heavily to a more malignant natural history of the alcoholism, or that effective intervention would, by alleviating depressive or dysphoric symptoms, alter the course of the alcohol dependence syndrome. The urge to find more effective treatments for dysphoria and persistent depressive symptoms must rest largely on the belief that until effective interventions are available, it is impossible to know what impact such interventions might have on the course of alcoholism or on any of the associated personality disorders that tend to occur concurrently.

RECOGNITION OF MULTIPLE CAUSES FOR DEPRESSIVE SYMPTOMS: A PREREQUISITE FOR RESEARCH

If the symptoms of depression in alcoholics can be due to multiple causes, it follows that some interventions may be useful in treating some varieties of depression, but not others. This now seems self-evident; however, much of the research on depression in alcoholism was done when antidepressant drugs were first introduced, and it did not take such patient and syndrome heterogeneity into account. In order to avoid this pitfall in future research, there must be a full recognition of the factors influencing mood and affect in this group of patients. Among the many potential causes of depressive symptoms are the following: (1) direct toxic effects of alcohol on the brain; (2) indirect toxic effects of alcohol (exerted by alterations in liver function, nutritional intake, or absorption of nutrients); (3) effects of alcohol withdrawal; (4) central nervous system (CNS) effects of drugs ingested to modify or enhance alcohol effects or to alleviate withdrawal; (5) CNS effects of injury and/or anoxia associated with alcohol-related accidental trauma and/or suicidal gestures; (6) social losses (jobs, friends, family, social status) caused by alcohol-related behavior; (7) a psychological response to the appreciation of the extent of physical impairment caused by alcohol use; (8) manifestations of several varieties of affective disorder transmitted independently of any vulnerability to alcoholism; (9) manifestation of any of several varieties of personality disorder that may have antedated alcohol problems; (10) manifestation of some genetically-transmitted vulnerability to both affective symptoms and alcoholism.

It is important to recognize that these factors do not usually operate in isolation, but generally interact in association with ethanol consumption. Figure 12-1 offers a picture of some of the generally accepted interrelationships among excessive alcohol use, alcohol dependence and withdrawal, alcohol-induced depression, alcohol-related CNS toxicity, antecedent depressive symptomatology and alcohol-induced social losses. Several of these factors are discussed at greater length in other chapters

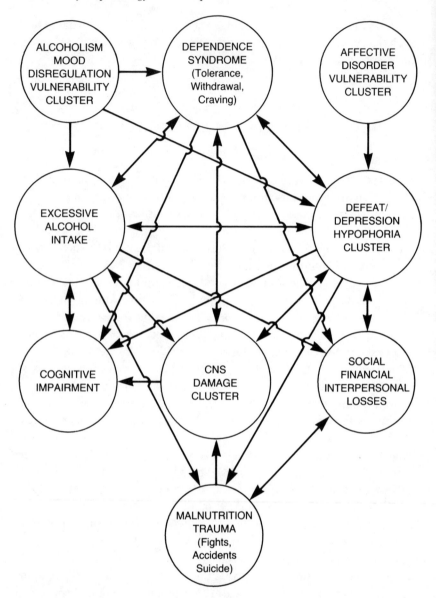

FIGURE 12-1.   Factors linked to depressive symptoms in alcoholics. (From "Drugs Used in the Treatment of Alcoholism" by J. H. Jaffe and D. Ciraulo. In J. H. Mendelson and N. K. Mello [Eds.], *The Diagnosis and Treatment of Alcoholism* [pp. 355–389]. New York: McGraw-Hill. Reprinted by permission.)

of this volume. In the next section of this chapter, we review some of the data supporting the idea that excessive alcohol use itself can cause a toxic organic depressive syndrome.

DEPRESSION IN ALCOHOLICS AS A TOXIC ORGANIC AFFECTIVE DISORDER

Considering the well-documented effects of alcohol on brain structure and cognitive function (see Brandt, Butters, Ryan, & Bayog, 1983; Parsons & Leber, 1981), it would be unlikely that the neural systems subserving mood would escape unscathed. Furthermore, given the degree of recovery of cognitive function that occurs, it would not be surprising to see some recovery in affective areas as well. These general observations and others are part of the evidence leading to the conclusion that some of the depressive symptoms seen during heavy drinking, or immediately following cessation, are due to the toxic effects of alcohol. The most persuasive evidence comes from laboratory studies in which alcoholics are permitted to ingest alcohol. In such studies, the initial sense of disinhibition, sometimes lasting only a few hours, is generally followed by reports of increasing irritability, dysphoria, and depression (Freed, 1978; Mayfield, 1979; Mendelson & Mello, 1970).[1] In some studies, however, even 1 week of drinking may not be long enough to produce significant dysphoria in all subjects (Persky *et al.*, 1977).

Also bearing on this question is a study by Birnbaum, Taylor, and Parker (1983) of 93 female drinkers. These investigators found that women randomly assigned to reduce their alcohol intake reported significant decreases in depression and anger during the sober state, as compared to women who were asked to maintain their usual level of alcohol intake. Since there were no changes in cognitive performance in this study, it is possible that the systems subserving mood are even more sensitive to alcohol-induced change than those subserving cognition. After examining plasma levels of amino acids in depressed and nondepressed alcoholics and controls, Branchey, Branchey, Shaw, and Lieber (1984) concluded that chronic alcohol use may induce depression

---

1. Increasing depression, irritability, and dysphoria have also been reported in laboratory studies of subjects given access to heroin (Meyer & Mirin, 1979).

in some situations by altering the metabolism of tryptophan, so that less of this amino acid precursor of serotonin enters the brain.

CAN BIOLOGICAL MARKERS HELP DIFFERENTIATE CAUSES OF DEPRESSION IN THE ALCOHOLIC?

Efforts have been made to develop biological measures that would differentiate among the varieties of depressive syndromes encountered in alcoholic patients. Most of these (the DST; measures of thyrotropin-releasing hormone [TRH]; and sleep electroencephalograms [EEGs]) have been adapted from measures originally aimed at differentiating depressive syndromes in nonalcoholic populations. Independent studies (Dackis *et al.*, 1984; Loosen *et al.*, 1983) have confirmed that some alcoholics continue to exhibit a "blunted" thyrotropin (thyroid-stimulating hormone or TSH) response to a dose of TRH. The test was initially used in recently detoxified alcoholic patients with and without secondary depression. Loosen *et al.* (1983) subsequently studied this response in members of AA who had been abstinent for at least 2 years, 30% of whom had histories of secondary depression and 19% of whom had family histories of depression, but none of whom were depressed (Hamilton scores were 10 or less) at the time of testing. Of 29 patients, 9 (31%) showed a blunted response that was unrelated to duration of abstinence of family or personal history of depression. Dackis *et al.* (1984) found a similar percentage (25%) of blunted responses in alcoholics without evidence of depression who had been sober for at least 3 weeks, and a higher percentage of blunting was seen earlier in the course of withdrawal. In short, the TRH test does not appear to be useful in categorizing types of depression.

The DST is markedly affected by liver function abnormalities and early stages of alcohol withdrawal. At the end of 2–3 weeks of abstinence, nondepressed alcoholics show no higher percentage of "escape" or nonsuppression than nondepressed control subjects (Dackis *et al.*, 1984; Khan *et al.*, 1984). Thus it could have some value in confirming the diagnosis of major depressive disorder among alcoholics without liver disease who have been abstinent for more than 3 weeks.

The characteristics of the sleep EEG found in depressed patients (decreased rapid eye movement [REM] latency; increased REM density) are also found in recently abstinent alcoholics with or without depression. Again, a 2- to 3-week period of recovery may be necessary before the sleep EEG can be utilized to assess the presence of major depression in alcoholics.

PHARMACOLOGICAL TREATMENT OF DEPRESSION AND DEPRESSIVE SYMPTOMS IN ALCOHOLICS

Pharmacological treatments for patients with alcoholism have been reviewed by Jaffe (1984), Jaffe and Ciraulo (1985), and Rada and Kellner (1979). Here the following drugs or drug groups are discussed: (1) tricyclic antidepressants; (2) monoamine oxidase (MAO) inhibitors; (3) phenothiazines and other dopaminergic blockers; (4) dopaminergic agonists; (5) lithium; (6) amphetamines and similar agents; (7) propranolol and other beta-adrenergic blocking agents.

TRICYCLIC ANTIDEPRESSANTS

Currently the tricyclic antidepressants are among the drugs most frequently prescribed for alcoholic patients (Ciraulo & Jaffe, 1981). Evidence for the efficacy of these drugs even among "primary depressives" with alcoholism is difficult to find, since patients with alcoholism have generally been excluded from participation in clinical trials of tricyclic drugs. One widely cited paper by Viamontes (1972) concluded that in 89 controlled studies of drugs for treatment of alcoholism, only one drug (a phenothiazine, not a tricyclic antidepressant) was found to be effective. However, the case for nonefficacy is "not proven." The interpretation of available studies is complicated by methodological problems, including failure to measure plasma levels to assure adequate dosage and compliance, and sometimes failure to measure changes in depression in addition to changes in drinking patterns. In most studies treatment was started immediately after withdrawal, when the rapid spontaneous improvement exhibited by many alcoholics would obscure any drug-related improvement. In most studies, doses used were inadequate to produce therapeutic blood levels even in nonalcoholic depressed subjects.

In a review of controlled studies of tricyclic drugs used in the treatment of alcoholics, we (Ciraulo & Jaffe, 1981) noted that despite these methodological problems, most of which would create a bias toward negative findings, four of six controlled studies of imipramine can be interpreted as showing some positive effect in terms of affect or clinic attendance. (In one of the four studies, low doses of chlordiazepoxide were also given.) Other reviewers have interpreted the same data on imipramine more negatively. One of three studies using amitriptyline, and one of two studies using doxepin, showed some positive effects.

Perhaps as a result of the effects of cigarette smoking and/or alcoholism, alcoholic subjects metabolize imipramine more rapidly than do nonalcoholic depressed patients. We have previously reported that alcoholics given 150 mg of imipramine per day had significantly lower steady-state concentration of imipramine and its metabolites than controls (with equal numbers of smokers in both groups) (Ciraulo *et al.*, 1982). The effects of alcoholism and smoking on pharmacokinetics of other tricyclic antidepressants are less clear-cut, as is the relationship between these other drug plasma levels and clinical response. Nevertheless, the studies of doxepin and amitriptyline in alcoholics used dosages that would currently be considered at the low end of adequacy for nonalcoholic depressed patients.

In our study of the pharmacokinetics of imipramine, we examined in a nonblind fashion the changes on various self-reported measures of depression in depressed alcoholics and nonalcoholic depressed veterans maintained on 150 mg/day of imipramine. As described above, at the end of 3 weeks of treatment, plasma levels of the drug and its metabolites were below accepted therapeutic levels in the alcoholic patients. There were some decreases in the BDI scores over this period, but when we compared these decreased scores with those of other alcoholics who had equally high initial BDI scores, but who for various reasons had not been referred for pharmacological treatment, we were surprised to find that the BDI scores of the subjects treated with imipramine were significantly higher than those of subjects treated with milieu therapy and psychotherapy alone. We were unable to find any differences between the drug-treated and untreated patients that would explain the difference in scores. After considering these findings, we elected not to proceed with a planned double-blind study of imipramine, designed to adjust dosage to yield higher plasma levels that would be closer to the therapeutic range. Another consideration in this decision was that most of the patients we encountered in our veteran population had patterns of depressive symptoms and anxiety that were more characteristic of those seen in atypical depressions and in patients with personality disorders.

If the advent of newer antidepressants, presumably with more selective neurotransmitter effects, stimulates a new look at the problem, it would be useful to look carefully at affects other than depression. The tricyclics (imipramine and amitriptyline) are effective antipanic agents in nonalcoholic patients (Ravaris, Robinson, Ives, Nies, & Bartlett, 1980; Zitrin, Klein, & Woerner, 1980), and it has been argued that the antipanic actions are distinct from the antidepressant actions (Zitrin *et al.*, 1980).

In summary, although the tricyclic antidepressants are widely used by clinicians, their efficacy is viewed with skepticism by a number of researchers. The tricyclics have no significant abuse potential, and are quite safe unless taken in deliberate overdosage. In nonalcoholics they have antidepressant and antipanic/antiagoraphobic effects. Since the most common affective disturbances among alcoholics are symptoms of depression, anxiety, and panic/agoraphobia, another look using better methodology may be in order, although some of the newer agents may hold more promise than agents such as imipramine.

MAO INHIBITORS

In a 1967 paper, Kissin and Charnoff (cited by Shaw *et al.*, 1975) found that isocarboxazide was not superior to placebo in producing abstinence for a 6-month period. If any other trials of MAO inhibitors in treating alcoholics have taken place over the past 12 years, they are not to be found in data bases used for computerized literature searches. There is now a renewed interest in the use of MAO inhibitors for the treatment of atypical depression, panic episodes, and anxiety syndromes (Liebowitz *et al.*, 1984; Quitkin *et al.*, 1984; Quitkin, Rifkin, & Klein, 1979; Ravaris *et al.*, 1980). Descriptions of some varieties of "atypical depressions" for which MAO inhibitors are said to be particularly effective have some features in common with the syndromes exhibited by many alcoholics in the weeks and months following detoxification (dysphoria, anxiety, and sensitivity to rejection, without the classic endogenous vegetative signs). The MAO inhibitors are logical candidates for therapeutic trials because of their demonstrated antipanic effects and the high prevalence of panic episodes (often in association with depressive features) among recovering alcoholics.

However, prescribing a drug for alcoholics that requires careful compliance with dietary restrictions and includes the potential for liver toxicity raises a number of concerns. Also, MAO inhibitors may sometimes be associated with disulfiram-like reactions when alcohol is ingested (Simmonds, 1982). While this side effect might be unacceptable to many patients, the need to warn alcoholic patients about the possibility of such a reaction could be seen as adding to the therapeutic value of MAO inhibitors. Concerns about side effects should not preclude clinical trials among those alcoholics without liver damage who, while still hospitalized, have persistent symptoms of depression and anxiety several weeks after withdrawal.

In our nonblind pilot trial of tranylcypramine in alcoholics who still had high BDI scores 3 weeks after admission for detoxification (Jaffe, Becker, Ciraulo, & Smith, 1984), we found that drug treatment produced a clear reduction in symptoms only in those alcoholics with high levels of anxiety as well as elevated BDI scores. Although the sample was small, we were not impressed by the antidepressant efficacy of tranylcypramine. A double-blind study now in progress may not reach completion, because so few potential volunteers remain who, after 2 weeks of hospitalization, still have BDI scores high enough to justify the risks associated with the drug and who also have no medical problems (hypertension, heart disease, liver disease) that contraindicate its use.

DOPAMINERGIC BLOCKERS

Dopaminergic blockers are important in the treatment of alcoholics with schizophrenia. What is at issue is their role in the management of non-schizophrenic affective disturbances beyond the period of acute withdrawal. Dopaminergic blockers have been compared with placebo on target symptoms of anxiety, tension, or depression during the postwithdrawal phase. Patients on placebo showed substantial improvement, and differences in favor of the drugs were not great (Behar & Winokur, 1979; Rada & Kellner, 1979). In one study, a low dosage of thioridazine was superior to placebo in reducing tension and insomnia, but the placebo group did better in terms of work and activity (Hague, Wilson, Dudley, & Cannon, 1976). As with the tricyclics, issues of design (dosage, criteria, timing) were biased against positive findings for dopaminergic blockers. However, the frequency with which tardive dyskinesia is seen with this group of drugs suggests that they are less benign than was previously appreciated. Although they have no abuse potential, there is reason to suspect that these drugs produce dysphoric symptoms and are therefore unlikely to be of significant help in the kinds of affective disorders encountered among alcoholics.

Dopaminergic Agonists

Apomorphine has been used in the treatment of alcoholism for many years, not only to induce vomiting in aversive conditioning, but also to reduce tension and craving. With the recognition that apomorphine acts as a dopaminergic agonist, there has been renewed interest in its therapeutic potential, as well as in that of other dopamine agonists such as bromocriptine (Anokhina, 1984). Feldmann (1983) has described in positive terms his experiences over a 35-year period treating more than 6000 alcoholics with apomorphine—experiences that were largely ignored because of the absence of appropriate controls. In parkinsonism, dopaminergic deficiency produces depression in addition to the characteristic motor signs, both of which are alleviated by L-dopa. In view of the postulated interactions of alcohol with catecholamine systems, it is possible that dopaminergic agonists might have some therapeutic value in affective states after alcohol withdrawal.

Lithium

Published control studies comparing lithium to placebo in alcoholic patients have the following in common: The subjects were recently detoxified alcoholics; the dropout rate was high, with the percentage completing the trial period ranging from 17% to 53%; and the measures of effectiveness included episodes of pathological drinking as well as measures of depression.

The studies have also differed in important ways. The initial study by Kline, Wren, Cooper, Varga, and Canal (1974) involved 73 male veterans who had high scores on the Zung Self-Rating Depression Scale. Thus all subjects were depressed by this criterion, but those with unipolar and bipolar depression were excluded from this study. The double-blind phase of the study lasted 48 weeks. At the end of this period, 16 lithium and 14 placebo patients were still in the study. The Zung scores for those remaining on lithium were comparable to those on placebo, but lithium patients had experienced significantly fewer days of pathological drinking and hospitalization for alcoholism (see also Kline & Cooper, 1979).

A study by Merry, Reynolds, Bailey, and Cooper (1976) began with 60 men and 11 women, 48% of whom had scores above 15 on the BDI and were considered depressed. At the end of an average of 41 weeks of treatment, BDI scores improved for both groups, but somewhat more for the lithium than for the placebo group. Among those categorized as depressed at the start of treatment, those on lithium had significantly fewer days spent drinking and fewer days on incapacitating drinking as compared to placebo. This conclusion was based on nine "depressed" patients on lithium and seven "depressed" patients on placebo.

A study by Pond *et al.* (1981) involved 47 patients and used MMPI profiles to assess depression. It was designed as a 3-month crossover in which the maximum period on lithium was 3 months. Nineteen subjects completed the study. No significant differences between conditions in terms of MMPI scores or drinking patterns were shown. The authors considered their own design to be inadequate to test the hypothesis.

There are several uncontrolled studies of lithium in alcoholics (Behar & Winokur, 1979; Keeler, 1980; Merry *et al.*, 1976), which indicate that alcoholics who are not being treated for manic–depressive illness do not find lithium reinforcing and do not take it regularly. However, compliance is a problem with lithium among others groups as well. There is little evidence that alcoholics who after detoxification show few signs of depression (as measured on either the BDI or the Zung scale) benefit from lithium. Controlled studies of lithium in alcoholic patients with more clearly defined affective illness (e.g., bipolar and unipolar cyclothymic affective disorders) have not been reported. A large-scale multicenter study of lithium in alcoholics is in progress.

In a recent controlled double-blind crossover study, Judd and Huey (1984) found that when alcoholics maintained on lithium for several weeks were given 1.32 ml/kg of 95% ethanol, they reported feeling less intoxicated, less cognitively impaired, and less desirous of continuing drinking than when maintained on placebo. This effect was not related to any additional diagnoses: The same general response was seen in those with (n = 16) or without (n = 19) lifetime histories of affective disorder.

Lithium has been studied in institutionalized young delinquents with histories of aggressive behavior, and in prisoners who had histories of recurrent patterns of violent behavior with minimal provocation. In these studies, violent, angry behavior decreased, while other forms of sociopathic behavior did not (Kellner & Rada, 1979). To the degree that alcoholism is particularly prevalent among these groups, and that among these groups the alcoholism has a particularly poor prognosis, these studies of lithium on prisoners and delinquents may have relevance for treatment. The findings that early signs of irritability and hostility are powerful predictors of later problem drinking (Lewis *et al.*, 1985) and of later suicide in alcoholics (Berglund, 1984) only offer additional indication of the potential value of lithium in selected subgroups of alcoholics. To the best of our knowledge, there have been no studies of lithium in alcoholics with ASP and histories of violent and aggressive behavior.

Among the drugs that are potentially available for treatment, lithium has two major advantages. The plasma levels that produce therapeutic effects are generally agreed upon, and there are readily available methods for monitoring both of these levels and compliance. Its safety range, however, is narrow, and the potential side effects are many. Judging from the available results, the number of alcoholics who would voluntarily take lithium long enough to benefit from it may be limited.

AMPHETAMINES AND RELATED DRUGS

Some studies indicate, and a number of physicians believe, that there is a useful place for amphetamines and related drugs in selected cases of depression resistant to other antidepressants. One rationale for considering the amphetamines and related drugs (e.g., methylphenidate) in the treatment of affective dysregulation in alcoholics is linked to the hypothesis that both mood and alcoholism may be linked to persistent minimal brain dysfunction (attention deficit disorder, hyperactivity) in many alcoholics. The one controlled trial of methylphenidate in groups that have included alcoholics has been disappointing (Mattes, Boswell, & Oliver, 1984), and even the proponents of this hypothesis concede that the abuse potential of these drugs probably rules out their general use in this population (Wood, Wender, & Reimherr, 1983).

PROPRANOLOL

Propranolol, a beta-adrenergic blocker, is superior to placebo in reducing tension with or without depression in recently withdrawn alcoholics (Rada & Kellner, 1979) and appeared to be superior to diazepam in a 2-week crossover study (Carlsson & Fasth, 1976). While there is little likelihood of dependence, propranolol is known to produce confusion and other cognitive impairments, and abrupt discontinuation (as might occur if an alcoholic returned to drinking) has been associated with potentially dangerous changes in cardiac function. The role of beta-blockers in affective disorders of alcoholics is yet to be clarified.

CONCLUSIONS

Depressive symptomatology is common among those who drink heavily; such symptoms are more likely to be seen and to be more severe in those who seek treatment, and are more common in female than in male alcoholics. In any given individual, the symptomatology can and usually does have multiple causes, ranging from toxic effects of alcohol to personality disorders antedating the onset of drinking. The many possible origins of depressive and dysphoric effects in alcoholics have been illustrated in Figure 12-1.

While practice effects associated with several of the common self-report instruments (e.g., the BDI and the Zung scale) used to measure depressive symptomatology in alcoholics may exaggerate the extent of the improvement that commonly takes place over the first weeks of treatment, most clinicians agree that the decrease in symptomatology is real and substantial. The trend toward improvement, however, should not obscure the observation that some alcoholic patients continue to report some symptoms of dysphoria and depression many months after treatment, and some may do so for years. Thus, the issue of differential diagnosis of dysphoria and mood disorder in alcoholics must be confronted during both the acute and the later phases of treatment. Neither the tools for making such a differential diagnosis nor the therapeutic procedures available if such a differential diagnosis is made are entirely satisfactory. In a patient with alcoholism and depressive symptoms of mild to moderate severity, there are no reliable methods to distinguish which depressive and dysphoric symptoms are part of a personality disorder, which stem from toxic effects of alcohol, and which may stem from some recurrent depressive diathesis equivalent to one of the Axis I affective disorders.

During the first few months of abstinence, when the symptom pattern in a given patient meets the criteria for one of the DSM-III affective diagnoses, it is often assumed that all symptoms in the cluster are etiologically related to that syndrome. Studies of intervention built on this foundation stand on shaky ground. While one would expect symptoms due to toxic effects to improve with the passage of time, the time course of recovery from these toxic effects is not well documented; continued recovery may continue over months. It should not be assumed that the mechanisms underlying drug-induced toxic affective disorder will respond to the same therapeutic interventions that have been successful with nonalcoholic patients who have major affective disorders meeting DSM-III criteria.

Alcoholic patients giving a clear-cut history of bipolar disorder or severe major depression have been treated using the psychopharmacological treatments applied to nonalcoholics. While there is no evidence to suggest that lithium is less effective in alcoholics, some studies suggest that alcoholics may metabolize some of the tricyclic antidepressants so rapidly that plasma levels may be less than optimal, even when patients are compliant about taking the medications. Many alcoholics giving less clear histories of major depression or depression of only mild to moderate severity typically receive no treatment aimed specifically at these symptoms. It is rare to find treatment specifically directed at depressive or dysphoric symptoms when these seem to be part of a personality disorder. This probably reflects varying mixtures of indifference to such patients, the patients' lack of interest in treatment, and a recognition that no established effective interventions exist. What is curious is how few interventions have been attempted.

The relationship of affective symptoms to excessive drinking is complex. It is not at all certain that altering dysphoric and depressive symptoms would alter pathological drinking patterns. Nevertheless, research on biologically oriented interventions directed at the varied affective problems experienced by alcoholics is fully justified by the frequency of the problems' occurrence, the associated impairments, and the likelihood that several varieties of affective disturbance are linked to genetically transmitted characteristics or to toxic effects of alcohol or other drugs of abuse. Future interventions will require greater attention to the heterogeneity of the affective syndromes under study, the effects of previous alcohol and drug ingestion on the metabolic disposition of the therapeutic agents being tried, the tendency of many subgroups of alcoholics to be noncompliant, and the likelihood that the very instruments used to measure the affective syndromes may themselves require improvement.

ACKNOWLEDGMENTS

This research was supported by grants from the National Institute on Alcohol Abuse and Alcoholism (No. 5P50AA03510), the Center for the Study of Alcoholism, and the Veterans Administration.

REFERENCES

Anokhina, I. P. (1984). Dopamine receptor agonists in the treatment of alcoholism. In, G. Edwards & J. Littleton, (Eds.), *Pharmacological treatment for alcoholism* (pp. 145–152). London: Croom Helm.

Beck, A. T., Steer, R. A., & McElroy, M. G. (1982). Self-reported precedence of depression in alcoholism. *Drug and Alcohol Dependence, 10*, 185–190.

Becker, J., Jaffe, J. H., Ciraulo, D. A. (1985). Unpublished manuscript.

Behar, D., & Winokur, G. (1979). Research in alcoholism and depression. A two way street under construction. In R. W. Pickens & L. L. Heston (Eds.), *Psychiatric factors in drug abuse* (pp. 125–152). New York: Grune & Stratton.

Behar, D., Winokur, G., & Berg, C. J. (1984). Depression in the abstinent alcoholic. *American Journal of Psychiatry, 141*, 1105–1107.

Berglund, M. (1984). Suicide in alcoholism. *Archives of General Psychiatry, 41*, 888–891.

Birnbaum, I. M., Taylor, T. H., & Parker, E. S. (1983). Alcohol and sober mood state in female social drinkers. *Alcoholism: Clinical and Experimental Research, 7*, 362–365.

Bohman, M., Cloniger, R., von Knorring, A. -L., & Sigvardsson, S. (1984). An adoption study of somatoform disorders: III. Cross-fostering analysis and genetic relationship to alcoholism and criminality. *Archives of General Psychiatry, 41*, 872–878.

Branchey, L., Branchey, M., Shaw, S., & Lieber, C. S. (1984). Relationship between changes in plasma amino acids and depression in alcoholic patients. *American Journal of Psychiatry, 141*, 1212–1215.

Brandt, J., Butters, N., Ryan, C., & Bayog, R. (1983). Cognitive loss and recovery in long-term alcohol abusers. *Archives of General Psychiatry, 40*, 435–442.

Cadoret, R. J., O'Gorman, T. W., Troughton, E., & Heywood, E. (1985). Alcoholism and antisocial personality. *Archives of General Psychiatry, 42*, 161–167.

Cadoret, R., Troughton, E., & Widmer, R. (1984). Clinical differences between antisocial and primary alcoholics. *Comprehensive Psychiatry, 25*, 1–8.

Carlsson, C., & Fasth, B. G. (1976). A comparison of the effects of propranolol and diazepam in alcoholics. *British Journal of Addiction, 71*, 321–326.

Choquette, K., & Hesselbrock, M. (1985). Unpublished raw data.

Ciraulo, D. A., Alderson, L. M., Chapron, D. J., Jaffe, J. H., Subbarao, B., & Kramer, P. A. (1982). Imipramine disposition in alcoholics. *Journal of Clinical Psychopharmacology, 2*, 2–7.

Ciraulo, D. A., & Jaffe, J. H. (1981). Tricyclic antidepressants in the treatment of depression associated with alcoholism. *Journal of Clinical Psychopharmacology, 1*, 146–150.

Dackis, C. A., Bailey, J., Pottash, A. L., Stuckey, R. F., Extein, I. L., & Gold, M. S. (1984). Specificity of the DST and TRH test for major depression in alcoholics. *American Journal of Psychiatry, 141*, 680–684.

Drake, R. E., & Vaillant, G. E. (1985). A validity study of Axis II of DSM-III. *American Journal of Psychiatry, 142*, 553–558.

Feldmann, H. (1983). Apomorphine in the treatment of alcohol addiction: neurophysiological and therapeutic aspects. *Psychiatric Journal of the University of Ottawa, 8*, 30–37.

Freed, E. X. (1978). Alcohol and mood: An updated review. *International Journal of the Addictions, 13*, 173–200.

Haertzen, C. A., Martin, W. R., Ross, F. E., & Neidert, G. L. (1980). Psychopathic State Inventory (PSI): Development of a short test for measuring psychopathic states. *International Journal of the Addictions, 15*, 137–146.

Hague, W. H., Wilson, L. G., Dudley, D. L., & Cannon, D. S. (1976). Post-detoxification drug treatment of anxiety and depression in alcoholic addicts. *Journal of Nervous and Mental Disease, 162*, 354–359.

Hamm, J. E., Major, L. F., & Brown, G. L. (1979). Quantitative measurement of depression and anxiety in male alcoholics. *American Journal of Psychiatry, 136*, 580–582.

Hatsukami, D., & Pickens, R. W. (1982). Posttreatment depression in an alcohol and drug abuse population. *American Journal of Psychiatry, 139*, 1563–1566.

Hesselbrock, M. N., Hesselbrock, V. M., Tennen, H., Meyer, R. E., & Workman, K. L. (1983). Methodological considerations in the assessment of depression in alcoholics. *Journal of Consulting and Clinical Psychology, 51*, 399–405.

Hesselbrock, M. N., Meyer, R. E., & Keener, J. J. (1985). Psychopathology in hospitalized alcoholics. *Archives of General Psychiatry, 42*, 1050–1055.

Jaffe, J. H. (1984). Alcoholism and affective disturbance. In G. Edwards, & J. Littleton (Eds.), *Pharmacological treatments for alcoholism* (pp. 463–490). London: Croom Helm.

Jaffe, J. H., Becker, J., Ciraulo, D. A., & Smith, L. (1984). Unpublished manuscript.

Jaffe, J. H., & Ciraulo, D. (1985). Drugs used in the treatment of alcoholism. In J. H. Mendelson & N. K. Mello (Eds.), *The diagnosis and treatment of alcoholism* (pp. 355–389). New York: McGraw-Hill.

Judd, L. L., & Huey, L. Y. (1984). Lithium antagonizes ethanol intoxication in alcoholics. *American Journal of Psychiatry, 141*, 1517–1521.

Kass, F., Skodol, A. E., Charles, E., Spitzer, R. L., & Williams, J. B. W. (1985). Scales ratings of DSM-III personality disorders. *American Journal of Psychiatry, 142*, 627–630.

Kay, D. C. (1980). The search for psychopathic states in alcoholics and other drug abusers. In W. E. Fann, I. Karacan, A. D. Pokorny, & R. L. Williams (Eds.), *Phenomenology and treatment of alcoholism* (pp. 269–304). New York: Spectrum.

Keeler, M. H. (1980). Lithium treatment of alcoholism. In W. E. Fann, I. Karacan, A. D. Pokorny, & R. L. Williams (Eds.), *Phenomenology and treatment of alcoholism* (pp. 207–216). New York: Spectrum.

Keeler, M. H., Taylor, I., & Miller, W. C. (1979). Are all recently detoxified alcoholics depressed? *American Journal of Psychiatry, 136*, 586–588.

Kellner, R., & Rada, R. T. (1979). Pharmacotherapy of personality disorders. In J. M. Davis & D. Greenblatt (Eds.), *Psychopharmacology update: New and neglected areas* (pp. 29–63). New York: Grune & Stratton.

Khan, A., Ciraulo, D., Nelson, W., Becker, J., Nies, A., & Jaffe, J. H. (1984). Dexamethasone suppression test in recently detoxified alcoholics: Clinical implications. *Journal of Clinical Psychopharmacology, 4,* 94–97.

Kline, N. S., & Cooper, T. B. (1979). Lithium therapy in alcoholism. In D. W. Goodwin & C. K. Erickson (Eds.), *Alcoholism and affective disorders* (pp. 21–29). New York: Spectrum.

Kline, N. S., Wren, J. C., Cooper, T. B., Varga, E., & Canal, O. (1974). Evaluation of lithium therapy in chronic and periodic alcoholism. *American Journal of Medical Science, 268,* 15–22.

Lewis, C. E., Robins, L., & Rice, J. (1985). Association of alcoholism with antisocial personality in urban men. *Journal of Nervous and Mental Disease, 173,* 166–174.

Liebowitz, M. R., Quitkin, F. M., Steward, J. W., McGrath, P. J., Harrison, W., Rabkin, J. G., Tricamo, E., Markowitz, J., & Klein, D. F. (1984). Phenelzine versus imipramine in atypical depression. *Archives of General Psychiatry, 41,* 669–677.

Loosen, P. T., Wilson, I. C., Dew, B. W., & Tipermas, A. (1983). Thyrotropin-releasing hormone (TRH) in abstinent alcoholic men. *American Journal of Psychiatry, 140,* 1145–1149.

Loranger, A. W., & Tulis, E. H. (1985). Family history of alcoholism in borderline personality disorder. *Archives of General Psychiatry, 42,* 153–157.

Mattes, J. A., Boswell, L., & Oliver, H. (1984). Methylphenidate effects on symptoms of attention deficit disorder in adults. *Archives of General Psychiatry, 41,* 1059–1063.

Mayfield, D. G. (1979). Alcohol and affect: Experimental studies. In D. W. Goodwin & C. K. Erickson (Eds.), *Alcoholism and affective disorders* (pp. 99–107). New York: Spectrum.

Mayfield, D. G., & Montgomery, D. (1972). Alcoholism, alcohol intoxication, and suicide attempts. *Archives of General Psychiatry, 27,* 349–353.

Mendelson, J. H., & Mello, N. K. (1979). Biological concomitants of alcoholism. *New England Journal of Medicine, 301,* 912–921.

Merikangas, K. R., Leckman, J. F., Prusoff, B. A., Pauls, D. L., & Weissman, M. M. (1985). Familial transmission of depression and alcoholism. *Archives of General Psychiatry, 42,* 367–372.

Merry, J., Reynolds, C. M., Bailey, J., & Coppen, A. (1976). Prophylactic treatment of alcoholism by lithium carbonate. *Lancet, 2,* 481–482.

Meyer, R., & Mirin, S. (1979). *The heroin stimulus: Implications for a theory of addiction.* New York: Plenum.

Midanik, L. (1983). Alcohol problems and depressive symptoms in a national survey. In B. Stimmel (Ed.), *Psychosocial constructs of alcoholism and substance abuse* (pp. 9–28). New York: Haworth Press.

Murphy, G. E., Armstrong, J. W., Hermele, S. L., Fischer, J. R., & Clendenin, W. W. et al. (1979). Suicide and alcoholism: Interpersonal loss confirmed as a predictor. *Archives of General Psychiatry, 36,* 65–69.

Murray, R. M., Gurling, H. M. D., Mernadt, M., Ewusi-Mensah, I., Saunders, J. D., & Clifford, C. A. (1984). Do personality and psychiatric disorders predispose to alcoholism? In G. Edwards & J. Littleton (Eds.), *Pharmacological treatments for alcoholism* (pp. 445–461). London: Croom Helm.

Nace, E. P., Saxon, J. J., & Shore, N. (1983). A comparison of borderline and nonborderline alcoholic patients. *Archives of General Psychiatry, 40,* 54–56.

O'Sullivan, K. B., Daly, M. M., Carroll, B. M., Clare, A. W., & Cooney, J. G. (1979). Alcoholism and affective disorder among patients in a Dublin hospital. *Journal of Studies on Alcohol, 40*, 1014–1022.

O'Sullivan, K. B., Whillans, P., Daly, M., Carroll, B., Clare, A., & Cooney, J. (1983). Comparison of alcoholics with and without coexisting affective disorder. *British Journal of Psychiatry, 143*, 133–139.

Parsons, O. A., & Leber, W. R. (1981). Alcohol, cognitive dysfunction and brain damage. In *Report on alcohol and health* (pp. 389–429). Rockville, MD: National Institute on Alcohol Abuse and Alcoholism.

Perry, J. C. (1985). Depression in borderline personality disorder: lifetime prevalence at interview and longitudinal course of symptoms. *American Journal of Psychiatry, 142*, 15–21.

Persky, H., O'Brien, C. P., Fine, E., Howard, W. J., Khan, M. A., & Beck, R. W. (1977). The effect of alcohol and smoking on testosterone function and aggression in chronic alcoholics. *American Journal of Psychiatry, 134*, 621–625.

Petty, F., & Nasrallah, H. A. (1981). Secondary depression in alcoholism: Implications for future research. *Comprehensive Psychiatry, 22*, 587–595.

Pond, S. M., Becker, C. E., Vandervoort, R., Phillips, M., Bowler, R. M., & Peck, C. C. (1981). An evaluation of the effects of lithium in the treatment of chronic alcoholism: I. Clinical results. *Alcoholism: Clinical and Experimental Research, 5*, 247–251.

Pottenger, M., McKernon, J., Patrie, L. E., Weissman, M. M., Ruben, H. L., & Newberry, P. (1978). The frequency and persistance of depressive symptoms in the alcohol abuser. *Journal of Nervous and Mental Disease, 166*, 562–570.

Quitkin, F. M., Liebowitz, M. R., Stewart, J. W., McGrath, P. J., Harrison, W., Rabkin, J. G., Markowitz, J., & Davies, S. O. (1984). 1-Deprenyl in atypical depressives. *Archives of General Psychiatry, 41*, 777–781.

Quitkin, F., Rifkin, A., & Klein, D. F. (1979). Monoamine oxidase inhibitors: A review of antidepressant effectiveness. *Archives of General Psychiatry, 36*, 749–760.

Rada, R. R., & Kellner, R. (1979). Drug treatment in alcoholism. In J. M. Davis & D. Greenblatt (Eds.), *Psychopharmacology update: New and neglected areas* (pp. 105–144). New York: Grune & Stratton.

Ravaris, C. L., Robinson, D. S., Ives, J. O., Nies, A., & Bartlett, D. (1980). Phenelzine and amitriptyline in the treatment of depression. *Archives of General Psychiatry, 37*, 1075–1080.

Schuckit, M. (1979). Alcoholism and affective disorder: Diagnostic confusion. In D. W. Goodwin & C. K. Erickson (Eds.), *Alcoholism and affective disorders* (pp. 9–19). New York: Spectrum.

Schuckit, M. (1983). Alcoholic patients with secondary depression. *American Journal of Psychiatry, 140*, 711–714.

Shaw, J. A., Donley, P., Morgan, D. W., & Robinson, J. A. (1975). Treatment of depression in alcoholics. *American Journal of Psychiatry, 132*, 641–644.

Simmonds, M. (1982). Letter. *New England Journal of Medicine, 306*, 748.

Stabenau, J. R. (1984). Implications of family history of alcoholism, antisocial personality, and sex differences in alcohol dependence. *American Journal of Psychiatry, 141*, 1178–1182.

Stangl, M. A., Pfohl, B., Zimmerman, M., Bowers, W., & Corenthal, C. (1985). A structured interview for the DSM-III personality disorders. *Archives of General Psychiatry, 42*, 591–596.

Viamontes, J. A. (1972). A review of drug effectiveness in the treatment of alcoholism. *American Journal of Psychiatry, 128*, 120–121.

von Knorring, A. -L., Cloninger, C. R., Bohman, M., & Sigvardsson, S. (1983). An adoption study of depressive disorders and substance abuse. *Archives of General Psychiatry, 40,* 943–950.

Weissman, M. M., & Myers, J. K. (1980). Clinical depression in alcoholism. *American Journal of Psychiatry, 137,* 372–373.

Wilkinson, D. A. (1982). Examination of alcoholics by computed tomographic (CT) scans: A critical review. *Alcoholism: Clinical and Experimental Research, 6,* 31–45.

Winokur, G., Rimmer, J., & Reich, T. (1971). Alcoholism: IV. Is there more than one type of alcoholism? *British Journal of Psychiatry, 118,* 525–531.

Wood, D., Wender, P. H., & Reimherr, F. W. (1983). The prevalence of attention deficit disorder, residual type, or minimal brain dysfunction, in a population of male alcoholic patients. *American Journal of Psychiatry, 140,* 95–98.

Woodruff, R. A., Guze, S. B., Clayton, P. J., & Carr, D. (1973). Alcoholism and depression. *Archives of General Psychiatry, 28,* 97–100.

Woodruff, R. A., Guze, S. B., Clayton, P. J., & Carr, D. (1979). Alcoholism and depression. In D. W. Goodwin and C. K. Erickson (Eds.), *Alcoholism and affective disorders* (pp. 39–48). New York: Spectrum.

Zitrin, C. M., Klein, D. F., & Woerner, M. G. (1980). Treatment of agoraphobia with group exposure in vivo and imipramine. *Archives of General Psychiatry, 37,* 63–72.

VI

Psychopathology and the Meaning of Addictive Disorders

13

Treatment Implications of a Psychodynamic Understanding of Opioid Addicts

EDWARD J. KHANTZIAN
ROBERT J. SCHNEIDER

A psychodynamic perspective of mental life attempts to examine the forces at work within an individual related to drives, affects, and those psychological structures that are responsible for regulating drives and affects. Such a perspective also attempts to take into account an appreciation of how developmental challenges have been handled and managed from the earliest phases of life. In infancy and childhood, particular emphasis is placed first on mother–child relationships, and subsequently on interpersonal relationships within the family. In adolescence and adulthood, increasing focus is placed on peer and interpersonal relationships in general.

Based on this perspective, a contemporary psychodynamic understanding of drug dependence attempts to explain how addicts' dependence on drugs is related to difficulties in coping with their internal emotional life and problems in adapting to their environment. This viewpoint takes into account psychological forces and structures from a developmental and adaptive perspective.

After a review of recent psychodynamic understanding of addictions, we delineate in this chapter some treatment implications of the vulnerabilities and psychopathology that have been found in narcotic addicts in treatment. Specifically, we hope to show how the difficulties addicts have in managing and regulating painful, emotional states, as well as in maintaining states of well-being and self-esteem, have important implications in considering treatment alternatives for such individuals.

BACKGROUND

Early psychodynamic theory placed heavy emphasis on the influence of drives in accounting for psychological and behavioral disturbances, including the addictions. This early perspective was based on an "id" or dual-instinct psychology that attempted to trace the influences of libido and/or aggression in explaining human thoughts, feelings, and actions. From this "id" psychology, the focus gradually shifted to the psychological structures responsible for regulating these instincts and adapting to the rigors of daily living. This "ego" psychology took particular note of defense mechanisms, often unconscious, which help manage the conflictual wishes and fears related to these instincts emanating from the id. More recently, theorists have explored the development of the ego and sense of self, and the ways in which these structures emerge from the infantile and early childhood experiences. It is only natural that psychodynamic theories of addiction have followed a similar developmental pattern.

Initial attempts to explain compulsive drug use emphasized the libidinal factors involved in addiction (Abraham, 1908/1960; Freud, 1905/1955; Rado, 1933). These formulations stressed the regressive, pleasurable states produced by drugs and linked them to the removal of subjectively experienced inhibitions and prohibitions. In these early discussions, few distinctions were made concerning the pharmacological properties of various addicting drugs.

Later formulations by Fenichel (1945), Savitt (1954, 1963), and Weider and Kaplan (1969) appreciated that the relief of anxiety and internal distress available through drugs was a powerful motive for drug use. However, all these theorists continued to view this relief as deriving from a return to pleasurable, regressive states. Although Glover (1956) continued to minimize the psychopharmacological effects of drugs, he did have an appreciation of the adaptive aspects of the addict's obsessional involvement with drugs. He believed that the addict defended against a regression to a more primitive, psychotic state by transferring conflicts concerning homosexual fears and paranoid–sadistic tendencies onto the drugs. This adaptive, or "progressive," view of drug use was a significant departure from earlier psychoanalytic emphasis on the regressive libidinal and erotic aspects of addiction.

The work of Chein, Gerard, Lee, and Rosenfeld (1964) marked a significant shift in the psychoanalytic literature on the addictions. Besides better appreciating the pharmacological effects of opiates, their work more appropriately focused on the addict's ego and superego pathology, as well as on problems with powerful narcissistic longings and other severe psychopathology. They emphasized that the use of narcotics represented an attempt to cope with painful feeling states, as well as with overwhelming developmental tasks and responsibilities in the outside world.

The works of Krystal (Krystal, 1977; Krystal & Raskin, 1970), Wurmser (1972, 1974, 1980), and Khantzian (1972, 1974, 1978) have further developed this adaptive and functional viewpoint of drug use. Wurmser has indicated that narcotics are used adaptively by addicts to compensate for defects in affect defense, particularly against feelings of rage, shame, hurt, and loneliness. Khantzian has stressed problems with drive and affect defense, and has proposed that narcotics can actually reverse regressive states through the direct antiaggressive action of opiates; this action counteracts disorganizing influences of rage and aggression on the ego. Both Wurmser and Khantzian have emphasized that the psychopharmacological effects of these drugs can act as a protection for defective or nonexistent ego mechanisms of defense.

Clearly, some of the pathology observed in addicts is the result of drug use and its attendant practices (Zinberg, 1975). However, it is our opinion that early developmental impairments in ego structures and the sense of self predispose these individuals to problematic adaptations such as drug addiction. More specifically, it is the behavioral problems most often associated with antisocial personality disorder that are more likely the result of drug addiction. Addicts' problems with the affects of depression, rage, and anger, however, probably stem from difficulties with drive and affect defense, self-care, dependency, and need satisfaction.

DISTURBANCES IN EGO AND SELF STRUCTURES

In the preceding and in what follows, we have made frequent reference to two concepts about psychological structure, the "ego" and the "self."

In many instances, the distinctions between these concepts are arbitrary, and there is considerable overlap in how they are used. Structure and function are stressed in relation to the ego, and subjective attitudes are stressed in relation to the self. Nevertheless, the ego has subjective elements associated with it, and the self has structural and functional aspects as well (Khantzian, 1981).

GENERAL DISTURBANCES IN SELF-REGULATION

Addicts' survival problems are formidable and derive from early developmental difficulties in managing their emotions and coping with external reality. Their limited capacity to manage affects is further exacerbated by the artificial drives and painful feelings resulting from the intoxication–withdrawal cycle of addiction. In addition, their involvement with illicit drugs often requires considerable time spent in a dangerous world of crime and violence. In such an existence, internal feeling states of comfort, security, and satisfaction are elusive or absent.

DISTURBANCES IN AFFECT AND DRIVE DEFENSE

Given addicts' unstable ego and self structures for regulating feelings, painful affects tend to trigger psychological fragmentation and disorganization. In our experience, the affects and drives associated with rage and aggression are particularly troublesome for these individuals. That is, uncontrolled (or fear of uncontrolled) aggression can disorganize the individuals from within by overwhelming their fragile ego structures, and can threaten them from without by jeopardizing needed relationships and provoking aggressive reactions in others. The appeal of opiates resides, then, in their capacity to mute or contain affective states that otherwise threaten addicts.

DISTURBANCES IN SELF-CARE

High-risk involvements, including the dangers of illicit drug use and related activities, are evidence of functional inadequacies in ego structures responsible for self-care and self-protection. These structures are acquired in early phases of development through a process of internalizing protective and caring parental behavior and attitudes. The capacity to anticipate harm and to avoid danger is the result of this internalization. Addicts, however, consistently fail to show caution or fear in the face of enormously risky activities. They also reveal a lack of awareness of the most basic "preventative maintenance" in attending to fundamental human concerns, such as health care, meaningful relationships, and productivity as workers.

DISTURBANCES IN SELF-ESTEEM, NEED SATISFACTION, AND DEPENDENCY

Besides these vulnerabilities in regulation of feelings and self-care, addicts are especially conflicted in regard to interpersonal dependency. They have a profound lack of self-esteem, which requires them to look to others for feelings of worth, comfort, and nurturance. Their demands and expectations of others are consequently excessive. When these unreasonable demands are not met, feelings of rage and frustration surface. Often their expressions of anger toward friends, family, and treatment providers result in guilt and depression, which leave them even more needy of others and thus more prone to resort to the mood-altering properties of drugs. In order to avoid this cycle, they often become counterdependent and totally disavow all their dependency needs. As a result, they alternate between a desperate, manipulative attitude to extract satisfaction from others, and distant, supercilious postures of utter independence and self-sufficiency. It is no accident that individuals who are so conflicted in regard to their needs would develop a symptom such as drug addiction. With this symptom, addicts can gain periodic relief from interpersonal needs while insuring a self-destructive dependency on a substance and on those from whom the substance can be acquired.

TREATMENT IMPLICATIONS

The nature of addicts' suffering and their need for regulation require enlightened treatment programs to place a premium on controls and safety, especially at the outset of treatment. Only then can we attend to the psychological disturbances associated with drug dependence. Our main allies for containment and treatment remain the traditional institutions (i.e., the courts, prisons, hospitals and treatment programs), human relationships (i.e., individual and group approaches), and drug substitutions. Once an addict is securely established in a program utilizing these resources, we can then go about the task of assessing the nature of his or her disturbances and developing suitable treatment approaches.

Obviously, good treatment rests on making correct diagnoses and identifying treatable target symptoms. We believe that an addict's "drug of choice" is a powerful indicator of his or her structural (i.e., ego–self) vulnerabilities and underlying psychopathology. Carefully reviewing with addicts their subjective feeling states before and after taking addictive drugs becomes an important step, and the information gathered thereby must be considered, with other factors, in establishing the nature of their suffering and in determining suitable treatment plans. Identifying environmental factors and precipitants for the initiation and maintenance of their drug use, and appreciating factors of chronicity and addictive mechanisms, are also important aspects of information gathering and treatment planning. However, we believe that addicts' subjective feelings of distress and the relief they obtain from opiates remain among the most helpful guidelines when considering their treatment needs. In probing their experiences with drugs in this way, we also learn much about the specific and general problems they experience with self-regulation that we have described in the first part of this chapter.

In order to successfully treat the impairments in ego and self structures, the behavior and impulsiveness associated with addicted individuals must first be sufficiently controlled. In many instances, institutional treatment/confinement is necessary or is imposed because of criminal offenses. Although the epidemic of drug abuse has increased the general awareness of proper treatment, it is still often the case that addicts are treated in prison, where there is too little understanding of addiction, or in hospitals, where there are perhaps too much understanding and insufficient controls (Khantzian, 1978).

Maintaining the balance between controls and understanding is a difficult task, particularly when treating large numbers of narcotic addicts in outpatient methadone clinics. The establishment of a program "structure," consisting of clear rules and regulations concerning behavior, is a practical necessity when working with this population. That is, program structure becomes a vitally important compensation (and basis for internalization) for the defects in ego and self structures that predispose these individuals to addictions. Without proper setting of limits, the violent and aggressive tendencies of these patients can make treatment impossible. In a more subtle vein, their manipulative and "splitting" activities must be kept to a minimum if they are to learn new, more adaptive ways of getting their needs met. This requires a treatment team that is cohesive and unified in its dealings with patients. It is in such an environment that these patients can feel safe in the face of their aggressive drives, and sufficiently nurtured to experience and verbalize painful affects such as depression, shame, loneliness, hurt, and fear.

Programmatic structures and setting of behavioral limits are also invaluable in addressing the other psychodynamic issues of these patients—namely, impairments in ego or self-care structures. As mentioned earlier, these functions normally develop as a result of early internalization processes in which the protective activities of the parents are gradually incorporated by the growing child. A similar acquisition of self-preservative skills can result from the internalization of program rules and the consequent development of an "observing ego." Though patients resent and break program rules on a regular basis, we have over time observed in them an increased ability to think before, during, and after their behavior. We believe it is the firm but caring imposition of limits and consequences for transgressions that promotes these new adaptive skills. Maintaining a consistent treatment posture and being patient with this process of internalization can be quite difficult, given addicts' enormous deficiencies in monitoring their behavior and striking lack of awareness concerning those deficiencies.

A similar process is involved when addressing problems of self-esteem. Subjective attitudes concerning one's self-worth and importance in relation to others are also derived from parental attitudes and attributes, specifically parental admiration and strength. The parents' demonstration of pleasure in the child and calmness in child rearing create an environment that responds to the child's needs for confirmation and security. These external sources of narcissistic sustenance are gradually transformed into intrapsychic resources. As treatment providers, we can meet some of these narcissistic needs in such a way that patients can eventually improve their sense of self-esteem and internal stability. This is not to suggest indiscriminate gratification of narcissistic longings; rather, it is a carefully administered therapy, during which sufficient amounts of care and security are provided for the purpose of eventual acquisition of these feelings within the self through a process of internalization and identification. Thus, extremes of aloofness or exaggerated friendliness are avoided by the treatment staff. Some of the patient's questions may be answered within a moderate relaxation of the traditional therapeutic "neutrality." Self-disclosure by the therapist and requests for assistance with daily living problems may be considered, though, again, extremes of withholding or giving are avoided.

The guidelines we offer above for program structure and management of the treatment milieu also have implications for the individual and group treatment approaches that we consider and offer for our patients. Similarly, such disturbances are often effectively modified in individual and group didactic approaches. Furthermore, the patients' problems with counterdependency, low self-esteem, self care and self-governance are particularly amenable to the sustaining, nurturing, and organizing benefits of self-help groups such as Narcotics Anonymous and Alcoholics Anonymous (Khantzian, 1981; Mack, 1981). In contrast, opiate addicts' lifelong problems with regulating their rage and aggression suggest that the aggressive–confrontative individual and group treatment approaches offered by other self-help groups might be not only risky, but in many cases contraindicated (Khantzian, 1974).

Similarly, in considering our human interventions, our patients' sociological situations (i.e., family, peer group, and socioeconomic environment) must all be carefully studied to determine what treatments are feasible, given these realities. For instance, a pathological family system that uses a member's addiction to avoid more fundamental and frightening interpersonal problems within the family will often undermine treatment as quickly as we can render it. It is an unfortunate side effect of considering addiction purely as a psychological problem that real problems such as social setting are often ignored, and consequently that the treatment provided is ineffective. This, of course, reinforces the exaggerated popular belief in the intransigence of addictive behavior. We suggest the work of Stanton, Todd, and Associates (1982) as a valuable entry point into the "systems" approach to drug abuse.

Beyond the institutional and human interventions that we have reviewed, we believe that one of the mainstays and treatments of choice in narcotic addictions remains methadone maintenance. We believe that it is also consistent with and a natural outgrowth of a psychodynamic understanding of opiate dependence. This conviction stems directly from our belief that the use of drugs has played a central role in regulating and controlling the addicts' otherwise overwhelming anxiety, depression, and rage. The long-acting properties of methadone provide ego support without the disruptive and regressive influences of the intoxication–withdrawal cycle. The prescription of the inexpensive and legally obtained methadone also eliminates the constant need to "hustle," which often leads to crime, danger, and the absence of other adaptive behavior such as work and meaningful relationships. Ironically, it is sometimes the case that patients initially worsen when they are treated with methadone, because the defensive, obsessional involvement with drug acquisition and usage is removed from their daily activities. This can allow the warded-off affects and drives to surface; in turn, these produce the feared, regressive state. This phase is typically short-lived, however, once the addicts' obsessive attentions are turned toward the various aspects of methadone treatment (i.e., quantity of dosage, other clinic members, therapists, weekly fees, etc.).

Although the evidence is only preliminary and based mostly on clinical trials with small samples, experience with substituting other psychotropic agents, especially tricyclic antidepressants and lithium, suggests that they may be of considerable benefit with many addicts (Khantzian, 1978; Woody, O'Brien, & Rickels, 1975). This is particularly relevant when underlying painful affect states and target symptoms of depression are identified. Still needed are controlled trials of psychotropic agents to better establish their efficacy with many of these patients.

SUMMARY AND CONCLUSION

We have delineated a number of vulnerabilities and defects in narcotic addicts and how they variably combine in a harmful way to predispose individuals to dependence on narcotics. We have also reviewed treatment implications of these disturbances. The therapeutic interventions that we have recommended cannot completely remove developmental impairments. They can, however, provide sufficient remedy for these defects to allow individuals to live life without the horrors of addiction and to attain considerable improvement in the quality of their lives, their regard for others, and their adjustment to external reality.

The dearth of longitudinal, prospective research in the addictions adds to the difficulty clinicians have in sorting out what are the causes of drug abuse and what are the effects. Having emphasized the multiple complexities that must be considered in addiction treatment and theory, we still find a psychodynamic perspective essential in our work with this population. Notwithstanding, we have included nonintrapsychic interventions in this chapter because they clearly are factors in making these patients physiologically and psychologically available for our more "in-depth" psychotherapeutic exploration and work.

REFERENCES

Abraham, K. (1960). The psychological relation between sexuality and alcoholism. In *Selected papers of Karl Abraham.* New York: Basic Books. (Original work published 1908)

Chein, I., Gerard, D. L., Lee, R. S., & Rosenfeld, E. (1964). *The road to H.* New York: Basic Books.

Fenichel, O. (1945). *The psychoanalytic theory of neurosis.* New York: Norton.

Freud, S. (1955).Three essays on the theory of sexuality. In J. Strachey (Ed. and Trans.), *The standard edition of the complete psychological works of Sigmund Freud* (Vol. 7, pp. 000–000). London: Hogarth Press. (Original work published 1905)

Glover, E. (1956). On the etiology of drug addiction. In *On the early development of mind.* New York: International Universities Press.

Khantzian, E. J. (1972). A preliminary dynamic formulation of the psychopharmacologic action of methadone. In *Proceedings of the Fourth National Conference on Methadone Treatment.* New York: National Association of the Prevention of Addiction to Narcotics.

Khantzian, E. J. (1974). Opiate addiction: A critique of theory and some implications for treatment. *American Journal of Psychotherapy, 28,* 59–70.

Khantzian, E. J. (1978). The ego, the self and opiate addiction: Theoretical and treatment considerations. *International Review of Psychoanalysis, 5,* 189–198.

Khantzian, E. J. (1981). Some treatment implications of the ego and self disturbances in alcoholism. In M. H. Bean & N. E. Zinberg (Eds.), *Dynamic approaches to the understanding and treatment of alcoholism* (pp. 163–188). New York: Free Press.

Krystal, H. (1977). Self representation and the capacity for self care. In *The annals of psychoanalysis* (Vol. 6, pp. 209–246). New York: International Universities Press.

Krystal, H., & Raskin, H. A. (1970). *Drug dependence: Aspects of ego functions.* Detroit: Wayne State University Press.

Mack, J. E. (1981). Alcoholism, A.A. and the governance of the self. In M. H. Bean & N. E. Zinberg (Eds.), *Dynamic approaches to the understanding and treatment of alcoholism* (pp. 128–162). New York: Free Press.

Rado, S. (1933). The psychoanalysis of pharmacothymia. *Psychoanalytic Quarterly, 2,* 1–23.

Savitt, R. A. (1954). Extramural psychoanalytic treatment of a case of narcotic addiction. *Journal of the American Psychoanalytic Association, 2,* 494.

Savitt, R. A. (1963). Psychoanalytic studies on addiction: Ego structure in narcotic addiction. *Psychoanalytic Quarterly, 32,* 43–57.

Stanton, M. D., Todd, T. C., & Associates. (1982). *The family therapy of drug abuse and addiction.* New York: Guilford Press.

Weider, H., & Kaplan, E. (1969). Drug use in adolescents. *Psychoanalytic Study of the Child, 24,* 399–431.

Woody, G. E., O'Brien, C. P., & Rickels, K. (1975). Depression and anxiety in heroin addicts: A placebo-controlled study of doxepin in combination with methadone. *American Journal of Psychiatry, 132,* 447–450.

Wurmser, L. (1972). Methadone and the craving for narcotics: observations of patients on methadone maintenance in psychotherapy. In *Fourth National Conference on Methadone Treatment, San Francisco, California, 1972: Proceedings* (pp. 525–528). New York: National Association for the Prevention of Addiction to Narcotics.

Wurmser, L. (1974). Psychoanalytic considerations of the etiology of compulsive drug use. *Journal of the American Psychoanalytic Association, 22,* 820–843.

Wurmser, L. (1980). Drug use as a protective system. In D. J. Lettieri, M. Sayers, & H. W. Wallenstein (Eds.), *Theories of addiction* (NIDA Monograph 30, pp. 71–74). Washington, DC: U.S. Government Printing Office.

Zinberg, N. E. (1975). Addiction and ego function. *Psychoanalytic Study of the Child, 30,* 567–588 (T).

14

Psychopathology Produced by Alcoholism

MARGARET BEAN-BAYOG

Few observers deny that drinking alcoholics have severe symptoms of disturbance in personality function. They are often impulsive, self-centered, self-destructive, irresponsible, isolated, repressed, guilty, depressed, irritable, and moody. Their judgment is poor. They use an elaborate defensive system based on primitive denial, rationalization, projection, and minimization. The sources of these symptoms have been controversial. Conventionally trained psychiatrists, mental health professionals, and many laypeople have usually made the intuitively appealing assumption that the character patterns seen during active alcoholism were present before the drinking began, and in fact caused the alcoholism.

Other chapters in this book discuss the relation between other mental illnesses, such as affective disorder, and alcoholism. This chapter approaches the issue from another perspective. It suggests that alcoholism itself is a traumatic experience that may *produce* psychopathology. This chapter pursues the thesis that some features of the so-called "alcoholic personality" are in fact a *complication* of the traumatic effect of the alcoholism, and not a cause of it, though once they occur they entrench and perpetuate the alcoholism. In order to do this, I refer to basic ideas in theory of character; discuss observations made in psychotherapeutic work with victims of a range of traumatic experiences; and show how the events in alcoholism are analogous to the disruption produced by other overwhelming human experiences, such as natural disasters (e.g., fire, flood, and famine), combat, incarceration in a prison or concentration camp, war, nuclear attack, life-threatening disease, and functional impairment such as stroke or dementia.

NOTES ON CHARACTER

In order to discuss psychopathology produced by alcoholism, it is necessary to refer to character development and function under normal conditions—that is, in the absence of trauma.

"Character" may be defined as predictable, stable behaviors, attitudes, interests, and relationships (Blos, 1968). Character development produces structures that perform crucial protective functions. The functions of character include maintenance of psychic homeostasis, regulation of self-esteem, preservation of ego identity, maintenance of automatic barriers to overstimulation from internal or external sources, and containment of fluctuations in affect. When character is formed, responses to danger situations become automatic, with the result that psychic energy is free for other uses. There are two types of situations where character is unable to carry out its functions; these are pathological states and stress or trauma. This discussion focuses on the latter.

In order to think clearly about character damage or psychopathology produced in adulthood, it is helpful to pose separate questions about development, trauma, and the capacity for healing. For instance, when is character formation final? What is the effect of trauma on character? Is this different during development and after character is fully crystalized? Once trauma has occurred, is it permanent or reversible? What constitutes the capacity for healing from a particular trauma, and how can healing be facilitated? For example, how can alcoholism treatment specifically work to heal the damage to character produced by the traumatic effects of alcoholism?

Character is formed slowly during childhood and adolescence. There is controversy about when its crystallization is complete. Blos (1968) contends that character is given its final shape by the end of adolescence, but Erikson (1950) reminds us that development and maturation continue throughout adulthood. A person may use successively more mature defense mechanisms over the decades of his or her adulthood (Vaillant, 1977).

THE EFFECT OF TRAUMA

"Trauma" may be defined as conditions that seem unfavorable, noxious, or drastically injurious to development (Greenacre, 1967). In adulthood, this definition should be expanded to include conditions injurious to *performance* of character functions, and not restricted to conditions that prevent development.

With these concepts and definitions of character development and trauma, we are now in a position to deal with the unusual case of what happens to character and personality if there is ghastly trauma after character is more or less firmly laid down.

The idea that adult trauma can produce disordered psychological functioning is a familiar one, which has been reported and described in a range of catastrophic human experience such as the following: knowledge that one is about to die or be killed (Becker, 1973; Kubler-Ross, 1969); combat (Brill & Beebe, 1955); normal grieving (Lindeman, 1944); natural disasters such as floods (Rangell, 1976; Titchener & Kapp, 1976); kidnapping and hostage experiences (Terr, 1983); concentration camp experiences (Frankl, 1959; Krystal, 1968; Niederland, 1968); nuclear holocaust (Lifton, 1968); and, of course, alcoholism (Bean & Zinberg, 1981).

The impact of trauma on character will vary with the characteristics of the trauma. And even with similar traumatic experience, the results will vary among people; for example, if 100 people are incarcerated in a concentration camp, each will bring to it his or her own history, strengths, and weaknesses, and will react in idiosyncratic ways. Nevertheless, the impact of the experience will be so overwhelming that it will be possible to make some generalizations about its effects. There will, for any trauma, be *many* symptoms and disturbances, variant survivor syndromes, and capacities for recovery, but there will also be consistent patterns.

For each trauma, one should identify the following:

1. The characteristics of the trauma.
2. Reactions and defenses during the traumatic experience.
3. The survivor syndrome.
4. The permanence and reversibility of change and the possibility of working through, repair, and healing.

EXAMPLES OF TRAUMA

Before attempting to identify the components of trauma and the response to alcoholism, I will briefly review for comparison two other overwhelming traumas: the Jewish holocaust during World War II, and the nuclear holocaust of Hiroshima and Nagasaki. This review relies on the extensive research with survivors in the work of Krystal (1968), Niederland (1968), and Lifton (1968), among many others.

One of the difficulties with understanding these traumas is that they were so overwhelming that they are almost unbearable to think about. The suffering and terror are nearly impossible to imagine, even when one details their components. Nevertheless, these two examples may be very helpful in understanding the impact of alcoholism, for two reasons. First, the enormous labor that has been invested in understanding the experience of these victims gives a basis of data for comparison with the experience of alcoholics. Second, since these human traumas took place at the far reaches of the extreme of imaginable or survivable experience, they both make the point that adult trauma *does* produce severe psychopathology. As such, they provide a scale or yardstick for conceptualizing the nature and severity of the trauma of alcoholism along a continuum from healthy nontraumatic adult experience through a range of threats all the way to these annihilating ultimate disasters.

CONCENTRATION CAMP VICTIMS

Niederland (1968) has itemized the main characteristics of concentration camp trauma as follows: a protracted life-endangering situation; chronic starvation; physical maltreatment with fear of total annihilation; degradation; dehumanization; recurrent terror episodes (selection of individuals for death in the gas chambers); total or near-total family loss; abrogation of causality; assaults on identity; and, finally, a prolonged "living dead" existence with no way out, leading to stupor and death.

In response to these factors, during the trauma, people used reactions and defenses such as emotional detachment; depersonalization and derealization; denial; automation of ego with robot-like numbness; regression to pregenital levels; identification with the aggressor; and more automatization, regression, adjustment, or death. After liberation, at which point there were often magical expectations and a symptom-free interval, a range of posttraumatic pathology appeared, including depression, anxiety, and survivor guilt. Other frequent symptoms included brooding, sadness, nightmares, and somatic complaints. These might crystalize into a "survivor syndrome," which might include reverberating terror, chronic depression, character changes, insomnia, nightmares, and somatic equivalents, withdrawal, helplessness, and other symptoms.

This radical disruption of mature character was even worse when the victims were children rather than adults. In addition to those symptoms, victims sustained a conviction of difference—the feeling that their experience could not be communicated—which isolated them even more.

NUCLEAR BOMB VICTIMS

By comparison, people who survived the atomic bombings in Hiroshima had another kind of overwhelming experience (Lifton, 1968). The major components of the trauma were overwhelming immersion in death; total unpreparedness and helplessness in the face of annihilation; the blast, heat, and destruction of the environment; and burns, radiation, and (for many) death. Later traumas included radiation sickness, genetic effects on the victims' posterity, late "A-bomb diseases" (e.g., leukemia), and fears about all of these.

In response, the victims exhibited the following reactions and defenses during the trauma: not panic, but ghastly stillness, slow motion, and a kind of "death in life" experience. After the bombing, people developed a "survivor syndrome" consisting of psychic closing-off (ceasing to feel, despite clear perception); denial, with everyone tending to gloss over, deny, or avoid the experience; isolation and apathy; guilt and shame, with a need to justify one's own survival; and horror at not having met requests of the dying (e.g., for water). In addition, there might be fears of being contaminated, somatic symptoms, weakness, self-focus, identification with death, a feeling of loss of immortality, and a sense of difference from the rest of humankind (Lifton, 1968).

COMMENTS

There were striking similarities in the survivors of the two disasters in their feeling that their experience could not be communicated and in their symptoms of depression, somatization, fearfulness, survivor guilt, and shame about the experience. In addition, survivors of both experiences tended to use denial to cope with trauma and communicated a sense of being different from the rest of the human race. These factors are also present in attenuated forms in alcoholism.

In the next section, I describe alcoholism according to the same model: the characteristics of the trauma, reactions during trauma, and symptoms afterward. This model offers implications for understanding alcoholics' behavior and helping them recover. I should stress first, however, the difference in scale of trauma between alcoholism and these two holocausts. Alcoholism attacks a single victim at a time, torments the victim's family and others immediately associated with him or her, and only distantly (though definitely and expensively) strains the social fabric. The Jewish and nuclear holocausts had far larger annihilating power; they affected not only each individual victim and family, but also two entire cultures.

ALCOHOLISM AS TRAUMA

INTRODUCTORY REMARKS

The present approach to the production of psychopathology by alcoholism ignores etiology and also pays little attention to how a person's actions produce the problem. The focus here is on the experience of developing alcoholism and the ways in which persons react to it.

Developing alcoholism is a complicated, confusing, and painful experience. It varies with age of onset, social and psychological setting, and presence of psychopathology. It usually begins gradually, without the people suffering from it realizing that they have symptoms of early alcoholism. They find their drinking going out of control, and feel guilty, bewildered, and frightened.

The central disturbance is inability to regulate alcohol consumption. This is partial and intermittent. The earliest symptoms of alcoholism include episodes of unplanned drunkenness; these may be clinically indistinguishable, especially early, from social drinking with deliberate intoxication. Individuals who lose control of their drinking do not realize what is happening to them. In order for them to diagnose themselves as alcoholics, they would have to label themselves with a stigmatized label, deal with family and professional myths about alcoholism, stop using alcohol, and enter treatment. Intuitively, from these people's perspective, this makes no sense. They do not fit the stereotype of advanced alcoholism; and, because their loss of control is partial, they know that *sometimes* they can control their drinking. They thus assume they always can do so if they redouble their efforts. They struggle against the loss of control, and, when they succeed, they feel "normal." Even when they fail, they still do not make the diagnosis of alcoholism. Instead, they feel helpless and guilty, and become demoralized.

Other symptoms of early alcoholism ensue—consequences of the drunkenness resulting from losses of control. People with alcoholism may have embarrassing episodes, causing shame, guilt, decreased self-esteem, trouble in close relationships, blackouts, or accidents. They develop anxiety, fear, and guilt when they drink, because they never know when they may go out of control.

As the disorder worsens, they may lose health and a sense of safety. Their psychological functioning will be distorted by the development of systems of denial designed to help them manage the feelings produced by these experiences. They may begin to lose or destroy things important to them. As these frightening and painful events occur, people developing alcoholism ought to realize that they have the disorder, instead, however, they fight to regain control, and rationalize each episode to explain their behavior to themselves and others. Their failure to regain control gradually destroys their self-esteem and the hope that they are worthwhile persons.

Insight and judgment into the danger are not only impaired by denial; they may also be damaged by repeated exposure to alcohol. Alcoholics remain "foggy" or "wet" for months after they stop drinking, "clearing up" slowly. Neurologically, they may resemble persons with a mild dementia; their symptoms may include disturbances in awareness, attention, affect regulation, memory, and ability to abstract. Their conscious experience may be markedly impaired much of the time, leaving them with a state of severe confusion, self-preoccupation, irrationality, and helplessness. At this time, they may additionally be physically ill from repeated drunkenness, or may have developed medical complications and addiction. The latter increases their psychological dependence upon alcohol.

From now on, if these people cannot assure themselves a supply of alcohol and an opportunity to use it, they will be physically sick. This intensifies their feelings of being helpless and out of control. Their experiences are increasingly terrifying. Prognosis at this stage is thought to be poor. The human response to this is similar to reactions to the development of other dreaded diseases, especially those that attack the integrity of personality (the ability to think, use language, and control feelings), such as stroke. Thought processes are at the core of the self, and people refuse to admit that they cannot control them (Kohut, 1972). Denial in these situations is particularly global and desperately held.

Having described the types of experiences alcoholics have, I now attempt to characterize the trauma, describe the patients' responses to it, and discuss the "survivor syndrome."

MAJOR COMPONENTS OF TRAUMA

Inability to regulate drinking leads to repetitive, unpredictable drunkenness. This produces the following traumatic disruptions:

1. Alcoholics undergo the experience of being destructively and repeatedly out of control, despite efforts to control the drinking.
2. These people are also subjected to a protracted life-endangering situation, with unpredictable dangerous or mortal events, such as car accidents and memory blackouts.
3. Short of actual danger, there are repeated threats and damage to personal integrity, self-esteem, and status. They are labeled alcoholic by others, and are thus subjected to stigma and prejudice, with marked degradation of social status.
4. Interpersonal relationships will be damaged or lost because of drinking. Alcoholics undergo multiple personal losses, especially family. There may also be losses of financial, legal, or work status.
5. Health may be damaged. Alcoholics may develop tolerance to alcohol, psychological dependence, physical dependence, and neurological impairment. Medical complications of alcoholism, such as hypertension, liver damage, and trauma from accidents or burns, also impair essential well-being.
6. Problem-solving responses to all of the preceding events are blocked by cognitive impairment, demoralization, defensive denial, social prejudice, and lack of resources.

MAJOR COMPONENTS OF THE PATIENTS' RESPONSES TO THE
TRAUMA

1. The impact of the experience of being unable to control the
drinking cannot be overestimated. Any incident demonstrating loss of
mastery, such as loss of control over bowel and bladder or over motor
movements, is devastating. The initial reactions include bewilderment,
anxiety, and growing dread as the experience is repeated. Helplessness
may spread from inability to control the drinking into other areas of
life. The persons react to the *meaning* of being out of control, not just
the dangerous consequences of it. Shame and guilt are intense and lead
the sufferers to isolate themselves, as well as to rely heavily on projection
of blame onto others. They may drink to blunt these feelings.

2. Dangerous consequences and threats of danger also evoke responses that include the use of a variety of defenses, especially denial,
magical thinking ("If I just have white wine, I'll never get cirrhosis"),
minimization, grandiosity, and omnipotence ("I can stop any time," or
"I'll just have one"). These defenses partly fail, and the persons experience fear, anxiety, helplessness, and increased psychological dependence on alcohol. The individuals may undertake various compensatory or safety measures, such as driving slowly when drunk, selling a
car to avoid accidents, and keeping notes of phone conversations as a
hedge against memory blackouts.

3. Threats and damage to self-esteem and degradation of status also
bring out emergency psychological maneuvers. The narcissistic injuries
of stigma and social degradation are handled by narcissistic defensive
maneuvers, devaluation of others, and reassuring gradiose self-con-
gratulation. (An example: "I couldn't have alcoholism because I'm a
doctor. If you suspect I have it, you must be poorly trained. The chair-
man of the department said I wasn't alcoholic, just overworked.") Alcoholics frequently attack the credentials of their caregivers or urgently
marshal their personal emblems of prestige, both to fend off the de-
graded diagnosis and to bolster battered self-esteem.

4. Alcoholics sustain terrible losses of integrity, self-esteem, crucial
relationships, financial status, career, and health. These may be denied,
sometimes at an almost psychotic level. One diabetic alcoholic, during
his 278th detoxification admission, claimed that his drinking was "like
being at a beach party. You don't mind sleeping under bridges in the
winter." His dispair at the horror, poverty, suffering, and risk of his

everyday experience was totally denied, and was handled instead by a lowering of his expectations. Most alcoholics, unlike this man, do register their losses at *some* level; they are often chronically depressed, with extremely high rates of suicide. Grieving and working through are usually aborted by continuing alcohol use and ongoing trauma.

5. Damaged health, especially the brain-impaired "foggy" state seen in a high proportion of drinking alcoholics, evokes a response similar to that of stroke victims or others with life-threatening illnesses that impair personality (as noted above). Intoxication, cognitive dysfunction, addiction with physical dependence, and physical complications of the alcoholism are threats to integrity, each of which produces responses. Patients react both to the illness and to the meaning of the illness—namely, that they are diminished persons.

6. Clear-thinking problem-solving responses are blocked by cognitive impairment, demoralization, and lack of resources, but the greatest obstacle is the patients' personality disruption and the reactive formation of a pattern of denial. The persons usually acknowledge the reality of the drinking episodes (though they may be denied or minimized), but the implication that the drinking is out of control is rejected. The goal is to make sense of each episode of aberrant drinking by explaining it as a result of extraordinary circumstances, while avoiding the added threat to psychic integrity of the alcoholic label and the loss of the alcohol. The price of this is that alcoholic people are forced to use a moral explanation of their drinking, which holds them responsible (as contrasted to the disease model, which implies that they need treatment), so their guilt and depression steadily increase.

THE ALCOHOLIC PERSONALITY

This configuration of defensive responses dominated by denial, but with breakthroughs of depression, guilt, anger, and anxiety as well as persistent and impulsive self-destructive drinking, is what I believe has been labeled the "alcoholic personality." I have tried to show how it might grow organically out of the experience of alcoholism, overlying and distorting but not replacing the original character of the alcoholic person. It also blocks a sensitive reaction to the dangerous reality of loss of control of drinking; acceptance of diagnosis; entrance into treatment; and stopping of the drinking.

Implications for Understanding Treatment and the
Work of Recovery: Permanence versus Reversibility of
Personality Damage

Over the past several decades, psychotherapists have realized that a
conventional model for treatment of alcoholism (seeing the drinking as
a symptom of underlying character disturbance, requiring psychotherapeutic treatment) has simply not worked well clinically. The model I
have described here implies a different approach to treatment. If alcoholism is traumatic and produces psychopathology, then the following
treatment approach makes better sense: First, the trauma must be stopped.
Then the recurrence must be prevented, and damage from the trauma
must be repaired and healed. Finally, any underlying or antecedent
character problem should be treated to prevent vulnerability to recurrence of the trauma in the future.

In order for the trauma to be stopped, the persons must enter some
kind of relationship to treatment or to helping persons. The drinking
must be stopped. This is necessary if the patients are to become safe
and secure enough to begin the work of recovery and to allow neurological healing to begin. To prevent the recurrence of the trauma, the
patients must learn *how* to get sober—a set of techniques taught in
Alcoholics Anonymous and any alcoholism treatment program. They
must also learn *why* to get sober—a revision in their conceptions about
themselves and their vulnerability to alcohol that allows them to protect
themselves from drinking. To heal the damage from the trauma, people
with alcoholism must cope with the effects of stopping drinking, such
as the protracted withdrawal syndrome, the slowly healing dementia,
family members' uproar and outrage at their own suffering, the loss of
the alcohol, the onslaught of shame, and the consciousness of ungrieved
losses now that daily experience is not dominated by the dangerous but
numbing drinking. They must also systematically dismantle the defensive
system that has been generated in reaction to the alcoholism: the denial,
projection, grandiosity, and other mechanisms they have used to help
themselves with the trauma. Finally, they must forgive themselves for
having been alcoholic, and must integrate the meaning of this experience
into their continuing lives.

The issue of reversibility or permanence of the effects of the trauma
and potential for full healing is much clearer, in light of the description
of the work that must be done to recover. The capacity for full recovery
will depend on length of alcoholism; extent of losses; presence or ab-

sence of permanent neurological damage; other resources, espeically of relationships; and the human drive to resolve, master, and integrate the experience. I ordinarily count on 6–18 months for the tasks of early recovery (stopping the trauma and learning how to keep it stopped), and 3 years for the work of advanced recovery (healing, grieving, remodeling psychic habits, forgiving oneself, putting the experience in perspective, and going on to reinvest one's attention in other things). Not all sober alcoholics accomplish all of these tasks. For many, it is a life's work. Sadly, too, many never enter sobriety, treatment, or recovery, so these healing processes can ensue. But for many, the ability to remain human and to restore a sense of integrity following the devastation that alcoholism has inflicted upon the thinking, remembering, feeling self is testimony to all that is most admirable in human nature.

REFERENCES

Bean, M., & Zinberg, N. (Eds.). (1981). *Dynamic approaches to the understanding and treatment of alcoholism.* New York: Free Press.

Blos, P. (1968). Character formation in adolescence. *Psychoanalytic Study of the Child, 23,* 245–263.

Becker, E. (1973). *The denial of death.* New York: Free Press.

Brill, N. W., & Beebe, G. W. (1955). *A follow-up study of war neurosis.* Washington, DC: U.S. Government Printing Office.

Erikson, E. H. (1950). *Childhood and society.* New York: Norton.

Frankl, V. (1959). *Man's search for meaning.* New York: Pocket Books.

Greenacre, P. (1967). The influence of infantile trauma on genetic patterns. In S. S. Furst (Ed.), *Psychic trauma* (pp. 108–153). New York: Basic Books.

Kohut, H. (1972). Thoughts on narcissism and narcissistic rage. *Psychoanalytic Study of the Child, 27,* 360–400.

Krystal, H. (Ed.) (1968). *Massive psychic trauma.* New York: International Universities Press.

Kubler-Ross, E. (1969). *On death and dying.* New York: Macmillan.

Lifton, R. (1968). Observations on Hiroshima survivors. In H. Krystal (Ed.), *Massive psychic trauma* (pp. 168–189). New York: International Universities Press.

Lindemann, E. (1944). Symptomatology and management of acute grief. *American Journal of Psychiatry, 101,* 141–148.

Niederland, W. (1968). An interpretation of the psychological stresses and defenses in concentration-camp life and the late aftereffects. In H. Krystal (Ed.), *Massive psychic trauma* (pp. 60–70). New York: International Universities Press.

Rangell, L. (1976). Discussion of the Buffalo Creek disaster—the course of psychic trauma. *American Journal of Psychiatry, 133,* 313–316.

Terr, L. C. (1983). Chowchilla revisited: The effects of psychic trauma four years after a school-bus kidnapping. *American Journal of Psychiatry, 140,* 1543–1551.

Titchener, J. L., & Kapp, F. J. (1976). Family and character change at Buffalo Creek. *American Journal of Psychiatry, 133,* 295–299.

Vaillant, G. (1977). *Adaptation to life.* Boston: Little, Brown.

Index

347